Essentials
of Textiles

Marjory L. Joseph

California State University, Northridge

Fourth Edition

Essentials of Textiles

HOLT, RINEHART AND WINSTON, INC.
New York   Chicago   San Francisco   Philadelphia
Montreal   Toronto   London   Sydney   Tokyo

Acquisitions Editor: Karen Dubno
Senior Project Editor: Lester A. Sheinis
Senior Production Manager: Pat Sarcuni
Senior Design Supervisor: Louis Scardino
Text Design: Caliber Design Planning
Cover Design: Albert D'Agostino

Library of Congress Cataloging-in-Publication Data

Joseph, Marjory L.
   Essentials of textiles.

   Bibliography: p.
   Includes index.
   1. Textile industry.   2. Textile fabrics.
   3. Textile fibers.   I. Title
TS1445.J63 1988   677   87–11946

ISBN 0-03-012598-7

Printed in the United States of America

8 9 0 1   016   9 8 7 6 5 4 3 2

Holt, Rinehart and Winston, Inc.
The Dryden Press
Saunders College Publishing

Preface

Essentials of Textiles is written for the general student and consumer who desires a fundamental understanding of textiles in order to improve the decision-making processes involved in the selection, use, and care of various textile products. Further, it aims to provide some understanding of the use of textiles in the world today and their importance to each and every person.

This text is based on *Introductory Textile Science* (Holt, Rinehart and Winston, 5th edition, 1986) but has eliminated the scientific details in that book. Although students may encounter terms and names that sound somewhat scientific, they should consider them as names and identifiers and not be concerned that chemistry or other sciences are necessary for textile knowledge at the consumer level. Whatever the background of the students or consumers reading this text, they will be making a variety of decisions concerning textiles during their lifetime. It is my hope that this text will provide some guidelines and directions to make such decisions well informed and satisfactory for the expected life of the product.

The specific goals for this textbook are:

To stimulate the reader's desire to recognize and appreciate textile fabrics and products.

To establish guides that will help the student in the selection, use, and care of textile products.

To facilitate an understanding of the interrelationships among fibers, yarns, fabric structures, finishes, and coloring agents; and to indicate the complexity of these relationships in terms of the selection, use, care, and application of textile products.

To understand the importance of textiles in the world, in the United States, and to each individual person.

Essentials of Textiles has been organized sequentially so that the student can better visualize the complete fiber-to-product cycle. The text begins with a general introduction to fibers and their importance in the economy; this is followed by an introduction to fiber classification, fiber theory, and fiber identification. Information concerning legislation affecting textiles is included in the first part of the book so that consumers have an idea of what information can be expected in the marketplace.

The second part of the text provides some details concerning the various textile fibers in use today; of particular interest are those fibers found in fabrics frequently used for home furnishings and for apparel.

Some mention is given to fibers used for specialized purposes or found in limited use either in the United States or in other countries of the world.

Part III discusses the manufacture of textile yarns and their characteristics. Part IV describes the various methods used in making fabrics and the various types of fabrics found on the market today in both general and special uses. Part V describes the various finishing processes used to make fabrics appeal to consumers and to perform the way consumers wish. It discusses the methods used in coloring fabrics and the techniques involved in producing designs on their surface. Part VI describes various methods used in testing fabrics and textile products to determine expected performance and the application of fabrics for a variety of end uses. Finally, there is a section on the care of textile products.

The text differs somewhat from previous editions. More emphasis has been given to the use of various kinds of fabrics in selected types of applications, or end uses, and to the matter of care. The last chapter is entirely new and describes the performance of textiles in end uses and the care of textile items.

There has been some rearrangement of chapters that will differ from previous editions, and some chapters have been combined. For example all testing has been combined into one chapter in Part VI. Also the discussion of textured and stretch yarns and fabrics has been consolidated as most stretch products available today are based on the use of textured yarns or elastomeric fibers.

Although the arrangement of material in this edition is not necessarily the same as that followed by all instructors of textiles, any part of this text can be taught as a unit in any order desired. Thus, instructors may start with fabrics rather than fibers, or finished consumer goods rather than fibers. In general, each part of the text can stand alone, although any consumer wishing to select, use, and care for textile products needs an understanding of all their aspects and component parts if they are to have the background required for making knowledgeable decisions.

This edition continues the organization used in the previous edition in relation to the fiber section. Chapters on finishes and coloring and applying pattern to fabrics remain in the same general order; however, considerable content has been changed to provide up-to-date information on fibers, finishes, and coloring procedures. The section on fabric structure has been updated to include the technology involved in making fabrics and the efforts of the textile industry to provide healthy environments for their workers.

The study questions, introduced in the third edition, have been retained; however, new questions have been introduced and some questions have been reworded; others have been dropped entirely if they no longer represented problems and concerns of the late 1980s and early 1990s.

Illustrations have been used profusely. Some are the same as in previous editions, particularly, if they are designed to provide help in conceptual understanding. The fashion illustrations have been changed unless they were uniquely specific.

The textile industry is one of the most dynamic in the world, with new fibers, processes, and refinements being introduced rather consistently. However, readers should be aware that new fibers are not appearing at the present time; rather, fiber modifications and combinations of various fibers into yarns and fabrics represent some of the most popular means for providing consumers with products they want. I have tried to give readers sufficient information for a sound understanding of textile fibers, yarns, fabrics, finishes, and coloring processes so that every person can make the best decision concerning the choice of a textile item and determine the recommended method of care. Of considerable importance to consumers is the knowledge of laws and regulations that affect the production and marketing of textile products.

I wish to thank the many individuals who have provided valuable input for this revision and previous editions of the text. Various instructors have shared their suggestions for changes and have indicated their general support of the book. For previous editions of this text the following individuals were helpful: Nancy Breen, Syracuse University; Carol E. Davey, Wayne State University; Eileen Francis, University of North Carolina–Greensboro; B. C. Gaswami, University of Tennessee, Knoxville; Kathryn E. Koch, University of Akron; H. Rex Richards, Colorado State University, Fort Collins; Janet T. Reimer, Douglass College; Clarence Rogers, Clemson University; Robert G. Steadman, Texas Tech University; Rachel Thomson, Bauder Fashion College; and Nancy L. White, California State University, Chico. For this fourth edition, the following individuals provided valuable help and direction: Louanne Antrim, Miami Dade Community College; Lillian Holloman, Howard University; Margery McBurney, Ashland College; Nancy Morris, Colorado State University; Sylvia Phillips, Phoenix College; Behnam Pourdeyhimi, University of Maryland; Marianne Williams, University of Utah; and Stephanie Winkler, Michigan State University.

I wish to thank my assistant, Nancy David, for her help in coordinating the illustrations, obtaining new ones, and seeking permission for their use. She also prepared the index for this text. In addition, my special thanks to my family, William Joseph, Dave David, and Nancy, for their help and understanding while I was writing this text.

For those who wish to use a manual, the *Illustrated Guide to Textiles,* Fourth Edition (1986), published by Plycon Press (6910 Deering, Suite E, Canoga Park, CA 91303), is designed to coordinate with this textbook. A set of sample fabric swatches that may be purchased to accompany the manual is also available from Plycon Press.

MLJ

Contents

PART V   Finish and Color Application   247

PART VI   Fabric Selection, Use, Care, and Testing   309

Essentials
of Textiles

Introduction to the Study of Textiles

A science has evolved in relation to the textile industry—one that has its own language, terminology, and methods of categorization. The scope of the textile industry, of textile knowledge, and of textile technology has expanded at a fantastic rate during the twentieth century. Thus, it has become necessary to refine the definitions and categories, to sharpen the tools of the trade so to speak, to provide a sound base for decision making concerning textile products. The following chapters provide an introduction to the industry; identify how fibers are classified, with emphasis on the Textile Fiber Products Identification Act; provide basic knowledge concerning fiber theory; indicate simple methods used in identifying different textile fibers; and describe textile legislation that has been implemented to make the selection, use, and care of textile products a process with which consumers can easily cope.

Fabric Economics and the Consumer

1

Every individual encounters textiles in some form almost every day of one's life. Consider for a moment what would be missing if there were no textile products. Visualize a world without textile fabrics for apparel and home furnishings, textile fibers and fabrics for business and industry, and textile products in various forms for the many different kinds of transportation vehicles. It is relatively easy to think about textiles for these various uses, but consider also the many uses of textiles in geotechnical applications (e.g., road beds and protection against landslides); recreation facilities and equipment (e.g., poles for pole vaulting, handles for golf clubs, sails for sailing vessels, and artificial turf); medicine in such applications as blood vessels and artificial organs; and building construction (e.g., fiber-reinforced and supported structures, roofs on arenas), as well as actual building components for selected types of insulation and reinforcements. It should be apparent that textile fibers, yarns, and fabrics are essential to life as we now know it (Figs. 1.1 to 1.3).

Consumers make choices regarding the selection, use, and care of textile products nearly every day. Many individuals base their decisions on inadequate information; they really do not have sufficient data in their mental data bank to make the best decisions concerning textiles. However, some individuals are interested enough to seek out the information needed for decision making, and these individuals do have the background for making adequate and informed choices. It is to help both groups of people that this textbook has been written. It is hoped that the topics discussed in the following chapters will provide the student and other interested consumers with the data that will make it easy and enjoyable to select, to use, and to care for textiles in the various forms and end uses encountered. It is also hoped that each and every reader will gain an appreciation for textiles and an enhanced understanding of their importance to all people.

Textile fibers and their use predate recorded history. Archeological evidence indicates that textiles of fine quality were made thousands of years before written records cite their existence. The early history of textile fibers and fabrics has been determined by such archeological finds as spinning whorls, distaff and loom weights, and fragments of fabrics found in such locations as the Swiss lake regions and Egyptian tombs (Fig. 1.4). Tales told by parents to children from generation to generation, designs and evidence of fabrics used in planning or constructing some pottery ware, and eventually, written records further testify to the early importance of fabrics.

The history of textiles is an integral part of the history of civilization. The legendary fig leaf in the Garden of Eden was supplanted by textile

1.1 Textiles in apparel. (Springs Industries)

1.2 left.   Textiles in home furnishings. (Springs Industries)

1.3 right.   Textiles in automobiles. (Courtesy Phillips Fibers Corporation)

1.4   Tapestry-woven linen rug with lotus pattern, from the tomb of Kha, Thebes, 18th dynasty (c. 14th century B.C.). (Museo Egizio, Turin)

body coverings, and textiles assumed a place of importance in the home. Early civilizations possessed both ingenuity and a desire to enhance appearance and environment. These factors contributed over the centuries to the development of complicated fabrics and ultimately to enormous technological expansion.

All early fibers derived from plant or animal life. Wool, flax (linen), cotton, and silk were the most important. Sometime in the early history of textiles, asbestos was introduced. Historical records indicate that in remote ages plant and animal fibers probably were made into fabrics by matting fibers together or by plying groups of fibers into yarns and then knotting or plaiting or interlacing groups of these fibers into some type of fabric.

Spinning and weaving seem to have emerged during the Stone Age. People at that time wrapped animal furs around themselves as body covering, but whether this was for warmth, modesty, prestige, status, decoration, or combinations of these factors remains a topic of discussion even today. Nonetheless, as techniques for fastening these skins together became more sophisticated, clothing was created; and as people began to appreciate the resultant warmth and decoration—as well as, perhaps, the prestige and status—the integration of fabrics with daily life increased. Not only were fabrics important for apparel but also they became important to decoration and to climate control of shelters. There is considerable evidence that weaving actually developed as part of the process of interlacing branches and leaves in the construction of shelters. Eventually, primitive peoples learned to spin yarn from available fibers and to weave, or interlace, these yarns to form cloth.

The Industrial Revolution of the eighteenth and nineteenth centuries transferred the processing of fibers and manufacture of fabrics from the home and small cottage shop to the factory. Mechanization gained importance, and gradually the textile industry expanded. Cotton and wool were especially affected; their growth and production became the concerns of governments throughout the world. Tariffs were levied, wars fought, and regimes toppled because of the political, social, and economic pressures that accompanied industrial advances in the production, marketing, and application of textiles.

The textile industry depended on the sources and forces of nature, combined with the ability of people to utilize them, as the only way to produce textile products until relatively recent decades. The first manufactured fiber, as a commercial product, is not yet one hundred years old. Rayon, which is the first manufactured fiber to be used successfully, was developed during the latter part of the nineteenth century and was introduced to the United States as a viable fiber during the first decade of the twentieth century. During this century the entire spectrum of manufactured fibers has been developed and modified; these have replaced a major proportion of the natural fibers.

Manufactured fibers required considerable research in their development and in determining what finishes and coloring agents would work effectively and produce fabrics that consumers found pleasing to the touch, attractive, and durable. Despite the development of manufactured fibers, however, natural fibers still have an important niche in the textile industry. Furthermore, many consumers want man-made fibers to look, feel, and perform like natural fibers and, in addition, to be easier to care for than natural fibers.

The decades of the 1960s, 1970s, and 1980s have seen many changes in manufacturing processes and in equipment technology involved in the manufacture of textile products. Modifications of manufactured fibers have created second-, third-, and fourth-generation fibers that are pleasing to consumers and provide products with a high level of performance. Research continues in the development of finishing and coloring processes and products, with the ultimate goal of providing consumers with products that meet their every need and desire.

The textile industry is one of the largest in the world. If all facets of this vast economic and industrial giant are considered, it probably involves more people and more money than any other industry. Even if we limit its scope to the growth, production, manufacture, and processing of fibers to fabrics, the textile industry ranks among the top in terms of number of workers and dollar value.

Production and consumption of textile fibers in the United States exhibited an impressive increase during the past few decades; however, it must be mentioned that current import patterns have negatively affected

TABLE 1.1 United States per capita availability of fibers (data in pounds)

	Per Capita			
Period	Man-Made Fiber	Cotton	Wool	Total
1920–1924	0.2	23.8	4.0	28.0
1925–1929	0.7	26.0	3.6	30.3
1930–1934	1.4	20.5	2.6	24.5
1935–1939	2.7	24.9	3.4	31.0
1940–1944	4.7	35.1	4.5	44.3
1945–1949	6.6	28.0	4.8	39.4
1950–1954	9.0	26.9	3.8	39.7
1955–1959	10.3	23.7	3.0	37.0
1960–1964	12.9	22.6	3.0	38.5
1965–1969	22.9	23.0	2.5	48.4
1970–1974	35.1	18.9	1.2	55.2
1975–1979	39.5	15.6	0.9	56.0
1965	18.3	23.9	2.9	45.1
1966	20.2	25.1	2.7	48.0
1967	21.4	23.5	2.2	47.1
1968	26.7	21.9	2.4	51.0
1969	27.9	20.9	2.2	51.0
1970	27.7	19.7	1.7	49.1
1971	32.9	20.4	1.3	54.6
1972	37.5	19.9	1.3	58.7
1973	41.7	18.3	1.0	61.0
1974	35.9	16.0	0.7	52.6
1975	34.7	14.9	0.7	50.3
1976	37.5	16.9	0.9	55.3
1977	41.1	15.8	0.9	57.8
1978	42.4	15.8	1.0	59.2
1979	41.6	14.8	0.9	57.3
1980	37.5	14.7	0.9	53.1
1981	37.9	14.5	1.0	53.4
1982	33.6	13.5	0.9	48.0
1983	41.7	15.8	1.2	58.7
1984	41.7	16.5	1.4	59.6
1985	37.3	17.0	1.4	55.7

the textile industry, as much fiber and fabric are being imported because they can be sold at low prices. Large-scale advertising campaigns have been launched by the American Textile Industry in recent years to encourage all consumers to buy American-made products. One of the most visible campaigns has the slogan "Crafted with Pride in the U.S.A." (Fig. 1.5).

Table 1.1 cites the per capita availability of fibers in pounds for selected years from 1950 through 1986. Although these data are called "fiber availability," the information actually identifies the mean average per capita consumption of textile fibers.

For the years cited the peak year was 1973, which had a per capita use of 61.0 pounds. Although there was a decline during the years since 1978, with 1982 particularly low, the per capita consumption of textile fibers remains relatively consistent. It is the change in the type of fibers used that must be considered. Natural fibers were the most used textile fibers until the late 1960s and early 1970s. By 1970 man-made fibers accounted for a greater proportion of textile fiber used in the United States than natural fibers; this trend has continued to the present time, with the use of man-made fibers nearly twice that of natural fibers. Sixty-seven percent of the fiber consumed on a per capita basis in 1984 was man-made. Specific information concerning man-made fibers indicates that polyester is the most used fiber in the United States.

Table 1.2 cites data for the world production of cotton, wool, silk, and man-made fibers excluding olefin and glass fiber. Again there was a slight drop during 1982 and 1983; however, data for 1984 show that world

1.5 Symbols used by manufacturers to promote textiles manufactured in the United States.

TABLE 1.2 World production of man-made fibers, cotton, wool, and silk (data in millions of pounds)

	Man-Made Fibers					
Year	Rayon and Acetate	Noncellulosic	Cotton	Wool	Silk	Total
1950	3,553	153	14,654	2,330	42	20,732
1955	5,030	587	20,926	2,789	64	29,396
1960	5,749	1,548	22,295	3,225	68	32,885
1962	6,315	2,381	23,052	3,257	73	35,078
1964	7,245	3,728	24,930	3,263	72	39,238
1966	7,370	5,473	23,274	3,387	78	39,582
1968	7,776	8,336	25,629	3,537	83	45,361
1970	7,573	10,871	24,947	3,449	83	46,923
1972	7,837	14,041	29,493	3,206	93	54,670
1974	7,787	16,505	30,966	3,375	99	58,732
1975	6,523	16,210	25,918	3,391	104	52,146
1976	7,076	18,963	27,513	3,278	106	56,936
1977	7,233	20,171	30,690	3,280	108	61,482
1978	7,314	22,121	28,600	3,369	112	61,516
1979	7,430	23,387	31,460	3,468	121	65,866
1980	7,151	23,118	31,166	3,485	123	65,043
1981	7,037	23,655	33,922	3,547	126	68,287
1982	6,485	22,355	32,274	3,591	121	64,826
1983	6,662	24,414	31,343	3,618	121	66,158
1984	6,785	26,220	36,330	3,688	121	73,144
1985	6,612	27,588	38,669	3,695	123	76,687

TABLE 1.3 Mill consumption of fiber, United States (data in billions of pounds)

Year	Rayon	Acetate[a]	Nylon[b]	Polyester	Acrylic[c]	Olefin	Glass[d]	Cotton	Wool	Total
1970	0.9	0.5	1.3	1.6	0.5	0.2	0.1	3.8	0.3	9.2
1971	1.0	0.5	1.7	2.0	0.5	0.3	0.1	4.0	0.2	10.3
1972	1.0	0.4	2.1	2.5	0.6	0.4	0.2	3.9	0.2	11.3
1973	1.0	0.4	2.3	3.1	0.7	0.5	0.2	3.6	0.2	12.0
1974	0.8	0.3	2.0	2.9	0.6	0.5	0.2	3.3	0.1	10.7
1975	0.5	0.3	2.0	3.1	0.5	0.5	0.1	3.1	0.1	10.2
1976	0.6	0.3	2.1	3.3	0.6	0.5	0.1	3.4	0.1	11.0
1977	0.6	0.3	2.3	3.6	0.7	0.6	0.1	3.2	0.1	11.5
1978	0.6	0.3	2.5	3.7	0.6	0.7	0.2	3.0	0.1	11.7
1979	0.5	0.3	2.7	3.8	0.6	0.7	0.2	3.1	0.1	12.0
1980	0.5	0.3	2.3	3.5	0.6	0.7	0.2	3.1	0.1	11.3
1981	0.5	0.2	2.2	3.5	0.5	0.8	0.1	2.7	0.2	10.7
1982	0.3	0.2	1.9	2.9	0.5	0.8	0.1	2.5	0.1	9.3
1983	0.4	0.2	2.4	3.4	0.5	0.9	0.2	2.8	0.2	11.0
1984	0.4	0.2	2.4	3.2	0.5	1.0	0.2	2.7	0.2	10.8
1985		0.5[e]	2.4	3.1	0.5	1.2	NA	2.8	0.1	10.6

NA means not available.
a. Includes triacetate. Cigarette tow is excluded.
b. Includes aramid for all years but 1983, 1984 & 1985.
c. Includes modacrylic.
d. Includes only glass fibers for Textile End Uses.
e. Rayon and Acetate combined.

production of fibers has surpassed all previous years. This increase may be explained in part by the increased population and by the increase in discretionary income for many peoples of the world.

Table 1.3 provides data on mill consumption of fiber for the years 1970 to 1985 by specific fiber. These data are cited in billions of pounds and apply to the United States only. This table clearly shows the shifting patterns of fiber use and indicates the popularity of polyester, with cotton and nylon in second and third place, respectively. This table also identifies the increase in the consumption of olefin during these years as well as the decrease in the use of rayon, acetate, and cotton.

Another important aspect of textile fibers and fabrics is their aesthetic properties. The constant search for new and different fabrics reflects an innate desire in most people for attractive surroundings and colorful, decorative apparel. Fabrics must be fashioned in innovative ways to form the many textile products found in our surroundings.

It appears that a majority of the consumers in the world want fabrics to be comfortable, to require minimum and easy care, to look attractive, and to perform in a particular situation for a desired period of time. The development and modification of new fibers, the combinations of various fibers in making fabrics, the development of special finishing compounds and procedures, the development and use of dyestuffs that provide long-lasting color, and advances in manufacturing technology all combine to provide consumers with considerable choice in the marketplace. This choice makes it possible for consumers to select, use, and care for textile products that meet the desired need.

Why is a knowledge of textiles of value to consumers? There is no brief answer to such a question, and some may argue that not everyone will find it of value. However, every individual normally is exposed to textile products in various forms, and a knowledge concerning these products will provide the data needed to make informed choices in the market-place. This book attempts to give the reader basic information concerning the properties and characteristics, the selection, the use, and the care of textile fibers, yarns, fabrics, and end-use products; further, such knowledge should make the selection, use, and care process somewhat easy, enjoyable, and satisfying.

Textile products are characterized by properties, components, or definitive parts. These include

Fiber or fibers—type and properties
Fiber arrangement and/or yarn structure
Fabric structure
Color—type and method of application
Finish—type, durability, method of application
Product assembly—how the textile fabric is constructed into an end-use product.

All fabrics are composed of fibers, some type of fiber arrangement or yarn structure, and some type of fabric structure. Many also have some type of color and finish applied. When textiles are formed into end-use products, the concept of product fabrication becomes part of the overall process; however, this aspect of textile production is not considered in this text except as it becomes important in terms of application.

The first five components or properties are given detailed discussion in this text, and the book has been organized around these components. The final portion of the text summarizes the combination or application of components in the ultimate textile end use and provides some guidelines to help consumers choose specific textile products for specific end uses.

As noted in the preface, little chemistry is used in this text. Where chemical terms are used they serve merely as names for products or processes and are not meant to be interpreted as chemical reactions. Thus, a background in chemistry is not required for this course; rather, when a term that appears to be chemical in nature is encountered, consider it the name of a product or procedure much like cotton is the name of a fiber.

In brief, Part I of this text provides the background and general information needed in the study of textiles. Part II is devoted to textile fibers and their properties; each fiber chapter includes a brief look at the history of the fiber, its production, and its characteristics and/or properties. Part III is devoted to yarn structure, the manufacture of yarns, and characteristics of yarns. Part IV describes fabric construction procedures and characteristics of various types of fabrics. Part V is devoted to finishing and coloring fabrics. Part VI attempts to summarize and combine the preceding information to make the selection, use, and care of textile products an enjoyable experience and a knowledgeable procedure.

Study Questions

1. What evidence identifies the importance of textiles in early civilizations?
2. When was the first man-made fiber introduced in the United States?
3. What has happened to world production and consumption of textile fibers since 1950? What factors have effected these changes?
4. What changes in proportional use of textile fibers have occurred since 1950?
5. Using Table 1.3 as a source, note changes in the use of man-made and natural fibers since 1970.
6. List the properties, components, or definitive parts that may be identified for textile products.

2 Fiber Classification

The magnitude of scientific development over the centuries made it obvious to scientists that some system of classification was needed to identify like objects and provide a basis for understanding these items and their characteristics. Thus, systems of classification were developed for a wide variety of things, and textile fibers were no exception. When the study of textile fibers was new, a very simple type of classification was sufficient; it was based on arranging fibers into the categories of animal, vegetable, and mineral matter, as these were the sources for the natural fibers.

With the development of man-made fibers this older system of classification became obsolete and new systems had to be devised. It was apparent to those scientists studying textiles that it would be impossible to remember and to describe individually all the various fibers available. Thus, these textile scientists reasoned that some system that would provide properties and characteristics for groups of fibers would be desirable. With such a method of grouping fibers it would be necessary to know only very special and specific properties and characteristics about any single fiber.

A major step in developing a sound classification system was taken when the federal government developed and passed the Textile Fiber Products Identification Act. This act, usually identified by the initials TFPIA, was passed in 1959 and became law in 1960. This legislation requires that most textile products sold at retail have labels securely attached that identify the fiber content. To help reduce consumer confusion this legislation, through several amendments, provides for twenty-one generic or family names into which all manufactured fibers of anticipated commercial value may be grouped. The law also specifies label format. It further provides for the labeling of natural fibers and for the continuation of previous legislation directed at wool fiber (see Chapter 5). Manufacturers' trade names may be used with generic names but should not be used without the generic identification. The excerpts from the law that follow describe each of the generic terms used for classification. In identifying textile fibers under the TFPIA it is important to note that the generic name is not capitalized although trade names are. In advertisements both terms may be written in capital letters, but this means that all letters in the names are capitalized. For the various tables and discussion in this text, the generic terms are not capitalized.

The following list defines each of the generic terms now used for the TFPIA. These definitions are not repeated in the fiber chapters but reference to them will be made. Natural fibers are not defined in the TFPIA, but the fiber must be identified, just as man-made fibers are identified.

The Generic Names

Federal Trade Commission Rules and Regulations under the Textile Fiber Products Identification Act.

Pursuant to the provisions of Section 7 (c) of the Act, the following generic names for manufactured fibers, together with their respective definitions, are hereby established:

acetate—a manufactured fiber in which the fiber-forming substance is cellulose acetate. Where not less than 92 percent of the hydroxyl groups are acetylated, the term *triacetate* may be used as a generic description of the fiber.

acrylic—a manufactured fiber in which the fiber-forming substance is any long-chain synthetic polymer composed of at least 85 percent by weight of acrylonitrile units.

$$(-CH_2-CH-)$$
$$|$$
$$CN$$

anidex—a manufactured fiber in which the fiber-forming substance is any long-chain synthetic polymer composed of at least 50 percent by weight of one or more esters of a monohydric alcohol and acrylic acid.

$$(CH_2=CH-COOH)$$

aramid—a manufactured fiber in which the fiber-forming substance is a long-chain synthetic polyamide in which at least 85 percent of the amide

$$(-C-NH-)$$
$$\|$$
$$O$$

linkages are attached directly to two aromatic rings.

azlon—a manufactured fiber in which the fiber-forming substance is composed of any regenerated naturally occurring proteins.

glass—a manufactured fiber in which the fiber-forming substance is glass.

metallic—a manufactured fiber composed of metal, plastic-coated metal, metal-coated plastic, or a core completely covered by metal.

modacrylic—a manufactured fiber in which the fiber-forming substance is any long-chain synthetic polymer composed of less than 85 percent but at least 35 percent by weight of acrylonitrile units,

$$(-CH_2-CH-)$$
$$|$$
$$CN$$

except fibers qualifying under subparagraph (2) of paragraph (j) (rubber) of this section and fibers qualifying under paragraph (q) (glass) of this section.

novoloid—a manufactured fiber containing at least 85 percent by weight of a cross-linked novolac.

nylon—a manufactured fiber in which the fiber-forming substance is a long-chain synthetic polyamide in which less than 85 percent of the amide

$$(-C-NH-)$$
$$\|$$
$$O$$

linkages are attached directly to two aromatic rings.

nytril—a manufactured fiber containing at least 85 percent of a long-chain polymer of vinylidene dinitrile

$$(—CH_2—C(CN)_2—)$$

where the vinylidene dinitrile content is no less than every other unit in the polymer chain.

olefin—a manufactured fiber in which the fiber-forming substance is any long-chain synthetic polymer composed of at least 85 percent by weight of ethylene, propylene, or other olefin units, except amorphous (noncrystalline) polyolefins qualifying under category (1) of Paragraph (j) (rubber) of Rule 7.

polyester—a manufactured fiber in which the fiber-forming substance is any long-chain synthetic polymer composed of at least 85 percent by weight of an ester of a substituted aromatic carboxylic acid, including but not restricted to, substituted terephthalate units

$$p(—R—O—\underset{\underset{O}{\|}}{C}—C_6H_4—\underset{\underset{O}{\|}}{C}—O—),$$

and parasubstituted hydroxybenzoate units

$$p(—R—O—C_6H_4—\underset{\underset{O}{\|}}{C}—O—)$$

rayon—a manufactured fiber composed of regenerated cellulose as well as manufactured fibers composed of regenerated cellulose in which substituents have replaced not more than 15 percent of the hydrogens of the hydroxyl groups.

rubber—a manufactured fiber in which the fiber-forming substance is comprised of natural or synthetic rubber, including the following categories:

(1) a manufactured fiber in which the fiber-forming substance is a hydrocarbon such as natural rubber, polyisoprene, polybutadiene, copolymers of dienes and hydrocarbons, or amorphous (noncrystalline) polyolefins; (2) a manufactured fiber in which the fiber-forming substance is a copolymer of acrylonitrile and a diene (such as butadiene) composed of not more than 50 percent but at least 10 percent by weight of acrylonitrile units.

$$(—CH_2—\underset{\underset{CN}{|}}{CH}—)$$

The term *lastrile* may be used as a generic description for fibers falling within this category; (3) a manufactured fiber in which the fiber-forming substance is a polychloroprene or a copolymer of chloroprene in which at least 35 percent by weight of the fiber-forming substance is composed of chloroprene units.

$$(—CH_2—\underset{\underset{Cl}{|}}{C}=CH—CH_2—)$$

saran—a manufactured fiber in which the fiber-forming substance is any long-chain synthetic polymer composed of at least 80 percent by weight of vinylidene chloride units.

$$(—CH_2—CCl_2—)$$

spandex—a manufactured fiber in which the fiber-forming substance is a long-chain synthetic polymer comprised of at least 85 percent of a segmented polyurethane.

vinal—a manufactured fiber in which the fiber-forming substance is any long-chain synthetic polymer composed of at least 50 percent by weight of vinyl alcohol units

$$(—CH_2—CHOH—)$$

and in which the total of the vinyl alcohol units and any one or more of the various acetal units is at least 85 percent by weight of the fiber.

vinyon—a manufactured fiber in which the fiber-forming substance is any long-chain synthetic polymer composed of at least 85 percent by weight of vinyl chloride units.

$$(—CH_2—CHCl—)$$

Each fabric or textile product shall have an attached label, tag, stamp, or some other identification that states the fiber, blend of fibers, or combination of fibers present.

Generic names must be in the same size type as trade names when used together, and the same size type shall be used for all fibers included in any textile fabric or product. The percentage of each fiber must be listed with the highest percentage first and others listed in order as they decrease. For example,

65 percent polyester
35 percent cotton

or

45 percent polyester
40 percent nylon
15 percent wool

Fibers present in amounts less than 5 percent may be omitted from labels; however, if a specific fiber is added in amounts less than 5 percent for some specific purpose it may be identified in the listing. The law permits up to a 3 percent variation between actual amounts of fiber present and what is stated on the label.

The tag, label, or stamp identifying the fiber content must also carry the name or some form of identification of the manufacturer of the product. This requirement is frequently fulfilled by using the number assigned to the manufacturer. Imported items have to be labeled with the country from which the product was processed or in which the item was made.

The Federal Trade Commission (FTC) has ruled that the TFPIA applies to the following products: wearing apparel, scarves, handkerchiefs, household linens, towels, washcloths, dishcloths, curtains, draperies, slipcovers, afghans, floor coverings, stuffing for furniture and mattresses, sheets, pillow cases, sleeping bags, and many more. To date, some products are exempted from this act. The exempted products include trimmings, upholstery on furniture sold as it comes from the manufacturer, ties, garters, diapers, shoelaces, and similar items.

The FTC enforces the TFPIA and can obtain an injunction to stop manufacturers and businesses that do not conform to the law. When guilt is proved, a fine up to $5,000 and/or imprisonment up to one year may be imposed. Consumers who have reason to believe that certain textiles are improperly labeled or are not labeled at all should contact the nearest FTC office. If consumers request accurate and adequate labeling, manufacturers and retailers will be forced to conform to the law and provide the desired information.

TABLE 2.1 Natural fibers

A. cellulosic fibers
  1. seed hairs
    a. cotton
    b. kapok
  2. bast fibers
    a. flax
    b. ramie
    c. hemp
    d. jute
  3. leaf fibers
    a. abaca
    b. pineapple
    c. agave (sisal)
  4. nut husk fibers
    a. coir (coconut)
B. protein fibers
  1. animal hair fibers
    a. wool
    b. specialty hair
      (1) alpaca
      (2) camel
      (3) cashmere
      (4) mohair
      (5) vicuna
    c. fur fibers
      (1) Angora rabbit
  2. animal secretion
    a. silk
      (1) cultivated silk
      (2) wild silk
    b. spider silk
C. mineral fiber
  1. asbestos
D. natural rubber

TABLE 2.2 Man-made or manufactured fibers

A. man-made cellulosic fibers
  1. rayon*
    a. cuprammonium rayon
      Bemberg
    b. viscose rayon
      1. regular and high-tenacity rayon
        Avtex
        Fibro
        Coloray, solution dyed
        Enkrome, solution dyed
      2. high-wet-modulus rayon
        Avril
        Zantrel (Fiber 700)
B. man-made modified cellulosic fibers
  1. acetate*
    a. secondary acetate
      Avtex
      Celanese
      Chromspun, solution dyed
      Estron
    b. triacetate**
      Arnel
C. man-made protein fibers
    azlon* (none currently produced in
    the United States)
D. man-made noncellulosic fibers
    (organic fibers)
  1. nylon*
    a. types 6 and 66
      Anso

Antron	
Astroturf	
Camalon	
Caprolan	
Cordura	
Enkalon	
Enkalure	
Lurelon	
Nypel	
Shareen	
Ultron	
Zefran	
b. type 11	
Rilsan	
c. type 6,10	
Nylex	
Quill	
d. bicomponent	
Cantrece	
2. aramid*	
Kevlar	
Nomex	
3. polyester*	
A-Tell	
Avlin	
Dacron	
Encron	
Enka	
Fortrel	
Golden Touch	

*Generic terms specified in the TFPIA.
**Terms that may be used as generic terms when the fiber meets special requirements as cited in the TFPIA.

Tables are included here to help in understanding fiber classification and to put similar fibers into categories. Table 2.1 presents a classification system for the natural textile fibers. The general headings of cellulosic, protein, mineral, and natural rubber have been used as they provide the most meaningful divisions for fibers grown and produced as a part of agricultural methods.

Table 2.2 presents the classification system for all manufactured or man-made fibers and is based on the generic terms identified by the TFPIA. Each generic term has been indicated by an asterisk, and selected trade names have been cited; these have been capitalized.

The system of classification used in this text and in these two tables is based on the following criteria:

1. The principal origin of the fiber. Fibers either occur as fibrous forms in nature or they are manufactured; thus, the first major breakdown indicates if the fiber is natural or man-made (see Tables 2.1 and 2.2, respectively).
2. The general chemical type. This is identified by dividing the fibers into

Kodel
Trevira
Ultra Touch
4. anidex* (none currently produced in the United States)
5. acrylic*
Acrilan
Creslan
Fi-Lana
Orlon
Zefran
6. modacrylic*
SEF
7. nytril* (none currently produced in the United States)
8. olefin*
a. polyethylene
Tyvek
b. polypropylene
Herculon
Marvess
Meraklon
Typar
9. saran*
Ametek
Saran
10. vinal*
Kuralon
Mewlon
11. vinyon*
Avtex

Rhovyl
12. novoloid*
Kynol
13. spandex*
Cleerspan
Glospan
Lycra
14. rubber*
15. lastrile** (none currently produced in the United States)
E. man-made mineral fibers
1. glass*
Beta
Fiberglas
PPG
2. metallic*
Brunsmet
Lurex
F. miscellaneous fibers not classified by the TFPIA
Lexan, a polycarbonate
PBI, polybenzimidazole
Avceram, carbon silica
Fiberfrax, alumina silica
Thornel, graphite
Boron
Sapphire wiskers
Tetrafluoroethylene fibers: Halar, Gore-Tex, Teflon, Telzel
Polychal fiber, Cordelan
Promix fiber, Chinon

the classes of protein, cellulosic, mineral, or synthesized (frequently called noncellulosics).
3. The generic term for all man-made fibers as identified by the TFPIA.
4. The inclusion of common names or trade names of fibers. Many people are familiar with common names and trade names; therefore, examples are included as a means of identifying the known fiber names and group names.

In using the tables it is important to remember that not all fibers are listed; rather the list identifies the most frequently found fibers and those with some special properties and characteristics. A recent trend in the marketplace has been to emphasize the generic term and omit trade names. This may be due, in part, to the amount of fiber imported into this country, which carries only the generic identification.

Specific fibers cited in the tables include those considered commercially important and easily recognized. Students wishing to study some of the less familiar fibers in detail will find additional data in references cited in the Bibliography.

It should be noted that although the TFPIA does not list or describe natural fibers, it does provide for their identification on fabric labels. This identification takes the form of the common name of the fiber, such as cotton, silk, or flax. Wool labeling is covered in the Wool Products Labeling Act, described in Chapter 5. The TFPIA refers to that legislation in relation to the labeling of wool fibers and uses the terminology described in that law.

The original TFPIA identified only seventeen generic names, but provision was made for the addition of new categories as new types of fibers were developed. Since the passage of the original law, it has been amended several times and now includes twenty-one generic categories. Although this legislation requires that generic terms only must be cited, many manufacturers use a trade name with the generic term or in attached advertising as a way to attract consumers who are familiar with the term and respect its quality. It is most important, however, for consumers to recognize generic terms of manufactured fibers and the properties and characteristics of generic groups in order to be informed in the marketplace. Informed consumers have the advantage of understanding why fibers react as they do to physical, chemical, and biological stimuli encountered in the daily use and care of textile products.

Study Questions

1. How should each of the following fibers be classified?
   cotton, jute, wool, mohair, camel hair
2. List eight generic terms for fibers that may be found in apparel or in home furnishings. For each term, cite at least one trade name.
3. What is the TFPIA? What does it do?
4. How would labels be prepared for fabrics with the following fiber composition?
   25 percent linen, 50 percent rayon, 10 percent silk, 15 percent jute
   15 percent silk, 85 percent triacetate
   85 percent wool, 15 percent nylon
   50 percent cotton, 50 percent rayon
5. What is the general rule for the proper order in listing fiber content on labels?

Basic Fiber Theory 3

The textile fabrics or products selected for use in apparel, home furnishings, or other end uses are made of "building blocks" just as houses and other structures are. These building blocks are the textile fibers, which are converted into final textile products by means of a series of manufacturing or processing steps. For consumers to be knowledgeable about the final textile product, they should be informed concerning the actual fibers used and their properties, characteristics, and behavior in use and care.

As discussed in the preceding chapter, textile fibers may be obtained from natural sources or they may be manufactured. Natural fibers include those taken from seed pods such as cotton, from animal coats such as wool, or from plant stems such as flax. Manufactured fibers are made from natural fibrous materials such as wood pulp (used for rayon) or from a variety of chemicals, which are then synthesized, or polymerized, to form fibers. Regardless of the source or process by which fibers are made, fibers do have various properties or characteristics.

Fiber Properties

To qualify for use as a textile fiber, materials must possess certain essential properties, or characteristics, or they must be capable of developing selected properties through various treatments or processes. Fiber properties may be grouped as primary properties or secondary properties. Primary properties include *high length-to-width (breadth) ratio; tenacity,* or fiber strength; *flexibility,* or pliability; *spinning quality,* or cohesiveness; and *uniformity.* Secondary properties are those that are desirable but not essential. Often their major role is to increase consumer satisfaction with the ultimate fabric. Characteristics in this group include *physical shape, density* or *specific gravity, color, luster, moisture regain and absorption, elastic recovery and elongation, resiliency, thermal behavior, resistance to biological organisms,* and *resistance to chemicals and other environmental conditions.* The following discussion includes definitions, brief descriptions, and tables showing the properties of selected fibers so that comparisons among fibers may be made.

Primary Fiber Properties

High length-to-width ratio Fibers must be considerably longer than they are wide to permit processing into yarns and fabrics. This quality is referred to as a *high length-to-width* or *high length-to-breadth ratio*. Because the property is essential for fabrication of fibers into textile fabrics and

TABLE 3.1 Fiber tenacity or strength

Fiber	Breaking Tenacity, Grams/denier, Dry
Natural Fibers	
cotton	3.0–5.0
flax	6.5
silk	2.4–5.1
wool	1.0–1.7
Man-Made Fibers	
acetate	1.2–1.4
nylon	3.5–9.5
triacetate	1.1–1.4
olefin	1.5–8.0
acrylic	2.0–3.6
polyester	2.5–9.5
aramid	5.3–22.0
rayon	2.4–5.0
glass	6.3–6.9
spandex	0.5–1.5
modacrylic	2.0–3.1

products, we can assume that all fibers on the market automatically possess an adequate length-to-width ratio.

Tenacity   Strength, or tenacity, of fibers varies among the different generic classes and within specific fiber types. In all cases, however, a textile fiber must possess sufficient strength to permit processing into the final textile product. Thus, it must successfully resist various physical procedures and those chemical processes required. Some fibers with minimal strength have other compensating properties that enable manufacturers to convert the fibers into yarns, fabrics, and end-use products. Table 3.1 cites the strength or tenacity of the major fibers or fiber types. An important advantage of strong fibers is that less fiber is required in producing durable yarns. Thus, fine yarns and sheer fabrics can be made from strong fibers, and they will usually provide a high level of satisfaction.

Flexibility   To make fibers into yarns and fabrics that can be creased, the fibers must be bendable, pliable, or flexible. These fibers have the quality of drapability, the capacity to move with the body and able to "give" when sat or walked on. Flexibility, or pliability, permits freedom of movement and the ability to shape fabrics to objects that are not flat. Forms that might resemble fibers in appearance but that lack adequate flexibility do not make satisfactory textile fibers for consumer goods; however, such forms may be of value in end uses where pliability is not desired.

It is generally accepted that a fiber must flex or bend repeatedly to be considered pliable. Fibers of different types vary in their degree of pliability. Relative pliability determines the ease with which fibers, yarns, fabrics, and end-use items will bend or give. The flexibility of fibers is directly related to the flexibility of an end-use textile product; therefore, fabric adaptation to the end use and fabric durability are closely related to the degree of flexibility of the fibers involved. This property, therefore, is important in evaluating fibers for specific end uses.

Spinning quality, or cohesiveness   Cohesiveness can best be described as the ability of fibers to stick together during fiber-arranging or yarn-manufacturing processes. The cohesiveness of fibers may be due to the contour of the cross-sectional shape, or it may result from the surface, or skin, structure of the fibers. When fiber shape and surface are not naturally cohesive, this property can be introduced by several alternative methods. The use of long filament fibers that twist easily into yarns is one technique that replaces natural cohesiveness; in this instance the fiber length becomes the equivalent of cohesiveness and provides the spinning quality needed for processing. Another method is to introduce crimp by means of texturizing, which builds in coils, zigzags, or other surface shapes and introduces adequate spinning quality to the fibers.

The spinning quality of a fiber influences such characteristics as yarn fineness, fabric thickness, snagging or pilling of surface textures, appearance, and fabric or textile product durability. Without adequate cohesiveness, fibers would not hold together properly in yarns and/or fabrics, and consumers would become unhappy with a purchase that did not retain the desired characteristics during use and care.

Uniformity   It is important that fibers be similar in length and width, in spinning quality, and in flexibility if they are to be processed without considerable caution. Uniformity produces even yarns and ultimately provides fabrics of uniform appearance that give relatively consistent service.

Consumers may not be aware of the primary properties in textile products they purchase. Because these properties are essential, fibers lacking them in an adequate degree are seldom converted into textile end-use products. Thus, most textile products are composed of fibers with a high length-to-width ratio, with adequate strength, with flexibility sufficient for the end-use application, with sufficient spinning quality, and with uniform structure. Nevertheless, consumers should be aware of, familiar with, and concerned about the primary fiber properties as they do influence product use, care, and behavior or performance.

Secondary Fiber Properties

Characteristics of fibers resulting from secondary properties vary among the different fiber types and even within each type. The amount of variation depends on the amount of modification introduced by the manufacturer or the effect created by environmental conditions. The level at which fibers possess secondary properties is responsible for much of the fibers' performance in end-use products. Secondary properties provide a basis for describing and classifying fibers, and they are important to the consumer as determinants of end-product performance, durability, maintenance, and appearance. Thus, secondary properties are frequently observed by consumers as being responsible for various characteristics of the textile product.

It should be noted that finishing processes can affect secondary properties noticeably. When a desirable secondary property is present at a low level, it may be possible to upgrade it through finishing. If a secondary property is completely absent from a fiber, it may be possible to introduce similar performance characteristics through various finishing procedures. Manufacturers, through various types of processing techniques, can modify, alter, or even eliminate undesirable qualities that result from various secondary fiber properties.

Physical shape   In addition to the primary property of a high length-to-width ratio, which is a part of the physical shape of the fiber, other factors involved in shape include the average fiber length, surface contour and irregularities, cross-sectional shape, and actual length and width. These elements provide the basis for both the macroscopic (low magnification) and microscopic (high magnification) appearance and description of a fiber. They are responsible for certain differences in yarn and fabric properties important to consumers that will be discussed in specific fiber chapters.

The length of the fiber can vary from approximately 1/2 inch, frequently considered to be the absolute minimum fiber length, to an endless, or nearly so, filament, which may be many miles in length. The diameter is always very tiny in relation to the length, but there is a difference in diameter among fibers. Whereas it is important that the diameter be kept tiny enough to permit flexibility and pliability, some fibers have larger diameters than others.

In cross-sectional shape there are many different types: Fibers may be trilobal, pentalobal, oviate, nearly flat, irregular, triangular, dog bone, or other shapes from flat to perfectly round. The cross-sectional shape will influence appearance and performance. Figure 3.1 illustrates some of the various cross-sectional shapes that may be found in textile fibers.

3.1 Various cross-sectional shapes of textile fibers.

TABLE 3.2 Density of selected fibers

Fiber	Density, Grams/cc	Fiber	Density, Grams/cc
Natural Fibers		acrylic	1.16–1.18
cotton	1.54	aramid	1.38–1.44
flax	1.50	glass	2.54
silk	1.25–1.34	modacrylic	1.30–1.37
wool	1.30–1.32	nylon	1.14
Man-Made Fibers		olefin	0.90–0.96
acetate	1.32	polyester	1.23–1.38
Arnel triacetate	1.30	rayon	1.50–1.53
		spandex	1.20–1.25

Density   Fiber density has sometimes been identified as specific gravity. The latter term may still be used, but the term *density* is preferred. Density identifies the relative weight of a fiber as compared to water. Water is given a rating of one. Density is correctly defined as *mass per unit volume,* whereas specific gravity is defined as *relative weight per unit volume.*

The differences among fibers in terms of density are reflected in such characteristics as fabric weight for identical fabric construction. Fabrics composed of fibers such as nylon or acrylic, which have low density, will be lighter in weight than fabrics of cotton or rayon, which have a relatively high density. To be valid, this comparison demands that all other factors in constructing the fabric remain identical.

Fibers with a density of less than one will float on water. For such products special consideration may be required in the choice of laundering and care techniques. Table 3.2 gives the density value for a selected group of fibers commonly found in consumer goods. Remember, the lighter the fiber, the lighter the fabrics, providing all other characteristics are the same.

Color   Fibers differ somewhat in their original or natural color. Natural fibers vary from almost white to nearly black, depending on type. Cotton fibers are creamy off-white to various levels of gray; wool varies from off-white to nearly black, depending on the type of sheep and pigment characteristics. Silk is nearly white when cultivated but may vary to deep yellow or light brown for various wild varieties; other natural fibers show wide variation in color as well.

Manufactured fibers may be pure white following manufacturing; however, some man-made fibers may be off-white until they are bleached. A few man-made fibers may be very dark; graphite fiber, for instance, is black.

The natural color of fibers may influence the results obtained when dyestuffs are added. Unless fibers are bleached to a pure white, dyestuffs will often react with the existing fiber color, and the dyed color will not be the same as that obtained on a pure white fiber. Therefore, most fibers are bleached as a part of processing prior to the addition of color in order to produce clear and pure colors. The typical natural color of fibers is included in the individual fiber chapters.

Luster   Luster refers to the gloss or shine that a fiber possesses. It depends on the amount of light reflected by a fiber and determines the fiber's natural brightness or dullness. The cross-sectional shape and surface contour of fibers influence the level of natural luster that a fiber exhibits as well as its chemical composition. Silk has the greatest luster of the natural fibers, whereas cotton is generally low in luster. Manufactured fibers can be produced with varying degrees of luster from high to low. The usual way to decrease luster of manufactured fibers is to add special pigments during the final processing. If luster is to be increased, special chemicals may be added. The ability to produce fibers, and the resulting fabrics, with varying degrees of luster is highly desirable for consumers, as it gives them a large number of aesthetic choices.

Moisture regain and moisture absorption   Except for a very few manufactured fibers, textile fibers have a certain amount of water as an integral part of their composition. This water is called *moisture regain* and is expressed as a percentage of the weight of the moisture-free fiber. The terms *moisture regain* and *moisture absorption* are sometimes used synonymously. However, *moisture absorption* is usually reserved to indicate the total amount of water that a fiber can absorb at the saturation point.

Fibers with good moisture regain will accept dyes and finishes more readily than fibers with a low regain. A few fibers have no regain at all, and this creates some serious problems in processing, particularly in the addition of coloring agents. The relation of moisture content to fiber strength is another factor that should be considered in evaluating fiber behavior. Some fibers are stronger when wet than when dry; others are weaker when wet; and still others demonstrate no change between the dry and wet state as far as strength is concerned. However, this relationship between moisture and strength is important in care, as fibers that are weaker when wet than when dry must receive special care during laundering or dry cleaning to prevent damage from the stress on the wet fiber. Cotton and other natural cellulosic fibers are stronger when wet than when dry and can be laundered with ease. Fibers with little or no moisture regain will wash and dry quickly. Fibers that are weaker when wet than dry, such as rayon, should be given careful handling during care periods to prevent damage.

Moisture regain also influences fabric comfort. Fibers that do have good moisture regain and moisture absorbency tend to be comfortable regardless of the outside environment; fibers with little or no absorbency tend to be uncomfortable when worn in hot and humid environments. Table 3.3 lists the standard moisture regain for a selected group of fibers.

Elastic recovery and elongation   The amount of stretch that a fiber will undergo is referred to as *elongation*. *Breaking elongation* is the amount of stretch a fiber undergoes to the point at which it breaks. *Elastic recovery* indicates the percent of return from elongation to the original fiber length. If a fiber returns to its original length from a specified level of stretch or attenuation, it is said to have 100 percent elastic recovery at that specific percent of elongation.

The amount of elongation is an important factor in evaluating elastic recovery. Some fibers with low elongation have excellent elastic recovery; however, this property is of little value because of the very low potential elongation. Thus, it should be obvious that elongation and elastic recovery must be considered together in fiber evaluation. A fiber with extremely high elongation but medium to low elastic recovery might be undesirable because the product would not return to size after extension or stretch. The interrelation between stretch and recovery, then, becomes extremely important to consumers in that it governs the shape retention, appearance, and comfort of textile products.

TABLE 3.3 Moisture regain of selected fibers

Fiber	Moisture Regain in Percent at 70°F and 65% Relative Humidity
Natural Fibers	
cotton	8.5
flax	12.0
silk	11.0
wool	13.6–16.0
Man-Made Fibers	
acetate	6.5
triacetate	3.2–3.5
acrylic	1.0–2.5
aramid	4.5
glass	0.0
modacrylic	0.4–4.0
nylon	3.5–5.0
olefin	0.0–0.1
polyester	0.4
rayon	10.7–16.0
saran	0.1
spandex	0.3–1.2

TABLE 3.4 Elastic recovery of selected fibers

Fiber	Percent Recovery Following 2 Percent Stretch
Natural Fibers	
cotton	75.0
flax	65.0
silk	92.0
wool	99.0
Man-Made Fibers	
acetate	94
triacetate	90–92
acrylic	80–99
modacrylic	86
nylon	100
olefin	100
polyester	85–100
rayon	82–95
spandex	100
glass	100

TABLE 3.5 Breaking elongation of selected fibers

Fiber	Percent Elongation at Break, Dry
Natural fibers	
cotton	3.0–10.0
flax	2.7–3.3
silk	10.0–25.0
wool	20.0–40.0
Man-Made Fibers	
acetate	25–35
triacetate	25–35
acrylic	20–55
aramid	22
glass	3.0–4.0
modacrylic	48
nylon	16–40
olefin	15–50
polyester	9.5–75
rayon	15.0–24
spandex	500–700

TABLE 3.6 Resiliency of selected fibers

Fiber	Resiliency Rating
polyester	high
wool	
nylon	
modacrylic	
acrylic	
olefin	
Arnel triacetate	
silk	
acetate	
cotton	
rayon	
flax	low

Table 3.4 provides data on elastic recovery of fiber stretch at 2 percent elongation. Table 3.5 identifies the percentage of stretch or elongation that a fiber will undergo to the breaking point. These two tables should be studied together to obtain maximum information concerning the interrelationships between elongation and elastic recovery.

Resiliency The ability of a fiber to return to shape after compression, bending, creasing, or similar deformation is called *resiliency*. It is useful in the determination of a fabric's crease recovery and smooth surface retention. Resiliency is evaluated on a comparative basis from excellent to poor. Elastic recovery is a significant factor in fiber resiliency; good elastic recovery usually indicates that the fiber or fabric will have good resiliency. Table 3.6 lists a group of textile fibers in terms of their resiliency, going from high to low. A review of the information in the table should help indicate why fibers such as polyester, wool, nylon, and acrylics are frequently used for floor coverings, where resiliency is a very important criterion.

Flammability and other thermal reactions The individual chapters concerning specific fiber types include sections describing thermal reactions. These sections indicate the behavior of individual fiber types at various temperatures.

Burning characteristics of textile fibers are of special concern to consumers. The news media and testing groups have acted as consumer advocates concerning flammable textiles, and the government has given the topic considerable thought, passing numerous laws relating to the level of flammability that textiles are permitted for specified uses. This legislation is discussed in Chapter 5. The flammability of textiles is an important characteristic and should be given high priority by consumers in making selections of textiles for apparel, home furnishings, and transportation

TABLE 3.7 Ironing temperatures for selected fibers

Fiber	Softens at °F	Suggested Ironing Temp. °F
cotton		425
flax		425
silk		300
wool		300
acetate	380	325
triacetate	460	400
acrylic	400	300
modacrylic	300	215
nylon 6	330	300
nylon 6,6	425	350
olefin	250	150
polyester	450	325
rayon		375
spandex	340	300

Temperatures are cited at the low end of the scale.

TABLE 3.8 Abrasion resistance of a selected group of fibers

Fiber	Abrasion Resistance
nylon	high
olefin	
polyester	
spandex	
flax	
acrylic	
cotton	
silk	
wool	
rayon	
acetate	
glass	low

vehicles. Obviously fibers with a low level of flammability will be safer than those with a high incidence of burning. It is important to recognize, however, that almost every fiber used by the general consumer will burn if in the direct path of flame.

Other thermal characteristics of textile fibers are important in the care of fabrics. These factors influence the temperatures that may be used during laundering, dry cleaning, and ironing. Table 3.7 provides a list of safe ironing temperatures for fibers commonly found in textile products that might require such care. Many irons use only the words *low, medium,* and *high*. It is recommended that temperatures of 400°F be considered high, temperatures between 250°F and 350°F be considered medium, and temperatures below 250°F be considered low.

Other secondary properties A fabric's abrasion resistance is important because it determines how a textile product will resist wear and subsequent damage from rubbing. Table 3.8 lists a group of commonly used fibers from high to low resistance to rubbing or abrasion damage.

Sunlight resistance is another important characteristic for textile fibers, especially for fabrics being used where exposure to sunlight is encountered, such as draperies and curtains, outdoor apparel, furniture for patios, and blinds or similar items that will be hung outside windows. Some fabrics will be damaged from sunlight even through window glass; thus, consideration of sunlight resistance is important here, too. Table 3.9 provides a comparative listing of selected fibers in relation to sunlight resistance.

The resistance of a fiber to various chemical agents is important in determining processing technology and care procedures. Table 3.10 gives fibers' resistance to acids, alkalies, and organic solvents. The consumer should be particularly alert to damage from organic solvents, as this will indicate possible problems in dry cleaning. Fibers damaged by alkalies require special care in the choice of detergents. Specific information is given in the fiber chapters.

Other properties and characteristics of fibers will be discussed in greater detail in the individual fiber chapters. Discussion will include reac-

TABLE 3.9 Sunlight resistance of selected fibers

Fiber	Resistance
glass	high
acrylic	
modacrylic	
polyester	
flax	
cotton	
rayon	
triacetate	
acetate	
olefin	
nylon	
wool	
silk	low

TABLE 3.10 Reactions of selected fibers to chemicals

Fiber	Reactions to Acids	Reactions to Alkalies	Reactions to Organic Solvents
cotton	harmed	resistant	resistant
flax	harmed	resistant	resistant
silk	harmed by mineral acids	harmed	resistant
wool	resistant	harmed	resistant
acetate	weakened	little effect	harmed by acetone, phenol, and chloroform; resistant to others
acrylic	resistant to most	resistant to weak	resistant
modacrylic	resistant to most	resistant	resistant to most
nylon	harmed	resistant	harmed by phenol and formic acid; resistant to most others
olefin	resistant	resistant	harmed by chlorinated hydrocarbons
polyester	resistant	resistant	resistant
rayon	harmed	resistant to weak	resistant
spandex	resistant	resistant	resistant

tion to chemicals, to environmental and climatic conditions, to microorganisms such as bacteria and fungi, and to insects.

A factor that plays a major role in the success or failure of a textile fiber is cost. The production and processing of a fiber must be sufficiently economical so that the final price of end-use products does not exceed the consumer's willingness or ability to pay. This does not prevent the expenditure of vast sums for research and development of new fibers, but it does tend to rule out the mass production of costly fibers. The same economic reality holds true for natural fibers. Whenever growth and processing costs result in exorbitantly expensive products, the competitive market will not support a successful sale.

Molecular Arrangement

The following brief discussion is designed to help students understand how fibers are formed and the influence of that formation on fiber properties. Fiber molecules are polymers; that is, they are large molecules produced by linking together many small molecules, or monomers, or small molecular units. These molecules link together to produce a large polymolecule, or polymer, that has a very long length and a very tiny diameter—just as the final textile fiber will have. One description of a fiber molecule states that if a fiber molecule were 1/8 inch in diameter it would be about 40 feet in length. Actually each fiber molecule is ultramicroscopic and can be seen only under electron microscopes.

Polymers differ in their arrangement within different types of fibers. Natural fibers do not permit the manipulation of the large molecules and cannot be altered during normal processing. Manufactured fibers may be manipulated so that the arrangement of the molecules can be modified or changed to produce fibers with slightly different molecular arrangements.

Fiber molecules can be arranged within a fiber so that they lay parallel to each other and parallel to the long dimension of the fiber. When this occurs, the fiber is said to be highly oriented (Fig. 3.2). These fibers tend to have a high strength, low elongation, and low moisture regain. In some fibers the molecules are arranged haphazardly; in other words the molecules are not in any systematic arrangement. Such fibers are said to

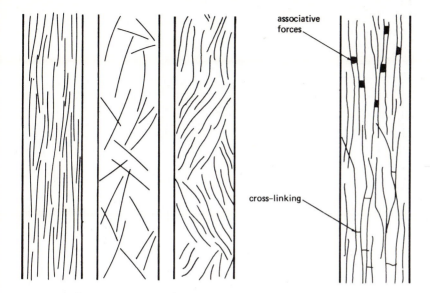

3.2 far left. Schematic diagram illustrating highly oriented molecules within a fiber.

3.3 second from left. Schematic diagram illustrating molecules in a random or amorphous arrangement.

3.4 second from right. Schematic diagram illustrating molecules in arrangements combining crystalline regions (regions where molecules are oriented with each other) and regions where molecules are oriented with the fiber axis as well as with each other.

3.5 right. Schematic diagram illustrating cross linking of molecules.

have low orientation and tend to be low in strength, high in elongation, and high in moisture regain (Fig. 3.3). Some fibers have both areas, one in which fiber molecules are systematically arranged and others where they are in no specific arrangement (Fig. 3.4). These fibers are described as having medium orientation and fall between the high- and low-oriented fibers in relation to strength, moisture regain, and elongation. Scientists have found ways to improve the molecular arrangement of fibers that have low or medium orientation. Some agent must be introduced into the fiber to produce cross linking of fiber molecules, which produces fibers with good elastic recovery and crease resistance but that maintain sufficient openness to permit easy coloring (Fig. 3.5).

Textile Fiber Production and Manufacture: An Overview

Fiber Forming and Spinning

Natural fibers are formed as they are grown or produced. Cotton fibers come directly from the cotton seed pod in the form in which they will be used for yarns and fabrics. Wool fiber comes directly from the sheep in the form required for converting to yarns and fabrics. Silk comes from the cocoon in the filament form that is taken directly to yarns and fabrics. Flax and other bast fibers are removed from the stems of plants in the form in which they will be used.

Manufactured fibers, however, must be processed to enable the fiber to be converted to yarns and fabrics. There are four basic processes involved: wet spinning process, dry spinning process, melt spinning process, and emulsion spinning process. Each will be described briefly, and diagrams of three of the processes are included to help understanding.

Wet spinning The polymeric material to be used in making the fiber is dissolved in some type of solution; this is forced through a spinning jet,

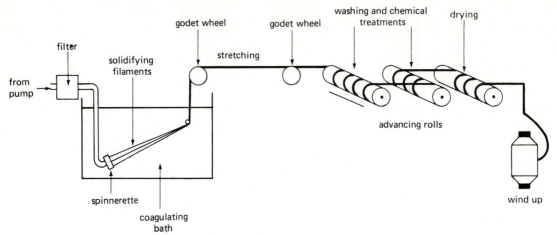

3.6 Diagram of wet spinning process.

called a spinnerette, into another liquid that reacts with the fiber solution. The process involves one of the following reactions: (1) The fiber polymer may be chemically changed to make it soluble in the solvent used; when this occurs, the fiber solution reacts with the second solution and the chemical reaction is reversed so that the material is re-formed in the shape of a fiber able to be made into yarns and fabrics. (2) There is no change in the chemical form of the fiber; rather the concentration is changed sufficiently to make the fiber soluble. It is extruded from the fiber solution into a second solution, usually water, where the solution concentration is reduced sufficiently for the fiber material to re-form; as it is forced through the spinnerette it takes the shape of a usable fiber. Fibers formed by the wet spinning process include rayons and some of the acrylic fibers (Fig. 3.6).

Dry spinning   In dry spinning the fiber solution is forced through the spinnerette into a warm air chamber. The warm air causes the solvent to evaporate, and the fiber solution forms into filaments and hardens. This process may involve converting the fiber polymer into a different chemical form that is soluble in a suitable liquid. As the solvent evaporates, the filaments take shape. Several fibers are made with the dry spinning process: acetate, triacetate, some types of acrylics and modacrylics, and some aramid fibers (Fig. 3.7).

Melt spinning   In melt spinning the fiber polymer is melted and the molten solution is forced through the spinnerette. As the soft filaments emerge from the spinnerette into a cooler environment, they harden into a usable filament ready for converting into yarns and fabrics. Melt spinning does require that the fiber can be melted without damaging the actual molecules. Nylon, polyester, and glass are examples of melt spun fibers (Fig. 3.8).

Emulsion spinning   This is a complex process that requires the fiber solution to be dispersed into a second liquid and then formed into the fiber as it is forced through the spinnerette. This process is used for only a very few fibers.

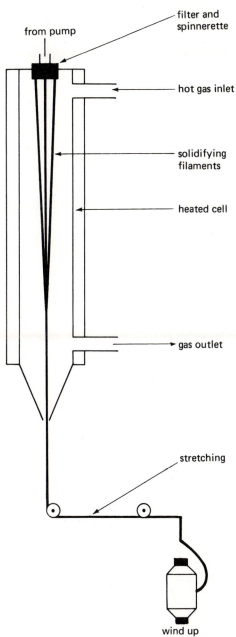

from pump

filter and
spinnerette

hot gas inlet

solidifying
filaments

heated cell

gas outlet

stretching

wind up

3.7 Diagram of dry spinning process.

hopper for
polymer chip

melting tank

pump

filter pack

spinnerette

emergent
filaments

cooling
air

convergence

duct

spinning finish
roll

traverse

wind up

3.8 Diagram of melt spinning process.

Fiber Modifications

Fiber manufacturers frequently create modifications or variants of the standard fiber polymers in order to produce fibers with special properties. These modifications can be the result of adding small amounts of other chemicals to the fiber during the conversion to a fluid state, adding small amounts of selected chemicals during the actual fiber-forming process, modifying the shape and size of the spinnerette openings during the spinning step, or modifying the composition of the bath into which the filaments pass as they leave the spinnerette. Some modification may occur after the fiber is formed by special processing techniques. The following describes, in brief, a few of the different types of modifications.

Delustering   Many man-made fibers are naturally very lustrous, or shiny. Since consumers do not always want shiny fibers, manufacturers have devised ways to reduce the shine when desired. This delustering process involves the addition of special substances, called *delustering agents,* to the fiber solution before the formation of the filaments. Delustering agents modify the way the fiber reflects light so that they appear to be dull or semidull.

Texturizing   Texturizing involves modification of the shape of the fibers (discussed more fully in Chapter 19). The purpose of texturizing is to build into fibers various shapes that make the filaments resemble yarns made of staple man-made or natural fibers. Texturizing creates fibers with built-in bulk and/or stretch.

Fiber variants   Since the early developments in man-made fibers, manufacturers have continued to investigate ways in which fibers would provide consumers with a variety of properties. Thus, fibers have been modified to alter the way in which they are dyed, to change the level of strength—either increasing or decreasing it—and to have different resistance to stress.

   The processes for achieving such variants involve adding small amounts of special chemicals to the fiber formula, modifying the polymeric compound, creating cross linkages between molecules within the fiber, altering the shape of the openings in the spinnerettes so that the fibers have different shapes, or changing the speed with which the material is forced through the spinnerette and drawn following extrusion.

Fiber forms   Natural fibers come from their source in the shape of a textile fiber; however, each natural fiber differs in appearance (these differences are described in the fiber chapters). Except for silk, natural fibers are available only in a staple form—that is, in a form that is relatively short, usually between 1/2 inch and 15 inches.

   Man-made fibers may be produced in several forms, as described in the following discussion (Fig. 3.9).

Monofilament   A monofilament is a single fiber or filament in a form ready for conversion into yarns and fabrics. Monofilaments tend to be somewhat stiff and lack draping qualities found in multifilament forms, but they have greater strength. Monofilaments can be as long as the manufacturer desires. Usually length is a matter of the size of the container on which the filament is wound following formation.

Multifilament   The typical yarn of man-made fibers is multifilament; that is, it is composed of several filaments that were extruded simultaneously through a spinnerette. The number in any group depends on the size the final single yarn is to be. As the filaments are combined, a slight amount of twist is inserted to hold them together. Multifilament yarns are flexible and soft and, in general, are preferred for fabrics used in apparel and home furnishings.

3.9 Filament and staple fibers.

Tow A considerable amount of man-made fiber is marketed in a form called *tow*. Tow is composed of many hundreds or thousands of filaments that have been formed simultaneously by extrusion through spinnerettes that have a very large number of openings. These many filaments are pulled together to form a large sliver of fibers.

Manufacturers can process tow into yarns by a direct process or by intermittent methods. In either case the filaments are broken into short lengths similar to staple fiber lengths.

Staple fiber Staple fibers are short fibers that resemble natural fibers, such as wool and cotton, in length. Man-made fibers may be cut into staple lengths for processing on the same type of machinery as that used for converting cotton or wool into yarns. The length of the fiber is determined by the type of machinery to be used and varies, usually, between 1 and 3 inches. Typically staple man-made fibers are cut from tow.

Bicomponent and Bigeneric Fibers

Bicomponent fibers are composed of two variants or modifications of the same generic fiber type. Bigeneric fibers are composed of two different generic fiber types. There are three basic methods for making these fibers: the side-by-side type, the sheath core type, and the matrix fibril type. These are diagramed in Figure 3.10. Special spinnerettes are used in making these types of fibers. Bicomponent fibers are made to provide textile products with varying shrinkage levels, bulk, or texture. Bigeneric fibers provide similar properties through the use of two different generic fiber types.

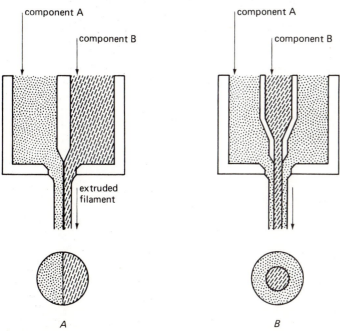 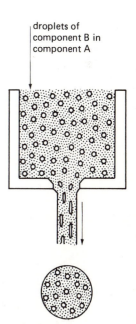

3.10 Diagram of three types of bigeneric and bicomponent fibers. **a.** Side by side. **b.** Sheath/core. **c.** Matrix.

There has been a change in terminology recently regarding bicomponent and bigeneric fibers. The term *bicomponent* may be used for any type of fiber composed of two different fiber variants of the same generic group or fibers made of two different generic fiber types. The term *biconstituent,* which used to be used to indicate fibers of two different generic types, is no longer acceptable. *Bigeneric* may be used for fibers of two different generic groups, but these fibers may also be identified by the use of the term *bicomponent.*

Study Questions

1. Give a brief description of each of the following primary fiber properties:
   a. Length-to-width, or length-to-breadth, ratio
   b. Tenacity
   c. Flexibility, or pliability
   d. Spinning quality, or cohesiveness
   e. Uniformity
2. List the secondary fiber properties and describe each briefly.
3. What is the relation of fiber density to consumer comfort?
4. How does luster affect the consumer and fabric choice?
5. Why is the property of moisture regain important to consumers?
6. Should elastic recovery properties influence consumer's choice of a textile product? Why?
7. Why should consumers be aware of the thermal reactions and behavior of textile fibers?
8. Why is sunlight resistance important for selected end uses of textiles? What specific end uses?
9. What end use would require fabrics with good abrasion resistance?
10. What fiber properties are associated with high molecular orientation?
11. Describe the various methods used to spin man-made fibers.
12. What is a fiber variant?
13. Describe monofilaments, multifilaments, and tow.
14. What is a bicomponent fiber? How is the term currently defined?

Fiber Identification 4

Qualitative identification of a fiber is difficult and usually requires several tests. It is not the intent of this chapter, or of this book, to provide a detailed summary of processes involved in fiber identification. Rather the purpose is to indicate the common tests used in identifying general fiber categories. A brief discussion of the complex processes used for specific fiber identification is given for information only. The major reason for including this information is to indicate the importance of knowing what fibers are in a particular product and how that information can be used to determine appropriate use and care procedures.

Much of the information is presented in chart form. The discussion cites the general procedures for identification and suggests interpretation and order of applying the tests.

Consumers should find the ability to identify fibers extremely valuable. It frequently helps in verifying label content, provides information concerning product care, and helps in recognizing legitimate complaints about performance of a textile product.

Tests for Fiber Identification

The Burning Test

The burning test is a good preliminary test for identifying categories of textile fibers, but it does not identify specific fibers themselves. It offers valuable data regarding appropriate care and indicates general fiber groupings. Problems arise when yarns or fabrics composed of two or more fibers are tested. The test will usually give the reaction of the fiber that burns most easily. But if a thermoplastic (heat-sensitive) fiber is involved, it might melt or withdraw from the flame and pull the other fibers with it.

Although the procedure for the burning test is simple, care must be taken when working with open flames to prevent injury to people or damage to property. The following steps will provide guidance.

1. Select one or two yarns from the warp, lengthwise (long direction), of a fabric if woven; snip a slender strip of fabric if knitted or of nonwoven constructions.
2. Untwist yarns so the fibers are in a loose mass when possible; for fabrics where it is impossible to obtain single yarns, the test must be performed on the sliver of fabric.
3. Hold the loosened fibers, or sliver of fabric, in forceps and move them toward the flame from the side.
4. Observe the reaction as they approach the flame.

TABLE 4.1 Burning characteristics of fibers

Fiber	Approaching Flame	In Flame	Removed from Flame	Odor	Residue
Natural Cellulosic cotton and flax	does not shrink away; ignites on contact	burns quickly	continues burning; afterglow	similar to burning paper	light, feathery; light to charcoal gray in color
Man-Made Cellulosic rayon	does not shrink away; ignites on contact	burns quickly	continues burning; afterglow	similar to burning paper	light, fluffy residue; very small amount
Man-Made Modified Cellulosic acetate	fuses and melts away from flame; ignites	burns quickly and evenly	continues to burn rapidly	acrid (hot vinegar)	irregular-shaped, hard, black bead
Natural Protein wool	curls away from flame	burns slowly	self-extinguishing	similar to burning hair	brittle, small, black bead
silk	curls away from flame	burns slowly and sputters	usually self-extinguishing	similar to burning hair	beadlike, crushable, black
weighted silk	curls away from flame	burns slowly and sputters	usually self-extinguishing	similar to burning hair	the shape of fiber or fabric
Natural Mineral asbestos	does not melt (safe fiber)	glows red if heat is sufficient	returns to original form	none	same as original
Man-Made Mineral glass	will not burn	softens, glows red to orange, may change shape	hardens	none	hard, white bead
metallic	*pure* metal has no reaction *coated* metal melts, fuses, and shrinks	glows red burns according to behavior of coating	hardens	none	skeleton outline hard, black bead

5. Move them into the flame for one or two seconds, and then pull them out. Observe the behavior the entire time.
6. Notice any odor given off by the fiber during the burning or charring.
7. Observe ash or residue formed.
8. Repeat for filling yarns when testing woven fabric.

Many fabrics either do not have a visible yarn structure or the yarns are difficult to remove, such as in knitted fabrics. When this occurs the use

TABLE 4.1 Burning characteristics of fibers (*continued*)

Fiber	Approaching Flame	In Flame	Removed from Flame	Odor	Residue
Man-Made Noncellulosic					
acrylic	melts and fuses away from flame; ignites readily	burns rapidly with hot flame and sputtering; drips, melts	continues to burn; hot molten polymer will drop off while burning	acrid	irregular, hard, black bead
modacrylic	fuses away from flame (considered safe)	burns slowly if at all; does not feed a flame	self-extinguishing	acrid, chemical odor	irregular, hard, black bead
nylon	melts away from flame; shrinks, fuses	burns slowly with melting; drips	self-extinguishing	celery	hard, tough, gray or tan bead
polyester	fuses, melts and shrinks away from flame	burns slowly and continues to melt; drips	self-extinguishing	chemical odor	hard, tough, gray or tawny bead
olefin	fuses, shrinks, and curls away from flame	melts, burns slowly	continues to burn	chemical odor	hard, tough tan bead
saran	fuses, melts, and shrinks away from flame	yellow flame burns slowly, melts	self-extinguishing	chemical odor	irregular, crisp black bead
vinal	fuses, shrinks, curls away from flame	burns with melting	continues to burn	chemical odor	hard, tough, tan bead
vinyon	fuses and melts away from flame	burns slowly with melting	self-extinguishing	acrid	irregular, hard, black bead
Elastomers					
spandex	fuses but does not shrink away from flame	burns with melting	continues to burn with melting	chemical odor	soft, sticky, gummy
rubber	shrinks away from flame	burns rapidly with melting	continues to burn	sulfur or chemical odor	tacky, soft, black residue

of the sliver of fabric is acceptable. However, if yarns have been used, it is always desirable to obtain single yarns for the burning test. As noted, if more than one type of fiber has been used in forming the product, the burning test will not give a meaningful result.

A further caution concerning the burning test: Dyes and finishes applied to fabrics may alter the flammability and the burning characteristics. Table 4.1 gives the typical reactions of common fibers when subjected to flame. Results will help identify broad categories but not specific fibers.

TABLE 4.2 Microscopic appearance of textile fibers

Fiber	Longitudinal Appearance	Cross-Sectional Shape
Man-Made		
acetate, triacetate	distinct lengthwise striations; no cross markings	irregular shape with crenulated or serrated outline
acrylic		
Acrilan, Courtelle, Creslan, Zefran	rodlike with smooth surface and profile	nearly round or bean shape
Orlon	broad and often indistinct length-wise striation; no cross markings	dog bone
bicomponent Orlon	lengthwise striations; no cross markings	irregular mushroom or acorn
modacrylic		
SEF	lengthwise striations	irregular round
Verel	broad and often indistinct lengthwise striation; no cross markings	dog bone
nylon		
nylon 6, nylon 6, 6 regular	rodlike with smooth surface and profile	round or nearly round
Antron and Cadon	broad, sometimes indistinct lengthwise striations; no cross markings	trilobal
olefin		
polyethylene, polypropylene	rodlike with smooth surface and profile	round or nearly round
polyester		
Dacron, Fortrel, Kodel, and Vycron	rodlike with smooth surface and profile	round or nearly round
Dacron type 62	broad, sometimes indistinct lengthwise striations; no cross markings	trilobal
Trevira	broad, sometimes indistinct lengthwise striations; no cross markings	pentalobal

Microscopic Evaluation

It is possible to be quite specific in fiber identification of several fiber types through the use of microscopes. For this test fibers should be mounted to obtain views of both the lengthwise and the crosswise dimensions. This test provides some degree of specificity and for some fibers is a positive identification. However, several of the man-made fibers are so similar that microscopic evaluation does not give a specific identification.

As consumers seldom have microscopes available, the microscopic test has little value outside the laboratory. This facet of fiber data does not play a part in normal use and care; therefore, it is not discussed in depth. However, a chart of microscopic characteristics is included for reference (see Table 4.2).

Solubility

The behavior of a fiber in specific chemical reagents is frequently cited as a definite means of fiber identification, especially when solubility data are combined with other test results. Knowledge of how a fiber reacts to selected chemicals is of value to the consumer when considering the use of stain removal agents, detergents, and other laundering and dry cleaning additives.

Acetone, which dissolves acetate and triacetate, is found in fingernail polish and polish removers; accidental spillage of acetone-containing

TABLE 4.2 Microscopic appearance of textile fibers (*continued*)

Fiber	Longitudinal Appearance	Cross-Sectional Shape
rayon		
viscose, regular	distinct lengthwise striations; no cross markings	irregular shape with crenulated or serrated outline
high-tenacity viscose	rodlike with smooth surface; indistinct striations or none	slightly irregular shape with few serrations
high-wet-modulus viscose; Avril, Zantrel	rodlike, smooth surface	round or oval shaped
cuprammonium	rodlike with smooth surface and profile	round or nearly round
saran		
Saran	rodlike with smooth surface and profile	round or nearly round
spandex	broad, often indistinct lengthwise striation; no cross markings	dog bone
Lycra		
Natural		
cotton, mercerized and not mercerized	ribbonlike convolutions (twists) sometimes change direction and are less frequent in mercerized fibers; no significant lengthwise striations, but lumen may appear as striations in some fibers	tubular shape with tubes usually collapsed, and irregular in size
flax, bleached	bamboolike, pronounced cross markings, nodes; no significant lengthwise striations	very irregular in size as well as shape; round and oval are most prevalent
silk, boiled off	smooth surface and profile, but may contain nodes; no significant lengthwise striations	mostly triangular with point of triangle usually rounded off; irregular in size and shape
wool, cashmere, mohair, and regular (Merino)	rough surface, cross markings due to surface scales; medulla or central fiber core sometimes apparent in coarse grades	round or nearly round; medulla may appear shaded

products would cause initial stiffening of acetate or triacetate fabrics followed by complete disintegration.

Vinegar, a 5 to 6 percent acetic acid, will not destroy fibers that would be dissolved by concentrated glacial acetic acid; however, vinegar could weaken fabrics made of affected fibers such as acetate.

Sodium hypochlorite with 5 percent available chlorine is standard undiluted bleach used in laundering. Chlorine bleaches dissolve wool and silk and may weaken other fibers. Thus, bleaches should be used with caution. Other chemical reagents used in fiber identification are seldom encountered in home-care procedures.

Table 4.3 provides an identification procedure using chemical solvents. The order of use *must* be followed carefully to obtain accurate results. Some of the chemicals used would dissolve prior fibers as well as the one(s) cited for specific identification. It is important to follow the directions that appear at the bottom of Table 4.3.

Instrumental Analysis

As stated previously, it is not the purpose of this text to provide sufficient detail for actual laboratory testing to determine fiber content. However, it is important to note the instrumental methods used in fiber analysis. The use of burning, microscopes, and chemical solvents is limited, in most laboratories, to preliminary steps. These procedures are then followed by such instrumental analyses as IR spectrophotometry, electron microscopy,

TABLE 4.3 Schema for identification of fibers by solubility

Chemical	Removes	Chemical	Removes
1. glacial acetic acid, 25° C (75° F)	acetate, triacetate	6. ammonium thiocyanate, at boil, 70% by weight	acrylics
2. hydrochloric acid 1:1, 25° C (75° F)	nylon 6, and 6,6	7. butyrolactone, 25° C (75° F)	modacrylics and nytriles
3. sodium hypochlorite, 25° C (75° F) 5% available chlorine	silk, wool	8. dimethyl formamide, 95° C (200° F)—not always effective	spandex
4. dioxane, 100° C (212° F)	saran	9. sulfuric acid, 75% by weight, 25% (75° F)	cellulosics
5. meta xylene, at boil	olefins	10. meta cresol, 95° C (200° F)	polyesters

When using the identification scheme cited, it is important to follow the procedure enumerated below very carefully.

1. Use the same sample of yarn or fabric until the total substrate, or sample, has been destroyed or put through every test.
2. Place the sample in the first reagent listed at the recommended temperature and leave the sample in the chemical for five minutes before continuing.
3. Remove any material that is left and rinse carefully in water.
4. Observe the amount of material left to determine whether some fiber has been dissolved or altered in any way.
5. In some cases, it may be helpful to look at the remaining fibers under the microscope to determine whether they have been damaged or if some in the sample have been destroyed.
6. Record the results of each step carefully.
7. Place the remaining fibers in solution 2 and repeat the steps above.
8. Continue this procedure until all of the sample has been dissolved or the 10 steps have been completed.

chromatography, X-ray diffraction, and differential thermal analysis (determination of the fiber melting point). Other instruments that might be used determine the refractive index of a fiber and the index of birefringence. Most laboratories have such instruments connected directly to computers and plotters so that records of identification are obtained during the actual testing.

Study Questions

1. What is the value of knowledge of fiber-burning characteristics to consumers of textile products?
2. List at least five test methods that might be used in fiber identification when laboratory facilities are available.
3. What fiber characteristics are involved in the tests given as answers to question 2?
4. The two following chemicals are found in household products. Cite the typical product and then identify fibers that might be damaged by each.
   a. Acetone
   b. Chlorine (sodium hypochlorite)
5. Why is it difficult to provide accurate fiber identification without the use of instrumental tests?
6. How could you determine if a fabric was made of wool or silk with simple household products?
7. Would it be possible to accurately identify silk by using only household products? Why?

Textile Legislation: Rules and Regulations

5

A variety of legislation has been approved during the past fifty years that has been designed to provide consumers with important information at the point of sale and to increase protection and safety in the selection, use, and care of textile products. Inasmuch as such legislation is important in all aspects of the study of textiles, it is included in the introductory portion of this text. As readers study about textile fibers, yarns, fabrics, finishing, and coloring, they may give consideration to the various rules and regulations the government has passed. Those of most importance to consumers are included in this discussion, with the exception of the Textile Fiber Products Identification Act, which has been discussed in Chapter 2.

Wool Products Labeling Act

The Wool Products Labeling Act (WPL) was passed in 1939 to protect producers, manufacturers, distributors, and consumers from the unrevealed presence of substitutes and mixtures in spun, woven, knitted, felted, or otherwise manufactured wool products. The act requires any textile product that has some wool fiber to be labeled to indicate the quantity and type of wool present. Several terms have been defined by the act and its amendments. Important definitions used in labeling wool products include the following.

Wool means the fibers from the fleece of the sheep or lamb or hair of the angora or cashmere goat. It may include the specialty fibers such as camel, alpaca, llama, and vicuna. These latter fibers must be labeled in some way, but they can either be called by the name of the animal from which they are taken or they can be called wool.

Recycled wool means (1) the resulting fiber when wool has been woven or felted into a wool product, which without ever having been utilized in any way by the ultimate consumer, subsequently has been reduced into a fibrous state, or (2) the resulting fiber when wool or reprocessed wool has been spun, woven, knitted, or felted into a wool product, which after having been used in any way by the ultimate consumer, subsequently has been converted back into a fibrous state.

Wool products means any product or portion of a product that contains, purports to contain, or in any way is represented as containing wool, reprocessed wool, or reused wool.

Reprocessed wool, the term used in the original legislation, fits the first definition for recycled wool, whereas *reused wool,* a second term used in the original legislation, fits the second definition. The term *recycled wool,* which was added to the law through amendments made in 1980, supersedes the use of *reprocessed wool* and *reused wool.* How-

LOOK FOR EITHER OF THESE
LABELS IN THIS GARMENT.

PURE WOOL

The sewn in Woolmark label
is your assurance of quality
tested fabrics made of the
world's best...Pure Wool.

WOOL BLEND

The sewn in Woolblend Mark
label is your assurance of
quality tested fabrics made
predominantly of wool.

5.1 Woolmark symbols.

ever, these latter terms still appear in some cross-references in the WPL.

The Federal Trade Commission is responsible for the enforcement of the WPL and provides both manufacturers and consumers with information concerning the act.

Other terms that may be used in relation to wool include the following: *Virgin* or *new* may be used with the term *wool* only when the fiber is new and has never been reclaimed from any type of woolen product. The term *fur fiber* may be used to identify fibers taken from animals normally used for fur such as mink. *Fur fiber* is not acceptable for use with fibers taken from sheep or the specialty animals such as goats, vicunas, llamas, or camels. The term *lamb's wool* is not defined in the rule as it now stands. However, it is frequently used to represent wool taken from animals less than eight months of age.

In general the quality of recycled wool is usually lower than that of new fibers. During the garnetting process that separates the fibers back into a fibrous mass from yarns or fabrics, some damage may occur. However, the warmth factor is not affected, and recycled wool is satisfactory in such products as interlinings, padding for carpeting, and inexpensive blankets.

The manufacturers of wool products may use the trademark for pure 100 percent wool products, called the Woolmark (Fig. 5.1). For fabrics that include other fibers in a blend or combination, the Woolblend mark may be used.

Consumers should seek labels to determine the fiber content—for either wool, covered by the WPL, or other textile fibers, covered by the TFPIA—to verify that labels have been securely attached to the product, and to have the information for use in decision making.

Pure Dye Silk Regulation

The Pure Dye silk regulation concerns the labeling of silk that has or has not been weighted. The regulation has been on the government books for many years. Although the legislation receives little recognition, it is still a requirement in the identification and labeling of silk products. Any silk item, other than black silk fabrics, must be labeled as "weighted silk" if the fiber has more than 10 percent weighting (see Chapter 26 for details on the process). Silk fabrics with 10 percent or less of weighting may be labeled as "pure dye silk." Black silk fabrics may have up to 15 percent weighting before the fabric needs to be called weighted silk. Weighting of silk tends to reduce the durability of silk fabrics and frequently results in cracks and splits, particularly at points where the fabric is bent, such as at cuffs, collars, and hemlines.

Fur Products Labeling Act

The Fur Products Labeling Act was passed in 1952. It has been amended slightly since that time but the basic requirements have not been changed. This law was passed to protect consumers and others against misbranding, false advertising, and false invoicing of furs and fur products.

The act requires that labels identify the true English name of the animal from which the fur is taken, the country of origin, and information about whether the fur product is composed of used, damaged, or scrap fur or fur that has been dyed or bleached. One amendment provided a set of names for identification of the animals, and a further amendment added the provision that furs that have been pointed, dyed, bleached, or artificially colored must be labeled as such.

Important terms defined by this act include the following:

Fur means any animal skin or part thereof with hair, fleece, or fur fibers attached thereto. This term does include skins that are to be converted into leather. *Used fur* means fur in any form that has been worn or used by the ultimate consumer. *Fur product* means any article of wearing apparel made in whole or in part of fur or used fur except that such terms shall not include such articles as the FTC shall exempt by reason of the relatively small quantity or value of the fur.

Care Labeling

Care labeling is required under a trade regulation rule first enacted in 1972; it was amended in late 1983 to be effective in 1984. This rule requires manufacturers and importers of textile wearing apparel and certain piece goods to provide regular care instructions through care labels or other methods described in the rule at the time such products are sold to consumers.

Before labeling products for care, the manufacturer must evaluate or test the product using the care instructions designated to determine their accuracy. Results of all such testing must be retained by the manufacturer and made available to consumers or others if requested. This will undoubtedly increase product cost.

Definitions of importance concerning this rule include the following.

Care label means a permanent label or tag, containing regular care information and instructions, that is attached or affixed in such a manner that it will not become separated from the product and will remain legible during the useful life of the product.

Certain piece goods means textile products sold by the piece from bolts or rolls for the purpose of making home-sewn textile wearing apparel. This term includes remnants, the fiber content of which is known, that are cut by a retailer but does not include manufacturer's remnants up to 10 yards in length that are clearly marked "pound goods" or "fabrics of undetermined origin."

Dry cleaning means a commercial process by which soil is removed from products or specimens in a machine that uses common organic solvents. The process may also include adding moisture to the solvent, up to 75 percent relative humidity, hot tumble drying up to 160° F (71° C), and restoration by steam press or steam-air finishing.

Machine wash means a process by which soil is removed from products in a specially designed machine using water, detergent or soap, and agitation. When no temperatures are given (e.g., warm or cold), hot water up to 150° F (66° C) can be regularly used.

Regular care means customary and routine care and not spot care.

The current Care Labeling Rule provides specific information concerning the labeling of wearing apparel. These include the following:

1. Manufacturers and importers must attach care labels so that they can be seen and easily found when the product is offered for sale to consumers. If the product is packaged, displayed, or folded so that consumers cannot see or easily find the care label, care instructions must also appear on the outside of the package or on a hangtag fastened to the product.
2. Care labels must state what regular care is needed for the ordinary use of the product. In general, labels for textile wearing apparel must have either a washing or a dry cleaning instruction. If a washing instruction is indicated, it must comply with the requirements set forth in paragraph a

cited below. If dry cleaning instruction is included, it must comply with the requirements cited in paragraph b below. If either washing or dry cleaning can be used on the product, the label must have only one of these instructions. If the product cannot be cleaned by any available cleaning method without being harmed, the label must so state.

a. Washing, drying, ironing, bleaching, and warning instructions must follow these requirements:

i. Washing: The label must state whether the product should be washed by hand or by machine. The label must also state a water temperature that may be used. However, if the regular use of hot water will not harm the product, the label need not mention any water temperature.

ii. Drying: The label must state whether the product should be dried by machine or by some other method. If machine drying is called for, the label must also state a drying temperature that may be used. However, if the regular use of a high temperature will not harm the product, the label need not mention any drying temperature. For example, the term *tumble dry* means that any temperature may be used; however, if the phrase *tumble dry at medium temperature* is used, drying cannot exceed the medium temperature setting.

iii. Ironing: Ironing must be mentioned on a label only if it will be needed on a regular basis to preserve the appearance of the product or if it is required under section v. Warning: If ironing is mentioned, the label must also state an ironing temperature that may be used. However, if the regular hot iron will not harm the product, the label need not mention any ironing temperature.

iv. Bleaching: (a) If all commercially available bleaches can be safely used on a regular basis, the label need not mention bleaching. (b) If all commercially available bleaches would harm the product when used on a regular basis, the label must say "No bleach" or "Do not bleach." (c) If regular use of chlorine bleach would harm the product but regular use of a nonchlorine bleach would not, the label must say "Only nonchlorine bleach, when needed."

v. Warnings: (a) If there is any part of the prescribed washing procedure that consumers can reasonably be expected to use that would harm the product or others being washed with it in one or more washings, the label must contain a warning to this effect. For example, if a shirt is not colorfast, its label should state "Wash with like colors" or "Wash separately." (b) Warnings are not necessary for any procedure that is an alternative to the procedure prescribed on the label. For example, if an instruction states, "Dry flat," it is not necessary to give the warning "Do not tumble dry."

b. Drycleaning:

i. General: If a drycleaning instruction is included on the label, it must also state at least one type of solvent that may be used. However, if all commercially available types of solvents can be used, the label need not mention any type of solvent.

ii. Warning: If there is any part of the drycleaning process that consumers or drycleaners can reasonably be expected to use that would harm the product or others being cleaned with it, the label must contain a warning to this effect. For example, if steam will harm the product, the label must state "Professionally dryclean, no steam." A warning is not necessary for any procedure that is an alternative to the procedure prescribed on the label. For example, if a label reads "Professionally dryclean, fluorocarbon," it is not necessary to add the warning "Do not use perchloroethylene."

Care labels must be provided for piece goods or yardage, except for certain exemptions. The label must provide information concerning regular care and must be available to give to customers at the time of purchase.

If a product carries no label it is to be assumed that any method of care can be applied without damage to the item—hot water, hot drying, hot ironing, bleaching with all types of bleaches, and dry cleaning by any method. Such products, however, must have some indication at the point of purchase that any care procedure can be used safely.

The regulation has provided a glossary of care terms. These definitions are included in the glossary of this text under the heading Care Terminology.

Figure 5.2 gives a few examples of typical care labels found in apparel items on the consumer market.

5.2 Care labels typically found in items of apparel.

Flammable Fabrics Act

The initial Flammable Fabrics Act was passed in 1953 to regulate the manufacture for sale in interstate commerce of all highly flammable wearing apparel fabrics. It was specifically designed to prohibit the sale of exceedingly hazardous or "torch"-type fabrics. At that time it was under the control of the Secretary of Commerce; the Secretary of Health, Education, and Welfare; and the Federal Trade Commission. Since then the jurisdiction for responsibility and enforcement has been given to the Consumer Products Safety Commission.

The original act was modified in 1967 to cover a wide range of clothing and interior furnishings. Since that time various standards have been added to provide for control of specific items such as carpets and rugs, mattresses and mattress pads, children's sleepwear sizes 0 to 14, and some upholstery fabrics.

There are a few terms used in relation to flammability that require careful definition.

Flame resistance (noun): The property of a material whereby flaming combustion is prevented, terminated, or inhibited following application of a flaming or nonflaming source of ignition with or without subsequent removal of the ignition source. (See ASTM yearbooks for current definitions.)*

Flame resistant (adjective): Having flame resistance.

Flame retardant (adjective): Undefined. This term should not be used except in the terms *flame-retardant treated* or *flame-retardant treatment*.

Flame retardant (noun): A chemical used to impart flame resistance.

Flame-retardant treatment (noun): A process for incorporating or adding flame retardants to material or to a product.

Current standards for control of fabric flammability cover clothing textiles, vinyl plastic films, large carpets and rugs, small carpets and rugs, children's sleepwear sizes 0 to 14.

Methods of testing each of these for their flammability will vary somewhat among products. For regular testing the flame used is 5/8 inch; for children's sleepwear the test flame is 1 and 1/2 inches. A special tablet is used for carpets and rugs.

*ASTM, *Annual Book of ASTM Standards,* Vol. 07.01, 1986, pp. 34–35.

It must be noted that treating fabrics to reduce flammability does not prevent them from burning. Nearly every fabric encountered in apparel or home furnishings will burn when in a flame; the only exception is glass, which will melt. Treating fabrics to reduce flammability reduces the danger of physical damage, but consumers must realize that it does not eliminate all danger.

Compliance with flame-resistance legislation has presented many difficulties. Technology concerning effective and safe finishing substances has encountered many problems, including the banning of one of the most popular and effective finishing compounds because it is a carcinogen.

Care of flame-treated fabrics poses some major problems. Detergents other than the phosphate type do not work well with flame-retardant finishes; and in some locations phosphate detergents are banned because of environmental concerns. Soap should never be used on flame-retardant treated fabrics because it masks the effectiveness of the finish and increases the flammability. Fabric softeners increase the flammability of fabrics; bleaches remove and/or destroy the finish. Fabrics that are made flame resistant through the use of fibers that have been made inherently flame resistant are the best choice. Whatever the item, care instructions should be followed carefully.

The legislation has been designed to increase human safety. Consumers may feel it is an infringement on their rights, as it does increase cost and reduce the amount of choice available for selected end-use items. However, for many consumers the safety is worth the added cost.

Consumers' Responsibility

The provision of information about the fiber content, care, and flame resistance of textile items is mandated by legislation. The success of such legislation is determined, to a great extent, by the consumer. If information required by law is not provided, the consumer has a responsibility to identify what is missing and request such information from the seller. If the seller shows no interest, it should be reported to the agency responsible for its enforcement.

Study Questions

1. Cite the various rules and regulations that are important in relation to the sale of textile products.
2. Describe each of the following in terms of what it does for the consumer:
   a. Wool Products Labeling Act
   b. Fur Products Labeling Act
   c. Care Labeling Rule
   d. Flammable Fabrics Act
3. Refer to Chapter 2 and indicate what the TFPIA is and what it requires in relation to textile product labeling.
4. What agency is responsible for the administration and control of the following rules and regulations?
   a. Wool Products Labeling Act
   b. Care Labeling Rule
   c. Textile Fiber Products Identification Act (TFPIA)
   d. Flammable Fabrics Act
5. Visit stores and observe the presence or absence of labels on textile items. What can be done to increase compliance with the various legal rules and regulations?

Textile Fibers

PART II

The study of textile fibers has expanded tremendously throughout the twentieth century. In 1900 a section on textile fibers would have probably included only chapters on the natural fibers, with a brief mention that research was underway to develop man-made cellulosic fibrous forms. Today, the study of textiles involves a wide variety of manufactured as well as natural fibers. Thus, this part of the book now has a total of eleven chapters and covers a broad field of different types of textile fibers.

References cited in the Bibliography provide much more information and detail about the various fibers. This text describes fibers by groups and includes a brief history; information on production; fiber properties; and discussion of selection, use, and care.

Chapter 6 describes the natural protein fibers; Chapter 7, the natural cellulosic fibers. Chapters 8 through 14 discuss generic groups of manufactured fibers that are of general interest. Chapter 15 describes special organic noncellulosic fibers that have limited interest to consumers but may increase in importance in the future. Chapter 16 treats the inorganic fibers, including glass and metallics.

Natural Protein Fibers

6

Natural protein fibers are obtained from animal sources—from the hair covering of selected animals and from animal secretions. Hair fibers include coverings from such animals as sheep, mohair goat, cashmere goat, camel, llama, alpaca, and vicuna; fur fibers come from animals more often valued for their pelts, such as mink, rabbit, beaver, and muskrat. Secretions are obtained from the larva, or worm stage, of the silkworm, which spins the cocoon from which silk fibers are obtained, and from the spider, which spins fine fibers in making its web. Hair and fur fibers have many properties in common; secretion fibers have some properties in common. Some properties or characteristics are similar within the entire protein fiber group; however, there are some obvious differences between hair and secretion fibers.

Fibers in this group have excellent moisture absorbency. Their standard moisture regain is high, and they absorb additional moisture at the saturation point. Protein fibers tend to be warmer than natural cellulosic fibers. The low degree of electrical conductance contributes to a buildup of static charge, so the resulting yarns and fabrics tend to release much static electricity, although this problem is reduced in the presence of moisture.

Natural protein fibers have poor resistance to alkalies and can be dissolved in a 5 percent solution of sodium hydroxide at the boiling point. Most fibers in this group show good resistance to acids, the exception being silk, which is damaged or completely destroyed by concentrated mineral acids. Protein fibers are harmed by many oxidizing agents, particularly chlorine-type oxidizing bleaches. However, hydrogen peroxide, also an oxidizing agent, is used safely and successfully to bleach wool and silk. Sunlight causes white fabrics of the natural protein fibers to discolor slowly and become yellow or light tan.

Fibers in this group have good resiliency and elastic recovery. All protein fibers except silk, from the silkworm, are comparatively weak, so care must be exercised in cleaning.

WOOL

Historical Review

The early history of wool is lost in antiquity. Sheepskin, including the hair, was probably used long before the discovery that the fibers could be spun into yarns or even felted into fabric. There is no evidence to support the theory that wool was the first fiber to be processed into fabric, but it seems certain that, as part of the skin, wool was used for covering and protection by prehistoric people.

Today, sheep are raised in every state of the contiguous United States and in most countries located in the temperate zones of both the Northern and Southern hemispheres. The center for sheep raising in the United States is in the West.

Although large areas of the United States are suitable for wool production, it produces less than 2 percent of the world's supply. Australia produces nearly 25 percent of the world's supply, followed by New Zealand with 14 percent. To meet consumer needs, approximately 30 percent of the wool used in the United States is imported.

Growth and Production

To provide the finest quality wool for the consumer, manufacturers control production carefully and scientifically. Sheep are inoculated against disease, dipped in chemicals to protect them from insects, and fed nutritionally balanced diets to produce healthy animals. Sheep in small herds live in sanitary, fenced-in shelters and are allowed to graze in clean pastures. Although large herds in the western United States, Australia, and New Zealand are free to roam open range land, sheepherders watch and protect the animals and make certain that the range land has adequate and nutritious food supplies.

Wool can be sheared from the living animal or pulled from the hide after the animal has been slaughtered for its meat. The sheared wool is called *fleece* or *clip wool*. Fibers taken from the slaughtered animal hide are called *pulled wool* and are frequently of lower quality than sheared wool.

Shearing takes place once a year in most locations; however, in areas where temperatures remain relatively warm throughout the year the sheep may be sheared twice. This practice tends to keep animals comfortable and reduces the amount of extra-long and coarse fibers, which are less desirable than the fine fibers. Experienced shearers can shear a sheep in fewer than thirty seconds (Fig. 6.1).

During the 1970s research workers in the United States and Australia developed a system of chemical shearing. The animals are fed a special chemical, which causes the wool to become loose from the skin, or fall away, and it can then be brushed together and removed without mechanical shearing. Under carefully controlled conditions there is no damage to the animal, and hair growth resumes within a short time. The advantages of this procedure are that it is easy to collect the wool, the fiber length is longer than that obtained from shearing, and there is less damage to the fiber. However, this process is still experimental, and most areas still depend on mechanical shearing.

Pulled wool is removed from the hide by one of two methods. It may be treated with a depilatory that loosens the fibers and permits them to be pulled away from the skin without damaging the hide, or it can be loosened by the action of bacteria on the root end of the fiber. Pulled wool, when used, is usually mixed with fleece wool before processing into yarns and fabrics.

Preliminary grading of wool fibers occurs while the fibers are still in the fleece because this step is important in determining cost. Fleeces are then shipped to the mill where they will be processed into yarns and/or fabrics.

6.1 Shearing sheep to obtain wool fibers.

Fiber Properties

Microscopic Properties

Under microscopic observation, the length of the wool fiber clearly shows a scalelike structure (Fig. 6.2). The size of the scales varies from very small to comparatively broad and long. Fine wool does not have scales as clear and distinct as coarse wool, but they can usually be identified under magnification as low as 100 power.

A cross section of wool shows three distinct parts of the fiber (Fig. 6.3). The outer layer is called the *epidermis* and is composed of the

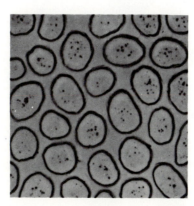

6.2 left. Photomicrograph of wool fiber, longitudinal view. Note scalelike surface. (E. I. DuPont de Nemours & Company)

6.3 right. Photomicrograph of wool fiber, cross section. (E. I. DuPont de Nemours & Company)

scales. The major portion of the fiber is the *cortex,* the central part, which accounts for about 90 percent of the fiber mass. In the center is the *medulla,* the area through which food reaches the fiber during the growth cycle. It also contains the pigment that gives color to the fiber. It could be noted that the hair fibers have characteristics very similar to human hair.

Physical Properties

Wool fibers vary in length from about 1 1/2 inches to 15 inches. Fine wools are usually from 1 1/2 to 5 inches long, medium wools from 2 1/2 to 6 inches, and coarse wools from 5 to 15 inches. The width of wool also varies considerably. Fine fibers such as Merino wool have an average diameter of about 15 to 17 microns; medium wool, from 24 to 34 microns; and coarse wools, about 40 microns. Some wool fibers are extremely coarse and stiff, and these may be called *kemp;* they are usually used in making industrial felts, carpeting padding, or inexpensive wool carpets.

Wool fibers have a natural crimp, or built-in waviness, similar to a curl in human hair (Fig. 6.4). The crimp increases the elasticity and elongation properties of the fiber and aids in yarn manufacturing.

Wool varies in the degree of luster. Fine and some medium fibers have enough luster to appear silky; coarse fibers are often dull. The color of the natural wool fiber depends on the breed of sheep and may vary from almost white to black. Most wool, after scouring, is a yellowish white or ivory color. (See Table 6.1.)

Compared to many other fibers, wool is weak. This weakness restricts the kinds of yarn and fabric construction to some degree; however, other properties such as resiliency, elongation, and elastic recovery compensate for the low strength and make it possible to produce wool yarns and fabrics that possess outstanding durability.

Wool has good elongation properties and elastic recovery, and resiliency is exceptionally good. As a result, wool fabrics will readily spring back into shape after crushing or creasing. Through the application of heat, moisture, and pressure, durable creases or pleats can be put into wool fabrics. The excellent resiliency of wool fiber gives it loft, which pro-

6.4 Varieties of wool fiber showing natural crimp.

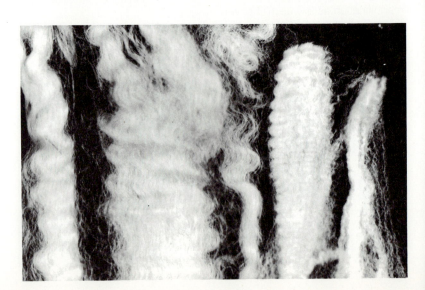

TABLE 6.1 Properties of wool fibers

Property	Evaluation
Shape	fiber length varies from 1½ inches to about 15 inches; width varies from 15 to 70 microns. Fiber has a natural crimp, or waviness
Luster	medium
Tenacity (strength)	
dry	1.0–1.7 g/d
wet	0.8–1.6 g/d
Elastic recovery	99% recovery at 2% extension
Elongation	
dry	20–40%
wet	20–70% +
Resiliency	excellent
Density	1.30–1.32 g/ccm
Moisture absorption	
20° C/65% R.H.	13.6–16.0% of fiber weight
saturation	29% +
Dimensional stability	subject to felting and relaxation shrinkage
Resistance to	
acids	good
alkalies	low; many alkalies destroy the fiber
sunlight	prolonged exposure deteriorates fiber
microorganisms	generally good
insects	damaged by moths and carpet beetles
Thermal reactions	
to heat	avoid prolonged exposure to temperatures over 140° C
to flame	burns slowly when in direct flame; is considered to be self-extinguishing

duces a wide variety of fabrics with good covering power that range from light and sheer constructions through heavy, thick fabrics. In general, wool fabrics tend to be warm.

Wool will absorb moisture to a high degree—approximately 30 percent of its weight. This ability is responsible for its comfort in humid, cold environments. As part of the moisture absorption function, wool produces or liberates heat, which helps keep the body warm in inclement weather. This same property also permits the fiber to accept color easily. However, in spite of the ability to absorb large amounts of moisture, the surface of the fiber has a hydrophobic property and tends to shed water and other liquids.

When wool yarns and fabrics are subjected to mechanical actions, such as agitation or abrasion combined with heat and moisture, they tend to become entangled and matted. This causes yarns to decrease in length and increase in diameter, which in turn results in fabrics that are dimensionally smaller in length but thicker than the original. This is called *felting shrinkage,* and it is used to advantage in making more compact, fuller, and more attractive fabrics than are obtained directly from the loom or other manufacturing machinery. However, it should be obvious that improper control of this process would result in fabrics that are highly unsatisfactory, and consumers must pay particular attention during the care of wool products to prevent this felting, which would severely damage the product.

Wool fabrics are likely to shrink after weaving or knitting as a result of yarn and fabric relaxation in addition to the felting shrinkage. This *relaxation shrinkage* must be considered by manufacturers of fabrics and, when possible, eliminated before placing products on the consumer market. Moisture tends to release any relaxation tension still remaining in yarns and fabrics, and thus, unless properly treated before use, shrinkage will occur during consumer care and result in an undesirable product.

Thermal Properties

Wool burns slowly in the presence of flame with a slight sputtering. It is self-extinguishing; that is, it stops burning when removed from the source of fire if it has its normal moisture regain. However, if the fiber is very dry, it will continue to burn even after the source of flame has been removed. It is possible to make wool flame resistant, but this involves the addition of special chemical compounds.

A crisp, brittle, black, bead-shaped ash is formed when wool burns; the odor given off may be compared to the smell of burning hair, meat, or feathers. Wool may be safely steamed with a damp press cloth. When pressing, or ironing, temperatures below 300° F (140° C) should be used.

Chemical Properties

Wool protein is particularly susceptible to damage by alkaline substances. Solutions of 5 percent sodium hydroxide will dissolve the fiber; strong detergents or soap, which are alkaline, should be avoided.

Wool is considered resistant to action by mild or dilute acids, but strong, concentrated mineral acids will eventually result in fiber decomposition.

Solvents used in cleaning and stain removal for wool fabrics have no damaging effects; however, chlorine bleaches damage the fiber and in concentrated form, as it comes from the bottle, will dissolve the fiber.

After prolonged exposure to direct sunlight, wool deteriorates. But if the fabric is properly protected and stored, there is no destructive effect; wools may be kept for many years when properly packaged for storage.

Biological Properties

Wool has good resistance to bacteria and mildew; however, microorganisms may attack stains on the fabric, particularly food stains. If wool is stored in an atmosphere where moisture is present, mildew will form and eventually destroy the fiber. Rot-producing bacteria will bring about the destruction of wool that has been subjected to moisture and soil for long periods of time.

Wool is a protein fiber and may be considered a food product for certain types of life. This makes it an appetizing meal for several types of insects. The larvae of the clothes moth and the carpet beetle are the most common predators on wool as a source of food. Various treatments used to prevent this damage include the following:

1. Spraying the fabric with chemicals that will kill the insects; these finishes need frequent renewing since dry cleaning or laundering tends to remove them.

2. Applying chemicals that react with the wool molecules and make the fiber unpalatable to the moth; this process is durable to laundering or dry cleaning and is the most successful.
3. Using substances in close proximity to wool that emit odors that are noxious to the insects

Use and Care

Care of Wool Products

A major problem with wool fiber and wool fabrics is a tendency to shrink during use and care. Considerable time, energy, and money have been directed toward the development of processing techniques and finishing operations that can be applied to wool fabrics to make them stable. As a result numerous woolen or worsted fabrics are available that do resist shrinkage during a normal life. However, even wool fabrics identified as washable require special handling during care procedures. During laundering, wool products should be handled as little as possible, not wrung, not agitated through regular laundry cycles, and not twisted, to remove excess water. Constant temperatures in both washing and rinsing cycles should be maintained. A neutral or mild soap or detergent should be used, and if bleaching is required, it should be hydrogen peroxide or perborate bleaches, not chlorine bleach. Wool products that are considered washable should be clearly labeled with care directions. Almost any wool can be dry cleaned, but if spotting or stain removal is required, the dry cleaner should be advised that the product is made of wool fiber.

Consumers should be aware of some basic guidelines in caring for wool apparel. After wear, woven wool garments should be placed on hangers and brushed carefully. This removes surface dust and soil and permits wrinkles to hang out. Knitted garments, especially loose knits such as sweaters and stoles, should be aired and then folded and stored in drawers to prevent sagging and misshaping from hangers. Frequent cleaning reduces insect damage and increases the life of wool fabrics. Wool carpeting should be cleaned frequently to keep soil out of the pile. At least weekly vacuuming should be done; and any stains should be removed as promptly as possible. Wool upholstery should be brushed and vacuumed often to remove soil and dust and prevent damage to the fibers from abrasion of the soil.

Use of Wool

Woolen and worsted fabrics are widely used throughout the world. They have special acceptance in many places because of their desirable properties of warmth, comfort, elastic recovery, flexibility, resiliency, and appearance. Both woolen and worsted fabrics can be tailored to fit well; they press easily and can be shaped by steam and pressing to conform to the body so they look and feel good (Fig. 6.5). They provide outstanding floor coverings that retain their appearance and give excellent wear. They make attractive and durable upholstery fabrics. *Worsted* fabrics are those made of fine yarns and long fibers, and they are usually smooth and crisp in feel. *Woolen* fabrics are usually made of shorter fibers and rough-textured yarns, usually have considerable bulk, and feel soft.

Despite the natural crease resistance of wool, additional finishes are applied by some manufacturers for special characteristics; these finishes provide a loftier fiber that returns to shape more easily than unfinished fi-

6.5 Wool fiber in apparel. (Hoechst Fibers)

ber. Researchers have also found that variations in fabric weight tend to affect creasing and recovery from wrinkling, with heavier, fuller fabrics performing better than lightweight ones.

Procedures for making wool fabrics both washable and flame resistant have been developed during the past decade and are used on a selected group of fabrics.

A variety of fabrics available to consumers are blends of wool and man-made fibers. The most common are blends of wool and nylon; wool and polyester; wool and acrylic; and some blends of wool and two other fibers such as wool, rayon, and nylon or polyester. Blends provide several desirable properties: They are usually easy to clean, hold creases and pleats satisfactorily, and are comfortable. Nylon in amounts as low as 12 to 15 percent will stabilize wool fabrics and prevent shrinkage during laundering, providing care is used in the laundering operations.

Wool products must be labeled to identify not only the fact that wool fiber has been used but also whether or not the fiber is new or recycled (see Chapter 5).

SPECIALTY AND FUR FIBERS

Textile fibers obtained from such animals as the goat, camel, alpaca, llama, and vicuna are referred to as *specialty fibers*. These fibers are available in limited quantities and are desired for special characteristics. Although these fibers may also be identified as wool, this is seldom done because the marketability of the specialty fibers is enhanced by the specific fiber or animal name.

Mohair

Mohair is the fiber of the Angora goat (Fig. 6.6). It is not to be confused with the fur fiber obtained from the Angora rabbit. Angora goats are raised in Angora, Turkey, from which they got their name; in areas of South Africa; in Australia; and in the states of Texas and Arizona.

Angora goats usually are sheared twice a year, in which case the

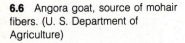

6.6 Angora goat, source of mohair fibers. (U. S. Department of Agriculture)

fibers are fine and silky in appearance and measure 4 to 6 inches in length. Occasionally, the goats are sheared only once a year to make the fiber longer for special uses.

Mohair resembles wool fiber in both physical and chemical properties. Its major advantages include remarkable resistance to wear and abrasion, a high degree of luster, excellent resiliency, and adaptability to complex yarns and textured fabrics. Mohair is found in such end uses as furniture upholstery, carpeting for special uses, some draperies, and suiting and sportswear fabrics; it may be blended with other fibers, including wool.

Cashmere

Cashmere is the fiber of the cashmere (Kashmir) goat, which is raised in the high mountains of Mongolia and China. High-quality cashmere is also available from herds in Iran, India, Afghanistan, and Turkey. Some cashmere goats are now raised in the United States, and fiber is available in small amounts from these animals.

The fiber is combed from the animal, and the yield per goat averages about 4 ounces of usable fiber. The short fibers, 1 to 3 1/2 inches, are very soft and fine; longer fibers, 2 to 5 inches, are somewhat coarse and stiff.

Yearly production of cashmere fibers is very small; thus, the fiber is relatively expensive. Cashmere fabrics are considered luxury items, but consumers who want very soft, warm, comfortable, and attractive products will pay the price.

Cashmere is similar to wool in most properties, except for the fact that it is finer and softer and more easily damaged by alkalies than wool. With proper care it will give good service. It can be used to produce fabrics that range from very thick to very sheer and fine. It tends to abrade more easily than wool and may loose its surface appearance if used in a product that encounters considerable rubbing. For best results dry cleaning is recommended as the best care procedure.

Camel Hair

Camel hair is obtained from the Bactrian, or two-humped, camel. This breed serves as a means of transportation in Asia and in the desert regions of China, Tibet, and Mongolia. The animal sheds about 5 pounds of fiber each year. This fiber is collected by those in charge of the animals and sent to centers where the fibers are available for purchase by fabric manufacturers. Camel hair is a natural golden brown color with a medium luster. The fabrics are warm, soft, and comfortable; they wear well and drape attractively.

There are two types of camel hair fibers: outer hair, which is long and coarse, and body hair, which is shorter and very fine. The short body hair is made into fine-quality yarns suitable for knitting and weaving into quality fabrics. The long, coarse hair is made into heavy yarns used in industrial fabrics for such products as transmission beltings. Fibers are also used in making artists' paintbrushes.

Fine camel hair products require the same careful handling as cashmere and mohair. Camel hair is used for coatings and sportswear fabrics and in some knitted products. The natural tan to reddish-brown color is attractive and frequently retained for final textile products.

Alpaca

The alpaca is a member of the camel family and is native to South America. It thrives in the Andes Mountain regions of Peru, Bolivia, Ecuador, and Argentina. The fiber is sheared from the animal once every two years. The fine fibers, which are separated from the coarse guard hairs, are used for textile fabrics. Long fibers may be matted into fabrics that are used for floor coverings.

Like camel hair, alpaca offers excellent warmth and insulation. The fibers are strong and glossy and make fabrics similar in appearance to mohair. Alpaca fabrics appear in suits, dresses, plush upholstery, and special linings. The natural color ranges from white to brown and black, and a variety of attractive fabrics can be created without additional dyestuffs.

Llama

Llama is also a member of the camel family. The llama produces fibers similar to those of the alpaca and is found in the same geographical area. The fibers, sheared once a year, are soft, strong, and relatively uniform in length and diameter but somewhat weaker than alpaca or camel hair.

South American Indians weave most of the pure llama fabrics. Some fiber is sold to wool manufacturers for blending with sheep's wool, other specialty fibers, or man-made fibers.

Vicuna

The most valuable and most prized hair fiber is that obtained from the vicuna, a small animal, about the size of a large dog, that is found in the Andes Mountains at elevations of approximately 16,000 feet. It is a member of the llama and the South American camel family. The vicuna is extremely wild, and attempts to domesticate it have been relatively unsuccessful to date; however, efforts by ranchers to raise the animal in captivity are continuing.

Vicuna is one of the softest fibers in the world; it is fine and lustrous, has a lovely cinnamon brown or light tan color, and is relatively strong. Fabrics of vicuna are lightweight and warm. The most frequent use for the fiber is for coat and suit fabrics and other types of outerwear.

Because the fiber can be obtained, usually, only by killing the animal, to protect the species from becoming extinct, the government of Peru limits the yearly kill. Each animal yields about 4 ounces of fine fiber plus 10 to 12 ounces of shorter, less choice fiber. The fine fiber is preferred for apparel fabrics; the shorter fibers may be used in various types of rough fabrics and in some matted floor covering materials. The total yearly production of vicuna fiber is just a few thousand pounds, so garments and fabrics of vicuna compare in price with expensive fur coats.

Fur Fibers

Fibers often blended in small amounts with wool or selected man-made fibers are obtained from several animals more frequently used for their fur pelts. These include mink, beaver, fox, chinchilla, muskrat, nutria, raccoon, and rabbit. Such fibers are added to fabrics primarily for softness, color, and prestige.

The angora fiber from the Angora rabbit appears frequently in knitting yarns and in knitted fabrics because it gives a fluffy, white, silky appearance to the end product. The Angora rabbit is raised in France, Italy, Japan, and the United States. The fur is combed and clipped every three months. Fibers are smooth, lustrous, fine, and resilient.

SILK

Historical Review

The history of silk combines both fact and myth, and it is difficult to separate the two. However, the legends concerning silk are all romantic and interesting. One of the most commonly told tales is as follows.

Emperor Huang-Ti, who ruled China sometime between 2700 and 2600 B.C., assigned his empress, Hsi-Ling-Shi, the task of studying a blight that was damaging the imperial mulberry grove. Tiny white worms were devouring the leaves, then crawling from leaf to stem to spin shining, pale (almost white) cocoons. Hsi-Ling-Shi gathered a handful of cocoons and carried them into her apartment, where she accidentally dropped one into a basin of hot water. The empress noticed that the cocoon separated into a delicate cobweblike tangle from which she could draw a slender tiny filament into the air. Further, she observed that the filament was continuous, and the more she unwound, the smaller the cocoon became. Thus, one legend, probably a combination of fact and fiction, records the discovery of silk fibers.

The move of a silk industry from China to other countries did not occur until about the time of Marco Polo, and even then, it involved considerable espionage to get silk culture into other countries. Today, silk is produced primarily in China Japan, and Thailand.

Throughout the development of the silk industry, this fiber has maintained a position of great prestige and is still considered a luxury. Silk is often called the "queen of fibers," a title well deserved by virtue of its association with royalty, the care required in its culture, and the properties and characteristics with which it has been endowed.

Sericulture (Growth and Production)

Silk is produced by the larvae of several moths, but the *Bombyx mori* is the only one raised under controlled conditions. These larvae live on mulberry leaves only, and each tiny larva consumes an extremely large number of leaves during its short lifespan. Raising these insects is a skilled occupation and requires countless hours of labor. The present-day industry is carefully controlled to prevent disease, and modern silk "factories" are as clean and frequently as sterile as hospital operating rooms. It should be noted that recent developments by researchers in Japan have made it possible to prepare a foodstuff based on the mulberry leaf that is proving to be as successful as the leaf itself. This modern food reduces the damage to the trees but, more important, makes it possible to have a food supply during an entire year.

The life cycle of the female *Bombyx mori* is relatively brief. Furthermore, domestication over the ages has resulted in a moth that does not fly. The cycle has been exploited further, so there is an orderly sequence in raising the worm that makes it possible to have a continuous industry. When it is not possible to have worms at the correct stages for continuous production, the cocoon can be held in storage until needed for reeling. The female moth lays between 400 and 700 eggs. Each egg is about the size of a pinhead, and each has a small dot on one end that is soft and permits the larva to hatch easily. The eggs are carefully screened and tested to ensure freedom from disease. They can be kept for long periods of time in cold storage without damage. When a supply of food is available, the eggs are warmed slightly; three to seven days later the worm hatches and begins to feed on the tender mulberry leaves or the manufactured food now used in some locations. A newborn larva is about 1/4 inch long. Although the larvae of the *Bombyx mori* are called silkworms, they are technically caterpillars.

During the growth cycle of the larva, it molts (sheds its outer skin) four times. Each time it grows a new skin to fit its larger size. After the fourth molting, it eats for about ten more days, making a total eating period of about twenty-five to thirty-five days. It is approximately 3 inches long and from 1/4 to 1/2 inch in diameter when it reaches full growth (Fig. 6.7).

Other moths are used for silk fiber; these are usually called wild silkworms, and they frequently feed on oak or other leaves. These wild silkworms tend to produce very large and irregular cocoons; color may vary from almost white to a very dark brown.

The cultivated larva attaches itself to a specially constructed straw frame, rears its head, and begins to spew the silk liquid, which hardens on contact with air. The larva spins by moving its head in a figure-eight motion and constructs the cocoon from the outside in (Fig. 6.8). As it spins, the larva decreases in size, and upon completion of the cocoon, it changes into the dormant chrysalis stage. Except for those used for breeding, the cocoons are subjected to heat, which kills the chrysalis. These cocoons can then be stored until they are unreeled in preparation for yarn manufacture.

The silkworm extrudes the liquid from two tiny orifices, or *spinnerettes,* in its head. As the liquid emerges into the air, it solidifes into the silk filaments (Fig. 6.9). The fibers, called fibroin, are coated with a sticky protein substance called sericin, which holds the filaments together in the cocoon.

6.7 left.   Silk worms on mulberry leaves.

6.8 below left.   Silk cocoons.

6.9 below right.   Silk filaments.

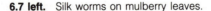

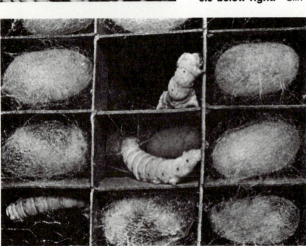

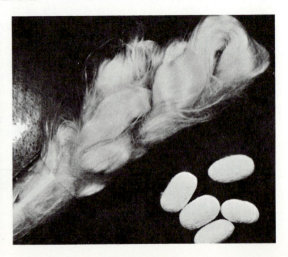

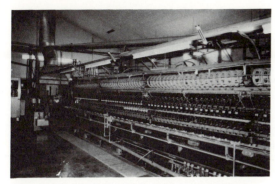

6.10 Reeling silk. (Sericulture Experiment Station, Japan)

Processing

Silk filaments are unwound from the cocoons in a manufacturing plant called a *filature*. Several cocoons are placed in hot water to soften the gum, and the surfaces are brushed lightly to find the end of the filaments. These ends are collected, threaded through a guide, and wound onto a wheel called a reel; hence the process is called *reeling*.

Reeling, until recently, has been largely a process done by people; even now much reeling is done by manual labor; however, new machinery has been developed that will do most of the work mechanically (Fig. 6.10). Even so, reeling of silk still demands considerable actual manual labor.

As the fibers are combined and pulled onto the reel, twist can be inserted to hold the filaments together. This operation is called *throwing,* and the resulting yarn is called *thrown yarn*. Fibers may be thrown in a separate operation, but the process remains basically identical.

The *sericin,* the gum that holds the filaments together, remains on the fibers during reeling and throwing; it is removed after these steps by a process called *degumming*. Sometimes the sericin may be left on the yarn until after the fabric has been completed. Before finishing, the gum is removed by boiling the fabric in soap and water. If stiffness is desired in the completed fabric, such as in taffeta, some of the gum may be put back onto the fabric; however, this is discouraged by many because it increases the tendency for silk to waterspot during use and care.

Silk filaments may be cut into short, staple fiber lengths and processed by using techniques similar to those used for cotton or wool (see Chapter 17). In addition to cutting silk filaments, short lengths of fiber are frequently obtained from the outer and inner edges of the cocoons and from broken cocoons.

Fiber Properties

Silk is a natural protein fiber. The actual protein is called *fibroin,* and it is composed of about fifteen amino acids hooked together in long molecular chains.

Microscopic Properties

Cultivated, degummed silk resembles a smooth, transparent rod when viewed longitudinally under a microscope (Fig. 6.11). If gum is still present, the fiber surface appears rough and irregular. Wild silk tends to be

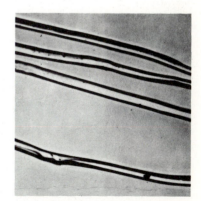

6.11 Photomicrograph of silk fibers, longitudinal view. (E. I. DuPont de Nemours & Company)

6.12 Photomicrograph of silk fiber, cross section. (E. I. DuPont de Nemours & Company)

uneven and darker than cultivated silk. It may exhibit longitudinal striations, or lines.

Cross-sectional views of silk show somewhat triangular-shaped fibers with little or no inner markings. Wild silks are larger than cultivated and tend to be somewhat uneven in cross section. See Figure 6.12 for typical cross-sectional views of silk fibers.

Physical Properties

Silk filaments are very fine and very long. They usually measure between 1,000 and 1,300 yards in length, but some may be as long as 3,000 yards. The width of silk ranges from 9 to 11 microns. The cultivated silk fibers are smooth, have a high luster or sheen, and are off-white to cream color. Wild silk is uneven, has less luster, and varies from cream through tan to light brown in color (see Table 6.2).

Silk is a strong fiber with good elastic recovery and moderate elon-

TABLE 6.2 Properties of silk fibers

Property	Evaluation
Shape	the fiber is fine, 9–11 microns in diameter; it is long—from 1,000 to 1,300 yards; the filament is smooth, even, white to cream color. Wild silk is uneven and dark in color
Luster	high
Tenacity (strength)	
dry	2.4–5.1 g/d
wet	2.0–4.3 g/d
Elastic recovery	92% recovery at 2% extension
Elongation	
dry	10–25%
wet	33–35%
Resiliency	medium
Density	1.25–1.34 g/ccm
Moisture absorption	
20° C, 65% R.H.	11%
saturation	25–35%
Dimensional stability	good
Resistance to	
acids	low; dissolves or is damaged by most mineral acids; organic acids do not damage
alkalies	strong alkalies damage fiber; weak alkalies have little or no effect
sunlight	prolonged exposure causes fiber breakdown
microorganisms	good
insects	destroyed by carpet beetles
Thermal reactions	
to heat	temperatures over 150° C result in yellowing and general discoloration
to flame	burns with a sputtering flame

gation. When it is wet, fiber strength is slightly reduced and elongation increases considerably. Silk has medium resiliency. Creases will hang out relatively well but not as quickly nor as completely as in wool.

The moisture regain for silk is relatively high; at saturation the regain is 30 percent, whereas at normal conditions it is about 11 percent. The absorption property of silk helps in the application of dyes and finishes, but unlike many fibers, silk will absorb impurities in liquids such as metal salts. These contaminants tend to damage silk by weakening the fiber or sometimes even causing ruptures.

Silk filaments, yarns, and fabrics have good resistance to stretch or shrinkage when laundered or dry cleaned.

Thermal Properties

Silk will burn when directly in the path of flame. After removal from the flame, it will sputter and eventually extinguish itself unless the fiber is extremely dry, and then it will continue to burn. It leaves a crisp, brittle ash and gives off an odor like that of burning hair or feathers.

Silk scorches easily if ironed with temperatures above 300° F (149° C), and white silk will turn yellow if pressed with a hot iron. The use of steam or a press cloth is recommended.

Chemical Properties

Silk is damaged by strong alkalies and will dissolve in heated caustic soda. Weak alkalies such as soap, borax, and ammonia cause little damage to silk unless they remain in contact with the fabric for a long time.

Whereas mineral acids can dissolve silk and cause fiber contraction and shrinkage, organic acids do no damage and are used in various finishing processes. Some authorities maintain that the scroop of silk—the characteristic rustling or crunching sound—is developed by exposure to organic acids.

Cleaning solvents and spot-removing agents do not damage silk, but chlorine bleaches will cause fiber disintegration. Hydrogen peroxide and perborate bleaches can be used safely on silk fabrics when needed.

Sunlight tends to accelerate the breakdown of silk, as does the oxygen in the atmosphere. Therefore, unless it is stored in sealed containers, the fiber will lose strength and eventually be destroyed.

Silk is a poor conductor of electricity, which results in the buildup of static charges. Like other protein fibers, it has a lower thermal, or heat, conductivity than cellulosic fibers. This factor, coupled with general compactness of construction, results in fabrics that tend to be warmer than comparative fabrics of cellulosic fibers.

Biological Properties

Silk resists attack by mildew and most other bacteria and fungi. It has good resistance to the clothes moth, but carpet beetles will destroy it. Destruction may be attributed to moths, but in actuality, it probably has been caused by carpet beetles.

Use and Care

Care of Silk

Dry cleaning has long been the recommended method for cleaning silk fabrics; home laundering can be done but it requires careful thought and minimum handling. When silk is to be laundered, a mild soap or synthetic detergent and warm water should be used. Thorough rinsing is needed to make certain that all detergent is completely removed, and instead of wringing, extra water should be removed by rolling the item in a towel and then hanging it in a cool location out of the direct sunlight. Silk should be ironed or pressed with a medium to low ironing temperature; steam and a press cloth are recommended.

When silk requires bleaching it is essential that hydrogen peroxide or a perborate bleach be used and not chlorine; chlorine compounds are destructive to silk. Silk fabrics tend to be damaged by perspiration, which weakens the fibers and causes alterations in the color. Deodorants and antiperspirants containing aluminum chloride should be avoided. It is advisable to wear protective dress shields when perspiration is a problem.

Silk in Use

Silk, often called the "queen of fibers," is used for luxury fabrics and for high-fashion items. Although use of silk is minimal compared with other fibers, it is a favorite of many consumers; and since travel has opened with China and expanded with other oriental countries, silk is finding its way into many consumer wardrobes and home furnishings.

Because silk can be used in either filament or staple form, it offers an incredible variety in yarn and fabric structures. In addition, silk colors exceptionally well, which provides the consumer with a wide choice of designs. Silk is versatile and can be found in a wide variety of apparel items and in many decorator fabrics for homes and offices.

Because of the fiber strength, silk textiles are durable and with proper care will last for many years. In apparel, silk is comfortable except on very hot and humid days; it maintains a neat and attractive appearance except when the fabric is very stiff, and then wrinkles tend to develop rapidly.

6.13 Silk blouses.

 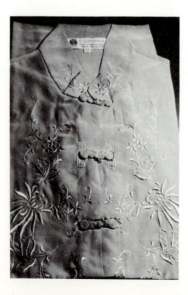 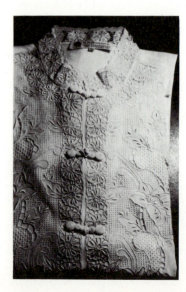

Man-made fibers have been used with great success to produce fabrics that look like silk. However, the consumer who likes silk typically is not satisfied with these "look-alikes." Consumers who like silk, and who can afford it, will pay high prices for silk items. In turn they receive a product that combines strength, flexibility, good moisture absorption, softness, drapability, warmth, luxurious appearance, and durability (Fig. 6.13).

Study Questions

1. List and discuss the properties of wool that make it desirable for either apparel or home furnishings.
2. Describe the procedures that may be used in wool care.
3. Compare wool with the specialty fibers in terms of fiber properties, typical end uses, and cost.
4. Why has consumption of wool dropped during the last thirty years?
5. What are the properties of silk that make it attractive to consumers?
6. How should silk products be cared for?
7. Discuss finishing procedures for wool that improve its behavior, particularly in apparel.
8. What care should be given wool carpeting?
9. What end uses are best for wool, and what end uses should be avoided? Why?
10. What are typical end uses for specialty fibers?
11. What end uses are desirable for silk, and what end uses should be avoided? Why?
12. Compare the properties of silk and wool; indicate how they are similar and how they are different.

7 Natural Cellulosic Fibers

Fibrous materials are found in nearly all plant life, but some plants have proved to be important sources of textile fibers for the manufacture of yarns, heavy cord and rope, and fabrics. These plant fibers consist largely of cellulose and, therefore, are classified as *natural cellulosic fibers*. This term indicates the simple composition of the fibers and provides a scientific method for comparing natural with man-made cellulosic fibers. The natural cellulosic fibers commonly encountered in consumer goods include cotton, flax (linen), jute, ramie, and hemp. Other natural cellulosic fibers may be found in small amounts and are mentioned in the discussion that follows.

COTTON

Historical Review

The origin of cotton is unknown. Archeologists have contributed valuable information concerning the fiber's early use, but there is a dearth of evidence to indicate exactly when or where cotton was first grown and used. Data suggest that cotton was raised in Egypt about 12,000 B.C.; but this information remains inconclusive. However, there is general agreement that cotton was used in India about 3000 B.C. and that it was the principal country in which cotton was utilized until 2500 B.C. There is evidence that cotton was made into fabrics in Peru about 2300 B.C.

Cotton culture in what is now the United States dates back about 2,500 years; evidence indicates that it was grown and used in the states of Utah, Texas, and Arizona about 500 B.C. Fragments of cotton fabrics have been found in dry caves and burial sites of the American Indians who inhabited the Southwest centuries ago, and anthropologists interpret this fact as indicating the importance of cotton fabrics to early Indian cultures.

Cultivation of the cotton plant for fiber use in the United States as a profit-making venture occurred in Virginia, where cotton was abundant between 1607 and 1620. Records show that cotton was grown through the Carolinas by 1665; by 1700 sufficient cotton was grown there to furnish clothing to one-fifth of the population of those states.

Most early cotton was of the Sea Island variety because the Churka, or roller gin, imported from India could separate seeds and fiber in this type of cotton only. However, as cotton culture moved inland, it was found that Sea Island cotton could not thrive and Upland varieties were adopted.

These were impossible to gin on the Churka, so hand separation of seed and fiber was required. After the invention of the saw-type gin by Eli Whitney in 1793, production of Upland cotton increased rapidly.

The economic effects of the invention of the cotton gin were revolutionary. Increase in cotton production and the subsequent development of low-cost textiles led directly to the industrialization of both Europe and America, as well as to the massive export-import business between the two continents. Indirectly, the effects were equally overwhelming but far from beneficial. Slavery, which had been dying out, was stimulated anew and became an adjunct of southern cotton culture, a subject of political controversy, and eventually a major reason for the American Civil War.

Originally, the factories for manufacturing and processing cotton into yarns and fabrics were located mostly in the New England states because of an abundance of water power and human power. Samuel Slater, a textile machinist from England, had opened the first spinning mill in the United States in 1791. By 1810 there were 226 mills in the New England area. After the Civil War, however, a changed economy dictated a movement of cotton manufacturing closer to the source of its fiber supply in the South. Not only did the move south reduce transportation costs and taxes, but it provided manufacturing plants with plentiful and cheap labor. It also, incidentally, brought social change to the hitherto agrarian society. For example, electricity was first used as a source of power in a cotton weaving plant in South Carolina. Cotton yarn and fabric manufacturing still remains a major business in the southern states of the United States.

Throughout the years the production of cotton has increased through improved farming procedures; more cotton of better quality is produced today on considerably less acreage than ever before. The production of cotton increased rapidly throughout the early part of the twentieth century; by 1926 the U.S. production was over 18 million bales per year. However, since that time production has dropped although it still remains an important agricultural crop.

The United States does import some cotton, mostly long staple varieties from Egypt and other Mediterranean and Asian countries. In 1984 and 1985 about 20 percent of the cotton used in the United States was imported.

Growth and Production

The cotton plant is a member of the same plant family that includes the hibiscus and hollyhock, the *Malvacae* family. The plant is grown most satisfactorily in warm climates where either rain or irrigation can provide sufficient water when needed.

The cotton blossom, which appears about one hundred days after planting, is a beautiful creamy white or light yellow color when it first blooms; the blossom changes to pink, lavender, or red on the second day. The petals drop off after forty-eight hours, leaving the boll, or seed pod, in which the fibers form. Fifty to eighty days later the pod bursts open, and the fleecy cotton fibers are ready for picking (Fig. 7.1).

Before picking the plants may be sprayed with defoliants, which cause the leaves to shrivel and fall off. As the cotton bolls mature and open, the fleecy fibers cascade out of the boll in the form of locks of fiber (Fig. 7.2).

Cotton is generally picked by machine. Picking machines are of two types: the picker and the stripper (Figs. 7.3 and 7.4). The picker pulls the fibers from the open bolls, whereas the stripper pulls the entire boll from the plant. Both machines are important in cotton farming. Pickers work

7.1 Cotton plant with fiber locks.

7.2 above left.   A single cotton boll; fibers are in a fluffy mass.

7.3 above right.   A mechanical cotton picker. (National Cotton Council of America)

7.4 left.   A cotton stripper. (National Cotton Council of America)

best on fields with lush growth and high yield; they are designed to pick two or four (or more) rows at the same time and can go over the fields several times if the crop warrants the additional pickings. Strippers are most effective on fields of low yields and low-growing plants; they pull from two or four rows simultaneously and go over a field only once.

Hand picking of cotton would produce the most uniform and best-quality fiber; however, in the United States the use of hand pickers is unlikely because of the high cost of labor, the size of the fields, and the fact that there is not adequate labor available. Some Asian countries may use hand picking, but this method is rapidly disappearing.

Processing

After cotton has been picked it is taken to the gin, where the fiber, called *cotton lint* by the trade, is separated from the seed. The gin used today is much the same, in principle, as the first saw gin developed by Eli Whitney; however, in size it differs considerably. The original gin was small and

7.5 above right. A modern cotton ginnery. (National Cotton Council of America)

7.6 above left. Cotton bales ready for shipment to textile mills. (National Cotton Council of America)

could easily fit onto a table; the modern gin is large and can handle a large amount of cotton at any one time (Fig. 7.5).

In addition to separating lint from seed, the modern gin will remove some foreign matter, such as dirt, twigs, leaves, and parts of the bolls. The seeds are a valuable byproduct of the cotton industry and produce cattle feed and cottonseed oil. The fibers, or cotton lint, are packed into large bales at the gin. Each bale weighs about 500 pounds gross (Fig. 7.6).

Samples of fibers are removed from the bales for determining fiber class. Factors used in this classification include the staple length of the fiber, the grade, and the character. *Staple length* refers to the length of the lint (fiber) and is determined to some degree by the variety of cotton plant. *Fiber grade* depends on color, amount of foreign matter present, and ginning preparation. The color can vary from white to gray or yellow. Cotton may be spotted or tinged, bright or dull. The spotted and tinged cotton is a frequent result of "one-time" picking, when bolls that have been opened for some time are mixed with newly opened bolls.

Foreign matter with the fiber includes leaves, twigs, broken parts of the boll or seed pod (called bract), dust, dirt, and sand. Hand-picked cotton has little foreign matter, whereas mechanically picked fibers can have much or little, depending on picking conditions and weather. If fibers are pulled off the ground, additional dirt and soil are present. Fiber grade involves the micronaire fineness, color, and foreign matter; and this, along with staple length, provides two of the three items used in the classification of cotton. The third factor is called *fiber character,* which includes fiber strength, uniformity, cohesiveness, pliability, elastic recovery, fineness, and resiliency. When all the information has been tabulated, the final quality of the cotton is established and a price is determined.

After ginning and classification are complete the cotton fiber is baled for shipment to manufacturers of yarns and/or fabrics.

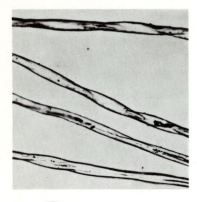

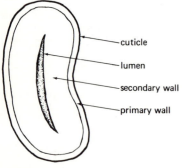

7.7 top. Photomicrograph of regular cotton, longitudinal view. (E. I. DuPont de Nemours & Company)

7.8 bottom. Diagram of the cross section of a cotton fiber.

Fiber Properties

Microscopic Properties

Cotton fibers are composed of an outer cuticle (skin) and primary wall; a secondary wall; and a central core, or *lumen*. Immature fibers exhibit thin wall structures and large lumen; mature fibers have thick walls and small lumen that may not be continuous because the wall forces the lumen to close in some sections.

The longitudinal view of the fiber shows a ribbonlike shape with twist, called *convolutions,* at irregular intervals (Fig. 7.7). The diameter of the fiber narrows at the tip. The lumen may appear as a shaded area or as striations; this is more obvious in immature fibers.

Fibers that have been swollen, as in mercerization, do not show the twist as clearly as untreated ones. Compared to the latter, swollen fibers appear smooth and round. Immature fibers also have few convolutions.

The cross section of the fiber usually shows three areas: the outer skin, or cuticle; the secondary wall; and the lumen (Fig. 7.8). The contour varies considerably; some fibers are nearly circular, some are elliptical, and some are kidney shaped. Immature fibers are more irregular in contour than mature fibers.

Physical Properties

The length of cotton fiber varies, depending on the variety, from about 1/2 inch to about 2 1/2 inches. Upland cotton, the major strain produced in the United States, has a diameter of approximately 18 microns and a length of less than 1 1/8 inches. American Upland varieties include such types as SJ-1 (Acala), Deltapine, Coker, Empire, and Stoneville. Long staple cotton is considered to be over 1 1/8 inches long; it is less than 15 microns in diameter. The major long staple cotton grown in the United States is raised in the Southwest, primarily in the states of California, Arizona, and New Mexico. It is often sold under the names of either Pima or Supima cotton. The amount of long staple fiber produced in the United States is small because it is costly to cultivate and process.

Fiber properties for cotton are cited in Table 7.1. The strength of cotton is moderate to slightly above moderate. It tends to be stronger when wet, which means it is easy to launder and process.

Because the resiliency and elastic recovery of cotton are low and elongation is comparatively low, fabrics wrinkle easily and do not recover from creasing. Therefore modern cotton fabrics require finishes to provide these properties at the level consumers seek. Finishes, however, may cause some side effects such as reduced strength and abrasion resistance. Nonetheless, consumers prefer cotton fabrics with special finishes in order to have easy care and other desirable properties.

An important property of cotton is its ability to absorb moisture. This is a major factor in fabric comfort. Fabrics made from cotton will pick up body moisture and remain comfortable when fibers that do not have good absorbency would be quite uncomfortable. Even fabrics in which cotton has been used as a part of a blend, such as polyester and cotton, tend to have absorbency because of the presence of the cotton fiber.

Cotton fibers are relatively stable and do not stretch or shrink. Cotton fabrics, however, do tend to shrink as a result of tensions encountered during yarn and fabric manufacture. Consequently cotton fabrics should be made shrink resistant if consumers are to have fabrics that will remain stable during use and care.

TABLE 7.1 Properties of cotton fibers

Property	Evaluation
Shape	fairly uniform in width, 12–20 microns; length varies from ½ to 2½ inches; typical length is ⅞ to 1¼ inches
Luster	low
Tenacity (strength)	
dry	3.0–5.0 g/d
wet	3.3–6.0 g/d
Elastic recovery	low; 75% at 2% extension
Elongation	
dry	3–10%
wet	3–10%
Resiliency	low
Density	1.54–1.56 g/ccm
Moisture absorption	
raw:conditioned*	8.5%
saturation	15–25%
mercerized:conditioned*	8.5–10.3%
saturation	15–27% +
Dimensional stability	good
Resistance to	
acids	damage, weaken fibers
alkalies	resistant; no harmful effects
organic solvents	high resistance to most
sunlight	prolonged exposure weakens fibers
microorganisms	mildew and rot-producing bacteria damage fibers
insects	silverfish damage fibers
Thermal reactions	
to heat	decomposes after prolonged exposure to temperatures of 150° C or over
to flame	burns readily

*Standard conditioned environment=65% relative humidity, 70° F±2°.

Thermal Properties

Cotton burns readily and quickly with the smell of burning paper. It leaves a small amount of a fluffy, gray ash. Long exposure to dry heat about 300° F (150° C) will cause the fiber to decompose gradually, and temperatures greater than 475° F (250° C) will result in rapid deterioration. Normal exposure to heat encountered in routine care and processing will not damage cotton, but fabrics will scorch if ironed with too high temperatures. Finishes, such as starch or durable press, increase the tendency to scorch.

Chemical Properties

Cotton is highly resistant to alkalies; in fact, they are used in finishing and processing the fiber. Most detergents and laundry aids are alkaline, so cotton can be laundered in these solutions with no fiber damage.

Strong acids destroy cotton, and hot dilute acids will cause disintegration. Cold dilute acids cause gradual fiber weakening, but the process is slow and may not be immediately evident.

Cotton is highly resistant to most organic solvents and to all that are used in normal care and stain removal procedures. Prolonged exposure to sunlight will cause the cotton fiber to become yellow and will gradually result in loss of strength. The damage is accelerated in the presence of moisture, some vat dyes, and some sulfur dyes. If properly stored in dry and dark areas, cotton will retain most of its strength and appearance.

Biological Properties

Cotton is damaged by various microorganisms. Mildew will produce a disagreeable odor and will result in rotting and loss of strength. Certain bacteria encountered in hot and moist conditions will cause decay. Moths and carpet beetles do not damage cotton, but silverfish will eat cotton cellulose, especially if it has been sized.

Use and Care

Cotton Care

Cotton is easy to care for. It can be laundered with almost any detergent or soap, unless finishes have been used that require special consideration. Any bleach may be used without damage to the fiber, except when special finishes would react with chlorine bleaches; then perborate or oxygen bleaches should be used. Dyes used may also influence bleaching, but perborate bleaches can be used on many colored fabrics without damage.

Cotton can be dry cleaned, if necessary, that is, if large products are difficult to handle in laundry equipment or require special pressing. Most spot-removal agents can be used safely on cotton. The major concern in the care of cotton fabrics is the presence of finishes that might require special care. It is wise to follow care labels attached to the product.

Cotton Use

Cotton has been the most universally used textile fiber throughout most of history. Only recently has it been surpassed in the United States by polyester. Worldwide it is still the most used single fiber. Fabrics of cotton and cotton blends are available in a wide price range. Inexpensive cotton fabrics are commonly found in standard fabric types such as muslins, percales, and broadcloth. Expensive cotton fabrics are available for use in high-fashion apparel, special home-furnishing fabrics, and other end uses. The relative cost of cotton fabrics is influenced by such factors as finishing processes, chemicals used, equipment costs, and labor costs. High-cost construction operations, such as Jacquard weaving, and the application of special surface designs developed by leading artists also increase the cost of the fabric.

Cotton and cotton blends have almost total consumer acceptance. They provide fabrics with varying degrees of comfort, easy care, and good durability for apparel (Fig. 7.9). They are used for a wide variety of home-furnishing fabrics, either in blends or as 100 percent cotton (Fig. 7.10). Blends of cotton with other fibers, such as polyester or nylon, may have as little as 20 percent or as much as 80 percent cotton. The higher

7.9 left.   Cotton fibers in apparel. (Springs Industries)

7.10 right.   Cotton in interior furnishings. (Springs Industries)

the cotton content, the more comfortable the fabrics will be; the higher the polyester or nylon fiber content, the easier the care will be.

Cotton fabrics are comfortable because of their softness, moisture absorbency, air permeability, and pliability. As a result of fiber strength, which increases when wet, cotton fabrics can undergo a wide variety of wet finishing operations and care procedures. The moisture absorbency makes it possible to use a variety of dyestuffs. For fabrics that are to be water repellent, stain and spot resistant, flame resistant, shrink resistant, and durable press, it is necessary to add special finishes. Cotton accepts these finishes and retains them through normal use and care.

FLAX

Historical Review

Flax, according to many authorities, may be the oldest fiber used in the Western world. Fragments of flax (linen) fabric have been found in excavations at the prehistoric lake regions of Switzerland, which date back to about 10,000 B.C.

The use of linen in Egypt before 3000 B.C. has been verified. The fiber was used for mummy wrappings until the practice of mummification declined. It was also used for ceremonial robes and decorative costumes. These early linen fabrics were of a fineness that has never been duplicated, even with sophisticated modern machinery. Examples have been found that were spun so fine that more than 360 single threads joined together formed one warp thread. Other fabrics were made with more than 500 yarns per inch, and these fabrics gave the appearance of sheerness.*

The use of flax spread from the Mediterranean region to parts of Europe. Belgium became one of the important centers for growing flax because of the chemicals in the River Lys.†

Linen fabric was introduced in Great Britain from Egypt about 1000 B.C., but actual use of the flax as a fiber probably did not occur until the first century A.D. At that time it is likely that Britons used flax fiber for coarse yarns and fabrics. However, at the same time Ireland was beginning to process flax into fine linen fabrics, and by A.D. 500 Irish linen was held in high esteem by the rulers of Europe.

Flax seed was brought to America by early settlers. Many colonists grew their own flax, spun their own yarns, and made their own fabric. A common fabric of that period was a combination of linen and wool, called "linsey-woolsey." The Industrial Revolution and development of the factory system took textile production out of the home, and as machinery most suitable for processing flax was developed in Europe, flax production for textile use in America came to a virtual halt.

Growth and Production

Flax is a bast fiber and is obtained from the stalks or stems of a plant called *Linum usitatissimum*. The flax plant requires a temperate climate with generally cloudy skies and adequate moisture. Flax seed is planted in April and May, and when fiber is to be obtained the seeds are planted very close together so that the stems will form foliage and seeds only at the top. The flax plant reaches a height of 2 to 4 feet. Its blossoms are a delicate pale blue or white. Fiber flax is pulled before the seeds are ripe (Fig. 7.11).

Processing

Pulling and Rippling

Flax for fiber is pulled by mechanical pullers (or in some areas by hand) so the root structure remains a part of the stem. Fibers extend below the ground surface, and if flax is cut the fibers become discolored.

Harvesting occurs in late August when the plant is a rich golden brown in color. After drying the flax is *rippled;* that is, it is pulled through special threshing machines that remove the seed pods.

Retting

To obtain the fibers from the stem, it is first necessary to remove the outer woody covering. The process, known as *retting,* can be accomplished by several procedures.

Dew retting involves exposing the fibers to the action of dew and sunlight; it requires four to six weeks. For *pool retting* the flax is packed in

*CIBA Review, No. 49, p. 1,766.
†CIBA Review, No. 49, p. 1,775.

7.11 Pulling flax. Stems are never cut to avoid damaging the fibers. (International Linen Promotion Commission)

sheaves and immersed in pools of stagnant water; the technique requires two to four weeks. In *tank retting* the fiber is stacked in large tanks and covered with warm water; this method requires only a few days. *Chemical retting* is accomplished by packing the fiber in tanks and covering with a chemical solution that will ret the fiber in a few hours (Fig. 7.12).

Most flax fibers grown in Europe today are retted by using a combination of dew and chemical retting. This process requires less time than other methods, except for the chemical process alone, and results in fibers of acceptable quality.

7.12 Bundles of flax are loaded into retting tanks. The soaking action combined with chemicals or bacteria loosens the flax fiber from the woody portion of the stalk. (International Linen Promotion Commission)

Breaking and Scutching

After retting is complete, the flax is passed between fluted rollers that break the outer woody covering into small particles. The fiber is then subjected to the scutching process, which separates the outer covering from the spinnable fiber. Since the early nineteenth century this has been done by a mechanical device.

Hackling

After scutching, the flax fibers are *hackled,* or combed. This separates the short fibers, called *tow,* from the long fibers, called *line*. It is accomplished by drawing the fibers between several sets of pins, each successive set finer than the preceding one.

Spinning

The flax fibers are drawn out into yarn, and twist is inserted. Flax fibers are spun either dry or wet, but wet spinning is considered to result in the best-quality yarn. Basically, the final yarn processing is similar to that used for other staple length fibers (Figs. 7.13 and 7.14).

7.13 left. Emerging from the combing process, these long wisps of fiber have passed over the series of graduated metal pins of the combing machine. The glossy flax now resembles switches of human hair. Left: fiber retted in water. Right: field-retted fiber. (International Linen Promotion Commission)

7.14 above. Hanks of combed flax pass through a drawing machine where they emerge in a continuous wide ribbon called a sliver. Repetition draws the flax thinner until all small fibers lay parallel, ready for spinning. (International Linen Promotion Commission)

Fiber Properties

Microscopic Properties

Flax fiber consists of fibrils or bundles of fiber cells held together by a gummy substance. Under the microscope the longitudinal view of the fiber shows the width to be quite irregular. The central canal, or lumen, casts a shadow, giving a slightly darker effect down the center. There are no convolutions, or twists, as in cotton, but longitudinal lines, or striations, can be seen. The points at which the fiber width changes are marked by swellings and irregular joint formations called *nodes*. These resemble the joints on bamboo (Fig. 7.15).

   The cross-sectional view clearly shows the lumen, the thick outer wall, and a somewhat polygonal shape. Immature flax may be oval in shape and usually has a larger lumen than mature fibers (Fig. 7.16).

Physical Properties

Flax fibers are not as fine as cotton because cells are held together in bundles. Line fibers are quite long—usually more than 12 inches and frequently from 18 to 22 inches—whereas tow fibers are less than 12 inches long and can be as short as a fraction of an inch (see Table 7.2).

   The natural color of flax varies from light ivory to dark tan or gray.

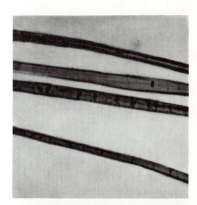

7.15 top. Photomicrograph of flax fiber, longitudinal view. (E. I. DuPont de Nemours & Company)

7.16 bottom. Photomicrograph of flax fiber, cross section. (E. I. DuPont de Nemours & Company)

TABLE 7.2 Properties of flax fibers

Property	Evaluation
Shape	width varies, mean diameter is 1/1200 of an inch; length of fiber varies from a few inches to 22 inches or more; average length 18 to 22 inches; average length after processing, 10 to 15 inches
Luster	medium to high
Strength	average tenacity, 6.5 grams per denier
Elastic recovery/ elongation	low elongation, 2.7 is typical; may extend as much as 3.3%; elastic recovery, 65% at 2% extension
Resiliency	poor
Density	1.5
Moisture absorption	good, approximately 12% at 20° C
Dimensional stability	good
Resistance to	
acids	good to cool, dilute acids; low or poor to hot, dilute; poor to concentrated either hot or cool
alkalies	high resistance
sunlight	good
microorganisms	mildew will grow on and damage fiber particularly in humid atmosphere
insects	good
Thermal reactions	
to heat	gradual decomposition after prolonged exposure at 150° C
to flame	burns readily

Choice fibers from Belgium and the other Low Countries are a pale sandy color and require little or no bleaching.

Flax possesses a high natural luster that produces attractive yarns and fabrics. It is a strong fiber, with a tenacity of 5.5 to 6.5 grams per denier. Flax is naturally stiff and resists bending. The fiber has little elasticity, elongation, and resiliency. Thus, linen fabrics are prone to crease and wrinkle badly. Finishes must be applied to offset these disadvantages.

Flax has a standard moisture regain of 12 percent. The saturation regain is comparable to that of other cellulosic fibers. This property makes for a comfortable apparel fabric.

Although flax fibers do not stretch or shrink to any marked degree, treated linen fabrics may do so as a result of the finishing processes or as a result of strain or stress placed on yarns during the fabric construction process.

Thermal Properties

Flax burns like any other cellulosic fiber. It will withstand temperatures to 300° F (150° C) for long periods of time with little or no change. Above 150° C prolonged exposure will result in gradual discoloration and degradation. Safe ironing temperatures may go as high as 500° F (260° C) as long as the fabric is not held at the high temperature for any length of time.

Chemical Properties

Flax is highly resistant to alkaline solutions, cool dilute acids, and dry cleaning solvents; but it is damaged by hot dilute and by concentrated acids. There is a gradual loss of strength when linen fabrics are exposed to sunlight. This is not serious—especially when the light is filtered through window glass. Linen, therefore, makes a good choice for curtain and drapery fabrics. Properly stored, flax will age remarkably well.

Biological Properties

Dry linen has excellent resistance to mildew and other microorganisms. In a moist or humid environment, however, mildew will grow rapidly and damage the fiber. Flax is generally resistant to household pests and insects.

Use and Care

Linen Care

Linen may be laundered or dry cleaned with no damage. Any type of detergent and any stain remover may be used, and laundry additives do little or no damage. If special finishes have been applied, care should be given to limit the temperatures used in ironing and to avoid the use of chlorine bleaches, particularly if a durable-press or wrinkle-resistant finish has been applied. Linen fabrics usually require ironing since they seldom come from the laundry or dry cleaning solvent without wrinkles. Because of its properties, linen does not soil quickly and unless stained seldom needs any bleaching. As with any textile product, the consumer should make certain that care label information is read and followed.

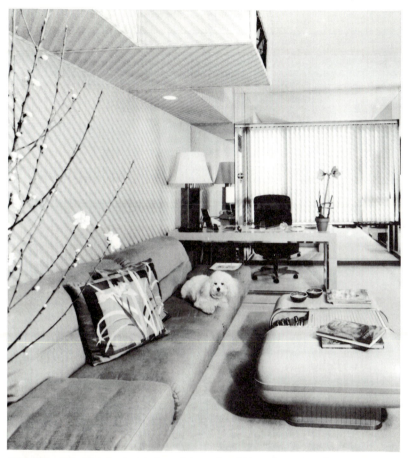

7.17 left. Linen fabrics in interiors. (International Linen Promotion Commission)

7.18 right. Linen and polyester fabrics in apparel. (Hoechst Fibers)

Linen Use

Because of the high strength of flax, it can be made into a variety of fabrics, from sheer to heavy, that have good durability. Other properties help create a fabric that is cool and comfortable in warm weather; the property of wicking—carrying moisture along the surface of the fiber so it moves away from the body—increases the comfort during humid, hot days.

Flax is used in fabrics for both apparel and home furnishings. It is often selected for table coverings, upholstery, draperies, and wall coverings (Fig. 7.17). The fiber can be made into a wide variety of fabrics by using many different fabric-construction procedures. It is a good choice for suiting fabrics for summer wear (Fig. 7.18). Because of its history, linen fabrics may have a high heritage and sentimental value since these fabrics tend to last for long periods of time.

Because of the moisture absorbency of linen and the fact that the fibers do not produce lint easily, many drying towels for glassware and fine china are made of flax (linen) fiber.

JUTE

Jute is a bast fiber obtained from the inner bark of the *Corchorus* plant. It is produced in greater amounts than any other fiber, with the exception of cotton, but is seldom used in fashion consumer goods. The fiber attained economic importance during the latter part of the eighteenth century; however, it had been used earlier and is considered to be the fiber referred to as "sackcloth" in biblical times.

The world's major growing area for jute is Bangladesh, followed by India and Thailand. The plant requires a hot, humid climate with fertile soil. When planted for fiber purposes, the seeds are sown close together, just as for flax, so that the stems develop into long, slender forms. Jute is made into fabrics in several Asian countries, Scotland, and the United States.

Jute is widely used in low-cost fabrics throughout the world. Fabrics made of jute are frequently called *burlap*. At one time, jute fiber was promoted as a fashion fabric in the United States; but because of the properties of the fiber, this use has not continued. However, it must be noted that jute of fine quality is used for apparel in Hong Kong and Singapore.

Jute is processed somewhat similarly to flax. It must be retted so that the fibers can be separated from the outer stem covering. After retting, the fibers are washed and dried and then sent to mills for spinning into yarns.

Jute varies in its natural color from yellow to brown or gray. It is difficult to bleach; thus, many jute fabrics tend to be the natural fiber color. It is a coarse fiber with a rough surface except for a limited amount of top-quality fibers, which are relatively smooth, fine, and soft. Though the fibers may be several feet in length following initial retting, they tend to break down to short fibers during processing into yarns (see Table 7.3).

The strength of jute is less than that of flax, hemp, and other bast fibers; the average tenacity of jute is 3.5 grams per denier. The elongation of jute is low, only about 1.7 percent, and there is little or no elasticity; the fiber is stiff because of the material that holds the fiber cells together. The density of the fiber is similar to that of other cellulosic fibers at 1.5. The moisture regain is 13.75 percent, and it has the added advantage of being able to absorb as much as 23 percent of its weight in water when there is high humidity.

The chemical properties of the fiber are similar to those of other cellulosic fibers, although some chemicals may react negatively if there is too much moisture in the fiber. For this reason, jute products should be kept dry for durability.

Jute has good resistance to microorganisms and insects. Moisture may increase the damage done by microorganisms, but dry jute will last for a very long time.

The fabric is widely used in the United States for bagging because it holds its shape well, and the rough surface tends to keep stacks of bags in position and resistant to slippage. It is used as a backing fabric for carpeting, where it prevents slipping and stretching of the surface carpet. Another use of jute is in the upholstery of furniture, where it provides a durable base. When used in furniture making, jute fabric is often referred to as *hessian*. It is also used in the manufacture of linoleum as a base on which the linoleum is built. Fine-quality jute can be made into attractive home-furnishing items, especially wall coverings and draperies; and it is used for a variety of craft activities.

TABLE 7.3 Properties of jute fibers

Property	Evaluation
Shape	irregular in diameter and length, 5 to 20 feet long
Luster	silky
Strength	3.5 grams per denier
Elastic recovery/ elongation	very low; elongation only 1.7–1.9%; elastic recovery, 74% at 1% extension
Resiliency	low
Density	1.5
Moisture absorption	13.7% at standard conditions
Dimensional stability	good
Resistance to	
acids	good to dilute; poor to concentrated
alkalies	very good
sunlight	good
microorganisms	good
insects	good
Thermal reactions	
to heat	similar to those of flax
to flame	burns readily

The production of jute is a labor-intensive industry; that is, it needs considerable manual labor rather than mechanical equipment. Consequently, it is doubtful if the production of jute will occur in countries with high labor costs such as the United States, Japan, and most European countries.

RAMIE

Ramie has been called *China grass* in many parts of the world; it is a bast fiber that has been cultivated for many centuries in China and Taiwan. Some evidence indicates that ramie was grown in the Mediterranean areas as early as flax, and some researchers believe that ramie was used for wrapping mummies as well. However, it is its history and popularity in Asian countries that has been most important.

Ramie is grown commercially in China, Japan, parts of Russia, Egypt, Indonesia, France, and Italy. For a period of time during the 1940s and 1950s, the plant was grown commercially in the United States; however, there is little or no production of ramie in the United States at the present time.

The ramie plant, a member of the nettle family, is a perennial shrub that can be cut several times a season after the necessary preliminary growth. It can be started from seeds, from which it reaches usable growth in three years; or it can be started from cuttings, which mature in two years.

After cutting, the ramie stalks are decorticated either by hand or machine. *Decortication* means peeling away or beating off the bark to free

7.19 Ramie stalks with decorticated and degummed fibers, (R. V. Allison, Everglades Experiment Station, Belle Glade, Florida, University of Florida)

the bast fibers (Fig. 7.19). Fibers are dried in the sun to make them white. They are degummed in caustic soda to remove pectins and waxes. Finally they are given a washing and are dried.

Ramie fibers are long, approximately 18 inches, and very fine. They are white and lustrous, almost silklike in appearance. Ramie is strong in terms of resistance to pull. However, the fibers are somewhat stiff and brittle and have lower pliability than other commonly used bast fibers. Their elastic recovery and elongation are also poor. Ramie reacts chemically in the same manner as other cellulosic fibers, except that it is not easily damaged by cold, concentrated mineral acids. The high degree of molecular orientation reduces the rate of acid penetration and thus the rate of damage. Of special interest is the fact that ramie is highly resistant to microorganisms, insects, and rotting.

Ramie fabrics frequently resemble fine linen. A considerable amount of fabric available on the market includes ramie as part of a blend of fibers, often blended with cotton or rayon or both or with fibers such as polyester or nylon. These blends are frequently found in knitted fabrics for apparel. The use of ramie adds strength; the blend of other fibers increases the flexibility of the fabric and reduces the potential damage from flexing.

HEMP

Hemp is a bast fiber that was probably used first in Asia. Records indicate that it was cultivated in China before 2300 B.C. Sometime during the Early Christian era, hemp was carried into Gaul and became an important fiber throughout Europe.

Today, hemp is grown on every continent and in nearly every country. A tough plant, it will grow at altitudes of 8,000 feet and in climates where temperatures are warm to hot.

The processing of hemp is similar to that of flax. The fiber requires retting to loosen the outer covering, followed by stripping or scutching to obtain the usable fibers (Fig. 7.20). Hackling, or drawing and spinning of the fibers into yarns, is the final step before fabric manufacture.

The fiber is dark tan or brown and is difficult to bleach, but it can be dyed bright and dark colors. Hemp fibers vary widely in length and diameter; some fibers may be no longer than 3/4 of an inch, whereas others may

7.20 Retting hemp. The fibers are laid in rafts and submerged with stone weights. *(Ciba Review)*

be 6 feet long. Short fibers are used for some domestic fabrics, especially in underdeveloped countries; longer hemp fibers are used in industrial yarns and fabrics in such end uses as canvas, twine, sacking, and rope. The specific gravity, or density, of hemp is 1.48. It exhibits low elongation and poor elasticity. Standard moisture regain is about 12 percent, and the fiber may absorb up to 30 percent of its weight in damp or humid environments.

Hot concentrated alkalies will destroy hemp, but hot or cold dilute alkalies or cold concentrated alkalies will not damage it. With the exception of cool weak acids, mineral acids will reduce the strength and eventually destroy the fiber completely. Organic solvents used in cleaning and bleaches, if handled properly, will not damage the fiber.

The thermal reactions of hemp and the effect of sunlight are the same as for cotton. Hemp is moth resistant, but mildew will attack and damage it.

Coarse hemp fibers and yarns generally are made into various types of ropes, cordage, and heavy-duty tarpaulins. Fine hemp fibers have been used in some countries for a variety of interior design fabrics, often for wall coverings.

MISCELLANEOUS PLANT FIBERS

A selected group of other plant fibers are described briefly, as they have limited use and limited interest to consumers. They may have special use for selected textile products.

Sisal, one of a group of fibers obtained from plant leaves, comes from a plant that belongs to the Agave family and is raised in Mexico. The fiber is also cultivated in Africa, Java, and South America. The leaves, which grow in a rosette from a short trunk, are cut when they are about four years old. Processing of the fiber involves separating them from the fleshy part of the leaf and removing pectins, chlorophyll, and other noncellulosic substances. Sisal can be dyed bright colors and has been widely used for such items as shopping bags, varicolored place mats, and novelty items (Fig. 7.21). Other uses include handbags or totebags, ropes, cordage, and hats.

Abaca derives from a plant that belongs to the banana family. In appearance it is often mistaken for the edible banana tree. The plant grows mainly in the Philippines, and most of the textile fiber is processed there. The leaf stalk from which the fiber is taken may reach a length of 25 feet. The fibers, therefore, are generally long; usable strands of abaca fiber may be up to 15 feet in length. Good-quality abaca has a natural luster and is off-white in color. Poor grades are dark gray or brown. The fiber can be bleached and dyed a wide variety of colors. The fiber is strong and flexible and exceptionally good for making rope, cordage, place mats for outdoor or indoor use, and selected items of clothing (Fig. 7.22). The fabric appears to be delicate, it is lightweight, and it is relatively strong and durable.

Pina fiber, from the leaves of the pineapple plant, is produced in several countries, but the Philippines provides the most. It is a white or light ivory fiber about 2 to 4 inches in length. The fiber is fine, lustrous, soft, flexible, and strong, as well as highly resistant to water. Fabrics of pina may be either soft and delicate or crisp. Considerable fiber goes into making "peasant"-type clothing, elaborately decorated accessories, and table coverings with elaborate embroidery. The fabrics are easily cleaned

7.21 Carpet tiles of sisal fiber woven with an inch-thick cut pile in stripes and solid color. (Larsen Carpet/Jack Lenor Larsen incorporated)

7.22   Place mats of abaca fiber.

and will retain their appearance for long periods of time. Substances with a high acid content or strong enzymes, such as cranberry juice, will cause rapid fiber degradation, however, and must be rinsed out of the fabric as soon as possible to prevent the formation of holes. With care, pina fabrics will last for a long time.

Coir is a fiber from the seed of the coconut. It is used in matting and cordage. It is taken from the outer shell of the coconut, between the outer hard covering and the actual nut. The natural color of coir is a rich cinnamon brown, and the fiber is frequently left undyed for floor mats and outdoor carpets or patio coverings. Because of a high degree of stiffness, coir is wrinkle resistant, strong, crush resistant, and impervious to abrasive wear. In addition, it can stand exposure to weather, especially rain, sleet, or snow, so it proves to be a practical fiber for doormats and similar products. The fiber can be dyed dark colors, but it is difficult to bleach and is seldom found in light colors.

Kapok, a seed hair fiber, comes from the Java kapok, or "silk cotton" tree. This huge tree grows in tropical regions and rises to a height of 50 feet or more. The seed pods, 3 to 6 inches in length, resemble the cotton boll. Ginning is not necessary, for after the fibers are dried, the seeds will shake away easily. Kapok is extremely light, buoyant, and soft. The fiber is difficult to spin into yarns, so its major use is for padding and stuffing, particularly in upholstered furniture and mattresses. As it is nonallergenic, it makes an excellent filler for pillows. One of the best known uses for kapok is in life preservers. Kapok-filled preservers will support up to thirty times their weight and will not become waterlogged.

Study Questions

1. *a.* What geographical locations are best for raising cotton?
   b. What climatic and environmental conditions are conducive to growing both high-quality and high-quantity cotton?
   c. Where is long staple cotton grown?
2. Cite the properties of cotton that are of particular value in providing products that please consumers.
3. Cite the properties of cotton that may create problems for consumers in the use and care of cotton fabrics.

4. Why is a large proportion of fabric made from blends of cotton with man-made fibers, such as polyester, rather than from pure cotton?
5. What are the properties of flax that make it desirable for table coverings? For draperies? For dish towels?
6. What are the disadvantages consumers may find in the use of linen fabrics?
7. Which retting process produces the best-quality flax fiber?
8. Where is most flax grown at the present time?
9. List and briefly describe the steps in processing flax.
10. How does the use of jute compare with the use of cotton and flax?
11. What is happening to ramie in relation to current usage? Why do you think this is occurring?
12. What are the properties of ramie that make it desirable for apparel fabrics?
13. List and describe the steps in growing and producing cotton, from planting the cotton seed to packing the fibers into bales.
14. What is the probable future of jute?
15. When and in what types of products will the average consumer find minor natural fibers such as pina, sisal, agave, and coir?
16. List end-use items you might select for each of the following fibers and discuss why you think that special use is appropriate:
    a. Cotton; list at least three different types of uses.
    b. Flax; list at least two different types of uses.
    c. Jute; list at least two different types of uses.
    d. Hemp; list at least one use.
    e. Ramie; list at least one use.
17. For the items you list in your response to question 16, describe how they might be cared for if they involve use by the typical consumer.
18. What are current trends in the use of cotton in blended fiber fabrics?

8 Man-Made Cellulosic Fibers: Rayon

Historical Review

The first written comment concerning the potential of creating man-made fibers is found in Robert Hooke's *Micrographia,* published in 1664. Hooke predicted that eventually there would be a way to duplicate the excrement of the silkworm. However, not until the nineteenth century did scientists actually make artificial fibers. In 1855 George Audemars made filaments from a solution of mulberry twigs in nitric acid. In 1857 E. J. Hughes created fibers from a solution of starch, glue, resins, and tannins.

The major breakthrough in the production of man-made fiber occurred in 1862 when Ozanam invented the spinning jet, or spinnerette. This remarkable device is the basis for all manufactured fiber production (Fig. 8.1).

In 1883 J. W. Swan produced filaments by forcing a solution of cellulose nitrate in glacial acetic acid through a spinning jet. However, credit for the invention of rayon is generally given to Count Hilaire Chardonnet, who produced a cellulose nitrate that he dissolved in alcohol. This solution was forced through a spinnerette into water or warm air. The filaments hardened, were stretched to orient the molecules and introduce sufficient strength, and finally were denitrated and purified to reduce flammability.

The viscose process for making rayon was discovered in 1891 by the English scientists C. F. Cross and E. J. Bevan. Since that time, the operation has been greatly modified and improved. The first American rayon operation, called the American Viscose Corporation, was opened in 1910. This organization merged with the FMC Corporation in the late 1960s; then in the mid 1970s the fiber-producing part of the company split from FMC and became Avtex fibers.

An important part of the mechanical development of rayon manufacturing was the invention of the spinning box by C. F. Topham in 1905. This box caught the fibers and imparted sufficient twist to hold the filaments together for further processing.

Between 1916 and 1930 companies such as DuPont, Industrial Rayon, Celanese, and American Enka joined the ranks of manufacturers of viscose rayon. In 1925 American Bemberg started production of rayon made by the cuprammonium process. The primary sources of rayon fiber in the United States at the present time are Avtex, Courtaulds, and North American.

Rayon received its name in 1925. Before that it had been called *artificial silk.* Because of general distaste at that time for things "artificial," many consumers avoided it. The fiber had other major drawbacks as well; it was inferior in many ways to the natural fibers. During the 1920s the fiber

8.1 Spinnerettes used in the formation of man-made fibers.

was modified to improve its properties, and with the new name, rayon, it gradually gained public acceptance.

Rayon was first used for automobile tire cord in 1927. To increase its practicality for tires, a group of manufacturers developed a unique high-strength rayon filament identified by the name *Tyrex*. This fiber is still produced today, although in very limited quantities. Other man-made fibers have become better suited to the manufacture of tires.

The decade of the 1950s saw many additional improvements in existing rayon fibers, including the development of high-strength or high-tenacity rayon, special carpet rayon, and high-wet-modulus rayon. Despite these developments, the use of rayon has decreased and at present accounts for a relatively small proportion of the man-made fiber market. Data for 1985 indicate that rayon and acetate combined account for only about 9 percent of the world's man-made fiber production.

During the early history of man-made fibers, the term *rayon* was used to indicate any type of manufactured fiber that was based on cellulose. As some fibers behaved quite differently from others, it was determined that some system was needed to indicate the type of fiber. Thus, in 1951 the Federal Trade Commission ruled that if named on labels, *rayon* was the term to indicate man-made cellulosic fibers, and *acetate* to indicate modified cellulosic fibers. These terms were incorporated into the TFPIA when it was passed (see Chapter 2).

Manufacturing Processes

Viscose Rayon

The principal raw material for viscose rayon is wood pulp. The pulp is processed to extract pure cellulose, which is then formed into thin sheets about 2 feet square (Fig. 8.2). These sheets are steeped in an alkali solution to convert the cellulose to soda cellulose. The alkali pulp is shredded into crumb form and aged for a specific time. After aging the cellulose crumb is treated with carbon disulfide to form a material called xanthate. The xanthate is dissolved in dilute sodium hydroxide to form a honey-colored liquid, which is aged until it reaches the correct viscosity, or thickness. It is then ready for conversion into fiber forms. Viscose rayon is made by the wet spinning process (Figs. 8.3 and 8.4). The viscose liquid is forced through spinnerettes into a solution, where the fibers coagulate into filament form.

When filament fibers are to be made into yarns, the spinnerette has the exact number of openings needed for the final yarn; if staple fibers are to be made, the spinnerettes have thousands of openings and the fibers are cut after they are formed. Viscose fibers are bright and shiny if not treated to reduce the luster. This process is accomplished by adding delustering agents to the viscose liquid before forcing it through the spinnerettes. The degree of dullness or brightness can be controlled through the amount of delusterant used.

Solution-dyed viscose is available. This is fiber that is colored while in the viscose solution before filaments are extruded. This product is more colorfast than fiber dyed after it has been made. A few of the solution-dyed viscose fiber trade names have been cited in Table 2.2.

Manufacturers may add crimp to viscose fibers to create staple fibers with better spinning quality. The crimp causes the fibers to hold together with ease and gives body and loft to the yarn.

8.2 Cellulose in sheet form being packed into steeping tanks. (Celanese Corporation)

8.3 above. Flow chart showing processes in viscose rayon manufacture.

8.4 below. Wet spinning. Viscose solution is forced through a spinnerette into a coagulating bath to form filaments. (Avtex Fibers, Inc.)

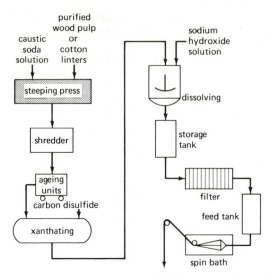

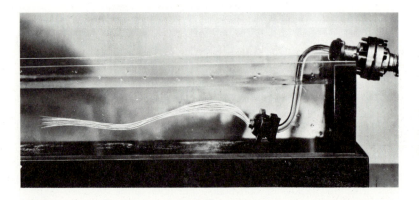

Modified Viscose Fibers   In addition to the regular viscose rayon, most producers manufacture viscose in medium and high tenacities (medium- and high-strength fibers). These fibers differ slightly from the regular rayon in both strength and elongation properties and in such factors as molecular orientation and molecular size. Fibers with high tenacity have less elongation than regular tenacity fibers.

High-wet-modulus rayon   High-wet-modulus rayon is considered desirable for many end uses, particularly for apparel and home-furnishing fabrics. Rayons of this type are obtained by changing the proportion of chemicals used in the manufacture and by reducing the aging time. These fibers are more like cotton than other rayons in their properties; they have good dimensional stability, strength, and elongation.

High-wet-modulus rayons are excellent in durable-press products, particularly if blended with polyesters. They accept minimum care finishes better than regular rayons. Other desirable properties of high-wet-modulus rayons include good stability to laundering and easy care; ability to be mercerized; and a crisp, lofty hand. *Hand* relates to the feel of a fabric.

Cuprammonium Rayon

E. Schweitzer, in 1857, discovered that cellulose would dissolve in a solution of ammonia and copper oxide. This reaction was finally applied to fiber manufacture in 1891 by Max Fremery and Johann Urban. They were successful in making cupra rayon in Germany. However, they did not have a successful venture, and it was not until 1901 that cupra rayon was made commercially. Edmund Thiele, who was working for the J. P. Bemberg Co., devised the stretch spinning process that made it practical to produce cupra fibers of good strength and fineness.

Cuprammonium rayon is not produced in the United States; however, it is produced in several European countries and is available on the U.S. market in limited quantities. The amount produced is very small, and it is used primarily for linings for suits and coats and for selected home-furnishing fabrics.

Fiber Properties

Microscopic Properties

Rayon is a manufactured fiber; thus, the manufacturer can control the size and shape to a great extent, and different types of rayon fibers can vary considerably in appearance.

The length or longitudinal appearance of regular viscose rayon exhibits uniform diameter and interior parallel lines, called *striations*. These striations are the result of light reflection by the irregular contour of the fiber (Fig. 8.5). If the fiber has been delustered it will have a grainy, pitted appearance; bright fiber is relatively transparent. The cross section of the fiber shows highly irregular or serrated edges (Fig. 8.6). Here, too, the presence of delusterants is indicated by a spotted effect, whereas bright fiber appears crystal clear.

High-tenacity viscose is similar to regular viscose in microscopic appearance except that it may have a smoother circumference and fewer striations. The cross section may appear almost perfectly round. High-wet-modulus rayon is similar in appearance to high-tenacity rayon (Fig. 8.7). Cuprammonium rayon has a clear longitudinal view and a nearly round, clear cross section (Fig. 8.8).

Physical Properties

The length, width (or diameter), and luster of rayon fibers may be controlled during manufacture; and the final characteristics or properties are

8.5 above. Photomicrograph of regular viscose rayon fiber, longitudinal view. (E. I. DuPont de Nemours & Company)

8.6 below. Photomicrograph of regular viscose rayon fibers, cross section. (E. I. DuPont de Nemours & Company)

8.7 far left. Photomicrograph of high-wet-modulus rayon, cross section. (American Enka Corporation)

8.8 left. Photomicrograph of cuprammonium rayon, cross section. (E. I. DuPont de Nemours & Company)

TABLE 8.1 Properties of rayon fibers

	Viscose					Cuprammonium
	Staple Fibers				Filament	
Property	Regular	Intermediate Tenacity	High Performance	High-Wet Modulus	High Tenacity	
Shape	shape can be controlled by the manufacturer; therefore, it is uniform in appearance; length and denier are determined by the manufacturer for the desired end use; available in both filament and staple; diameter varies from 12 to 40 microns					
Luster	controlled by manufacturer; can vary from dull to bright					
Tenacity (g/d)						
conditioned*	2.4–3.0	3.1–3.4	3.8–4.4	4.0–5.0	4.0–6.5	1.7–2.3
wet	1.1–1.5	1.5–1.8	1.9–2.8	2.2–3.0	3.5–4.3	0.9–1.4
% Elastic recovery at 2% stretch	82	97		95		75
Wet modulus at 5%	2.3–2.0	2.3–3.0	4.0–5.5	6.0–9.5		
% Elongation at break						
conditioned*	19–24	20–23	24–27	15–23	9–26	10–17
wet	21–28	21–28	20–26	24–28	14–30	17–33
Resiliency	low	low	low	low	low–medium	low
Density (g/ccm)	about 1.5 for all types of rayon					
% Moisture regain						
conditioned*	10.7–16 for all viscose types					12.5
saturation	25–27 for all viscose types					27.0
Resistance to						
acids	generally not good, but under some circumstances it may be acceptable					
alkalies	generally not good, but under some circumstances it may be acceptable					
sunlight	average	average	average	good	good	good
microorganisms	mildew will destroy all types of cellulosic fibers					
insects	silverfish will damage all types of cellulose fibers					
Thermal reactions						
to heat	extended exposure to high temperatures will eventually degrade the fiber					
to flame	flame-resistant rayon resists burning, other rayons burn					

*Conditioned environment = 65 percent relative humidity, 70° F ± 2°.

based on planned end-use requirements. The strength of most rayons is relatively low and is further decreased when fibers are wet, which means that rayon fabrics require careful handling in any wet processing operation and in care procedures. High-tenacity and high-wet-modulus fibers are considerably stronger than regular rayon and have both a wet and dry strength similar to cotton (see Table 8.1).

Elastic recovery and resiliency of regular viscose rayons are low; elongation is high. Fabrics of these fibers tend to wrinkle and stretch easily; however, finishes can be applied to correct these faults. High-wet-modulus fibers are less subject to stretching and wrinkling, but even these fibers produce fabrics that tend to crease unattractively unless they have been given special minimum care finishes.

Rayon fibers have good moisture absorbency, which makes them accept dyes well. The same property also contributes to the high degree of comfort in rayon apparel. Regular rayon fabrics are subject to stretching followed by relaxation shrinkage after laundering; however, the high-wet-modulus fibers do not stretch easily and exhibit less relaxation shrinkage.

Fabric construction as well as fiber characteristics contribute to the degree of relaxation shrinkage. Tightly woven fabrics will exhibit less size change because of the compact arrangement of yarns and fibers. Loosely woven or knitted fabrics will have more size change because there is space into which the yarns and fibers may contract. Most rayon fabrics receive some finishes to control dimensional stability or size.

Thermal Properties

Rayon is cellulose, so it burns rapidly with a yellow flame, leaving a small amount of light gray residue. When the flame is extinguished there may be a slight afterglow. Hot water and iron temperatures from 300° F to 350° F (149° C to 177° C) can be used safely on rayon fabrics. Exposure to high temperatures, greater than those cited, for extended periods of time does result in fiber breakdown.

Chemical Properties

As rayon is chemically identical to cotton, it responds in much the same manner to chemicals. Minor differences stem from the reduced molecule size that accompanies manufacturing.

Strong alkali solutions cause rayon fibers to swell and eventually result in a loss of strength; weak alkalies do not damage them. High-wet-modulus rayons can receive the same types of chemical treatments as cotton and thus can be mercerized.

Hot and cold concentrated acids cause rayons to disintegrate. Hot dilute acids result in fiber deterioration, but cold dilute acids have little or no effect. Resistance to dry cleaning solvents and stain removal agents is good. Bleaches will not harm rayon fabrics unless finishes have been applied that are damaged by the bleach solution.

Regular rayon fibers will deteriorate from extended exposure to the sun, whereas high-wet-modulus fibers will withstand it well enough to give adequate service in drapery fabrics and other home-furnishing fabrics.

Biological Properties

Rayons resist all insects except silverfish, which are injurious to fibers unless protected by special finishes. Mildew will destroy rayon of all types as the fiber is cellulosic, and soil increases the ease with which mildew forms. Regular rayon fibers are subject to harm by rot-producing bacteria. High-wet-modulus fibers are fairly resistant to bacteria.

Use and Care

Rayon Care

Rayon care is more demanding than natural cellulosic fibers because of the difference in strength and other properties that result from the manufacturing operations. If caution is used, rayon fabrics can be laundered successfully, and they can be dry cleaned without damage. Any detergent can be used, and bleaches can also be used except when finishes are present that might react with them. The consumer should read care labels carefully when laundering rayon fabrics. Because of the low strength of

8.9 Women's apparel of rayon and polyester. (Hoechst Fibers).

rayon, they should not be twisted or wrung following laundering; rather water should be padded out by using a towel or a gentle cycle on an automatic washer. Dry cleaning does not damage rayon fabrics under normal procedures.

Regular viscose tends to stretch when wet, then shrink when it dries; this poses care problems for the consumer. It is important to handle regular rayons carefully during laundering to reduce this size change.

Rayon can be ironed at medium to high temperatures unless finishes have been applied that require medium- to low-temperature ironing. Again, reading care labels is essential.

Rayon Use

Rayon is used in apparel and home-furnishing fabrics (Fig. 8.9). It may be used in some industrial fabrics. Because rayon can be produced in either filament or staple form, this fiber offers versatility in yarn and fabric construction; certainly it provides greater variety than natural fibers available only in one physical form. Fabrics can be made that are very sheer to very heavy, very soft to very firm, and very limp to very stiff. Yarns can be simple, complex, or textured.

Blends or combination fabrics that combine rayon with one or two other fibers are available on the market. These blends mix such fibers as polyester, acrylic, nylon, acetate, cotton, flax, wool, and ramie with rayon—both regular and high-wet-modulus. Rayon contributes absorbency, comfort, and softness when blended with polyester, acrylic, or nylon fibers. With cotton, it may alter appearance to create a soft luster; with wool, rayon will decrease the cost; with flax and ramie, it can reduce cost and help produce appearances that are typically associated with linenlike fabrics.

Though high-wet-modulus rayon fibers are frequently used in blends with polyester or cotton, there are a few uses for the fiber by itself. These include the construction of knit or woven fabrics when a soft silky hand is desired for apparel and home furnishings and of selected industrial fabrics when a combination of low cost and properties similar to cotton is desirable. A fashion item during 1985 and 1986 was a challis-type fabric made of rayon fiber.

To provide consumers with rayon fabrics that are flame resistant, manufacturers have developed special modifications of the fiber that involve the addition of fire-retardant chemicals to the solution before the fiber filaments are formed. These modified fibers, more expensive than other rayon, do perform satisfactorily. They are usually labeled FR rayon.

Although there has been a steady decline in the use of rayon fiber during the past two decades, the industry has tried to regain some of its market through prestige products that appeal to the middle and upper economic levels. Leading designers have introduced high-fashion apparel items made of rayon fabric and promoted the fiber for its pleasing hand and drape.

Study Questions

1. What are the favorable properties of rayon?
2. What are the disadvantages or negative properties of rayon?
3. What is high-wet-modulus rayon, and how does it differ from regular rayon?

4. What is high-tenacity rayon and in what type of products is it usually found?
5. List a few trademark names for high-wet-modulus rayon. Remember to refer to Chapter 2.
6. Compare the properties of regular rayon and cotton and of high-wet-modulus rayon and cotton.
7. Describe the care methods recommended for textile products made from
   a. Regular rayon fibers
   b. High-wet-modulus fibers
   c. Blends including high-wet-modulus fibers
   d. Blends including regular rayon fibers
8. In addition to fiber content, what factors influence the care of fabrics made of rayon?
9. When were the various types of rayon introduced to the commercial consumer market?
10. List typical textile products that may be made of various types of rayon fiber.

Modified Cellulosic Fibers: Acetate and Triacetate

Historical Review

Acetate, which is properly called cellulose acetate, was first made by Paul Schutzenberger in 1869. At that time there was neither a practical nor a safe process for converting the substance into something useful. In 1904 Henri and Camille Dreyfus developed a safe and relatively inexpensive process for producing cellulose acetate. The first use for this substance was as a coating on cotton fabric or as a film similar to cellophane or plastic wrap. As a coating the substance was applied to fabric used in early airplanes. The Dreyfus firm finally produced acetate in fiber form in 1921 in England; in 1924 an allied organization started production of the fiber in the United States. During the years since, several companies established manufacturing facilities to make acetate fiber. As other, newer man-made fibers were developed the use of acetate declined, and today the only companies producing acetate in the United States are the Celanese Corporation, Avtex Fibers, and Tennessee Eastman.

Triacetate fibers were developed along with regular acetate. However, manufacture of triacetate into fiber form was delayed until the middle of the twentieth century, when safe solvents became available in sufficient quantity to make production economically profitable. Arnel, the only triacetate fiber made in the United States, was introduced by the Celanese Corporation in 1952, and large-scale production started in 1955. Both acetate and triacetate continue to be respected fibers for selected types of fabrics; however, their use has continued to decline over the years, and they account for a relatively small proportion of all fiber used in the United States.

Manufacture of Acetate: Secondary Acetate and Triacetate

The materials required for manufacturing acetate include cellulose, acetic acid, and acetic anhydride, plus sulfuric acid as a catalyst. Cellulose is obtained primarily from wood pulp; it is purified, bleached, and shredded. The shredded cellulose is fed into pretreatment tanks, where it is thoroughly mixed with glacial acetic acid and held for a specified length of time. The pretreated pulp is transferred to kneading machines called *acetylators,* and the acetic anhydride is added. During this step the cellulose is dissolved and becomes cellulose acetate. It is a clear liquid called *acid dope.* The dope is aged, or ripened, in special storage tanks; water is added as needed to reduce the acid concentration. Hydrolysis occurs during the ripening, resulting in the formation of acetate. When this secondary acetate solution is mixed with water, the acetate precipitates out in the form of small flakes. The flakes are washed thoroughly and dried.

The cellulose acetate flakes are dissolved in acetone to form a *spinning dope.* This spinning solution is forced through filters to remove any undissolved acetate and impurities and then through the spinnerette into a warm air chamber. Here the acetone evaporates and the acetate coagulates as it falls through the chamber (Fig. 9.1). The filaments traveling downward are twisted together to form yarn. The method of fiber manufacture is called *dry spinning.*

Triacetate is manufactured from the same raw materials, but the ripening stage, in which hydrolysis of the acetate occurs, is omitted. A spinning solution is made by dissolving the triacetate flakes in methylene chloride; this solution is dry spun into a warm air chamber, just as is secondary acetate.

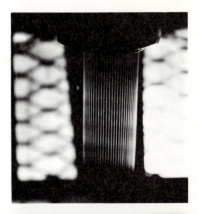

Fiber Properties

Microscopic Properties

When viewed longitudinally under the microscope, acetate appears to be uniform in width with several lines parallel to the fiber length (Fig. 9.2). These lines, called striations, are farther apart than those found in rayon fibers. Bright acetate is clear, whereas dull, or delustered, acetate appears speckled or pitted. The cross section of acetate is lobed with irregular curves but with no sharp serrations, or edges, like those frequently observed in viscose rayon (Fig. 9.3).

Triacetate is very similar in microscopic appearance to acetate. It may have clearer striations and the cross section may have sharper lobes or serrated edges. Positive distinction between triacetate and secondary acetate by microscopy is not possible.

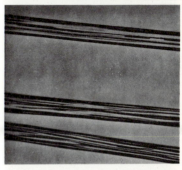

Physical Properties

The length, diameter, and luster of acetate and triacetate depend on end use. Manufacturers can produce a wide variety of fiber shapes and conformations. The makers of spinning jets have developed spinnerettes with orifices of different shapes that can turn out modified fibers such as flat filaments, oval filaments, and irregular filaments (see Table 9.1).

Both acetate and triacetate have low strength and require careful handling. But the desirable properties of hand, drape, and appearance make the fabrics manufactured from these fibers attractive to designers and consumers.

The low elastic recovery of acetate, coupled with its low resiliency, results in fabrics that become easily wrinkled and permanently deformed. Triacetate has better elastic recovery than regular acetate, and the resiliency is good. Triacetate will hold its shape and appearance and wrinkles hang out.

The moisture regain of acetate is slightly less than cotton; that of triacetate is fairly low. Generally, it is adequate for comfort in fabrics. But the lower moisture regain, coupled with the molecular arrangement, makes dyeing of both fibers difficult, and the process requires special dyes.

Acetate and triacetate fibers are comparatively resistant to stretch or shrinkage unless fabric relaxation occurs as a result of excess tension on yarns during the fabric construction process. Fibers will tend to shrink if exposed to high temperature.

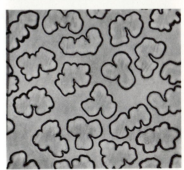

9.1 top. Acetate fibers are dry spun. The solution is forced through the spinnerette into an air chamber, where the fibers are formed as the solvent evaporates in a heated environment. (Celanese Corporation)

9.2 middle. Photomicrograph of acetate fiber, longitudinal view. (E. I. DuPont de Nemours & Company)

9.3 bottom. Photomicrograph of acetate fiber, cross section. (E. I. DuPont de Nemours & Company)

TABLE 9.1 Properties of acetate and triacetate

Property	Acetate	Triacetate
Shape	shape can be controlled by the manufacturer—therefore, uniform in observed appearance; length and denier are determined by manufacturer for end use	
Luster	controlled for both; can vary from dull to bright	
Strength (in grams per denier)		
dry	1.2–1.4	1.1–1.4
wet	0.9–1.0	0.8–1.0
Elastic recovery	100% at 1% extension	90–100% at 1–2% extension
	48–75% at 4% extension	80–84% at 4% extension
% elongation		
dry	25–35	25–35
wet	35–45	30–40
Resiliency	low	good
Density	1.32	1.32
Moisture absorption		
20° C/65% R.H.	6.5	3.2–3.5
saturation	14.0	9.0
Dimensional stability	good	good
Resistance to:		
acids	both fibers have fair resistance to dilute acids and poor to concentrated acids	
alkalies	both fibers have good resistance to dilute alkalies; both are eventually destroyed in concentrated alkalies	
sunlight	loss of strength for acetate; triacetate has superior resistance	
microorganisms	both discolor; acetate will lose strength, but triacetate retains strength	
insects	silverfish will eat sized acetate or triacetate	
Thermal reactions		
to heat	softens and melts at temperature over 175° C	softens at temperature over 235° C
to flame	both fibers burn easily and quickly	

Thermal Properties

Acetate and triacetate are thermoplastic fibers (easily affected by heat) and will soften at temperatures over 175° C and 235° C, respectively. The fibers melt and burn, forming a hard, black bead ash. They give off an odor similar to that of hot vinegar. Triacetate can be *heat treated* to withstand higher temperatures without damage. The same treatment also permits setting permanent pleats and creases in triacetate fabrics.

Chemical Properties

Dilute alkalies have little effect on acetate or triacetate. Concentrated alkalies cause saponification of both and eventually a loss in fiber weight and a reduction in the soft hand of fabrics.

Concentrated acids weaken the fibers drastically and in most instances cause complete disintegration. Dilute hot acids may cause decomposition or, at least, a loss of strength. Cold dilute acids weaken the fiber if exposure is prolonged.

Petroleum solvents used in dry cleaning do not damage acetate or triacetate. However, such solvents as acetone, phenol, and chloroform will destroy the fibers. Consumers should be cautious when using fingernail polish remover, paint remover, and similar products, as they often contain acetone that will destroy the fiber.

Sunlight causes a loss of strength in acetate fiber but has little or no effect on triacetate. Storage may result in weaker acetate fibers; triacetate has good to excellent stability to aging and storage.

All acetates develop static charges, especially when dry, because they are poor conductors of electricity.

Biological Properties

Fungi such as mildew and bacteria may discolor acetate fibers. Some weakening of acetate may occur, but triacetate retains its strength.

Moths and other household pests do not damage acetates or triacetates. However, silverfish may attack heavily sized fibers in order to eat the starch sizing. Naturally, this will damage the fiber and alter its hand and appearance.

Use and Care

Care of Acetate and Triacetate

Both acetate and triacetate have low strength and tend to be weaker when wet than dry. Thus, fabrics from either type of fiber require careful handling in laundering or dry cleaning. Acetate tends to wrinkle badly during care, and twisting or wringing should be kept to a minimum; triacetate performs somewhat better than acetate in this respect. Because of this property, when washing machines are used, it is best to select a gentle cycle for acetate and triacetate items.

Almost any type of detergent may be used on acetate and triacetate. Bleaches can be used with care; however, unless there are stains, bleaching is not required because standard laundering procedures usually remove most soil and return the fabric to its original appearance. If bleaching is considered necessary, it is important to follow directions on the bleach container and any care labeling information provided with the textile product. The low moisture regain of acetate results in fibers that are relatively resistant to staining and to size change during care.

Acetate may be dried in automatic dryers if they have temperature controls; only a medium to low temperature should be used. Although triacetate can tolerate higher temperatures than acetate, drying temperatures should still be kept low.

Triacetate may not require any ironing, or at most a light touch-up, as the fiber characteristics result in fabrics that tend to regain their original shape following care procedures. However, acetate does not regain its appearance without ironing. Medium to low ironing temperatures should be used; steam and a press cloth are suggested to prevent damage to

9.4 Chiffon jersey dress of Arnel triacetate.

the fabrics. Because of the difficulty in care, many labels will suggest that acetate products be dry cleaned.

Special dyestuffs were developed for acetate and triacetate. These dyes produce relatively good color durability when applied correctly. Thus, laundering or dry cleaning does not tend to cause any color loss.

Use of Acetate and Triacetate

Both acetate and triacetate are selected by designers for the outstanding drapability and desirable hand of the fiber. These fibers are used in a variety of applications, but most uses are either for apparel or home furnishings. They are frequently chosen for drapery or curtain fabrics, for which they provide good durability. They may also be used as upholstery materials, frequently as part of a blend of fibers. Triacetate has not been used as widely in home furnishings, but it is popular in apparel because it provides a fabric that is comfortable and that has some easy care properties. Permanent pleats can be built into triacetate fabrics that will withstand normal use and care. Triacetate has a crisper hand than acetate, but it can be made into fabrics that are soft and drape well (Fig. 9.4).

Both acetate and triacetate have been used in blends with other fibers. Depending on the other fibers in the blend, acetate or triacetate may contribute stability to the fabric. Both acetate and triacetate are used in knitted fabrics; the triacetate is especially successful because it holds its shape, retains permanent pleats, packs well, and hangs out quickly to its original appearance.

Triacetate is more expensive than acetate, and both fibers are more expensive than either rayon or cotton; in fact they are frequently more expensive than polyester fibers. Acetate and triacetate are generally sold only as filament fibers and are made into fabrics from filament yarns. A solution-dyed acetate is available, and these fabrics have superior colorfastness.

Several important modifications of acetate and triacetate have been introduced to the market during the past decade. Flame-resistant acetate and triacetate are available for manufacture into children's sleepwear. Other modifications include the development of fibers with antistatic and antimicrobial properties. For typical trade names for acetate and triacetate see Table 2.2.

Study Questions

1. What are the properties and characteristics of acetate and triacetate fibers?
2. How do acetate and triacetate fibers differ in properties and characteristics? How are they similar?
3. When was acetate introduced to the public? When was triacetate available to consumers?
4. What was acetate used for before it was successful as a fiber for apparel and home furnishings?
5. What is the major difference in the manufacture of acetate and triacetate fibers?
6. Describe care procedures and care problems for acetate and triacetate fibers and fabrics.
7. Indicate some of the modifications of acetate that are available on the market.
8. How does the use of acetate and triacetate fibers compare with other man-made fibers? With natural fibers?

Polyamide Fibers: Nylon and Aramid

10

NYLON

Historical Review

The history of nylon is a story of scientific research and development. In 1927 the DuPont Company gave a small group of scientists unrestricted funds for basic research in the hope that new scientific information would ultimately lead to chemical advancement. A year later the research team, headed by Wallace Carothers, began to study long-chain molecules such as those found in natural fibers. This phase of their work resulted in the creation of a number of giant molecules called *macromolecues, polymolecules,* or *polymers*. The team also determined that linear polymers, composed of relatively small molecules linked end to end—much like a chain of paper clips—could be man-made.

In the 1930s the chemists discovered an unusual characteristic in one of the substances under investigation. They found that when a glass rod in contact with some viscous materials in a beaker was pulled away slowly, the substance adhered to the rod and formed a fine filament that hardened as soon as it was exposed to cool air. Furthermore, they observed that the cool filaments could be stretched several times their formed length to produce a flexible, strong, and attractive fiber. After this discovery the scientists set out to produce such a fiber in a practical and economical manner.

The next few years were devoted to improving the polymer, finding efficient methods for manufacturing it, developing necessary mechanical equipment for its production, and perhaps of most importance, finding possible uses for it. In 1938 DuPont set up a pilot plant, and one year later a large-scale plant was placed "on stream" at Seaford, Delaware.

Nylon, in the form of knitted hosiery for women, was test marketed in various parts of the United States in late 1939 and early 1940. Introduction of the fiber to the general public was well planned and coordinated; it was a classic example of successful mass marketing (Fig. 10.1). Throughout the nation, heralded by uniform advertising, nylon stockings were launched on May 15, 1940. They were an immediate success, and despite their temporary absence during World War II, they retained their popularity; today women's hosiery is frequently referred to as "nylons."

The first nylon was referred to as type 6,6. The numbers derive from the fact that each of the two chemicals used in making this type of nylon has six carbon atoms. Nylon type 6,10 was developed at the same time, and it is composed of one chemical with six carbon atoms per molecule and ten carbon atoms per molecule for the second chemical. Nylon 6,6 was considered desirable for apparel and selected home furnishings; nylon 6,10 was used in making brushes and similar items. Since the intro-

10.1   Advertisement used to introduce nylon, October 30, 1938. (E. I. DuPont de Nemours & Company)

duction of nylon 6,6, other types of nylon have been developed and marketed, of which the most common type is nylon 6. In many countries nylon is identified by the term *polyamide*.

Manufacturing

Early advertising of nylon proclaimed that the fiber was made from coal, air, and water. This, of course, was an oversimplification, but it is true that the elements found in nylon are also found in coal, air, and water—that is, carbon, hydrogen, oxygen, and nitrogen.

Nylon 6,6 is a linear condensation polymer made from hexamethylene diamine and adipic acid. Specific amounts of the two chemicals are combined in solution to form *nylon salt*. This salt is purified, polymerized, extruded in ribbon form, and chipped into small flakes or pellets. These flakes or pellets are melted and extruded through a spinnerette into cool air, and the nylon filaments are formed. After cooling, the filaments are stretched or cold drawn to orient the molecules in the fibers and develop the necessary fiber strength and fineness (Fig. 10.2).

Nylon 6 is manufactured in a similar manner except that the chemical used is called caprolactum.

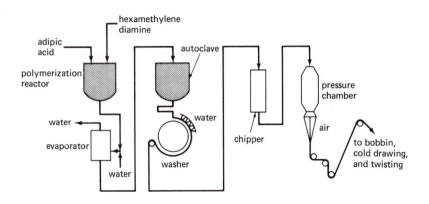

Fiber Properties

Microscopic Properties

Nylon filaments are usually smooth and shiny. When viewed in cross section they are either round or multilobal with smooth edges. Special trade names have been developed for multilobal fibers and include Cadon, Enkaloft, Ultron, Cumuloft, and Antron. Longitudinal magnification shows relatively transparent fibers of uniform diameter with a slight speckled appearance (Figs. 10.3, 10.4, and 10.5).

Physical Properties

Like other man-made fibers, nylon can be extruded in a variety of diameters and lengths, and its transparency and luster can be controlled (see Table 10.1).

One of the major advantages of nylon fibers is their strength and

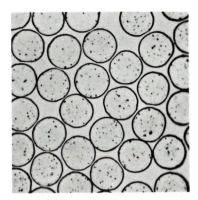
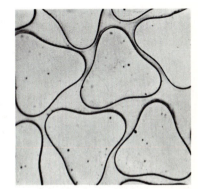

10.3 Photomicrograph of nylon 6,6 fiber, longitudinal view. (E. I. DuPont de Nemours & Company)

10.4 Photomicrograph of nylon 6,6 fiber, cross section. (E. I. DuPont de Nemours & Company)

10.5 Photomicrograph of trilobal nylon, cross section. (E. I. DuPont de Nemours & Company)

TABLE 10.1 Properties of nylon 6,6 and nylon 6

Property	Nylon 6,6	Nylon 6
Shape	shape is controlled by the manufacturer; filaments are uniform; length and diameter are determined by the manufacturer for specified types; available in filament or staple; bright, semidull, or dull	
Luster	controlled from bright to dull	
Tenacity (strength)		
dry	4.3–9.0 g/d	3.5–9.0 g/d
wet	4.0–7.6 g/d	3.2–8.0 g/d
Elastic recovery	100% recovery at 4% extension	
Elongation		
conditioned*	19–40%	16–50%
wet	20–46%	18–55%
Resiliency	good	good
Density	1.14 g/ccm	1.14 g/ccm
Moisture regain		
conditioned	3.8–4.5%	3.5–5.0%
wet	8.0%	8.5%
Dimensional stability	excellent	excellent
Resistance to		
acids	all nylon has poor resistance to acids; some mineral acids and some organic acids dissolve nylon fiber	
alkalies	all nylon has good resistance	
organic solvents	generally good for both types	
sunlight	sunlight is generally destructive unless special finishes have been added	
microorganisms	high	high
insects	resistant to most; may be damaged by ants, crickets, and roaches	
Thermal resistance		
to heat	all nylon softens and melts if temperatures are above	
	250° C	210° C
ironing temperature	150° C	150° C
to flame	heat-sensitive; shrinks from flame, melts, drips, burns in open flame; frequently self-extinguishing; some finishes and dyestuffs may alter behavior in flame	

*Conditioned environment = 65% relative humidity, 70° F ± 2°.

abrasion resistance. Nylon's strength or tenacity ranks high among man-made fibers, and because it retains much of its stretch when wet, it requires no special care. Its resistance to abrasion makes it appropriate for many different uses.

Nylon is a highly elastic fiber with excellent elongation and elastic recovery. These qualities assure outstanding shape retention of nylon fabrics. Nylon has good to very good resiliency, and fabrics recover easily from crushing or wrinkling.

Compared with natural fibers, nylon has rather low moisture absorbency. In spite of this characteristic, nylon accepts dyes well and dries quickly after exposure to moisture. However, the low moisture absorption and poor electrical conductivity tend to cause an accumulation of static electric charges on nylon, which can be very uncomfortable to consumers.

Nylon fibers will stretch under stress but will return to their original size after release.

Thermal Properties

It is in thermal properties that the differences between nylon 6,6 and nylon 6 are most apparent. Nylon 6,6 will melt at approximately 259° C, whereas nylon 6 melts at about 210° C. All nylon can withstand temperatures to about 300° F (about 140° C) for long periods of time without damage. However, as temperatures rise above these limits, discoloration and loss of strength occur fairly rapidly.

Nylon melts away from a flame and forms a gummy gray or tan ash that hardens as it cools. The fiber will burn if held in an open flame, but it does not support combustion. However, some dyestuffs and finishes may cause the fiber to burn more readily.

Because nylon is heat sensitive, or thermoplastic, it can be heat set during processing so that it will retain its shape during use and care. Application of temperatures higher than those used for heat setting may cause fiber deformation and shrinkage; therefore, it is important to avoid temperatures that might exceed those used in processing. Safe ironing temperatures for nylon 6,6 should not exceed 350° F, and for nylon 6, not over 300° F.

Chemical Properties

Nylon is not affected by alkalies, but acids—whether of the mineral or organic type—will destroy the fiber. Most organic solvents have little or no effect on nylon. Stain-removal or dry cleaning solvents do not damage it. Soaps, synthetic detergents, and bleaches can be used safely.

Sunlight is destructive to nylon and causes a marked loss of strength after extended exposure. For that reason nylon is not recommended as a window curtain or drapery fabric. Specially developed dyes, however, can inhibit sunlight damage in nylon to a certain extent. Age appears to have no effect on the fiber, and it may be stored, if away from light, for many years without noticeable deterioration.

Biological Properties

Nylon is highly resistant to attack by most insects and microorganisms. However, some insects normally found outdoors, including ants, crickets, and roaches, will eat nylon if they are trapped in folds or creases. Mildew may attack finishes used on nylon, but it does not damage the fiber.

Other Nylons

A variety of other types of nylon, or polyamide, fibers are manufactured throughout the world. A few have been popular in the United States, and some have been manufactured here.

Nylon 6,10

Nylon 6,10 has been mentioned earlier. It is used primarily as a bristle in various types of brushes—paintbrushes, clothes brushes, and tooth-brushes, for example.

Nylon 11

Rilsan, or nylon 11, is produced in Europe, Asia, and South America. It is a polymer with properties very similar to those of nylon 6 or nylon 6,6. However it has a lower moisture regain and a lower melting point. It does not discolor as quickly and is frequently used for bulky yarns and fabrics.

Nylon 7

Nylon 7 is made in the Soviet Union. It, too, is similar to nylon 6,6 and nylon 6; however, it has better stability to heat and to light. The moisture regain is slightly lower.

Nylon 46

Nylon 46 is a relatively new fiber, introduced in the mid-1980s. It is reported to have superior dimensional stability and high strength and better heat resistance than other nylons. To date, it is limited to industrial applications.

Qiana

Qiana was a popular nylon fiber for several years. It was used in high-fashion fabrics for both apparel and home furnishings. In the mid-1980s, DuPont eliminated Qiana as a trade name for a fiber, using the name now to indicate a special fabric certified by DuPont for use in certain items. That is, the term now refers to fabrics and not fibers.

Nylon Modifications

Many modifications of nylon are available for different types of consumer goods. One of the most common modifications is to produce the fiber in different cross-sectional shapes. These shapes produce many different qualities, such as increased cover; a crisp, silklike hand; reduced pilling; increased bulk; sparkle effects; and increased resistance to showing soil. Trilobal and other multilobal nylons are particularly popular for home-furnishing fabrics such as floor coverings.

Nylon can be modified by texturizing (see Chapter 19). This process changes the bulk and loft of nylon yarns and fabrics.

Chemical additions can be made to nylon to increase the strength and abrasion resistance, to provide antistatic properties, and to increase the resistance to soiling.

A common bicomponent nylon available on the market is called Cantrece and is recommended for women's hosiery.

Use and Care

Nylon Care

Nylon is easy to launder. It can be washed safely at all temperatures, drip dried, spun dried, or dried in the dryer. However, low to medium temperatures should be used to reduce the chance of wrinkles being formed that are difficult, if not impossible, to remove. Drying in dryers at medium or low temperatures, followed by prompt removal, is recommended as the best method for keeping the original appearance of the fabric.

Bleaches can be used, when needed; however, consumers should read care labels carefully because some types of dyes or finishes may negate the use of bleach. Any type of soap or detergent can be used safely. Antistatic rinses, such as fabric softeners, are recommended.

A major problem that might be encountered in laundering is that nylon tends to scavenge color and soil from other products in the same laundry operation. This produces gray, yellow, or otherwise discolored items that may be difficult, if not impossible, to restore to their original appearance. Proper care, however, reduces this buildup of grayness and helps retain the original appearance of the product. White nylon is particularly vulnerable to discoloration. There is some evidence that colored detergents may discolor white nylon if not thoroughly rinsed away during rinse cycles.

Because it is very difficult to identify which type of nylon one might have, unless the label has given a trade name that is recognized as type 66, low ironing temperatures are recommended for all nylon products if ironing is necessary. Many nylon fabrics have been processed so that they retain their appearance during use and care, and ironing or pressing is not required.

When used with fibers that require dry cleaning, nylon responds without problems. However, laundering is the recommended care when possible.

Home-furnishing items made of nylon, such as carpeting and upholstery, should be spot cleaned whenever spots or stains occur. Removing these stains as soon as possible helps the textile item retain its original appearance and not become dingy or gray.

Nylon Use

Nylon is popular for apparel, home furnishings, and industrial products (Figs. 10.6, 10.7, and 10.8). It is the leading fiber in the manufacture of hosiery and has considerable importance in the lingerie market. For outer-

10.7 Nylon in home furnishings. (Carpet and platform coverings of Allied's Anso IV nylon fibers)

10.6 Nylon knit running suits. (Allied's Caprolan nylon fibers)

10.8 Nylon carpeting. (Allied's Anso IV nylon fibers)

wear it is blended with other fibers to contribute dimensional stability, elastic recovery, shape retention, and abrasion resistance. It is used, frequently, for apparel that has to resist various environmental conditions such as extreme cold and wet weather.

Many carpeting and upholstery fabrics are made of nylon, for the fiber wears well, is easy to clean, and does not require special protection against moths and carpet beetles. Trilobal nylons, such as Cumuloft and Ultron, are popular in carpeting because they resist showing soil and crushing and retain an attractive appearance for many years.

If dyestuffs are selected wisely, nylon fabrics exhibit good color retention. However, it is extremely important that proper techniques be used in applying dyes to avoid streaky or uneven dyeings.

Pilling, the formation of tiny balls of fiber on the surface of the cloth, is a severe problem with fabrics made of spun nylon yarns and, to a lesser degree, with filament fiber fabrics. Because the nylon fibers are extremely resistant to abrasion, the pills are not rubbed off after they form, as they would be on the surface of fabrics with low abrasion resistance such as wool.

Because of the low moisture absorbency of nylon, fabrics must have adequate spaces, or interstices, between yarns to permit water vapor passage and thus ensure the wearers' comfort. Various finishing techniques may be used to improve surface absorbency; these increase comfort by drawing moisture away from the body. These properties are advantageous when nylon is used for such items as carpeting. The low absorbency reduces the amount of moisture that the carpet might pick up on humid days; furthermore, it reduces the amount of waterborne soils that the carpet picks up.

The capacity for nylon to be heat set makes it possible to build into the fabric surface designs such as crinkled and embossed effects. It is also possible to build in puckered or crinkled effects through the use of finishing agents such as weak solutions of phenol.

ARAMID FIBERS

A polyamide quite different from regular nylon is called aramid. There are two aramid fibers currently available in the United States, Nomex and Kevlar. Both are manufactured by DuPont. These fibers have some properties that are similar to nylon and some properties that are very different.

Nomex

Nomex is a fiber with an irregular cross-sectional shape; it is strong, has high elongation and good elastic recovery, medium low moisture regain, excellent dimensional stability, and good resistance to high temperatures. Probably the most important property of Nomex is its behavior in flame. The fiber resists damage from heat and has a very low flammability. It has good resistance to chemicals, similar to nylon fibers. Nomex is difficult to dye, but it is available in a limited range of colors.

The care of Nomex is similar to that for nylon except that it will tolerate higher temperatures. Nomex is used where resistance to combustion and low smoke generation are required, and where chemical stability and durability and high temperatures are needed. Typical uses for Nomex include protective suits for firefighters, race car drivers, and employees in plants where heat and fire pose a hazard; aircraft furnishings; hot gas filtration fabrics; electrical insulation; covers for laundry presses and ironing boards; selected components for space vehicles; and portions of apparel for space personnel.

Kevlar

Kevlar fibers have extremely high tenacity (strength)—approximately five times the strength of a steel wire of the same weight and more than twice the strength of high-tenacity industrial nylon. It has an unusually high initial modulus, that is, resistance to distortion or stretch under high stress. Moisture regain is about 7 percent, which is similar to acetate; elongation is low.

Thermal properties are superior; it has outstanding stability to heat. Chemical properties are also good.

Kevlar is used in a variety of specialized applications (Fig. 10.9). One of the most important is as body armor, or bulletproof vests. It was used as structural reinforcement in making the *Gossamer Albatross,* the first man-powered aircraft to fly the English Channel. It is used in a wide variety of industrial applications for such products as hoses, conveyor belts, ropes, cables, booms, and reinforcement for concrete.

Care of Kevlar is similar to Nomex and nylons. It can be laundered and dried without damage.

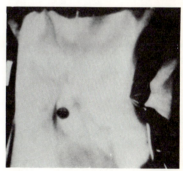

10.9 Kevlar aramid fiber used as protection against bullets. (E. I. DuPont de Nemours & Company)

Study Questions

1. Identify the differences and similarities between nylon 6,6 and nylon 6 (refer to Table 10.1).
2. How do the properties of nylon influence its care?
3. Prepare care instructions for nylon fibers that would be appropriate for care labels on apparel or home-furnishing items.
4. List five typical end uses for nylon fibers, and discuss the properties that make the fiber appropriate for each end use cited.
5. What did the development of nylon fibers contribute to the history of man-made fibers?
6. What are typical end uses for aramid fibers? Why is the fiber appropriate for such uses?
7. Why is nylon so successful in hosiery?
8. How do the two polyamide fibers, nylon and aramid, differ? How are they similar?
9. What textile items do you or your family own that are made of nylon? Why do you think nylon was chosen for these products?
10. Why would a police officer want to have a vest made of aramid fiber?

11 Polyester Fibers

Historical Review

The initial research on polyester fibers was done by Carothers and his research team as a part of their work for DuPont. However, the polyamides, particularly nylon, appeared to show more promise, and the research team directed their efforts to the development of those materials. Polyester research was set aside, partly because the properties of early polyester fibers appeared to be less desirable than those of nylon; also it seemed they would be too expensive to produce.

While Carothers and his assistants directed their emphasis to the polyamides, chemists in Britain began experimenting with long-chain polyester polymers. In 1941 J. R. Winfield and J. T. Dickson, of Calico Printers Association, introduced a successful polyester fiber. Development of this fiber was delayed by World War II, and public announcement of the discovery was withheld until 1946. Imperial Chemical Industries (ICI) purchased the rights to manufacture polyester fiber in all countries except the United States, for which DuPont obtained the manufacturing rights.

DuPont, after several trial names, called their polyester Dacron, and it was made available to consumers in 1951. A large manufacturing plant was completed in Kinston, North Carolina, in 1952, and since that time polyester has become one of the most widely used fibers. Since 1975 polyester has accounted for approximately 30 percent of all fiber consumed yearly in the United States.

While Dupont was making Dacron polyester popular in the United States, ICI was making their polyester, called Terylene, popular in Great Britain and the rest of Europe. Since the 1960s several companies have developed and marketed polyester fibers. A look at Table 2.2 will illustrate a few of the many trade names used for polyester fibers, which are made in nearly every fiber-producing country.

Polyester fibers found immediate consumer acceptance because of their easy maintenance and excellent crease resistance. When the fiber was first previewed for the press, several products were exhibited, the most impressive being a man's business suit. To dramatize the superior wrinkle resistance and easy care properties of the new fiber, its manufacturers arranged for the suit to be worn for sixty-seven days without being pressed. During that time it was submerged twice in a swimming pool and washed once in an automatic washer. When shown at the press conference, it was still considered wearable.

Polyester is the single most used fiber in the United States and ranks among the top in world consumption.

Fiber Production

Polyesters are made by reacting a dihydric alcohol with a dicarboxylic acid. The generic definition was modified in 1973 (see page 12) so that

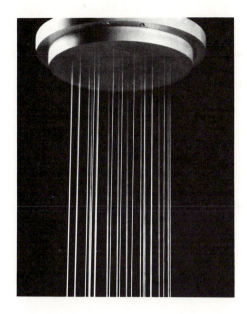

11.1 Melt spinning; polyester filaments emerging from spinnerettes. (Hoechst Fibers)

no specific acid is identified; thus, the definition can cover a variety of polyesters.

As the acid and alcohol are polymerized, they are extruded from the polymerizing vessel in the form of a ribbon. This ribbon is cut into small chips; the chips are diced and conveyed to a hopper from which they are fed to the melt spinning tank. The hot solution is forced through spinnerettes and solidifies into fiber form on contact with cool air (Fig. 11.1). It is stretched while hot; the stretching contributes strength to the fiber and controls elongation characteristics. The greater the amount of molecular orientation obtained during this stretching step, the stronger the fiber and the lower the elongation.

Fiber Properties

Microscopic Properties

A longitudinal view of polyester fiber exhibits uniform diameter, smooth surface, and a rodlike appearance (Fig. 11.2). The cross section may be perfectly round (Fig. 11.3) or lobal in shape. The modifications in which trilobal- and pentalobal-shaped filaments are formed are the most popular.

Physical Properties

Polyester can be made in any length or diameter required for potential end uses. The fiber is partially transparent and white or slightly off-white in color. Pigment can be combined with the spinning solution, which permits control of the degree of luster—not color. Optical brighteners are frequently added to produce clear, bright fibers.

The strength of polyesters varies widely. It, too, depends on end use and is controlled by manufacturing procedures. Some fibers have a low tenacity similar to rayon, whereas others may be as strong as nylon. The strength of polyester fibers is the same wet and dry.

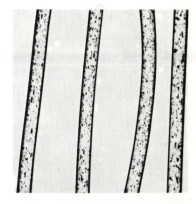

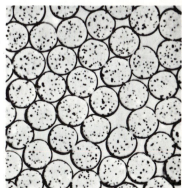

11.2 Photomicrograph of regular polyester fiber, longitudinal view. (E. I. DuPont de Nemours & Company)

11.3 Photomicrograph of regular polyester fiber, cross section. (E. I. DuPont de Nemours & Company)

TABLE 11.1 Properties of polyester fibers

Property	Evaluation
Shape	shape for polyester fibers is controlled by manufacturers; it may be of a wide choice of diameters and either round or multilobal in cross section
Luster	controlled from semibright to dull
Strength	
dry	ranges from 2.5 to 9.5 grams per denier
wet	little or no difference from dry
Elastic recovery	varies in elastic recovery but typically has 90 to 100% recovery at 2% extension
Elongation	varies by type, 9.5–75%
Resiliency	excellent
Density	1.38
Moisture absorption	0.4%, very low
Dimensional stability	excellent
Resistance to	
acids	strong acids destroy fiber; weak acids have little or no effect
alkalies	resistance is good to weak alkalies and moderate to strong
sunlight	behind glass, resistance is excellent; in direct sun, medium
microorganisms	excellent
insects	excellent
Thermal reactions	
to heat	will melt at temperatures from 238° C to 290° C
to flame	will burn, but slowly, and melting fibers tend to drop off, preventing further burning

Elongation is another controlled property. The fiber's elastic recovery is very good, and its resiliency is excellent. When properly heat set, polyesters require ittle or no pressing to retain a smooth appearance (see Table 11.1).

The moisture regain of polyester fibers is very low—less than 0.5 percent. Because of this low regain, moisture has little effect on fiber strength, and static electric charges are accentuated. Furthermore, the low moisture absorption demands special techniques in dyeing and finishing. Like cotton and linen, polyesters have a high degree of wickability. This wicking property can produce end-use products that carry exterior moisture through to the inside or body perspiration through to the outside.

When polyester is properly heat set it will not shrink or stretch during normal use and care.

Thermal Properties

Polyester fibers melt at temperatures from 460° to 550° F (235° C to 290° C), depending on type and modification. As the fiber melts, it forms a gray or tawny-colored bead that is hard and noncrushable. Polyesters will burn and produce a dark smoke and an aromatic odor. In light fabric constructions, the fibers frequently melt and drip away from the source of ignition, preventing the propagation of flame.

Ironing temperatures for polyesters vary with fiber type. Generally, however, a medium to low temperature should be used when any ironing or pressing is needed.

Heat setting of polyester yarns and fabrics is essential if they are to have the easy care, wrinkle-free properties associated with the fiber. Once heat set, polyester will hold creases, pleats, or any other shaping lines, as long as proper care procedures are followed.

Chemical Properties

Polyester has good resistance to weak alkalies but only moderate resistance to strong ones. Weak acids do not affect the fiber, nor do strong acids at room temperatures. Strong acids at high temperatures, however, will destroy polyester.

In general, the fiber resists organic solvents. Chemicals used in stain removal and cleaning do not damage polyester; bleaches have no destructive effect.

Direct sunlight weakens polyester, but the fiber has good resistance to sunlight when behind glass. It is, therefore, satisfactory for window curtains and drapes.

Biological Properties

Insects will not destroy polyesters if there is other food available. However, if trapped, beetles and similar insects will cut their way through the fabric as a means of escape. Though microorganisms will not harm the fiber, they may attack finishes that have been applied.

Modified Polyester Fibers

Polyester fibers are available in a variety of types; some of them are considered to be second-, third-, and fourth-generation fibers. Each type has at least one special characteristic that alters fiber behavior in some way. These new fibers are created by altering the cross-sectional shape, by changing the chemical formulas, or by varying the physical processing.

The changes in shape produce fibers with hand and appearance different from those of regular polyester. Trilobal and pentalobal (or other variant) cross sections contribute several desirable properties to polyester fibers. Yarns and fabrics constructed from lobal fibers are characterized by a silklike hand and appearance. They tend to soil less quickly, or appear to, because dirt lodged in the valleys between the lobes is less conspicuous. Lobal fibers have improved covering power, and their luster and surface sheen are pleasing to the eye.

Chemical modifications change the dyeing properties and alter the types of dyes that are used on the fiber (Fig. 11.4). These modifications can alter the fiber strength, and thus the pilling behavior, and the crush resistance.

Physical modifications have resulted in hollow fibers, which are designed for use as fiberfill and which provide excellent bulk, resiliency, and insulating properties. Another physical modification is achieved by altering the spinning speed, which changes the degree of orientation and affects properties such as strength and pilling. Crimp can be set in the filaments during manufacture to increase bulk and resilience.

11.4 Cross-dyed polyester fabric. Modification of polyester fibers can control dye acceptance to permit formation of checks, plaids, or stripes after fabric is woven. (E. I. DuPont de Nemours & Company)

A major problem with polyester fibers is their tendency to absorb oily substances and become stained. Researchers claim to have developed oil-resistant polyester, but there is little label information that would indicate this fiber is commonly used.

POY Polyester

Polyester filaments are frequently textured to provide yarn with greater bulk and to be more like natural fibers such as cotton or wool. POY polyester is designed so that final orientation occurs during the actual texturizing operation. The resulting polyester yarns are said to be easier to handle in both knitting and weaving than other types of polyester textured yarns.

Flame-Resistant Polyester

Inherently flame-resistant polyester is desired because the property becomes an integral part of the fiber and cannot be removed through use and care. This effect is achieved by adding special chemicals to the fiber solution before the filaments are formed.

Other Modifications

Two modifications of polyester were announced during 1985. One, called Mawus-M, has a high bacteriostatic performance that is durable and has good moisture absorbency. A second, called Mawus-R, is a heat-resistant polyester that remains free from holes even if a lighted cigarette is held against the fabric for three minutes.

Benzoate Polyesters

A polyester made from benzoic acid and ethylene oxide was developed by a Japanese corporation although the trade name, A-Tell, was not included in the latest listing of foreign-made fibers. However, the fiber was considered desirable because it gave the appearance of silk. It had high strength, good elongation, superior dimensional stability, excellent elastic recovery, low moisture regain, excellent resistance to chemicals, good temperature resistance, resistance to abrasion, resistance to damage from sunlight, and easy care.

Use and Care

Polyester Fiber Care

The most important characteristics of polyester fibers might well be their wrinkle-free appearance and ease of care. Fabrics of these fibers require little or no ironing, are easy and safe to launder, and dry quickly.

Care requirements for polyester fabrics are minimal. Soaps, synthetic detergents, and laundry aids do not damage fabrics made of these fibers. If the fabric has become heavily soiled or stained with oil-based substances, the areas should be pretreated before laundering with special stain-removing laundry aids, liquid detergent, or clear liquid shampoo; these should be rubbed into the stained or soiled area before any laundering. If laundered without some type of substance to loosen the oil and lift it from the fibers, chances are high that the stain will become permanent.

Polyester products can be dried in dryers or drip dried; however drying in automatic dryers is considered best because of the fluffing action, which tends to bounce any wrinkles out. The fabric, however, must be removed as soon as the dryer stops; otherwise, wrinkles that are extremely difficult to remove will be set into the fabric.

Blends of polyester with other fibers may require special handling although blends of polyester and cotton are easy to care for and respond well to laundering. Nonetheless, consumers should read care labels before laundering or dry cleaning any textile product made of blends.

Despite the easy care properties of polyester fabrics, some consumers have had problems with shrinkage of polyester knits. These problems are probably caused by polyester that has not been properly heat set. Users of knit polyester fabric may wish to wash the yardage before use to minimize any shrinkage that might occur after it is made into end-use items. High temperatures should also be avoided in the care of polyester because they increase the possibility of shrinkage. In general, however, polyester is considered a stable fiber, and polyester fabrics are considered dimensionally stable, that is, resistant to stretch or shrinkage.

Polyester Use

Fabrics of polyester are popular for apparel for men, women, and children (Fig. 11.5). There are limitless varieties available, ranging from very heavy fabrics to very sheer and from very smooth to highly textured surfaces.

Blends of wool, cotton, rayon, or linen (flax) with polyester fibers are popular. In blended fabrics the polyester contributes easy maintenance, strength, durability, abrasion resistance, wrinkle-free appearance, and shape and size retention when properly stabilized. Protein or cellulosic fibers contribute comfort, moisture absorbency, reduced static charge, and enhanced ability to take on dyes.

Polyester is widely used in home-furnishing fabrics (Fig. 11.6). The use of polyester for upholstery, draperies, and floor coverings continues

11.5 Women's apparel of polyester and rayon blend. (Hoechst Fibers)

11.6 Polyester in fabrics for interiors. (Hoechst Fibers)

to be strong. Polyester is also widely used in industrial fabrics such as conveyor belts, fire hoses, laundry bags, ironing board covers, fishing nets, ropes, and sailcloth. Polyester is used in some tires, particularly automobile tires, because it provides good durability and eliminates flat spotting that was associated with nylon.

An interesting and important use of polyester is for surgical implants, where it does not cause physiological reactions. It has been used for blood vessels, as components in artificial hearts, and for other selected implants.

Some polyester is being used in the building trades in nonwoven mats as part of roofing installations; needled polyester fabrics are used for some geotextile applications for erosion control and stabilization in road beds.

Study Questions

1. What was the first polyester marketed for consumer use and where was it first available?
2. List the properties of polyester and relate them to end-use potential.
3. Why do you think that polyester is the most frequently used fiber?
4. Discuss the care methods suitable for 100 percent polyester fabrics, for blends of polyester and cellulosic fibers such as cotton or rayon, and for blends of polyester and wool.
5. Cite several different uses for polyester fibers and indicate why the fiber is suitable for each of the uses cited.
6. Identify some of the modifications of polyester. How do they affect the polyester in terms of end use?

Acrylic and Modacrylic Fibers

12

ACRYLIC FIBERS

Historical Review

The early success of nylon was so phenomenal that many manufacturers began experimenting with a variety of potential polymeric-forming chemicals in an attempt to identify other man-made fibers. During World War II, DuPont announced a new type of man-made fiber, which eventually became *Orlon* acrylic. This acrylic fiber had several interesting characteristics; but in the beginning the fact that the staple fiber form resembled wool, whereas the filament fiber form resembled silk, appeared to be of most interest to researchers.

While DuPont worked on their acrylic fiber, other chemical companies began experimenting also, and by the early 1950s Chemstrand, a joint operation of Monsanto and American Viscose, was producing an acrylic fiber named *Acrilan.* Monsanto eventually purchased all rights to the joint organization and is one of the leading manufacturers of acrylic fibers today.

Other companies to develop and produce acrylic fibers were American Cyanamid, who introduced *Creslan* in 1958, and Dow Chemical, now BASF Corp., who introduced *Zefran* also in 1958. These remain the major acrylic fibers on the U.S. market, although a considerable amount is imported.

Production

Acrylic fibers are linear polymers formed by addition polymerization of at least 85 percent by weight of *acrylonitrile (vinyl cyanide)*. Solvents dissolve the polymer to permit spinning. The dissolved polymer is extruded through spinnerettes into a heated spinning container or into a coagulating bath, where the filaments solidify (wet or dry spinning). The filaments are stretched while hot to introduce molecular orientation and fineness.

Fiber Properties

Microscopic Properties

Acrylic fibers viewed longitudinally show uniform diameters, a rodlike appearance, and some irregularly spaced striations, or parallel lines (Fig. 12.1). Cross-sectional views of the various acrylics exhibit considerable

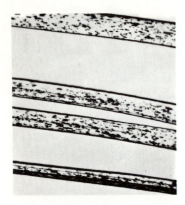

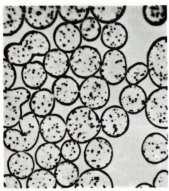

12.1 Photomicrograph of Orlon acyrlic fiber, longitudinal view. (E. I. DuPont de Nemours & Company)

12.2 Photomicrograph of Creslan acrylic fiber, cross section. (E. I. DuPont de Nemours & Company)

differences. Orlon possesses a dumbbell or acorn-shaped cross section. Acrilan is round or bean shaped, and Creslan and Zefran are nearly round (Fig. 12.2).

Physical Properties

Like all man-made fibers, acrylics can be controlled for length and diameter. In general, the fiber is marketed in staple or tow form and is used as a staple fiber. Acrylics are available in bright, semidull, or dull lusters (see Table 12.1).

Most acrylics are marketed in pure white. However, Zefran can be obtained in producer-dyed colors.

The strength of acrylics is slightly lower than that of cotton, but it is still adequate for a variety of end uses. Although the fibers' tenacity is reduced when wet, this does not pose any problem in use and care.

The elongation of acrylic fibers varies from 20 to 55 percent. When fibers are wet, elongation increases. The elastic recovery of acrylics is good at extensions of 1 to 2 percent, but at higher degrees of extension the recovery drops sharply. Bicomponent acrylics have good to very good

TABLE 12.1 Properties of acrylic fibers

Property	Evaluation
Shape	controlled by manufacturer; may be filament or staple in length; round, dog bone, or other irregular shape in cross section
Luster	from bright to dull depending on planned end use
Strength (in grams per denier)	
dry	2.0–3.6
wet	1.6–2.9
Elastic recovery	elastic recovery is good at low levels of elongation; 90–95% at 2% extension
Elongation	20–60%
Resiliency	good
Density	1.16–1.18
Moisture absorbency	1.5–2.5%
Dimensional stability	good with correct care procedures
Resistance to	
acids	good resistance to weak acids; fair resistance to strong
alkalies	good resistance to weak alkalies; poor resistance to strong
sunlight	excellent
microorganisms	excellent
insects	excellent
Thermal reactions	
to heat	maintain at temperature below 160° C; do not subject to boiling
to flame	burns readily unless specially treated

elastic recovery; they can be tumbled dry after laundering and will recover their original size.

Acrylic fibers have good resiliency. Bulky fabrics are especially resilient and lofty; they retain their shape very well.

The moisture regain of acrylic fibers is relatively low, which results in speedy drying but contributes to difficulty in dyeing. Static electricity will build up in acrylics, a problem that increases when the humidity is low.

With proper heat setting and appropriate care, acrylic fibers show little dimensional change. However, the application of excess heat and steam will cause shrinkage and a loss of loft or bulk. This characteristic can be quite evident when knitted acrylic sweaters receive improper care.

Thermal Properties

Acrylic fibers have good resistance to heat. The fibers are thermoplastic and respond to heat-setting procedures. Upon exposure to fire, they burn with a yellow flame and form a gummy, hot residue that drips away from the burning fibers. This residue is hot enough to ignite combustible substances on which it may fall.

Manufacturers recommend that these fibers not be subject to boiling water because excessive shrinkage can occur. Ironing temperatures should be kept at medium to low settings—325° F (160° C).

Chemical Properties

Acrylic fibers have good resistance to weak alkalies, but strong ones cause rapid degradation. Weak acids have no destructive effect whatsoever; concentrated acids cause a loss of fiber strength.

The solvents used in cleaning and stain removal are not damaging to acrylic fibers. The same is true for soaps and detergents. Bleaches can be used if directions are followed. Acrylics have excellent resistance to sunlight.

Biological Properties

Mildew, other microorganisms, and common household pests will not attack or eat acrylic fibers.

Fiber Modifications

Modifications of acrylic fibers include changes in the physical shape of the cross section, changes in dyeing characteristics, development of bicomponent filaments, and changes in flame resistance.

One of the most important types of modification has been the development of bicomponent fibers. These are made of two different chemical formulations extruded simultaneously (see page 29). The resulting cross section may be round, acorn shaped, or mushroom shaped. Each of the components differs in selected properties. A typical bicomponent acrylic has one component that curls during finishing and gives a spiral crimp or coil to the fiber. The second component may have a high moisture regain that makes it possible for the fiber to accept more varieties and/or deeper shades of dyestuffs. Most bicomponent acrylics, particularly Wintuk and Sayelle, must be dried without tension so that the spiral crimp develops properly and the yarns and fabrics return to their original size.

A second important acrylic modification is the incorporation of special chemicals that render the fiber flame resistant. These fibers may use the same trade name, with the letters FR attached to denote the added property.

Other fiber modifications include the production of pigmented fiber—fiber that is already colored before extrusion—which has excellent colorfastness. This modification is recommended for both indoor and outdoor carpeting, outdoor furniture, and recreational fabrics. Another modification incorporates chemicals that reduce the buildup of static electric charges.

Most acrylic fibers with modifications carry some type of informative labeling to inform consumers of the added characteristics. It is important that consumers read any labels attached to the product.

Use and Care

Acrylic Fiber Care

The care of acrylic fibers is relatively easy and simple. Consumers should be aware that most acrylic fibers can be washed and dried in home laundry equipment provided that there is a variable temperature control for the dryer. Acrylics are somewhat heat sensitive, and when dryers are used, low or medium temperature settings must be selected. Any type of soap or detergent may be used successfully; bleaches can be used when necessary providing care information is observed. Fabric softeners help to reduce the buildup of static electricity.

Dry cleaning is not recommended for acrylic fibers.

Fabrics of bicomponent acrylic need a dryer for best results. The combination of tumbling and temperature is required to restore the fabric to its original size. Fragile and delicate items of acrylic fibers should be hand laundered to reduce the amount of agitation during care; however, even these fabrics perform better if tumbled dry. It is important to read care labels and adhere to recommended procedures.

12.3 Apparel of acrylic fibers. (Monsanto Fibers)

12.4 Acrylic fibers in interiors. (Monsanto Fibers)

Acrylic Fiber Use

Acrylic fibers are popular in knitted products such as sweaters and other items of apparel; they are frequently used in woven fabrics in which softness is important, such as challis fabrics. Acrylics are used in a variety of home-furnishing fabrics including floor coverings, upholstery, and blankets.

Acrylic fibers have low density; they are soft, provide bulk with light weight, and are warm (Fig. 12.3). They are popular in sportswear and when soft, bulky, light, and warm fabrics are desired. For home furnishings the fabrics have excellent crush resistance, are light in weight, and easy to maintain. They are made into deep pile fabrics that resist crushing and retain their attractive appearance over a long period of time (Fig. 12.4).

Bicomponent yarns of acrylic fibers are widely used in knitted products and are popular for hand knitting (Fig. 12.5).

Special flame-retardant acrylics are used in carpeting and rugs.

12.5 Knitting yarns of Orlon Sayelle and Wintuk.

MODACRYLIC FIBERS

Historical Review

Dynel, the first modacrylic fiber introduced to the public, was produced in 1950; in 1956 Tennessee Eastman brought out Verel. These modacrylics resulted from attempts to produce a fiber that could withstand higher temperatures than previous vinyl chloride fibers. Legislation calling for flame-resistant textile products for children also fostered further development of the modacrylics. Presently, the only modacrylic fiber produced in the United States is SEF, made by Monsanto and introduced in the 1970s. Some modacrylics are produced by foreign countries, notably Japan; many of these are used for such items as wigs and toys.

Production

Modacrylic is an addition polymer composed of vinyl chloride and acrylonitrile. The two substances are polymerized; the polymer is dissolved in acetate, filtered to remove any solids, and extruded into a water bath where the filaments coagulate. The fibers are dried and stretched to impart strength and control elongation.

Fiber Properties

Microscopic Properties

The longitudinal view of modacrylics shows clear, transparent striations. Cross sections are irregular: They may be C-shaped, peanut shaped, or somewhat flat (Fig. 12.6).

Physical Properties

Length and diameter, that is, fineness, of the fiber are controlled by the manufacturer. SEF is a white fiber with a slightly yellowish cast. It can be bleached to a pure white and obtained in bright or dull lusters.

The strength of modacrylic fibers is similar to that of cotton. The fibers have high elongation with good elastic recovery, and the resiliency

12.6 Photomicrograph of modacrylic fiber, cross section. (E. I. DuPont de Nemours & Company)

TABLE 12.2 Properties of modacrylic fibers

Property	Evaluation
Shape	controlled by manufacturer; irregular cross sections for all types
Luster	controlled from bright to dull
Strength	2.0–3.1 grams per denier no difference between wet and dry
Elastic recovery	recovers 80–99% at 2% elongation
Elongation	35–45%
Resiliency	very good
Density	1.30–1.37
Moisture absorption standard	0.4–4.0%
Dimensional stability	good
Resistance to acids alkalies sunlight microorganisms insects	good to excellent good excellent excellent excellent
Thermal reactions to heat to flame	softens and shrinks at temperatures from 150° C to 190° C shrinks away from flame; does not support combustion; difficult to ignite; self-extinguishing and dripless

of modacrylics is very good. Moisture regain is low, and because of this the fiber requires special handling to dye or print it satisfactorily (see Table 12.2).

Thermal Properties

Modacrylic fibers do not support combustion. They will burn when placed directly in a flame, but they self-extinguish as soon as the source of flame is removed. The fibers do not drip when burning. Modacrylic fibers are sensitive to heat and should not be ironed or treated with temperatures over 375° F. Because of their heat sensitivity they should not be exposed to boiling water for any length of time. Although they do not support combustion they will, of course, be destroyed by fire. However, they are considered to be flame resistant and meet federal legislation for flame-resistant textiles.

Chemical Properties

Modacrylic fibers have good resistance to most alkalies. Although concentrated solutions may cause some discoloration, there is minimal or no loss in strength. The modacrylic fibers have good to excellent resistance to acids. Most organic solvents used in cleaning and stain removal do not damage modacrylics. However, acetone will dissolve the fibers, and some paint solvents may stiffen them.

The fibers have excellent resistance to sunlight and to all types of soaps, synthetic detergents, and bleaches. These cleaning agents may all be used with no harm to the fibers.

Biological Properties

Modacrylic fibers are highly resistant to microorganisms and insects. Tests indicate that moth larvae will starve to death rather than eat their way through modacrylic fabric to reach desirable food.

Use and Care

Modacrylic Fiber Care

Fabrics of modacrylic fibers and blends including modacrylic fibers can be laundered in automatic washers and dried in automatic dryers providing that temperatures can be controlled and that other fibers in a blend are washable. Low-temperature drying is necessary to prevent shrinkage. Any type of soap or synthetic detergent is safe on modacrylic fibers, and they can be bleached when necessary without damage. The use of some type of fabric softener is encouraged to reduce the static charge formation. It is essential to read care labels to make certain that any special care procedures are followed.

Modacrylics can be dry cleaned without damage, but cleaners should be informed that the fiber is modacrylic or a blend containing modacrylics.

Stain-removal agents normally used will not damage modacrylic fibers; however, acetone should be avoided because this chemical can stiffen modacrylic fiber fabrics and eventually cause disintegration.

Modacrylic Fiber Use

The major end use for modacrylic fibers has been as part of a blend for children's sleepwear and other items of apparel that must meet flame-resistant regulations (Fig 12.7). It is also widely used in "fake" fur coat or jacket fabrics; it has been used in wigs and other hairpieces. For the home, modacrylic fibers are used for draperies and carpeting.

Fabrics made from modacrylics are soft, resilient, stable in size unless subjected to high temperatures, low in pilling properties, and flame resistant. Modacrylic is used for draperies and carpeting for commercial buildings and commercial aircraft because of its flame-resistant properties.

Modacrylic fibers are frequently blended with other fibers, especially acrylics or polyester. These blends are widely used in knitting yarns, high-pile fabrics, carpeting, and draperies (Fig. 12.8).

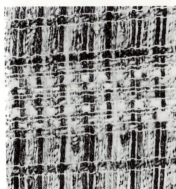

12.7 Sleepers of a flame-retardant fabric containing SEF modacrylic and polyester fibers. (Monsanto Fibers)

12.8 Drapery fabrics of fiber blend including modacrylics.

Study Questions

1. List and describe the properties of acrylic fibers; make special note of properties that make them popular with consumers.
2. What properties of acrylics may result in consumers' dissatisfaction?

3. How do acrylic and modacrylic fibers compare? How are they alike? How different?
4. What are the recommended care procedures for acrylics? For modacrylics?
5. What modifications of acrylic fibers enhance their appeal to consumers?
6. What is the major contribution of modacrylic fibers in textile products today?
7. What are the properties of modacrylics? What are typical end uses?
8. Refer to Table 1.3 and compare the use of acrylic and modacrylic fibers with other manufactured fibers.

Olefin Fibers

13

Historical Review

Olefin fibers were developed in the 1950s and early 1960s. Polyethylene in fiber form was the product of Imperial Chemical Industries of England; polypropylene was developed by Montecatini of Italy. Today there are more producers of olefin fibers than of any other fiber. Most of these producers do not use trade names for their fibers; however, a few well-known trade names have been cited in Table 2.2. In the United States, in 1985, over 11 percent of the fiber used was olefin fiber; the only fibers to exceed olefin in use are polyester, cotton, and nylon.

Production

The olefin raw materials are polymerized under pressure with a catalyst. To produce fiber filaments the manufacturers melt spin the polymer into a current of cooling gas. After the filaments are cool, they are drawn or stretched to six times the spun length; this drawing process introduces molecular orientation and makes the fiber fine and pliable.

There are two basic types of olefin fibers. The polyethylene type is made from ethylene, and the polypropylene type from propylene. The following discussion emphasizes polypropylene fibers because they are the type commonly found in consumer goods.

Fiber Properties

Microscopic Properties

Olefin fibers resemble glass rods in both longitudinal and cross-sectional views (Fig. 13.1). They are even, clear, and round. Polypropylene may be extruded through specially shaped spinnerettes; it will then have irregular cross sections, depending on the type of opening in the spinnerette.

Physical Properties

The length and diameter of olefin fibers are controlled by the manufacturer. Polyethylene tends to be waxy; polypropylene does not. Both types are smooth and white.

The strength of olefin fibers is good, but it varies with the degree of polymerization and molecular orientation from about 3.5 to 8.0 grams per denier. The top strength is comparable to high-tenacity nylon.

Polyethylene has a wide range in elongation, and its elastic recovery is excellent. If it is stretched more than 10 percent, however, it can lose some of its shape and will not return to its original size. The elongation of propylene also varies widely, but the elastic recovery is good at nearly any level of elongation or extension. Olefin fibers will retain their size and

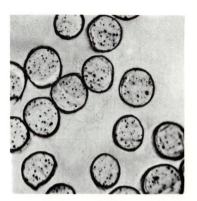

13.1 Photomicrograph of polypropylene olefin fiber, cross section. (E. I. DuPont de Nemours & Company)

119

shape when properly heat treated for stabilization. They will stretch or shrink only if subjected to temperatures higher than those used in the heat-setting operation.

Olefin fibers have good resistance to crushing; therefore polypropylene gives good service in carpeting.

The fibers have little or no moisture absorption, which creates some difficulties in dyeing. However, modifications in the formulas have corrected this problem to some degree, and considerable fiber that is to be sold colored is solution dyed—the dye is a part of the material forced through the spinnerette. The fibers do have a wicking property, which helps to compensate for the lack of absorbency and tends to carry moisture away from the body to help create comfortable apparel fabrics (see Table 13.1).

Thermal Properties

Olefin fibers burn slowly and give off a sooty, waxy smoke. They shrink at low temperatures unless heat set; even then the fibers soften at temperatures above 150° F to 160° F (65° C to 70° C). Olefins should be ironed, if necessary, at the lowest setting on an iron, and a press cloth should always be used.

TABLE 13.1 Properties of olefin fibers

Property	Evaluation	
	Polyethylene	*Polypropylene*
Shape	controlled during manufacture, but usually olefin fibers are round	
Luster	controlled and may be bright to dull	
Strength (in grams per denier)	1.5–3.0	3.5–8.0
Elastic recovery	100% recovery at 2% extension	100% recovery at 2% extension
Elongation	20–80%	15–50%
Resiliency	good	good
Density	0.92–0.96	0.90–0.91
Moisture absorbency	less than 1% for both types	
Dimensional stability	if stabilized, good resistance unless subjected to temperatures over 120° C	
Resistance to		
acids	excellent	excellent
alkalies	excellent	excellent
sunlight	both fibers slowly degrade in sunlight	
microorganisms	good	good
insects	good	good
Thermal reactions		
to heat	shrinks at 75° C; melts at low temperatures	shrinks at 120° C; melts at 170° C (335° F)
to flame	both fibers burn and emit heavy, sooty, waxy smoke	

Chemical Properties

Olefin fibers are highly resistant to alkaline substances. They have good resistance to acids, except for oxidizing acids, which weaken them.

Cleaning solvents containing chlorinated hydrocarbons should never be used because they cause the fibers to swell and eventually to disintegrate. Soaps and detergents, as well as bleaches, can be used safely.

Olefins will lose strength after prolonged exposure to sunlight. They are subject to staining by oil and grease, but normal care usually removes such stains.

Olefins do exhibit static buildup, but it is considered to be less than that of nylon or polyester.

Biological Properties

Olefin fibers are seldom attacked or damaged by mildew, microorganisms, or insects.

Use and Care

Olefin Care

Olefin fabrics launder well, dry quickly, and require little or no ironing. Floor coverings are easily cleaned: Stains wipe off with a sponge or cloth and water. Detergents can be used successfully for stubborn stains.

In general, olefin fibers should be machine washed in warm water. Fabric softeners will improve the hand and reduce static electricity. Olefin fabrics may be dried in automatic dryers if they have low temperature settings; otherwise they should be air dried.

Stains should be removed before laundering, if possible. Fabrics should not be ironed unless they are blends that permit it or a press cloth, along with the lowest iron setting, is used. Care labels should be followed carefully.

Dry cleaning of olefin fibers is not recommended. If products seem to require professional care, the cleaners should know what the fiber content is and be aware of the danger of using some cleaning agents such as chlorinated hydrocarbons.

Olefin Use

Olefins, particularly the polypropylene fibers, have a variety of uses, such as industrial applications, apparel, home furnishings, and specialized recreational uses (Figs. 13.2 to 13.4) The olefins continue to increase in usage throughout the world; however, much of that increase is in industrial applications.

For apparel, knitted fabrics are made from olefin fibers; frequently a blend of olefin with other fibers is used. Some woven fabrics made of olefin fibers or blends that include olefins are available. Typical end uses for olefin fibers in apparel include sportswear, especially knitted sweaters, suits and coats, and dresses. Because of a wool-like hand and feel, low density, good wicking property, and low cost, the polypropylene fibers are increasing in use for apparel. Trade names for olefin fibers found in apparel, particularly lingerie, are Lita and Pliana.

Olefin fibers are used in home furnishings in an increasing amount. They are widely used for indoor-outdoor floor coverings, for tufted carpet-

13.2 Marvess olefin fibers used for pile in carpeting. (Courtesy Phillips Fibers Corporation)

13.3 Furniture upholstered in Marvess olefin. (Courtesy Phillips Fibers Corporation)

13.4 Marvess olefin indoor-outdoor carpet in auto showroom. (Courtesy Phillips Fibers Corporation)

ing for such areas as kitchens and family rooms, and for blankets. Advantages of its use in carpeting include the facts that it is easily cleaned, it does not crush easily, and stains can be easily removed. A major advantage of the fiber for blankets is its light weight.

Nonwoven olefin fabrics have many industrial and geotechnical applications, particularly for road bed stabilization and erosion prevention. Other uses for olefin fibers include disposable diapers, artificial ski slopes, craft yarns, particularly for macramé, and a variety of end uses in industry and business.

One of the major problems with olefin fibers is the difficulty in dyeing, and the use of solution or pigment dyeing is increasing in order to provide a wide choice of durable, colorfast products. Modifications of the fibers to permit the application of color, either solid colors or prints, following fabric construction have been successful.

Olefin fiber is relatively low in cost, which is part of the reason for its increased use throughout the world.

1. What are the major differences between polyethylene and polypropylene?
2. What are typical consumer products that might be made of olefin fibers?
3. What care procedures are recommended for products made of polypropylene olefin fibers? What care should be avoided when possible and why?
4. Why is olefin a good choice for carpeting for both indoor-outdoor and regular indoor pile carpeting?
5. What properties of olefin fibers make them satisfactory, or even desired, for apparel items?
6. What characteristics of olefin fibers, particularly polypropylene, may cause dissatisfaction with apparel items?
7. How does the use of olefin fibers compare with other commonly used fibers in the United States?
8. What do you think the future of olefin fibers will be? Why?

14 Elastomeric Fibers

Elastomeric fibers are elastic, rubberlike substances. They can be prepared in various forms, but discussion here is limited to fibrous forms used in textile products. All elastomers are characterized by extremely high elongation and outstanding elastic recovery.

Rubber

Rubber is the thick, gummy liquid obtained from trees of the *Heavea* species. Although it has been used for centuries, it was not until the nineteenth century that scientists became aware of the unusual characteristics of the substance and the potential for use in industry and in consumer goods. In 1839 Charles Goodyear discovered that the properties of rubber were greatly changed when it was heated with sulfur. Strength and elasticity increased, and cold temperatures no longer hardened the fiber. For the TFPIA definition of rubber see page 12. Goodyear's process, now known as vulcanization, set the scene for the development of rubber in many forms. Consumption of rubber remained small until the beginning of the twentieth century and the growing automobile industry. Rubber was suddenly required in large quantities for tires.

As a fiber, rubber dates from the 1920s, when the U.S. Rubber Company found that fine rubber filaments could be used as a central core for other fibers. Such fibers as cotton were wrapped around the rubber core, and the resulting yarn could be used for elasticity in various fabrics. Synthetic rubbers were developed in the 1930s, but it was not until the natural source of rubber was cut off by World War II that synthetic rubber gained consumer acceptance. Today, there is a good market for many products in both natural and synthetic rubber.

The properties that make rubber desirable in certain end uses include the following: a high degree of elasticity, flexibility and pliability, strength, toughness, impermeability to water and air, resistance to cutting and tearing, and resistance to many chemicals.

Rubber yarns contribute support and improved fit to selected apparel products. Fabrics with rubber are comparatively crease resistant and require a minimum of ironing.

There are, however, several properties of rubber that can cause problems: deterioration by sunlight and smog, loss of strength and elasticity through aging, damage from body oils, damage caused by solvents commonly encountered in cleaning and laundering, and sensitivity to temperatures over 200° F (93° C) and to low temperatures—which cause deterioration, loss of pliablity, and the development of a brittle fiber.

Rubber Care

Rubber products can be laundered in warm water. Strong soaps and synthetic detergents are recommended because they remove oily dirt better than mild detergents. Drying in a dryer at medium temperatures is considered safe by some authorities, but others maintain that air drying is the only acceptable method. Probably the most important fact about cleaning rubber items is that they should be laundered after each wearing to reduce damage from body oils and perspiration. Bleaches should be used sparingly; care labels should be checked to determine if bleaches can be used safely. It is best to avoid dry cleaning.

Rubber Use

Rubber yarns are used in foundation garments, swimwear, surgical fabrics such as elastic bandages and support hose, underwear, elastic yarns for decorative stitching, shoe fabrics, tops of socks and hosiery, and elastic tape.

During the 1960s one company sought a new generic term for an elastomeric fiber other than spandex, which was a part of the original TFPIA. The FTC considered the proposal, redefined rubber, and specified the term *lastrile* as a substitute generic term for one group of synthetic rubber fibers. There has been no additional development of these fibers to date.

Spandex

DuPont introduced the first spandex fiber in 1958. That fiber is now called Lycra and is the most commonly encountered spandex fiber in the United States. Two other fibers, made by Globe Manufacturing, are available—Cleerspun and Glospan. On the world market there are a few other spandex fibers. For the most part the spandex fibers all have similar properties and end uses.

In the 1960s several textile researchers predicted that spandex would ultimately be a part of every fabric. This prediction, however, did not materialize. Spandex is used to add special properties to a variety of fabrics but built-in stretch in all fabrics has not occurred.

Fiber Properties

Microscopic appearance of elastomeric fibers varies considerably. Lycra has a dark, spotted longitudinal appearance under magnification (Fig. 14.1). The cross section is somewhat dog bone in shape (Fig. 14.2). Other spandex fibers may be rounder than Lycra. All spandex fibers tend to be larger in diameter than other generic fiber groups.

Spandex fibers are relatively weak, but because of their tremendous elongation—500 to 800 percent—they have good durability. Their elastic recovery is excellent, and they accept dyes easily and evenly.

Spandex fibers will burn and form a gummy residue. They can be ironed safely at temperatures below 300° F (150° C).

The resistance of spandex to chemicals is good. Concentrated alkalies at high temperatures cause eventual degradation. Acids have little effect. Soaps and synthetic detergents do not damage the fiber; however, chlorine bleaches may cause yellowing and some loss of strength. Dry cleaning agents with chlorine compounds may alter colors.

Spandex has several advantages over rubber, including resistance to degradation by sunlight and smog and to damage from body oil and perspiration. Spandex has superior flex life, is easily dyed, and requires only easy care.

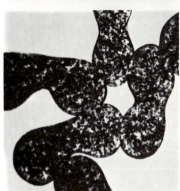

14.1 Photomicrograph of Lycra spandex fiber, longitudinal view. (E. I. DuPont de Nemours & Company)

14.2 Photomicrograph of Lycra spandex fiber, cross section. (E. I. DuPont de Nemours & Company)

Use and Care

Spandex Care

Spandex can be laundered with nearly any type of soap or detergent; bleach may be used if care is exercised. Automatic washers and dryers may be used safely providing temperatures are kept at a medium to medium-low setting. As spandex is normally used in small amounts and blended with other fibers, it is best to identify care procedures appropriate for the other fibers and then determine if additional caution should be taken for the spandex.

All producers of spandex fibers state that the normal concentration of chlorine in swimming pools will not damage the durability of the fiber; however, it may cause a color loss, and white spandex may yellow as a result of chlorine, smog, body oils, and perspiration. Frequent laundering is recommended to reduce this damage.

Spandex Use

Spandex is used either as bare filament or in core spun yarn constructions (Fig. 14.3). The core spun yarn is the more popular although both have uses in various types of textile products. The ultimate amount of stretch in fabrics containing spandex is based on the elongation of the other fibers and, of most importance, the method by which yarns have been made. The amount of stretch can be controlled by yarn spinning adjustments.

Spandex is found in such end use products as swimwear; foundation garments; bras; lingerie straps; sock tops; support and control-top hosiery; medical products requiring elasticity; and home-furnishing fabrics such as fitted sheets, upholstery, and slipcovers (Fig. 14.4).

Spandex is never used as 100 percent of any fabric construction; the typical amount of spandex in blends is between 3 and 8 percent.

14.3 Core spun yarn, showing the staple covering fibers pulled away at each end to reveal the core.

14.4 Swimsuit with spandex in a blend of fibers.

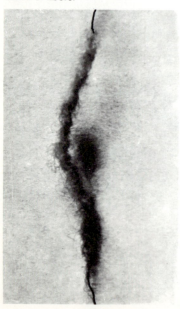

Anidex

The FTC added the term *anidex* to the TFPIA in 1969. At that time a fiber called ANIM/8 was produced by Rohm and Haas. The company has since ceased production, and there is no known production of this type of fiber anywhere in the world.

Study Questions

1. What properties of spandex make it an easy care fiber?
2. What major property (or properties) of elastomeric fibers makes them desirable for fabrics that require some level of stretch?
3. What is the major difference between spandex and rubber that would be of concern to consumers?
4. Why is spandex preferred in such items as support hosiery?
5. Why is spandex a good choice for foundation garments? What problems could occur because of its use in these apparel items?
6. In what types of home-furnishing fabrics might you find spandex fibers? Why?

15 Other Organic Noncellulosic Fibers

The fibers discussed in this chapter are not well known and are seldom used by the general public. However, they may have specialized uses for certain types of apparel and/or home furnishings, and they often have application for specialized industrial textiles. The following discussion identifies the remaining generic categories of fibers and other special noncellulosic organic fibers that are important to the textile industry.

For some of the generic groups identified by the TFPIA (see p. 11), there are no longer any fibers in production in the United States; for a few there is no known production anywhere in the world. They are mentioned here for the reader's information.

Saran

Saran fibers were introduced to the retail market by Dow Chemical Corporation in 1940. Subsequently, other saran fibers were introduced, but in 1985 only Ametek Corp. was producing a saran fiber.

Saran is manufactured from vinylidene chloride and vinyl chloride or vinyl cyanide. The filaments are melt spun and cold drawn.

Saran fibers are transparent, even, smooth, and almost perfectly round in cross section. They are lustrous and silky in appearance. Luster is reduced when the fibers are cut into staple length; crimp is built in when staple length fibers are to be used so that the fibers will hold together in making yarn.

Saran is not strong but it has good elongation, very good resiliency, and excellent elastic recovery. These properties help make the fiber a good choice for carpeting and selected types of upholstery and draperies. The moisture absorbency is very low, which increases the difficulty in dyeing the fiber.

The fiber is virtually nonflammable, which makes it highly desirable for home-furnishing fabrics for commercial and contract use. However, the fibers do have a relatively low melting point, and thus care requires low temperatures for drying and for ironing if needed.

Saran is highly resistant to acids and most alkalies. They may be damaged by sodium hydroxide and ammonium compounds. Most cleaning solvents, spot removers, and laundry aids will not damage the fiber; however acetone, carbon tetrachloride, and alcohol may cause a loss in strength at high temperatures.

Sunlight causes saran to discolor, but there is little or no loss in strength. Saran does develop static electric charges. The fiber is not affected by mildew, microorganisms, or household pests of any kind.

Care of saran fibers is much like many other man-made fibers such as polyesters and nylons. As long as high temperatures are avoided, it may be laundered and dried safely with most types of laundry equipment and supplies.

The most frequently encountered use of saran is in the home-furnishings field for upholstery, draperies, and carpeting. It is sometimes used in upholstery for vehicles. Originally it was used for outdoor furniture because of its excellent resistance to sunlight; however, that end use has been disappearing because olefin fibers are much less costly and are considered satisfactory for outdoor furniture. Much fabric that contains saran is composed of blends (Fig. 15.1).

The use of saran has not expanded as originally expected, primarily because the fiber is more costly than competitive fibers, such as the olefins.

Vinyon

The first vinyon fibers were made in 1933 by the Carbide and Carbon Corporation; however, commercial quantities were not available until 1939, when American Viscose bought the rights to produce the fiber. Only one vinyon fiber is currently being produced in the United States, but there are a variety in production in foreign countries.

The fiber has round, dog bone, dumbbell, or irregularly shaped cross sections (Fig. 15.2). The longitudinal appearance is smooth and even and relatively clear. It can be made in any length or diameter.

The tenacity, or strength, of vinyon is similar to that of dry rayon, but there is no difference between wet and dry strength. There is a tremendous variation in elongation—from low to high; resilience is good, but elastic recovery is only fair.

Vinyon fibers are heat sensitive and soften at temperatures above 150° F. However, this property is the basis for use of the fiber in various processes by industrial concerns.

The fibers made in European countries are noted for their high flame resistance, and this property is responsible for considerable usage in apparel and accessories in those countries. It has been suggested as a potential fiber for children's sleepwear because fabrics made from imported vinyon fibers do pass the flame-resistance test for children's sleepwear. Fibers made in the the United States are designed for industrial use only.

Vinyon has good resistance to chemicals. Acids and alkalies have no effect, and solvents used in cleaning do not damage vinyon except for ketones such as acetone and aromatic hydrocarbons. Soaps and synthetic detergents are safe to use.

Vinyon fibers have been used in fabrics for accessories such as handbags and hats and for floor matting. Nonwoven fabrics made of vinyon are used as bonding agents in the manufacture of special textile products.

Vinal

Vinal is not currently manufactured in the United States; however it is available in limited quantities from foreign countries such as Japan.

Under magnification, vinal fibers appear smooth, somewhat grainy, and characterized by faint striations. They are bean shaped, U-shaped, or nearly round in cross section. The fibers are white or nearly white in color.

Vinal does not support combustion; it softens at 390° F (200° C) and melts at 425° F (220° C). Vinal has good resistance to chemicals. Chlorine bleaches as well as soaps and detergents can be used safely. The fiber has good tolerance to sea water and excellent resistance to microorga-

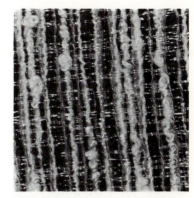

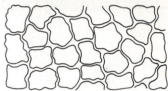

15.1 Fabric containing saran fibers.

15.2 Sketch of microscopic cross section of vinyon fibers.

nisms and insects, which make it highly adaptable to uses involving exposure to these environmental conditions.

Except for limited industrial applications, vinal has not been used in the United States in any sizable quantity. In Japan and some other countries it is employed in protective apparel such as raincoats, jackets, hats, and umbrellas; in suiting fabrics; in lining fabrics; and in socks and gloves. Blends of vinal with other fibers such as cotton, rayon, or vinyon are silky in appearance and soft. Industrial uses include fishing nets, filter fabrics, tarpaulins, and bristles for specialized brushes. The blend of vinal with vinyon gives a soft fabric that is highly flame resistant, and this combination has been made into children's sleepwear (Fig. 15.3).

As extruded, vinal fibers are water soluble and must be treated with formaldehyde to make them insoluble. Some quantity of the fiber is marketed in the soluble form for specialized uses such as in some surgical applications, after which it is dissolved; and as a base for embroidery; after the embroidery is finished the base is dissolved, leaving a lacelike, open structure that is decorative.

Nytril

Nytril was introduced to the market in 1955. It offered consumers several highly prized properties including easy care, softness, no pilling, resilience, bulk, and warmth. However, production of this fiber stopped during the late 1960s, and there is no evidence that it will be on the market in the near future.

Novoloid

Novoloid is currently produced by the Kynol Corporation. It is marketed for specialized uses in which there is a demand for high resistance to flames and chemicals, easy care, and minimal shrinkage.

15.3 Infant's garment of vinyon and vinal blend. (Macy's)

15.4 Protective apparel of Kynol novoloid fiber. (American Kynol, Inc.)

Novoloid is used where flame-resistant products are required, such as in garments for firefighters, welders, and the military and in manufacturing plants where heat and flame are potential hazards. It has been made into protective apparel for race car drivers, fabric for airplanes and lighter-than-air craft, protective apparel for workers in laboratores with a high fire and chemical hazard, and wall coverings in which flame resistance is a priority (Fig. 15.4).

Azlon

Azlon fibers are man-made protein fibers, and at the present time there are no azlon fibers available anywhere in the world. These fibers had many good properties, but they also had some negative characteristics. They are probably not being manufactured currently because they are relatively weak and cannot compete successfully with other man-made fibers.

Polychal

These fibers are not defined by the TFPIA. They are made of 50 percent polyvinyl chloride (vinyon) and 50 percent polyvinyl alcohol (vinal) produced in a matrix bicomponent structure (see p. 29). The fiber is currently made in Japan and is called Cordelan.

Cordelan has gained consumer importance and acceptance because it is flame retardant and meets the federal standards for children's sleepwear. These fabrics are soft and pleasant to the touch.

The strength of Cordelan is similar to that of cotton; it has good elongation and fair moisture regain. It can be laundered with almost any type of soap or detergent, but chlorine bleaches should not be used. If bleaching is necessary, hydrogen peroxide or perborate bleaches should be employed. It can be laundered in automatic washers and dried in automatic dryers. It is available, primarily in Japan, in children's sleepwear, blankets, and selected home-furnishing fabrics.

Polybenzimidazole (PBI)

Polybenzimidazole is made by Celanese Fibers. It is available in limited quantities for specialized uses in which a high temperature- and chemical-resistant fiber is required. PBI resists temperatures greater than 350° F (177° C) for long periods of time, and it is stable to 935° F (500° C) for limited periods of time. The fiber has good tenacity, density similar to cotton, relatively high moisture regain, and good elongation. Chemical resistance to most acids and alkalies is excellent; however, alkalies at high temperatures will eventually result in a loss of strength. The fiber does not burn in air, is dimensionally stable, does not melt, does not give off smoke until it reaches 560° C (1040° F), and retains flexibility even when charred.

PBI is used as a substitute for asbestos in applications requiring high thermal stability, chemical resistance, and flame resistance. Thermal protective apparel made of PBI provides comfort, flexibility, and resistance to high temperatures.

PBI is used in firefighters' turnout coats, proximity clothing, industrial protective apparel, high-temperature protective gloves, welders' apparel, aircraft seat encapsulates, and parts of astronauts' apparel. It is a high-cost fiber and will probably be limited in use to those applications in which the special properties are required.

Polycarbonate Fibers

Polycarbonates are designed for specialized uses. Currently the only fiber available on the market is Solvex, which has been developed and marketed for a very specialized use. The fiber disintegrates in dry cleaning solvents; thus, it is used as basting for tailored garments during construction. The operation of pulling the basting threads is unnecessary because the thread becomes brittle in cleaning solvent and breaks into small pieces that are easily rinsed away. A saving of more than 50 percent in labor costs for this part of the tailoring operation results from using threads of this fiber.

Chinon

Chinon is called a *promix* fiber and is made in Japan. It is composed of 70 percent acrylic and 30 percent azlon. Although information on its manufacture is not available, it has been described as a graft fiber.

The fiber is similar to silk in density, has a moisture regain slightly higher than nylon, and has a tenacity similar to polyester. Probably the most publicized property is the similarity of this fiber to silk in appearance and hand but with easy care properties. It can be laundered or dry cleaned safely; however, chlorine bleaches should not be used. Ironing, when needed, should be done with a low to medium-low temperature setting.

Mirafi

This fiber is identified as a bigeneric fiber of propylene and nylon. The fibers are made into nonwoven fabrics for specialized geotextile uses such as ground stabilization, road building, erosion control, and land reclamation.

Celiox Fibers

Celiox fibers are made from acrylonitrile that has been subjected to special processing, which results in a cross-linked structure. The fiber has high heat resistance, is nonmelting, resists flame, and has the hand of normal textile fibers so that it can be used in making standard textile fabrics.

The fiber has high moisture regain and can be made into comfortable apparel items; it has a low density, which produces lightweight fabrics. However, of most importance is the fact that it has the heat resistance of a ceramic fiber. The major use of this fiber is as a substitute for asbestos, where it provides many of the same properties of asbestos fiber without any of the health hazards associated with it.

Teflon (Fluoro) Fibers

Fluoro fibers are made from tetrafluoroethylene. They are relatively inert; resist very high temperatures; and are unaffected by acids, alkalies, and other solvents. The most common trade name is Teflon, although the fiber is available under other names (see Table 2.2). The fiber is not used in fabrics for general consumer use; rather it is made for industrial and commercial applications in which high chemical and heat resistance are the most important characteristics. Some typical end-use products of this type of fiber include filter fabrics in smokestacks, gaskets, packing fabrics, and covers for press units in commercial laundries. A new development based on fluoro fibers called Gore-Tex is being used as a barrier to bacteria and in protective clothing for people who will be exposed to dangerous bacteria or insecticides. It has been used for medical purposes, but little is known of this use as yet.

Study Questions

1. Why are these miscellaneous organic noncellulosic fibers of importance in the study of textiles?
2. What are the properties of saran that would appeal to general consumers?
3. What are typical end uses for saran?
4. Why has saran not been more widely used in recent years?
5. What are the important characteristics of vinyon, and what are some of the typical end uses for this type of fiber?
6. What is polychal? Chinon? How do they differ from generic fiber terms?
7. In what products is novoloid fiber found and why is it successful in such uses?
8. Briefly describe each of the following generic fiber types and identify the major advantage of each:
   a. Saran
   b. Vinyon
   c. Vinal
   d. Novoloid
9. What generic groups have no fibers in current production? What do you believe are the reasons for this?
10. Why are PBI and polycarbonate fibers important? What are their primary uses?

16 Mineral and Miscellaneous Fibers

NATURAL MINERAL FIBERS

Asbestos

Asbestos is the only mineral fiber used in the form in which it is obtained from natural sources. A fibrous vein in serpentine or amphibole rock (Fig. 16.1), it has been known and used since the early days of Greece and Rome.

The use of asbestos was recorded by Pliny the Elder in the first century A.D. Legends concerning this amazing fiber have been told for centuries. It is said that Emperor Charlemagne delighted in mystifying guests by throwing a tablecloth of asbestos into a roaring fire and then removing it, unharmed and clean, from the flames. A few centuries later Marco Polo told his friends in Italy about a substance he observed in Siberia that could be woven into attractive textiles that would not burn, even in direct flame. These stories all emphasize the important property of asbestos—it is completely resistant to fire.

Early uses of asbestos included cremation fabrics, wicks for lamps, table coverings, and even handkerchiefs. Chrysotile is the asbestos most often used as a textile fiber because the fibers have good strength, flexibility, toughness, low conductivity, and adequate length for spinning into yarns. They have a silky appearance and texture (Fig. 16.2).

However, the popularity of asbestos is rapidly declining, and in the United States, at least, its use is being curtailed drastically. There is considerable evidence that asbestos is carcinogenic, particularly when bits of

16.1 Asbestos rock, showing both rock and fiber form. (Johns-Manville Incorporated)

134

16.2 Fire-resistant coverall, hood, and gloves of aluminized asbestos and cotton fabric. (American Crafts Council's American Craft Museum, New York City)

fiber break off from yarns and are absorbed into the lungs. For this reason asbestos is on the list of products that are banned for use in the United States. Other fibers, such as Celiox and PBI, have been promoted as substitutes for asbestos. Consumers should avoid any product in which asbestos is used.

MAN-MADE MINERAL FIBERS

Glass Fiber

The origin of glass and glass fibers is uncertain. One legend credits Phoenician fishermen with the discovery of glass fiber. It is said that these men noticed pools of a molten substance under fires they had built on a sandy beach on the Aegean Sea. Natural curiosity caused them to poke at the molten material; and as they withdrew the sticks, the substance pulled out in a long, stringlike form. This was, perhaps, the first glass fiber. During the Middle Ages, Venetian artisans developed spun glass, which they used as decoration on blown glass forms such as goblets and vases.

Serious efforts to create glass fibers for textiles began in the late nineteenth century. Edward Drummond Libbey succeeded in attenuating glass into fiber and made sufficient yarn to manufacture fabric for a dress, which was exhibited at the Columbia Exposition of 1893. The garment was attractive and not transparent as the public had anticipated. However, the fibers were coarse and low in strength and flexibility. A concentrated development plan for glass fiber began in 1931, and by 1938 usable glass textile fibers were available in commercial quantities. The Owens-Corning Fiberglas Corporation was formed, and glass fibers were placed on the market in the late 1930s.

Production

The raw materials for glass fiber are primarily silica sand and limestone with small amounts of modifiers such as aluminum hydroxide, sodium carbonate, and borax. These materials are melted at high temperatures and formed into fibers by either of two processes. The traditional procedure produces clear marbles from the melt; these marbles, called *cullet,* are melted a second time and forced through a platinum bushing, a type of spinnerette, and the fibers form as they hit the cooler air. A newer process forms the fibers directly from the original melt and bypasses the marble step. Both operations produce fibers of good quality.

If staple fibers are desired, the filaments are blown with a current of steam under high pressure as they leave the spinnerette. This process causes the fibers to break into small lengths, which are then caught on a revolving drum. The fibers are pulled from the drum into a sliver and processed as any staple fiber (see Chapter 17).

Fiber Properties

Glass fiber is strong; elongation is low—only 3 percent—and elastic recovery is 100 percent. It has outstanding dimensional stability. The fibers do not absorb moisture, and they have excellent resistance to wrinkling. Glass fibers are smooth, even, and transparent. The cross section is round.

Glass fibers will not burn although they soften at about 1500° F (815° C), and strength begins to decline at temperatures over 600° F (315° C). However, as soon as the heat is reduced, fiber strength returns unless the fiber has actually been melted out of shape.

Glass fiber has a high chemical resistance to most acids; only hydrofluoric and hot phosphoric attack glass fibers; resistance to alkalies is poor. The fiber is not damaged by organic solvents nor by mild laundry agents.

Although glass fibers are pliable and flexible, they lack abrasion resistance. When folded, as for hems in draperies or window curtains, the edge will tend to crack or break. A fine glass fiber, Beta, has better resistance to abrasion because of fiber fineness. This fiber has been tried in a variety of applications such as upholstery, draperies, bedspreads, and table coverings. Glass can be colored or printed by means of special treatments.

Although glass fibers are considered nonallergenic, there is growing evidence that the fibers produce serious allergic reactions in some people because of the cut fiber ends or finishing procedures. There is also some evidence that the fiber can be a health hazard because of the small bits of glass that break away from yarn ends during use and care.

Coloring glass fabrics does involve special care. The Coronizing process is the most successful. It makes it possible to create either solid colored fabrics or prints. The fabric is saturated with a dispersion of silica, dried, and then heat set; pigment is applied to the surface with a resin solution, dried, treated with a final finishing compound to improve colorfastness, and given a final drying. Because the process tends to flatten the yarns, the fabric has improved drapability and retains shape and appearance during use and care.

Use and Care

Glass fiber care   The care of glass fibers may be considered difficult or easy. They can be laundered with any mild detergent or soap and dried by simply wiping the fabric with a cloth or letting it hang to dry. But when the fibers are laundered in an automatic washer, it is essential to run several rinses through the machine after the fabric is removed to make certain any residue from the fibers has been removed before being transferred to other fabrics in the next washer load. Glass fabrics should not be dry cleaned.

The major points to consider in care are these: They should never be wrung or spun dry in a dryer; they should not be rubbed to remove stains; strong alkalies should be avoided; care labels should be followed carefully. Curtains or draperies can be washed in tubs or similar containers and then rehung immediately after wiping with a soft cloth. If it is not possible to rehang, the fabrics may be laid across padded lines; but the amount of folding should be kept to an absolute minimum.

Glass fiber use   The use of glass fibers in consumer goods is decreasing. It is difficult, in fact, to find glass fabrics for home furnishings for residential use (Fig. 16.3). The major use for glass is in commercial applications in the form of fiber mats, fiber reinforced plastic or metal, or coated fabrics. Glass fabrics coated with some materials, such as Teflon, have been used successfully for "roofs" on air-supported domes such as sports arenas, shopping malls, and airport structures (Fig. 16.4). As a fiber mat or woven or knitted fabric, glass is used in building boats and automobiles (Fig. 16.5), where it serves as a reinforcement for the plastic base. It is used for some geotextile applications.

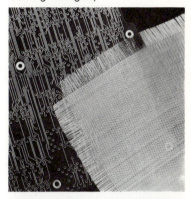

16.3   Glass fiber in fabric for printed circuit board substrate. (Owens-Corning Fiberglas)

16.4   Glass in building construction, Fiberglas dome. (Owens-Corning Fiberglas)

16.5   Glass-reinforced composite body panels. (Owens-Corning Fiberglas)

Metallic Fibers or Yarns

Metallic yarns are among the oldest forms of fiber and probably should be considered the oldest form of man-made fiber. The first metallic fibers were not real fibers but were the result of slitting very thin sheets of metal into narrow ribbonlike forms. Even today many metallic yarns are manufactured by using variations of this old slitting process.

Gold, silver, and aluminum are the metals most often used in textile products. Gold and silver yarns have been used since ancient times; aluminum is a modern product. Gold and silver yarns are costly. Usually they are made by wrapping a fine copper wire, or even silk or nylon filaments, with thin strips of the gold or silver. Because silver and gold both discolor over time, and because they are expensive products, aluminum has replaced these fibers in most countries. Some fabrics from Asian countries may still include gold or silver threads; but these are few and expensive.

Aluminum yarns are made by one of two basic procedures. The aluminum may be encased in a plastic coating of either a polyester, such as Mylar, or cellulose acetate-butyrate; or finely ground aluminum, color, and polyester are mixed together and then the mix is laminated to a clear polyester film and cut into thin slivers for use as yarns. In the first process the polyester is the better of the two products, but it is more expensive than the cellulose acetate-butyrate. Color may be added either to the plastic coating or directly to the aluminum by using an adhesive to seal it to that metal.

Both types of metallic yarns can be obtained in a variety of colors including those that give the appearance of gold and silver. The plastic coatings protect the yarn from damage from water, chlorine, and detergents.

Metallic yarns are not especially strong, but they are quite adequate for the typical decorative purpose for which they are used. Polyester-coated yarns are stronger than those coated with acetate-butyrate.

The care of metallic yarns is determined to a considerable degree by the plastic coating material, the core substance when yarns are wrapped, or other materials that might be used with the metallic yarns. Careful observance of all care labels is a must. Warm, never hot, temperatures should be used in both laundering and drying operations.

Metallic yarns are widely used in home-furnishing fabrics for such items as drapery and curtain materials (Fig. 16.6), upholstery materials, bedspreads, towels (for decoration), and tablecloths and place mats. In apparel, metallic yarns are used for their decorative character and may appear in apparel for almost any type of occasion, from evening gowns and cocktail dresses to sportswear such as slacks, shorts, and bathing suits, depending on current fashion (Fig. 16.7).

Stainless Steel Fiber

Another important metallic fiber is stainless steel. It is used in textiles either as a monofilament or in combination with other fibers in filament or staple form. Stainless steel in fabrics contributes strength, tear and abrasion resistance, and thermal conductivity. Steel fibers reduce static buildup in floor coverings. It is incorporated in small amounts, usually less than 5 percent, with fibers such as nylon, wool, polyester, or acrylic; it is then made into yarns that are used to form the carpet pile. Steel filaments may also be woven into the carpet base, where it carries away static electric charges.

Stainless steel is also used as a resistance filament and is incorpo-

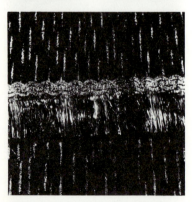

16.6 Fabric for home furnishings with metallic fibers for accent. (Larsen Textiles/Jack Lenor Larsen incorporated)

16.7 Metallic fibers or yarns in apparel fabrics.

rated into draperies, floor coverings, and upholstery. The stainless steel becomes a resistance wire that radiates heat when properly connected to a source of electric energy. One of the best known trade names for steel fibers is Brunsmet.

MISCELLANEOUS FIBERS

Carbon Fibers

Carbon or graphite fibers have been developed for use in various types of industrial textiles and in some types of consumer goods. These fibers are made up of 95 to 99 percent carbon. *Graphite* is the term reserved for fibers that are 99 percent carbon.

Carbon and graphite fibers are continuous filaments and are made by converting acrylic or regenerated cellulose filaments into nearly pure carbon. These fibers are strong and stiff and resist high temperatures. When carbon fibers are added to a plastic base, a reinforced product is produced that has superior properties, including high strength, light weight, and an engineered balance between stiffness and flexibility that meets the needs of the planned end use.

Carbon fibers are used in numerous industrial and consumer products. Some of the typical end uses for carbon are as reinforced plastics or metals for structural materials—where high strength, stiffness, and light weight are needed characteristics—such as rotor blades for helicopters, compressor blades in jet engines, golf club shafts, crossbows for archery, bicycle parts, skis, keels for canoes, and machinery parts. Carbon filaments may also be used to make flameproof fabrics for protective apparel. They have been used by the military where nuclear, biological, and chemical resistance is necessary. They are being used as a substitute for asbestos.

Alumina Fibers

Alumina fibers, made from aluminum oxide, are available for the specialized use of embedding in metal. The resulting matrix is used for automotive and jet engines, aerospace structures, and batteries. These fibers have a high modulus and good strength and resist temperatures to over 1000° C.

Boron and Boron Nitride Fibers

Fibers of boron or boron nitride are soft, white in color, strong, and flexible. They are used where heat resistance and flame resistance are important. Boron nitride is the most common of the two fibers. It is used in fabrics for aerospace applications, for certain types of protective apparel, and for heat- or thermal-resistant shields. Uses are limited to industrial applications in which high performance is demanded.

Other Mineral Fibers

Several other mineral substances are important for use in fibrous forms. These fibers are strong, stiff, and light in weight. They are often used as reinforcement for plastic or metal bases and include fibrous forms of aluminum silicate, silicon oxide, potassium titanate, and aluminum oxide.

These fibers are used when the product must have outstanding resistance to high temperatures.

Study Questions

1. What were some of the uses of asbestos? Why is it no longer used in the United States?
2. What environmental and health problems are associated with the use of asbestos fiber? With glass fiber?
3. What are the basic properties of glass fibers?
4. What are typical end uses for glass fiber and why?
5. Name several end uses for metallic fibers and describe why they are found in such products.
6. What are typical uses for carbon fibers? Why?
7. What problems are involved in caring for glass fiber fabrics? Why?
8. How would you care for fabrics in which metallic yarns have been used? What should guide your choice of care procedures?
9. Indicate a special use of steel fibers for residential situations.

Yarn Structure

Yarns are required if fabrics are to be woven or knitted. Thus, the making of yarns is as old, or nearly so, as the manufacture of fabric; yarn making does predate recorded history. In prehistoric times fibers were twisted together in simple ways to form yarns. It is reasonable to suppose that the first technique for yarn making involved rolling fibers together between the palms of the hands, between fingers, or between a hand and another part of the body such as the thigh. This latter process is still used by some peoples in isolated parts of the world; it may be used by craftspeople in preparing special yarns for craft and art.

The next development was the invention of spindles. Various types of spindles have emerged from archeological digs, but the most common device seems to have employed a distaff, a spindle, and a whorl. Loose fibers were tied to a distaff. The spindle was a short stick notched at one end and pointed at the other. The spinning whorl was secured near the pointed end. The spinner held the distaff under the arm to free both hands for the actual spinning. Fibers were attached to the spindle notch, and the whorl pulled the fibers and spindle downward in a twirling motion. As the spindle dropped, the spinner drew out the fibers and formed them into a thread with the fingers while the whirling spindle twisted them into a tight strand or yarn. When the spindle neared the ground, the spinner took it up, wound the finished thread around it, and caught the new yarn in the notch. The process was then repeated. Illustrations of these operations have been found in a variety of sources, but some of the best were on pottery that dates to very early years (Fig. III.1).

Yarns were spun by hand methods until late in the fourteenth century, at which time a crude spinning wheel was developed. The Saxony wheel (Fig. III.2), seen in many antique shops and museums today, was introduced in the sixteenth century. It is still used in some parts of the world and is currently enjoying a revival among artisans. This spinning

III.1   Design on an early Greek vase (c. 560 B.C.) clearly showing a spindle, whorl, and distaff used in spinning yarns. (Metropolitan Museum of Art, New York: Fletcher Fund, 1931)

III.2   Spinning wheel. (Don Cyr)

wheel forms the yarn mechanically, but the power is human. Either a hand-propelled wheel or a foot treadle operates the wheel.

During the eighteenth century multiple spinning frames were developed, and shortly thereafter water power was incorporated. The basic machine-spinning techniques are still used today. A number of men played major roles in the perfection of spinning processes and equipment. Lewis Paul and John Wyatt developed the roller method of spinning in 1737; James Hargreaves invented the spinning jenny in 1764; Richard Arkwright introduced the water power spinning frame about 1770; and Samuel Crompton created the spinning mule in 1779. Theirs are the basic inventions on which all modern spinning depends.

Today yarns are manufactured by several processes. The type of fiber will influence the process selected, as will the appearance desired.

The following four chapters describe methods by which yarns are constructed, different types of yarns and yarn modifications, and blended or combination fiber yarns and/or fabrics.

Yarn Construction: Simple Yarns 17

Basic Principles

To convert textile fibers into fabrics some type of fiber arrangement is required. Probably the most common method is to convert fibers into yarns, which are then constructed into fabrics. Yarns are essential for woven, knitted, or knotted structures and for many braided ones. This chapter describes the basic procedures involved in making yarns, discusses simple yarns, and notes their basic properties.

Yarn is defined by the American Society for Testing and Materials (ASTM) as

> A generic term for a continuous strand of textile fiber, filament, or material suitable for knitting, weaving, or otherwise intertwining to form a textile fabric. Yarn occurs in the following forms:
> a. a number of fibers twisted together
> b. a number of filaments laid together without twist
> c. a number of filaments laid together with more or less twist
> d. a single filament . . . a monofilament
> e. one or more strips made by the lengthwise division of a sheet of materials such as a natural or synthetic polymer, paper, or metal foil.*

Insertion of the phrase "or strands" following "continuous strand" in the first part of this definition will serve to broaden and clarify the use of the word *yarn* as it is interpreted in this text. There are different types of yarns available, and these include single yarns, plied yarns, cord yarns, simple yarns, complex or fancy yarns, and thread.

Yarns can be made either from short staple length fibers or from filament fibers (Fig. 17.1). If filaments are used, the yarns may be either *multifilament* (composed of several filaments) or *monofilaments* (made from one single filament). The staple fibers may derive from natural fibers that are available only in short staple lengths; they may be made from the natural fiber silk, for example, by using the silk filaments; or they may be made from man-made fibers, which can be used in either filament or staple length form. Staple fibers require considerably more processing to form into yarns than do filament fibers.

*ASTM, *Annual Book of Standards,* Part 07.01, 1985, p. 76.

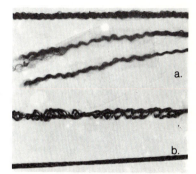

17.1 a. Staple yarns. b. Filament yarns.

YARN PROCESSING

Yarns composed of staple fibers are frequently called *spun yarns,* and this term will be used interchangeably with the term *staple fiber yarn.* In general, spun yarns are manufactured by either the cotton or the wool system. There are differences between them that relate to the typical fiber length used.

The Cotton System

The basic cotton system is called the *ring spinning process.* Although there are a variety of other methods for preparing cotton yarns, the ring process remains the most widely used and the one best adapted to preparing yarns of varied sizes and from various types of fibers cut to the typical length of cotton fiber.

Modern yarn-making mills use several types of automated systems. This automation may involve all the steps from opening the fiber bale to the final yarn spinning, or segments of the process may be automated. The general steps in ring spinning are cited in the following discussion; the use of automated procedures are identified when appropriate.

Opening, Cleaning, and Blending

Cotton and/or other staple fibers of similar length arrive at the processing unit or mill in a large bale. To make cotton system yarns of man-made fibers they are cut to the typical length of cotton fibers. Whatever fiber or fiber types to be used in making the yarn, they need to be well blended prior to yarn formation; this is necessary to produce uniform-quality yarns.

The first step, therefore, is to combine fibers from several different bales and sources. Once the bales are opened, thin layers of fibers from different bales are fed into the blending machine. These machines loosen and separate the closely packed fibers and remove dirt and other heavy impurities, either by gravity or by centrifugal force. This step ensures that fibers are well blended into a uniform mix. In general, this first step of opening, cleaning, and blending mixes only fibers of the same type. Blending fibers of different fiber types usually occurs later in the process.

Figure 17.2 is an illustration of one type of opening unit that is auto-

17.2 Opening and blending machine. The blending unit runs along the top of the bales and plucks tufts of fiber from each bale. Fibers are collected in the upright chamber to the back. When full, the unit returns to a transfer point where the fibers are blown into a duct to a large blending chamber. (American Textile Manufacturers Institute)

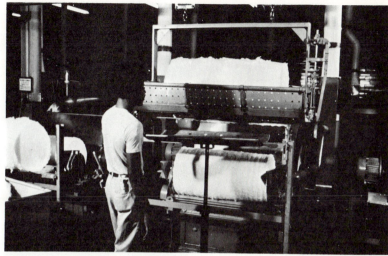

17.3 Close-up of metal "fingers" that pull small tufts of fibers from the bale, loosen them, and free them for processing. These fingers are used in a karousel opening machine. (Springs Industries)

17.4 The picker lap is delivered to the card frame, where it supplies fibers to form the card sliver. (Springs Industries)

matic. The opened bales of fiber are set into position, and metal fingers (Fig. 17.3) pull fibers from the base of the bale. These fibers are then blown to separate and fluff them and are next fed directly to the carding unit.

Picking

The intermittent ring spinning system requires the fibers from the opening units to be transported to the *picker frame* in some compact form or on some type of conveyor system. The picker frame additionally cleans the fibers and then forms them into a rolled mat that is ready for setting in place on the card frame (Fig. 17.4).

This roll of fibers is called a *lap;* it is about 45 inches wide and of randomly oriented or arranged fibers that resemble absorbent cotton in form and shape. Quality of the yarn is dependent to a considerable degree on the thoroughness of the picking operation and the uniformity of the picker lap.

In automated systems the fibers are sent directly from the opening units to the card frame.

Carding

In the intermittent process the picker lap is transported and placed at the end of the carding frame (Fig. 17.5). In automated systems, fibers are fed directly to the carding frame by either air systems or a combination of air and gravity (Fig. 17.6).

Carding continues the cleaning process, removes fibers too short for yarns, and separates and partially straightens the fibers so that their longitudinal axes are somewhat parallel to each other. These fibers are then

17.5 A carding frame. At the back, or right, is the picker lap; at the front, or left, is the card sliver as it is taken from the carding unit. (Springs Industries)

17.6 Automated high-speed carding machine. Fibers are fed directly to the card frame through ducts from opening and blending machines. (Springs Industries)

17.7 Fibers leave the carding frame in a filmy, sheer layer.This web is pulled into the sliver for the next step in manufacturing yarns. (Springs Industries)

spread into a thin, uniform web (Fig. 17.7). The web moves into a funnel-shaped device where it is gathered into a soft mass and formed into the *card sliver*. This sliver is not completely uniform in diameter, and the fibers are considerably more random in arrangement than a combed sliver. When carded yarns are to be made, the card sliver goes directly to the

17.8 Slivers are fed together into the drawing frame, at back, where they are combined and drawn into a new sliver ready for combing. (Springs Industries)

17.9 Rolls of slivers from the drawing frame are fed into the combing machine, where new comb slivers are formed. (National Cotton Council of America)

drawing machines; if combed yarns are desired, additional processing, called combing, is required before the drawing operation.

Combing

For high-quality yarns of outstanding evenness, smoothness, fineness, and strength, the fibers are combed as well as carded. In the combing operation several card slivers are combined and then *drawn* onto the comb machine, where they are, once again, spread into a web. As the web is formed there is further cleaning and straightening of the fibers. Short fibers are removed during combing. After the combing the fibers are pulled from the combing wires and formed into a comb sliver. This sliver will be used in making yarns with high levels of fineness, uniformity, and quality (Figs. 17.8 and 17.9).

Drawing

Depending on the quality of yarn desired, drawing follows either carding or combing. Several slivers are combined and conveyed to the drawing machine, where they are pulled together and drawn out into a new sliver no larger than one of the original single slivers.

If the final yarn is to be an intimate blend of two or more fibers, the drawn sliver will be composed of different fibers. For example, one sliver of cotton fibers for each sliver of polyester fibers will produce a blend of approximately 50 percent cotton and 50 percent polyester. Drawing does not set any twist into the drawn sliver (Fig. 17.10).

17.10 Slivers from either the carding or combing machines are fed into a drawing frame, where they are blended in preparation for the roving frame. (Cotton Incorporated)

Roving

The sliver from the drawing frame is taken to the roving frame, where it is attenuated until it measures from 1/4 to 1/8 of its original diameter. As the roving strand is ready to leave the roving frame, a slight twist is imparted to the strand of fibers, and it is then ready for the spinning frame (Fig. 17.11). The fineness and intimacy of blending depend to some degree on the number of times the slivers are doubled and redrawn prior to the roving operation.

Spinning

The final process in the manufacture of spun yarns is the actual spinning operation. In the spinning frame the roving is further stretched and drawn to the ultimate diameter of the final yarn. During this operation, twist is inserted. Several methods are used for inserting twist into the final yarn, but

17.11 Roving frame. Slivers from the drawing frames are pulled out to form the roving. A slight twist is imparted to hold fibers together. (Springs Industries)

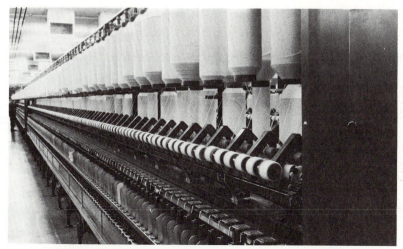

17.12 A conventional spinning frame, which converts roving, at the top, to a spun simple single yarn. An average frame holds 360 spindles of roving, each supplying a spinning area. The roving is guided into the spinning area, center, where it is stretched and pulled out to form a fine yarn. (Springs Industries)

17.13 Close-up of spinning area where roving is reduced in size to form a yarn. (National Cotton Council of America)

the most common for fibers of the length of cotton is called *ring spinning* (Figs. 17.12 and 17.13). In ring spinning the drawn-out roving is guided in a downward direction and through the *traveler,* a small inverted U-shaped device. The spindle on which the completed yarn is wound rotates approximately 13,000 revolutions per minute; the traveler moves around the ring at a rate between 4,000 and 12,000 revolutions per minute. As the spindle revolves to wind the yarn, the yarn passes through the traveler, which carries it around the ring. This process imparts the desired amount of twist. The yarn formed on the spinning frame is a simple single yarn.

The Wool System

Wool fibers and manufactured fibers that have been cut to the typical length of wool fibers can be spun into yarns by the woolen or worsted systems. Woolen yarns are carded and spun; worsted yarns are carded, combed, drawn, and spun.

Sorting

Spinning wool fibers into yarns requires some special procedures. The fibers must be sorted and graded according to fineness (or diameter), length, and strength. Each fleece is opened and the fiber is graded, which determines the type of product for which the fiber will be used. Fine fibers are relatively long and are reserved for sheer wool fabrics and for worsted fabrics; medium fibers of short lengths are suitable for woolen fabrics for apparel and home furnishings; coarse fibers, both long and short, are used for rough textured fabrics and for carpeting. The best-quality wool comes from the sides and shoulders of the sheep. Lambs' wool is very fine wool that has been sheared from young animals not more than eight-months old; it is reserved for fine-quality sweaters and similar products.

Scouring

After sorting and grading, the wool is scoured, that is, washed in warm, soapy water several times and thoroughly rinsed and dried. Scouring is essential for it removes the natural grease in the fiber, the suint or body secretions, dirt, and dust. Natural grease is recovered and purified and becomes lanolin, an oil used in the cosmetic industry. Scouring is not required for man-made fibers that are to be processed on woolen or worsted equipment.

Woolen Yarns

To make woolen yarns the wool fibers are fed to the carding machine where the fiber mass is opened or separated, tangles are removed, fibers are straightened to some degree, impurities are removed, fiber from various supply stocks are mixed, and the fibers are finally pulled from the card in a form called roving or roping. The carding machines are similar in appearance to those used in carding cotton fibers, but the carding wires are somewhat longer. The carding operation may use several sets of carding cylinders (Fig. 17.14).

The roving or roping goes directly to the spinning frame, where the roving is drawn out to the desired size, twist is inserted, and the woolen yarn is wrapped onto packages for use in weaving or knitting. Because of the absence of drawing in making woolen yarns, the yarns have less fiber orientation than carded cotton yarns. They are characterized by nonuniformity, bulk, resilience, good insulation, and a rough, hairy surface.

Worsted Yarns

Following scouring and lubrication, wool fibers are carded, which straightens the fibers, removes impurities, and blends fibers from different batches to provide for uniformity in length and quality. Fibers are arranged in a relatively parallel manner. The card frames are similar to those used in other processes, but many systems use two cylinders and several feed rolls. The card sliver is drawn and then combed. These steps are similar to processes used in spinning fibers on the combed cotton system. The wool at this point may be referred to as *wool top* (Fig. 17.15).

17.14 below. Woolen carding. Fibers are opened or loosened, mixed, made into a uniform web, and condensed into roping. (Wool Bureau)

17.15 right. Worsted carding. Carding teases out the fibers and removes impurities. The wool in a filmy web, see lower right, is gathered together into a sliver. (Wool Bureau)

After combing, the comb sliver is drafted or drawn to form a roving; this roving is delivered to a spinning frame, where the final worsted yarn is made. Worsted yarn can be spun by several methods, but most modern worsted yarn is made on ring spinning frames.

Worsted yarns are characterized by a relatively smooth and even surface, a highly parallel fiber arrangement, a compact structure, resiliency, and good strength. Yarns can be made in various sizes.

Staple Fiber Yarns From Man-Made Fibers

It has been noted in previous paragraphs that man-made staple fibers may be converted into yarn by using the cotton system or the woolen/worsted system. The key is to make certain that the manufactured fibers have been cut into the length appropriate for the machinery to be used. When cotton yarn-spinning equipment is to be used, the man-made fibers should be cut the average length of cotton fibers; if wool yarn spinning is desired, the man-made fibers should be cut the average length of wool fiber.

When blends of natural and man-made fibers are to be made, or blends of different types of staple length man-made fibers are to be produced, the blending of the different types of fiber usually occurs during the drawing operation.

Yarns of staple length fibers can be made to differ in diameter, surface texture, strength, amount of twist, and uniformity. Yarns for use in the warp direction of woven fabrics will require a higher amount of twist and strength than those to be used in the filling direction; this is to provide sufficient strength to tolerate the action of the loom during weaving. Knitting yarns may differ from those intended for weaving. Knitting yarns may have different levels of twist, bulk, and diameter depending on the type of knit fabric to be made.

Filament Yarns

The manufacture of yarns from filament fibers, whether natural or man-made, is a simple and direct process. Silk is the only natural filament fiber; and silk yarn depends on the number of cocoons reeled off at one time (see Chapter 6).

Filament yarns of man-made fibers are made by either a continuous or discontinuous process. In the continuous process the number of openings in the spinnerette and the number of filaments in the final yarn are the same. The filaments are extruded; drawn to develop stretch, molecular orientation, and fineness; and then combined with the desired amount of twist and wound onto take-up bobbins or containers (Fig. 17.16). The discontinuous process differs in that filaments, without twist, and for some types, without drawing, are wrapped onto packages, cakes, or cones. When needed, these filaments are rewound from the package, twist is added, and they are drawn if necessary. The yarn is then rewrapped onto bobbins or beams ready for use in fabric construction.

Filament yarns are smooth and even unless they have been deliberately made irregular for novelty effects. Simple yarns of filament fibers are lustrous and somewhat silky in appearance. The luster can be controlled by the addition of delusterants to the fiber solution before filament formation or by the addition of finishing agents to the filaments following production.

Filament fibers have no protruding fiber ends, so they do not pill unless the filaments are broken, and lint is not formed. Round filaments tend

17.16 Filament fibers are combined with minimal twist to produce multifilament yarns. All the filament fibers required for a specific size simple single yarn are extruded simultaneously through the spinnerette. (Celanese Corporation)

to shed soil, whereas multilobal filaments tend to hide or camouflage soil.

The strength of filament yarns is determined by a combination of factors: fiber tenacity, number of filaments combined to make the yarn, and denier or size of each filament and of the final yarn. Because filaments are long, they receive equal pull in the yarn and fiber strength is maximized.

The amount of twist in filament yarns is usually relatively low, but high-twist crepe yarns are made successfully from filament fibers.

Other Yarn-Manufacturing Processes

Several new methods have been developed over the past few decades for converting staple fiber yarns and/or tow into yarns. The processes are important because they represent considerable economies in speed of production, labor costs, overhead, space requirements, and energy requirements.

Open-End Spinning

The term *open-end spinning* applies to fiber systems in which a break occurs in the fiber system. Break spinning and open-end spinning are synonymous (Fig. 17.17). The essential steps in open-end spinning include

17.17 The basic principle of break spinning.

fiber supply   break   fiber   break   yarn

the following: A coarse sliver of fibers is fed to an opening system, which opens the sliver to the point where the fibers are individual entities; the individual fibers are fed forward; they are collected on a small surface and pulled from the surface as a thin layer, constantly adding to the open end, or tail, of the forming yarn. The thin layer is attenuated, twist is inserted, and the resulting yarn is wound onto bobbins. There are two methods commonly used in open-end spinning: aeromechanical, or rotor spinning; and fluid, air, or water jet systems.

Rotor spinning   Rotor spinning involves the contact of fibers in or on rotating devices such as funnels, cones, baskets, sieves, or needled surfaces. A sliver of fibers is fed into the unit, a current of air forces the fibers into a loose form, and they are collected on the rotating device. As they collect, they are pulled off the rotor by mechanical means to form the yarn, and the new yarn is wound onto packages. Twist is inserted as the yarn is removed from the rotor.

Rotor spinning is a popular process and has replaced some ring spinning units. There are some differences in quality and characteristics between ring spun and rotor spun yarns, but both have some advantages. Many of the disadvantages associated with early rotor spun yarns are disappearing as the process is improved and perfected. Rotor spun yarn requires considerably less plant space, less energy, and less labor; the operation is cleaner, and production of yarn is considerably faster than for ring spinning.

Modern rotor spinning equipment produces yarns that are very fine as well as medium to coarse yarns. Yarn defects have been reduced. In general, it can be stated that rotor spun yarns compare favorably with ring spun yarns. Typical end uses for yarns made by rotor spinning include apparel, home furnishings, and industrial fabrics. In fact, they can be used in nearly every product in which ring spun yarns have been used.

Jet spinning   Spinning of yarns by air or water jet systems is similar to the rotor process except that the yarn is formed in moving air rather than on a rotating surface. The method is increasing in use; yarns have good uniformity, appear to be stronger than rotor spun yarns, and do not pill as quickly as staple fiber yarns of other types (Fig. 17.18).

Friction Spinning

The friction system of making yarns is a modification of a system originally called DREF. In this process the sliver enters the system and the fibers are separated and spread onto a combing or carding roll; they are doffed or removed from this roll and transported by air to the friction zone. Two cylinders rotating in the same direction pull the fibers together to form the yarn. The angle of the feed into the friction rolls affects fiber alignment; the smaller the angle, the better the fiber alignment and the more parallel the fibers will be.

Yarns made by this process tend to be free of impurities and to have more body and less strength than ring spun yarns. They are used successfully in apparel fabrics, home-furnishing fabrics, and industrial fabrics in which high strength is not a requirement.

Twistless Yarns

Twistless yarns are made by using an adhesive to hold fibers together. A roving is made and drawn to a fine strand; during the drawing an adhesive

17.18 Air jet spinning machine produces yarn directly from drawn sliver. (Springs Industries)

is applied by rollers. The drawn yarn, coated with adhesive, is wound onto packages; the packages are steamed, and the adhesive bonds the fibers together. Twistless yarns are stiffer, have increased luster, have less elongation, have better covering power, and are more uniform than ring spun yarns.

Self-Twist Yarns

Self-twist yarns are essentially two-strand or two-ply yarns (see p. 156). They may involve one ply or strand of staple fibers and one of filament, two strands of staple fibers, two of filament fibers, or multiple combinations of these fibers. A common type is the Selfil yarn, which is composed of one strand of staple fibers with some twist and a filament strand wrapped around the staple strand. The filament strand alternates S and Z twist.

Core Spun Yarns

Core spun yarns have a central core with a second layer or sheath of fibers wrapped around it. Both core and wrapping may be of the same fiber type, or two different fiber types (or more) may be used. One part may be of filament fibers and the other of staple fibers; or both parts may be of

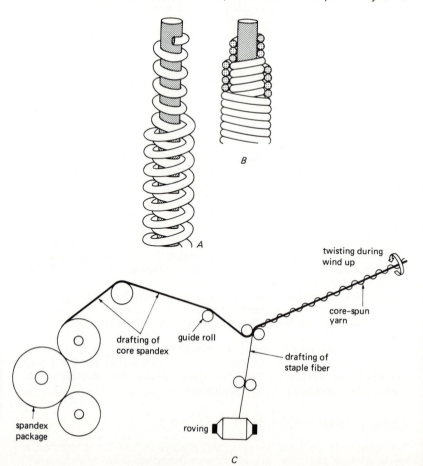

17.19 Diagram showing core spun yarn and core spinning process. a. double-covered spandex with the core extended. b. Double-covered spandex with core relaxed. c. Core spinning operation.

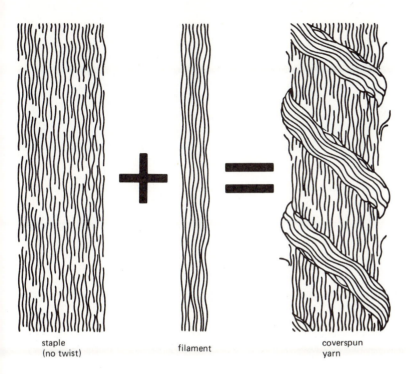

staple
(no twist)

filament

coverspun
yarn

17.20 Steps in making a coverspun yarn.

either filament or staple length fibers. The outer sheath may completely cover the core. When the outer sheath does not cover the central core, it is possible to create interesting effects in appearance. One of the most common types of core spun yarns is that involving a core of a stretch filament, such as spandex, with a covering of staple fibers (Fig. 17.19). A new method of making core spun yarns is called Coverspun. It can use any type of staple fibers, but it is especially desirable for wool, and it uses any type of filament fibers. The outer wrapping does not hide the central core (Fig. 17.20).

Tape Yarns

Split film or tape yarns are produced from thin sheets, or films, of polymer that are cut into narrow strips, or ribbons. These thin strips of material, much like plastic wrap, are drawn, stretched, and then twisted into the final yarn. Tape yarns have good strength, good abrasion resistance, and good stability. They are frequently used for carpet-backing fabrics; for making sacks and bags; for tarpaulins; for webbings; and for such miscellaneous products as blinds, travel goods, swimming pool covers, and ropes.

SIMPLE YARNS

Descriptions and Terminology

Simple yarns are even in size throughout their length, they have an equal number of turns or twists per inch throughout their length, and they are

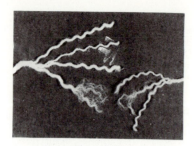

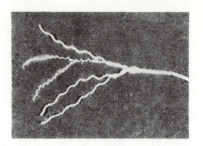

17.21 left. A simple single yarn; one end is untwisted to show individual fibers.

17.22 center. A simple four-ply yarn and a three-ply yarn. The ply has been untwisted to show the individual simple single yarns.

17.23 right. A cord yarn composed of four plies, each ply with two single yarns.

relatively smooth and uniform throughout. Simple yarns may be single, ply, or cord types. They may have little twist to a great amount of twist. Simple yarns are considered to be relatively durable, although durability is affected by such factors as yarn size, amount of twist per inch, and structure—single, ply, or cord. A very highly twisted simple yarn may be called a crepe yarn when it is characterized by sufficient twist so that it tends to kink, producing a rough surface texture in the fabric.

A simple single yarn is made directly from fibers and involves giving the assemblage of fibers sufficient twist to hold them together during processing into fabrics, use, and care (Fig. 17.21). These simple single yarns are uniform in structure throughout. A simple ply yarn is made by combining two or more single yarns (Fig. 17.22). These yarns are also uniform in structure throughout. A simple cord yarn (Fig. 17.23) is made by combining two or more simple ply yarns to form the final yarn.

A simple single yarn is the most basic assemblage of fibers suitable for making into fabrics. When a single yarn is untwisted it will break apart into the individual fibers from which it has been made. These yarns can be made from any fiber and by the yarn construction processes previously described.

A simple ply yarn is composed of a combination of two or more simple single yarns. The ply yarn is uniform throughout. In naming or identifying ply yarns the number of plies involved precedes the term *ply*. Thus a yarn made of two singles would be a two-ply yarn; a yarn made of five singles would be a five-ply yarn. To verify that the yarn is a simple yarn, the word *simple* would precede the number, for example, a simple two-ply yarn, a simple five-ply yarn.

Cord yarns are composed of two or more ply yarns combined. For simple cord yarns, the singles used to make the ply yarns and the ply yarns used to make the cord are simple or uniform yarns. To identify the number of singles and the number of plies used in making cord yarns the following system is used. The first number given would indicate how many plies have been used in making the cord; the second number indicates how many single yarns were used to make the plies. Thus, a 4,7 ply cord would mean that seven single yarns were combined to make each ply; then four plies were combined to make the cord. Again, using the word *simple* before the first number indicates that the yarn is uniform throughout.

Yarn Properties

Thread and Yarn

Thread and yarn are basically similar. *Yarn* is the term usually applied when the fiber assemblage is employed in the manufacture of fabric;

17.24 An assortment of thread. (Consumer and Educational Affairs Dept., Coats & Clark)

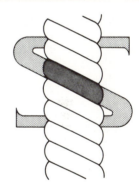

17.25 A crepe yarn. The high twist causes the yarn to kink and gives fabrics a crinkled surface.

thread is used to indicate a product that joins pieces of fabric together to create textile products. Thread is frequently of plied construction and is even and strong. One might explain the difference by saying that thread is always a yarn, but a yarn may not be a thread.

Thread must be so constructed that it can be adapted to either hand or machine sewing as well as to embroidery or lace making. A satisfactory thread must have high strength and adequate elasticity, a smooth surface, dimensional stability, resistance to snarling, resistance to damage by friction, and an attractive appearance. Several types of thread are available: simple ply threads, cord threads, elastic threads, monofilament threads of man-made fibers, and multifilament threads of silk and man-made fibers (Fig. 17.24).

Yarn Twist

In most methods used to make yarn, twist is inserted to help hold the fiber together. The amount of twist is sometimes identified rather broadly by such terms as *low, medium,* and *high.* It is more accurate, however, to identify the twist by citing the number of turns per unit length. As the yarn becomes finer in diameter, it requires more twist per unit length. Heavy, coarse yarns can have very low twist and still be durable because of the amount of fiber involved. Typically the more twist the stronger the yarn will be; however, beyond an optimum point additional twist causes yarns to kink and actually lose strength (Fig. 17.25).

Yarn twist may be identified as either S or Z twist. This describes the direction of the twist. When the yarn is twisted so that the lines of twist would conform to the central part of the letter S, it is said to have a right-hand twist; if the twist conforms to the central part of the letter Z, it has a left-hand twist (Fig. 17.26). The direction of twist is important when considering yarns for manufacture into ply and cord yarns.

The balance of yarns is another important factor associated with yarn twist. If yarns are *balanced,* the twist has been inserted in such a manner that a length of yarn will hang in a loop without kinking or doubling on itself (Fig. 17.27). *Unbalanced yarns* have sufficient twist so that a torque effect develops and the yarn will untwist and retwist in the opposite direction, leaving it twisted upon itself. Smooth fabrics require balanced yarns; crepe and textured surfaces may be created from unbalanced yarns.

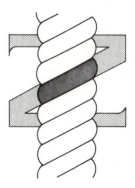

17.26 Diagram of S- and Z-twist in yarn.

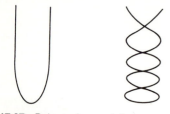

17.27 Balanced yarn, left; unbalanced yarn, right.

A variety of effects can be obtained by combining single yarns or ply yarns of different twist direction, level of balance, and amount of twist.

Yarn Number

Yarn number is a measure of linear density, or in simple terms, yarn size. *Direct yarn number* is the mass-per-unit length of yarn; *indirect yarn number* is the length-per-unit mass of yarn. Yarn number is frequently called yarn count in the indirect system. To some extent the yarn number is an indication of diameter when yarns of the same fiber content are compared.

Over the years various methods of determining yarn number have been developed. Cotton yarns are numbered by measuring the weight, in pounds, of one 840-yard hank of yarn. The yarn number is the number of hanks required to weigh 1 pound. If one hank weighs 1 pound the yarn is called a number 1, usually identified as 1s. If thirty hanks are required, it would be a 30s yarn. The higher the number the finer the yarn. A very fine yarn would be a 160s, a medium yarn a 30s, and a heavy yarn a 1s.

Woolen yarn is measured by the number of 300-yard hanks per pound; worsted yarn is measured by the number of 560-yard hanks per pound. Silk and man-made fiber yarns are typically measured by the denier system. The denier is equal to the weight in grams of 9,000 meters of yarn. This is an example of a direct system, whereas the numbering of cotton, wool, and worsted is indirect yarn numbering.

The present systems of determining yarn size may be summarized as follows: In the indirect system, the higher the yarn number the smaller the yarn diameter. In the direct system, the higher the number the larger the yarn.

In attempts to arrive at some uniform system of yarn numbering, some groups, including ASTM, have suggested that a system called *tex* be adopted. This numbering system is based on the weight in grams of 1 kilometer, 1,000 meters, of yarn. The weight becomes the tex number. This system would eliminate some of the confusion and provide the same kind of measurement for all types of yarns from any type of fiber.

Study Questions

1. List the steps in the conventional ring spinning system of constructing yarns made from fibers such as cotton.
2. Name the ways in which the traditional system of ring spinning has been modified during the past twenty-five years to provide for more rapid construction with less manual labor.
3. How does the ring spinning system as used for cotton differ from the systems used for making woolen or worsted yarns?
4. What are the differences in yarn construction procedures between carded and combed yarns? Where do these differences occur?
5. What are the differences between construction procedures for staple yarns and for filament yarns?
6. What is open-end spinning? What is the difference between rotor and air jet spinning?
7. What are the advantages of the open-end methods of making yarn as compared with ring spinning?
8. Describe at least three other processes for making yarns.
9. What are simple yarns?
10. Describe simple single, simple ply, and simple cord yarns.

11. How does yarn twist affect yarn properties? What is the difference between balanced and unbalanced yarn?
12. What is yarn number? What are the differences between direct and indirect yarn number? Give an example of each. Why would adoption of the tex yarn-numbering system be of value?

18

Complex or Fancy Yarns

Complex or fancy yarns are made primarily for their appearance. They differ from simple yarns in that their structure is characterized by irregularities. ASTM defines a *fancy yarn* as

> A yarn that differs significantly from the normal appearance of single or plied yarn due to the presence of irregularities deliberately produced during its formation. In single yarns the irregularities may be due to the inclusion of knots, loops, curls, slubs, and the like. In plied yarns the irregularities may be due to a variable delivery of one or more of its components or to twisting together dissimilar single yarns.*

The terms *fancy, complex,* and *novelty* are considered synonymous.

As noted from the definition most fancy yarns are either single or plied. However, cords or modified cord complex yarns are used in some special fabric constructions.

Types of Complex or Fancy Yarns

Several systems have been used in classifying, describing, and naming complex or fancy yarns. There are discrepancies among these systems in both definitions and names given to various complex yarn structures. The descriptions used here appear to be typical of the majority; but they may differ among authors, partly because of changes that result from the interpretations of historical data.

Fancy Single Yarns

Slub yarns A slub yarn may be either a single yarn or a two-ply yarn. However, the majority are single yarns. These yarns are made by uneven twisting of the fibers as they are spun into the final yarn. At intervals, which may be irregularly or regularly spaced, the yarn is left either untwisted or slackly twisted to produce soft, bulky areas (Fig. 18.1). Ply slub yarns are described in the section on fancy ply yarns.

Slubs may be of any length; however, as the amount of twist in the enlarged portion of the yarn is low, strength in that section of the yarn may also be low. Thus, for durability it is advisable to keep the bulky sections in a single slub yarn to a relatively short span. The lack of twist in the enlarged areas results in yarns that are fluffier and softer at those points than in the remainder of the yarn. Single slub yarns are found in such fabrics as shantung; butcher cloth; and selected knitting yarns for sportswear, coats, and other apparel.

18.1 A single slub fancy yarn.

*ASTM, *Annual Book of Standards,* Vol 07.01, 1985, p. 77.

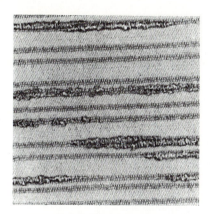
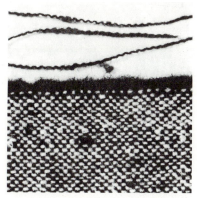

18.2 above left. Fabric using thick-n-thin yarns.
18.3 above center. Tweed with flake yarns and separate flake yarn.
18.4 above right. Diagram of the basic units in a three-ply complex or fancy yarn: the core, or base yarn; the decorative, or effect yarn; and the binder, or tie yarn.

Thick-n-thin yarns Thick-n-thin yarns are similar in appearance to slub yarns, except thick-n-thin yarns are usually much thinner or finer. However, the manufacturing process differs, as does the length of the fiber used. Slub yarns are made from staple length fibers; thick-n-thin yarns are made from filament fibers. As the filaments are extruded, the pressure forcing the solution through the spinnerette openings is varied so that filaments are thicker in some sections than in others. The resulting group of filaments forms a yarn of irregular size with thick and thin characteristics (Fig. 18.2).

Flock or flake yarns Flock or flake yarns are usually single fancy yarns in which small tufts of fiber are inserted at irregular intervals and held in place by the twist of the base yarn. These tufts may be round or elongated. Flock yarn is used for special effects in suiting and dress fabrics and for some home-furnishing fabrics. Tweeds, for example, usually contain flock or flake yarns (Fig. 18.3). One drawback to these yarns is that the tufts of fiber may be easily removed from the base yarn. However, as this problem occurs over a long period of time, it is not considered serious. Some authors classify flock or flake yarns as one type of slub yarns.

Fancy Ply Yarns

The majority of fancy ply yarns involve three or more single yarns. The common exception is the ply slub. Other exceptions occur when the fancy yarn becomes a cord construction. The typical construction of a fancy ply involves three single yarns: a base yarn, an effect yarn, and a tie or binder yarn (Fig. 18.4). The base yarn controls the length and stability of the final yarn; the effect yarn forms the design apparent in the final yarn; the tie or binder yarn holds the effect yarn securely in place around the base yarn to provide durability in use and care.

Ply slub yarn Ply slub yarns are made by using one ply to form the slub, or fluffy, areas and a second yarn to hold the enlarged slubs in place. In a ply slub the enlarged, or fluffy, areas may alternate between the two single yarns used; thus in some places one single forms the slubs with the other holding fibers in position, whereas in other locations the reverse occurs. Ply slub yarns have somewhat better durability than single slub yarns because of the holding ply (Fig. 18.5).

18.5 Complex ply slub yarns.

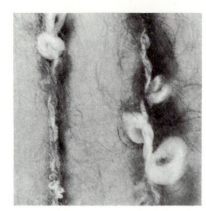

18.6 Loop-type fancy yarns.

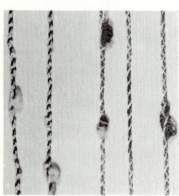

18.7 top. Ratine fancy yarns and fabric.

18.8 bottom. Nub or knot complex yarns.

Loop and curl yarns The loop complex or fancy yarn is one of the easiest to identify (Fig. 18.6). There are always loops or curls of some size extending away from the base yarn. The base yarn may be of any size, but the typical is relatively coarse and heavy. The effect yarn, which forms the loops, is usually made of fibers that give the appearance of fluffiness. The effect yarn may be of single or ply construction. Loops are held securely in place on the base yarn by means of a tie or binder yarn. This yarn is usually fine and is designed to blend into the base yarn so that it is not obvious.

Bouclé Bouclé yarns are characterized by tight loops projecting from the body of the yarn at fairly regular intervals. These yarns are of three-ply construction. The effect yarn that forms the loops, or bumps, that protrude from the yarn is wrapped rather tightly around the base yarn, and the loops are relatively tiny. Bouclé fabrics can be constructed by either knitting or weaving techniques; the yarn is available also for hand knitting or weaving. It is used for both apparel and home furnishings, but usually bouclé yarns are found in either apparel or accessories.

Ratiné and gimp yarns Ratiné and gimp yarns are similar to each other and, in addition, are somewhat like bouclé yarns. The major difference is that the loops or extensions from the base yarn are close together in ratiné and gimp, whereas they are spaced farther apart in bouclé. They can be differentiated from loop yarns because these have obvious loops that are relatively large and open. Most ratiné or gimp yarns use highly twisted singles in their construction. The manufacture of these yarns requires two distinct twisting operations; after the yarn is first made it is twisted in the opposite direction to establish the desired effect for the final yarn (Fig. 18.7).

Nub or spot and knot or knop yarns The terms *nub, spot, knot,* and *knop* are frequently used interchangeably; however, there are minor differences. A nub or spot yarn is made on a special machine that permits the base yarn to be held almost stationary while the effect yarn is wrapped around it several times to build up an enlarged segment. Sometimes the effect yarn is held in position by a tie, but in many cases the nub or spot is secure enough so that a tie or binder yarn is not needed. The knot or knop yarn is produced in much the same way except that brightly colored fibers are frequently added in the effect knot (Fig. 18.8).

Seed or splash yarns Although seed or splash yarns are similar to nub or knot yarns, there are minor differences. In splash yarns the added seg-

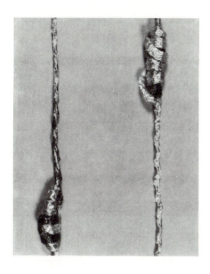 

ment is elongated in shape and very tightly twisted around the base yarn. Seed yarns may differ in that the effect is a very tiny nub that is tightly twisted and not as long as the splash segment (Fig. 18.9).

Spiral or corkscrew yarns   Spiral or corkscrew yarns are fancy yarns in which the desired effect is obtained either by twisting together yarns of different diameters or different fiber content or by varying the speed or the direction of twist. A spiral yarn is comprised of two or more single yarns of different size, one fine with a hard twist, the other bulky with a slack twist. The heavy yarn is wound spirally around the fine yarn. A corkscrew yarn is made by twisting together two yarns at an uneven rate, twisting together two yarns of different size, or loosely twisting a fine yarn around a heavy yarn so that it gives the appearance of a corkscrew (Fig. 18.10).

Chenille yarn   Chenille yarn creates special effects in fabrics for apparel or home furnishings. The yarn resembles a hairy caterpillar—*chenille* is French for caterpillar. A special doup weave, a leno weave construction (see p. 196), is built and then slit into narrow warp-wise strips that serve as yarn. This yarn is then used as filling in chenille fabrics. As the special fabric is slit, the loose ends of the crosswise yarns, which are soft and loosely twisted, form a pilelike surface. The yarn can be folded so that the pile is all on one side of the final fabric, or it may be arranged so that the loose ends form a raised surface on both sides of the fabric (Fig. 18.11).

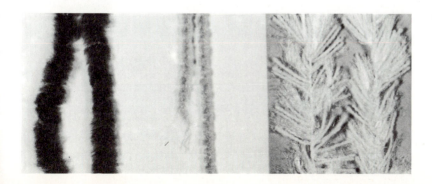

18.11   Chenille-type complex yarns.

Chenille yarns are often used in making carpeting, bedspreads, and upholstery fabric.

Core and Metallic Yarns

Core and metallic yarns are identified here, in brief, because they may be fancy yarns and provide surface design, although they do not strictly fit into the accepted definition of fancy yarns.

Core spun yarn A core spun yarn was described in the previous chapter. It is a yarn in which a base or foundation has been encircled or wrapped by a second yarn. The core may be of rubber wrapped with cotton to provide highly elastic properties; or it may be of silk wrapped in metallic yarns, which give durable decorative accents to fabric. Other types of core yarns may be used that are often decorative or fancy in nature.

Metallic yarns Metallic yarns are much the same as metallic fibers, discussed in Chapter 16. Metallic yarns are used primarily for decoration; the yarn itself may be fancy or the effect of the metallic yarn in the fabric may create the decorative effect.

Complex Yarns in Use

Complex or novelty yarns add texture and design to fabric and are valued for their appearance and the effect they create. However, there may be problems in comfort, maintenance, and durability because of the yarn's construction. Some complex yarns are rough and harsh, so they may actually be uncomfortable in wearing apparel or in upholstery fabric. On the other hand, many loop yarns are soft and pleasant to touch and increase the warmth of an item, making these yarns ideal for sweaters or fabrics where warmth is desirable.

The rough surface of fancy yarns and the irregular twist create characteristics that may cause them to snag easily, to be damaged by abrasion, and to show wear more rapidly than smooth fabrics. However, the appearance of fancy or complex yarns is sufficient to ensure that they will be chosen for a variety of different types of fabrics. Figure 18.12 includes examples of fabrics with complex yarns that are commonly used for apparel; Figures 18.13 and 18.14 illustrate fabrics that may be marketed for upholstery or draperies.

18.12 below left. Fabric made with chenille complex yarns.
18.13 below right. Fabrics made, in part, with complex yarns.

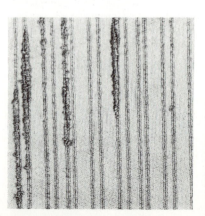

 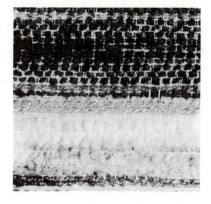 

18.14 Drapery fabrics made, in part, with complex yarns.

Study Questions

1. Describe the following fancy or complex yarns:
   a. Slub yarn, single
   b. Slub yarn, ply
   c. Loop yarn
   d. Bouclé yarn
   e. Corkscrew yarn
   f. Gimp yarn
   g. Knot yarn
   h. Ratiné yarn.
   Why is it difficult to describe these yarns? What problems would you en-counter in trying to locate examples of fabrics in which each of these types of yarn have been used?
2. What are some of the problems in use and care that are associated with fancy or complex yarns?
3. What are the reasons for using complex yarns in fabric?
4. What are typical end uses for complex or fancy yarns?
5. What are the limitations in the use of complex or fancy yarns?

19 Textured and Stretch Yarns

Textured Yarns

Textured yarns are characterized by the presence of crimp, zigzag shapes, or other configurations that contribute bulk and/or stretch to the filaments that comprise the yarn. Textured yarns can be made from either filament fibers or staple fibers cut from filaments that have been given a textured configuration of some type. The majority of textured yarns are made from filament fibers. Texturizing occurs following the spinning of the fiber material through the spinnerette. It may be done immediately following fiber formation and be a part of a continuous operation, or it may be done some time after the filaments have been made.

Textured yarns may be uniform in shape and smooth in appearance—like simple yarns; or they may be irregular so that they have some resemblance to complex yarn structures. Because textured yarns have special properties that make them sufficiently different from other yarns, they are discussed as an individual type of yarn in this text.

There are three types of textured yarn: stretch, modified stretch, and bulked. Although each has specific characteristics, it is possible for yarns to have some properties of all three.

Stretch yarns have extremely high levels of elastic extensibility and elastic recovery. Modified stretch yarns have some degree of stretch or extensibility, but they have been stabilized by processing to control the stretch and keep it at a preestablished amount. This control maintains a predetermined amount of extensibility at a level below that of regular stretch yarns but with sufficient stretch to provide desired properties in the end uses selected.

Bulk yarns are special textured yarns designed to contribute bulk to a fabric. These yarns have moderate to low levels of stretch and fluffy, bulky properties. Bulked yarns are common, and they have a variety of end uses including sweaters, knit fabrics, and carpeting.

Most textured yarns are manufactured from thermoplastic fibers. The ability of filament fibers or staple fiber yarns to be heat set is a necessary property for the majority of texturizing processes but not for all. Heat setting, described in some detail as a finish on page 258, involves building into fibers different characteristics than the product had before such processing. Heat setting, therefore, makes it possible to modify the fibers through the use of heat and to produce fibers with a different configuration than they had when first made.

There are several different processes used in the manufacture of textured yarns. These include stuffer box crimping, gear crimping, tunnel crimping, knit-deknit crimping, false twisting, and edge crimping—all of which utilize heat in some form. The air jet method of texturizing does not require heat and can be used on fibers that are not heat sensitive.

Texturizing Processes

False Twist Methods

False twist textured yarns are manufactured by inserting twist into simple filament yarns, setting that twist by the application of controlled heat, and untwisting as the yarns cool. As the twist is removed, the yarns kink or crimp in a spiral manner because of the distortion that results from the presence of the heat-set twist. When stretchy yarns are desired, the yarns are heated during the initial twisting process only; for yarns that are to be bulky only, the yarns are passed through a second heating zone after the untwisting occurs (Fig. 19.1).

Simple yarns made by this method are characterized by either a left- or right-hand torque, so they tend to be unbalanced and subject to distortion in the final fabric. To prevent this effect, manufacturers frequently combine a yarn with left-hand twist and a yarn with right-hand twist—which does produce balanced yarns. The best known yarn made by the false twist process is *Helanca*. Originally Helanca yarn was made from nylon filaments, but today it is made of several different types of thermosensitive fibers; the two most commonly encountered are nylon and polyester.

When stretch yarns are to be made, the degree of stretch in the final yarn is controlled by the number of turns per inch that are heat set into the filaments. Yarns are available in a wide range of stretch, from those that can be elongated up to 400 percent of the original length and still return to the original size down to yarns with a relatively low amount of stretch. Bulk can also be controlled, and fibers can be heat set to have considerable bulk or none at all. Proper finishing ensures that the desired amount of stretch and/or bulk will remain in the fibers and fabrics during use and care. Yarns made by the false twist systems are generally softer and more uniform than those made on other texturizing equipment (Fig. 19.2).

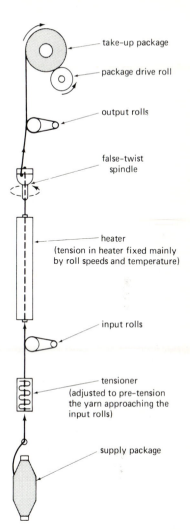

labels: take-up package; package drive roll; output rolls; false-twist spindle; heater (tension in heater fixed mainly by roll speeds and temperature); input rolls; tensioner (adjusted to pre-tension the yarn approaching the input rolls); supply package

19.1 Schematic drawing showing the yarn path through a typical false twist machine. (National Knitwear and Sportswear Association)

19.2 False twisting equipment. (American Barmag Corporation)

Knife Edge Method

Textured yarns made by the knife edge method possess a spiral-like curl or coil. The yarns are passed over a heated knife edge, or the yarns are heated and, while still hot, then passed over a knife edge. It is easy to visualize this process if one remembers how to build curl into some types of gift-wrapping ribbon by drawing it over the blade of a pair of scissors or over a knife edge. This process has been widely used for yarn for women's hosiery. One trade name that has been used for this type of yarn is *Agilon.*

The usual technique consists of drawing a thermoplastic yarn, such as nylon, over a hot, sharp knife blade. The resulting yarn has properties similar to wool. These yarns show a high degree of elasticity but retain their sheerness. Some of this type of textured yarn is now being used in such products as power-control hosiery, knit fabrics for sweaters, and some types of upholstery and carpeting.

The amount of stretch built into these types of yarns can be controlled. Because they are nontorque in nature they can be used either as singles or as plied yarns—which makes it possible to create very sheer fabrics when desired.

Stuffer Box Method

In the stuffer box method fibers are forced into a narrow box or tube that causes them to develop a saw-toothed crimp. The crimp is heat set, and when the filaments are removed from the tube the crimp remains a part of the fiber properties. The greatest amount of bulk and a controlled amount of stretch can be created by this method. Yarns are torque free and produce satisfactory single as well as ply yarns. The best known process for making these yarns is called *Ban-Lon.* It is important to note that Ban-Lon yarn may be made from any thermoplastic fiber; further it should be emphasized that Ban-Lon is not a name for a fiber; it is the name of a process. Ban-Lon is made from either nylon or polyester filaments. Filament fibers, rather than staple fibers, are preferred because they do not pill as badly as staple fibers (Fig. 19.3).

Ban-Lon fabrics are soft, strong, and easy to care for. They have a

19.3 Diagram of stuffer box texturizing: 1. Filament yarn feeding into the unit. 2. Crimping rolls. 3. Stuffer box. 4. Control to release textured yarn. 5. Textured yarn leaving unit. (E. I. DuPont de Nemours & Company, Patent 3,237,270)

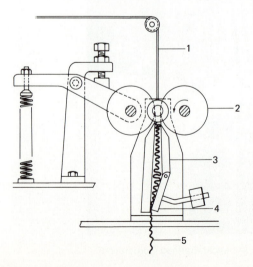

lively hand, excellent moisture absorption, controlled stretch, minimum pilling, dimensional stability, and adequate air circulation for comfort.

Another product that utilizes the stuffer box method is called *Spunize*. Spunize may be of ply construction as well as single; it usually uses a high number of filaments in making the yarn. As it is usually thicker than Ban-Lon, Spunize is more common in carpets, upholstery fabrics, and industrial applications.

Gear Crimping

Gear crimping involves feeding yarns, under controlled tension, between intermeshing gears that impart a saw-tooth configuration to the filaments. Novelty textured yarns can be formed by this method as well as uniform crimped yarns (Fig. 19.4).

Knit-deknit Yarns

The knit-deknit process requires that filament yarns be knitted into a tube of fabric; the fabric is then subjected to heat to set the knit loops. After the knit loops are set, the fabric is deknitted and the filaments are rolled onto packages ready for use in making fabrics (Fig. 19.5). A variety of textured patterns can be obtained by using this method because the knit-deknit character can be heat set in irregular designs to make the yarns behave in an irregular manner.

Draw Texturizing

Draw texturizing is similar to false twist methods. The difference lies in the fact that the filaments to be used have not been completely oriented during fiber manufacture. These partially oriented yarns (POY) make it possible to reduce cost in the manufacture of textured yarns and produce yarns of high quality.

Draw texturizing combines the operation of drawing the filament fiber to orient the molecules and produce strength and the operation of texturizing.

This method is limited, primarily, to polyester fibers (see p. 104). Draw-textured yarns are said to have superior dyeability, a crisp hand, durable appearance, and good thermal stability.

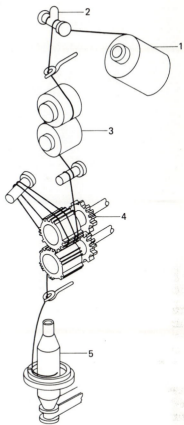

19.4 above. Diagram of gear crimping process for texturizing: 1. yarn supply. 2. Tension controls to maintain uniform yarn feed. 3. Thread advancing rolls, which pull yarn from supply and feed it to the texturizing area. 4. Gears used to produce crimp. 5. Take-up spindle.

19.5 left. Knitted tubing that has been heat set and is being deknitted to produce textured yarns. (Celanese Corporation).

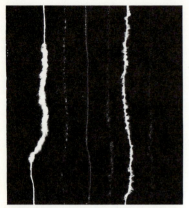

19.6 Taslan textured yarns made by air jet texturizing. These examples have been made to simulate complex yarns. (E. I. DuPont de Nemours & Company)

Air Jet Method

The air jet process is a highly refined rewinding operation that provides for a brief exposure of multifilament yarn to a turbulent stream of compressed air. One of the best known examples of this process is *Taslan*. The air jet process involves the exposure of the multifilament yarn to the concentrated jets of air that blow the filaments apart and form loops in each of the individual filament fibers. The resulting yarn is bulky, but it does not exhibit much stretch. Because no heat is involved, filament yarns of any type can be bulked by the air jet method.

This process has been successful on a wide variety of fibers. It works well on glass fiber yarns that are to be used for drapery fabrics. It is successful on any fiber that is in filament form when bulk is the characteristic desired. Taslan yarns have been made to simulate complex or fancy yarns by some manufacturers (Fig. 19.6).

Yarns that are bulked or textured by this method exhibit the following properties: a permanent change in the physical structure of the yarn; a unique appearance, hand, and texture; increased covering power; subdued luster; and low yarn strength and elongation processes.

Multicomponent Texturizing

Two different fiber types or modifications of a single generic type can be extruded simultaneously (see p. 29). Depending on the choice of components, it is possible to form fibers with various levels of crimp and, thus, with various levels of stretch or bulk. Cantrece nylon, Sayelle, and Wintuk acrylics are examples of multicomponent texturizing.

Spinnerette Modifications

A spiral or helical crimp can be introduced into filaments by modifying the shape of the spinnerette openings, changing the speed with which the fiber solution is forced or pulled through the spinnerette, or vibrating the spinnerette. Each of these produces textured yarns with characteristics similar to those obtained by other processes.

Stretch Yarns and Fabrics

The discussion of stretch is located in the yarn structure section of this book because most stretch products are the result either of yarns made from some elastomeric fiber or the texturizing of yarns to introduce stretch characteristics.

The concept of stretch originated in 1589, when the first knitted fabrics were introduced. Since that time knits have been an important method for creating fabrics that had some stretch. In the early part of this century researchers found that elasticity, or stretch, could be built into yarns by using some of the elastomeric or stretch fibers—either natural rubber filaments or, after the development of man-made elastic fibers, the elastomeric products.

The word *stretch* has not acquired a specific meaning. In modern terminology, a true stretch fabric has the ability to extend, or stretch, under tension plus the equally important capacity to return to its original length after release of strain. The degree of potential stretch, sometimes called elongation, varies from as little as 5 percent to as much as 500 percent. Most fabrics fall within the 10 to 25 percent category or the 30 to 50 percent range. In stretch fabrics this amount of elongation occurs at low amounts of pull or stress. Suggested standards from various testing organizations specify a load of 4 pounds per 2-inch-wide strip or 2 pounds per 1-inch-wide strip as the force to be used in determining the percent of stretch. It is generally held that any test specimens that fail to stretch 20 percent or more under the load or pull applied should not be called stretch fabrics. Figure 19.7 illustrates the test procedure used to determine the percent of stretch in any fabric.

Stretch fabrics are classified into two major categories: comfort stretch and power stretch. *Comfort stretch* describes stretch fabrics that go into clothing for everyday use with a stretch factor of up to about 25 percent. It also applies to fabrics used for home furnishings, such as slip covers and fitted sheets that have some stretch in the fabric. *Power stretch,* sometimes called action stretch, describes stretch fabrics that have more snap and muscle power, more extensibility, and quicker recovery than comfort stretch fabrics. The stretch factor generally ranges from 30 to 50 percent and is best adapted to various types of sportswear such as ski wear, swimwear, and other active sports apparel; to foundation garments; and to professional products that require a high level of stretch.

There is an area between these two types where there is overlap. Fabrics may have up to 40 percent stretch and still be designed primarily for comfort; they may be as low as 25 percent and still have some power. Comfort stretch is designed for use under low loads of stress such as 2 pounds per inch, whereas power stretch is designed for higher loads of stress.

Stretch can be imparted to textile products at varying stages of manufacture. It can be created by using elastomeric fibers; textured stretch yarns; fabric construction, such as knitting; and finishing processes. However, as noted, the most commonly encountered stage is at the yarn-manufacturing process, in which stretch can be introduced either as the result of elastomeric fibers or of textured stretch yarns.

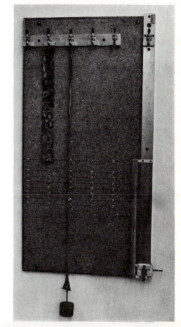

19.7 One sample with weight attached to measure amount of stretch.

Fiber Stretch

Stretch has been produced through the use of elastomeric rubber fibers since the early 1920s. Fine filaments of rubber were covered with cotton, rayon, or silk and then woven, knitted, or braided into fabrics with other yarns. Rubber core yarns were early examples of elasticity and stretch. Modern stretch core yarns usually depend on the presence of spandex fibers, which can be used in several ways to create stretch fabrics. They can be made into yarns in an uncovered or bare form; these are primarily power stretch end-use products or those demanding a high resistance to stress. Typical uses for yarns using bare spandex include elastic bandages and other medical products. Spandex or other elastomeric fibers can be made into core spun yarns (see p. 154) and used for either power or comfort stretch. Core spun yarns in which spandex has been used for the core make up a large proportion of the stretch yarns used in making power stretch end-use items. These yarns can be designed to have up to 500 percent stretch, 200 percent being fairly common. Characteristics of the final fabric depend mainly on the other fibers used and not on the spandex, except for the stretch property.

Spandex fibers are also used in *intimate blend* spinning. This use of spandex is limited but it does involve the cutting of spandex fibers into staple lengths and then blending these fibers with other staple fibers, such as cotton or polyester, and making yarns.

Bicomponent fibers may also provide some stretch; these filaments are designed to have a high degree of coil and, as a result, a high degree of stretch. The amount of stretch can be controlled by varying the amount of coiling that occurs as a result of the two modifications of the fiber.

As noted, even with the use of elastomeric fibers, the final stretch depends on the way these fibers have been constructed into yarns, and they cannot be used without some type of yarn structure.

Yarn Stretch

The majority of stretch products depend on yarn stretch. Although the use of elastomeric or stretch fibers has been discussed briefly in the preceding section, it has been emphasized that the presence of stretch in any end-use product in which elastomeric fibers are involved has been created through the use of yarns of some type. The other type of stretch yarn is the product of texturizing. The major processes used for texturizing that creates stretch yarns have been described in the preceding section. As noted, stretch can be developed by using many of the texturizing techniques; however, the two most important processes are false twisting and the knife edge process. The stuffer box process can introduce some stretch but it is relatively low compared with the other methods.

Stretch yarns can be used in making knitted, woven, or braided fabrics. Furthermore, stretch yarns in which heat-sensitive or thermoplastic fibers are present, in general, are more durable than stretch yarns using non-heat-sensitive fibers.

Fabric Stretch

Stretch can be introduced into fabric by the fabric construction process. The most satisfactory method, in this case, is knitting, which is discussed in Chapter 22. Knit fabrics have been popular for centuries because of their give, or stretch characteristics. However, unless the product has been well designed and engineered, knit fabrics may stretch during use and care. Thus, stretch created by the use of yarns is preferred.

Finishing Stretch

Some research has been directed toward the development of stretch in fabrics through various finishing procedures. This method has not been developed to any degree, and at the present it is doubtful if any stretch fabric is available that depends on finishing processes.

Textured Yarns in Use

Textured yarns are found in a wide variety of fabrics. They can be uniform in appearance or plied in special ways to resemble fancy or complex yarns. The major factors in the development and acceptance of textured yarns include comfort, appearance, and versatility.

Man-made fibers, primarily in filament form, often prove to be uncomfortable as apparel fabrics because the filaments pack together tightly and prevent the movement of moisture or air through the fabric. However, texturizing creates bulk and space between the filaments, so the yarn itself will absorb moisture and provide a greater degree of comfort. In addition, fabrics of textured yarns may be considerably warmer than those of smooth, closely packed yarns because the bulk acts as insulation.

Maintenance of fabrics made from textured yarns is basically the same as the care given the same fiber in any other form. The added moisture retention increases the drying time for these fabrics, but washing procedures are the same as for any fabric made from the particular fiber or fibers involved. The surface texture of these yarns are rougher than flat filaments, and they may be easily abraded or damaged from rubbing or snagging. Durability, apart from the potential for snagging and abrading, is the same as for any fabric made from the particular fiber. Care should be exercised in relation to the snagging problem because snagging can lead to broken filaments, and broken filaments increase the pilling that can occur, which reduces the attractive life of the product.

Stretch Yarns and Fabrics in Use

Stretch can be built into fabrics so that it occurs in either the horizontal (filling) direction or the vertical (warp) direction, or it can occur in both directions—commonly called two-way stretch. Most power stretch and action sportswear fabrics tend to be of the two-way stretch construction, whereas fabrics designed for comfort stretch tend to be the one-way type, using either the warp or filling direction.

Most stretch fabrics do not completely return to their original measurements after elongation. The difference between the original size and the measure after elongation (involving wear and care) is referred to as *growth* or *unrecovered stretch*. This growth is frequently eliminated in laundering, but it can lead to temporary, or in some cases permanent, deformation. A growth or increase in size of 2 to 3 percent would result in an unattractive product, especially when apparel items are involved. A maximum growth rate of 2 percent is considered standard.

Several research studies have examined stretch and identified the amount of stretch needed for various end uses. Studies related to apparel have been based on determining the amount the body stretches in various positions. Data from these studies have been summarized and provide the following recommendations:

Tailored clothing, 15 to 20 percent stretch
Spectator sportswear, 20 to 35 percent stretch
Active sportswear, 35 to 50 percent stretch
Stretch pants, 40 to 60 percent stretch

None of these items of apparel should have more than 5 percent unrecovered stretch, and the 2 percent indicated previously is considered best.

The problem of where and how stretch should be used has received considerable attention over the past fifteen years. Power stretch is involved for foundation garments, swimwear, active sportswear, and other items in which considerable holding power is required or considerable action is involved (Fig. 19.8). These apparel items require figure shaping as well as providing for considerable body movement. Although the amount of stretch should be relatively high, stretch should occur only when considerable force is exerted.

Considerable attention has been given to the potential for using comfort stretch in the manufacture of garments that are sized so that "one size fits all," but this policy is not generally accepted. Comfort stretch apparel items should be sized by using the same standards as those used for fabrics without stretch. Only in this way can comfort really be a part of each item for each individual.

Stretch fabrics have been used in a variety of applications other than apparel. They are used in items for home furnishings, particularly for upholstery and slipcover fabric (Fig. 19.9) and in some fitted sheets. Stretch fabrics provide a textile item that fits well, lies smoothly, and gives

19.8 Apparel for running with comfort stretch, a blend of polyester, cotton, and Lycra spandex. (E. I. DuPont de Nemours & Company)

19.9 Furniture covered with stretch fabric. (Turner, Ltd.)

a neat appearance. Stretch should be avoided in such home furnishings as curtains or draperies where the weight of the fabric could stretch the product out of shape.

Stretch fabrics are used in a variety of medical and therapeutic products such as bandages and support hose.

Stretch has never quite reached the potential expected during the 1970s. However, it is used in a variety of items where it can provide the following characteristics: comfort, good fit, retention of shape, design flexibility, psychological appeal, wrinkle resistance, attractive appearance, longer wear, and reduced seam puckering.

Study Questions

1. List and describe at least four techniques or processes used in producing textured yarns.
2. Which of the processes used to make textured yarns is the most frequently used?
3. Which texturizing process can be used on yarns that are not heat sensitive or thermoplastic?
4. What special, if any, procedures should be used in the care of textured yarns?
5. Why is texturizing important? Are consumers really aware that yarn has been texturized? If not, why not?
6. What is the most often used process for producing stretch in fabrics?
7. How can stretch be developed in fabrics and end-use items?
8. What are the differences between action and comfort stretch?
9. What is unrecoverd stretch? What limits should be placed on it for apparel that is to remain attractive?
10. How much stretch should be provided for various types of apparel items?
11. Why should manufacturers avoid making products of stretch that have not been sized properly?
12. Identify properties or characteristics of textured yarns that influence care that the product can receive. Repeat for stretch yarns and fabrics.

Blends and Combination Yarns and Fabrics

20

Blends and combination yarns and fabrics are those in which two or more generic types of fibers are used. These different types of fibers can be combined in the following ways:

1. Two or more different types of fibers can be blended into a single yarn.
2. Single yarns, where each single is of a different fiber type, can be plied together to form a combination ply yarn.
3. Single or ply yarns of one fiber type can be used with single or ply yarns of another fiber type and woven, knitted, braided, or knotted into a fabric. As many different fiber types as desired can be used, but each single yarn would be of the same fiber content.

The accepted definition of a blend as stated by ASTM is "a blended yarn is a single yarn spun from a blend or mixture of different fiber species"; a combination yarn is defined as a "ply yarn twisted from single yarns of different fibers."*

These definitions support the first two items in the preceding list. One of the major difficulties in definitions and in understanding blend and combination fabrics is that many manufacturers and consumers believe that all fabrics in which two or more fibers have been used are *blend* fabrics. Labeling does not help, and the TFPIA requires only that the fibers present in a fabric be identified; it does not require that any information be given concerning how the fibers are arranged in that fabric.

Fortunately most fabrics manufactured today with two or more fibers are blends. It is important, however, to identify possible combinations, particularly in woven fabrics, that represent combination fabrics of either the second or third type just listed. Woven fabrics may be constructed by using single yarns of one fiber in the warp direction and single yarns of a second fiber in the filling direction. Another type of combination occurs when a blend yarn is used in one direction of the woven fabric and a single fiber type yarn is used in the other direction. Fabrics in which blended yarns are used throughout the construction are more likely to give desired performance characteristics during use and care than fabrics made with single yarns of one specific fiber but with different fibers used in different yarns.

Knit fabrics may be a true blend; they may be made from a combination of yarns of different fiber types; or they may be made of ply yarns, each with a single component of different fiber types. The typical knit fabric with two or more fibers has been made from true blend yarns; however, as with all textile products exceptions are found on the market. Again,

---

*ASTM, *Annual Book of ASTM Standards,* Vol. 07.01, 1985, p. 76.

care and performance may be somewhat different for knits made from blended yarns and those that represent combinations.

Nonwoven fabrics of two or more fiber types will be blends because the fiber types must be mixed together before the fabric is actually made.

Blended fiber fabrics may be made from a variety of proportions of each of the fibers involved. A typical fiber blend is cotton and polyester, and the amount of each may vary widely. Cotton may exceed the polyester, they may be equal, or the polyester may exceed the cotton. Amounts found in fabric in 1986 varied from 20 percent cotton and 80 percent polyester to 80 percent cotton and 20 percent polyester. The most typical blends of these two fibers are the 50/50 blend, or the 65 percent polyester and 35 percent cotton. The properties of fabrics that are most influenced by the various percentages of fibers include comfort and ease of care. The more cotton in a blend the more comfortable the fabric, whereas more polyester increases the ease of care.

For a majority of blends on the market, optimum percentages have been established for the fibers involved. For example, textile scientists generally agree that in blends of polyester and cotton, the percentage of cotton should range between 35 and 50 percent if the fabric is to combine the properties of easy care, durability, and comfort. If easy care and durability only are most important, the polyester component might be as high as 80 percent; when comfort is the most important factor, cotton may reach the 80 percent level.

A blend of 55 percent acrylic with 45 percent wool, or a blend of 50 to 65 percent polyester and 35 to 50 percent wool, results in fabrics that provide comfort, can be washed instead of dry cleaned, and give good durability. A fabric in which as little as 12 to 15 percent nylon is blended with 85 to 88 percent wool and given proper finishing is considered to be a washable wool fabric, providing it is handled carefully. In addition, the nylon increases the resistance of the fabric to abrasion damage and helps prevent a high loss in strength that might occur because of the effect of the finishing processes on the wool fiber.

Blends can be developed to provide consumers with special performance characteristics and/or to meet predetermined end-use requirements. They may be designed specifically for appearance, to combine appearance and performance, to emphasize easy care, to attract consumers who want to buy luxury fibers for prestige but who can only afford small amounts, to reduce cost, or to provide durable-press and easy care properties. Some typical examples of blend fabrics and the reasons often posed for their development include the following: polyester and cotton to provide easy care, durability, and comfort; rayon and acetate to provide appearance and draping qualities; silk, vicuna, and cashmere to add prestige; linen with rayon or polyester to provide stiffness and appearance. Table 20.1 indicates some of the properties that various fibers may impart to a blend.

A variety of blends have been available in the market, with new blends appearing each year. Ramie is being used in blends, particularly in fabrics imported from the Far East. A variety of fibers are used in curtain and drapery fabrics. Modacrylics may be used to increase flame resistance; rayon and acetate, to improve draping qualities; polyester and cotton, for durability and ease of care.

Blends or combination fiber fabrics are the result of considerable research, development, and testing. Instead of developing new fibers, manufacturers during the past fifteen years have concentrated on mixing or blending different fibers to produce yarns and fabrics with desirable properties. A blend that has been properly engineered exhibits properties that represent the best of each fiber involved.

TABLE 20.1 Properties of Fibers Used in Blends

Property	Acetate	Acrylic	Cotton	Modacrylic	Nylon	Olefin	Polyester	Rayon	Wool
Abrasion Resistance	d	d	c	c	a	a	a	d	b
Absorbency	c	d	a	d	d	d	d	a	a
Bulk and Loft	d	a	d	a	d	d	d	d	a
Press Retention	c	c	d	c	b	c	a	d	c
Resistance to Heat	b	b	a	d	c	d	c	a	b
Resistance to Pilling	a	d	a	d	c	b	d	a	c
Stability	a	a	b	a	a	a	a	d	d
Strength	c	c	b	c	a	a	a	c	c
Wrinkle Recovery	b	b	d	b	b	b	a	d	a

Key: a, superior; b, good; c, average; d, poor.

Combination fabrics and yarns may produce outstanding results if the combining process creates yarns with properties that work well together. In the case of a combination yarn using two or more singles, each of a different fiber type, the fabric may give outstanding use and be easy to care for. When made into fabric, the yarns should give good wear and performance. The major problem with combination fabrics occurs when the yarns in one direction are of one type of fiber and the yarns in the perpendicular direction are of a different fiber type. Such combinations can produce fabrics that give poor performance; they may wrinkle badly in one direction or both; they may shrink in one direction or both; and they may require complicated care procedures.

Strength is introduced into combination fiber fabrics by using yarns of high breaking load in the direction that requires extra resistance to force or by spacing strong yarns among yarns of low tenacity fibers. Strong fibers will increase resistance to breaking. Fibers may also be chosen because of their elongation and elastic recovery. Fabrics in which spandex fibers have been used to provide a high level of elongation and elastic recovery are often made from core yarns, which, technically, are combination yarns; further, the spandex may be used in one direction only.

Blends and combination fiber fabrics are usually produced for special end uses in which the fabric can be designed to bring out the very best of each of the fiber's properties. However, it is possible to manufacture some fabrics that are not suitable for chosen end uses; in such cases consumers are seldom satisfied with their purchases.

It is particularly important for the fiber content to be clearly identified. Although fiber content labels do not indicate how the fibers are used—a blend or a combination—they do provide some help in determining the care procedures.

The following example using polyester and rayon fibers illustrates why a combination might be less desirable than a blend. If polyester and rayon fibers have been carefully blended, the entire fabric should perform the same, and in general, such a fabric has a good appearance, is easy to care for, and has adequate strength and dimensional stability. However, if the fabric is a combination in which polyester fibers are used in the warp direction and rayon fibers are used in the filling direction, performance might well be poor. For example, although the polyester yarns help provide easy care and good appearance, the rayon yarns might shrink and/or wrinkle, which would create a very unattractive product.

Consumers should notify retailers and/or manufacturers when merchandise does not perform as desired. Such reporting helps to inform manufacturers about what does or does not work in a combination or a blended fiber fabric. Also, it could provide backup information that might, ultimately, require labeling to identify blends or combination fiber fabrics.

Study Questions

1. Define a blend yarn and a combination yarn.
2. Describe a blend fabric and a combination fiber fabric.
3. How might blended fiber fabrics and combination fiber fabrics differ in performance? Why?
4. How might blended fiber fabrics and combination fiber fabrics differ in care procedures used? Why?
5. Indicate some of the recommended levels of selected fibers in a blend and the advantages or disadvantages of each.
6. What are the reasons for the popularity of blends of polyester and cotton? What proportion of each fiber is typically found in these fabrics? Why?

Fabric Construction

Fibers, yarns, layers of fabrics, and combinations of these are combined in different ways to produce the wide variety of fabrics available to the consumer. Part IV describes the various processes used in the manufacture of fabrics.

fabrics from one thread

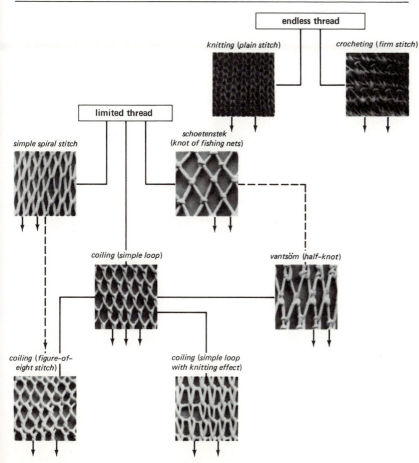

endless thread

knitting (plain stitch)

crocheting (firm stitch)

limited thread

simple spiral stitch

schoetenstek
(knot of fishing nets)

coiling (simple loop)

vantsöm (half-knot)

coiling (figure-of-
eight stitch)

coiling (simple loop
with knitting effect)

IV.1 Examples of early fabrics made from one continuous yarn, such as knitted or knotted fabrics. (*Ciba Review*)

179

Woven fabrics are discussed in Chapter 21. Knitted fabrics are described in Chapter 22. Chapter 23 is devoted to information concerning the production of fabrics directly from fibers, and Chapter 24 describes various other types of techniques used in producing fabrics including knotting, braiding, and multicomponent structures.

Figures IV.1 and IV.2 illustrate a number of time-honored methods of fabric construction. Fabrics can be knitted, knotted, and coiled from one yarn; or they may be made using two or more sets of yarn by weaving, plaiting, and tapestry methods. Many of the methods of producing fabrics that have been used in the past are still in use today; the difference lies in modern technology which makes it possible to create a variety of fabrics in less time than older methods required.

IV.2 Examples of early fabrics made from several yarns including plaited and braided fabrics. (*Ciba Review*)

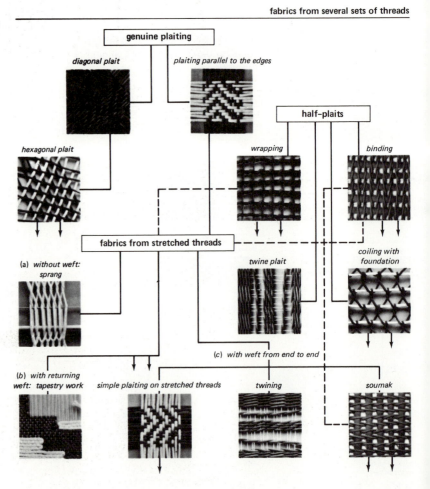

fabrics from several sets of threads

genuine plaiting

diagonal plait

plaiting parallel to the edges

half–plaits

hexagonal plait

wrapping

binding

(a) *without weft: sprang*

fabrics from stretched threads

twine plait

coiling with foundation

(c) *with weft from end to end*

(b) *with returning weft: tapestry work*

simple plaiting on stretched threads

twining

soumak

Woven Fabrics

21

Weaving is one of the oldest arts known. Though no actual looms from early civilizations have survived, fabrics of fine quality have been found in various archeological excavations. Fabrics were discovered in the tombs of ancient Egypt, in the Swiss lake region of Europe, and in excavations of early American Indians such as the Anasazi. Illustrations on pottery and other art forms have testified to the fact that weaving is a very old art. One illustration found on a pottery vase, dated during the fifth century B.C., shows the use of an early loom of that period and, further, depicts part of the legend of Odysseus and Penelope, his wife. While Odysseus was traveling for Greece, Penelope refused to marry anyone else despite the demands of her family. She started weaving a *winding* sheet for her father-in-law and promised that she would not marry again until that sheet was finished. During the day she continued to weave, but each night she would unravel everything she had done. At last, betrayed by a servant, she was compelled to finish the shroud and choose a suitor. But Odysseus returned just before the fateful decision had to be made, and the two were reunited. Figure 21.1 is an illustration of Penelope seated at the loom.

Early looms were very crude compared with modern mechanical weaving equipment. Nonetheless, all looms, old and new alike, have the same basic principles in their operation. There is a system to hold the warp yarns under tension, there is a way to spread yarns apart so that the

21.1 Vertical warp-weighted loom. Penelope at her loom, Greek, 5th century B.C. (Chiusi Museum, Italy)

crosswise thread can be placed through the opening or shed, and there is a device to pack the crosswise threads tightly together.

Woven fabrics consist of sets of yarns interlaced at right angles in established sequences. The yarns that run parallel to the selvage, or to the longer dimension of a bolt (or length) of fabric, are called the *warp yarns* or *ends;* those that run the crosswise dimension of the fabric are called *filling yarns, weft yarns, woof yarns,* or *picks. Warp* and *filling* are the terms found most often in discussions of woven fabrics for consumer goods. The terms *ends* and *picks* are used by the industry.

Until the early nineteenth century weaving was primarily a hand process. In the late 1700s and early 1800s scientists and inventors such as Joseph-Marie Jacquard and Edmund Cartwright developed weaving looms that were partially machine powered. Soon scientists had developed looms that were entirely power driven. During the nineteenth and early twentieth centuries, developments in weaving involved the addition of automatic features to existing looms to increase the speed of operation and reduce the frequency and amount of damage due to faulty functioning.

The twentieth century, particularly since mid-century, has seen tremendous advances in the technology of weaving. Looms that are faster, wider, and more efficient than previous equipment are becoming commonplace in the textile industry. These looms use various methods to lay the filling or pick yarns as well as improved technology to increase the speed of weaving and the width of the woven fabric as it emerges from the loom. These improvements are described, in brief, following the description of the basic weaving process.

Basic Weaving Technology

The parts of the basic loom are shown in Figure 21.2. The *warp beam* holds the lengthwise yarns and is located at the back of the loom; this beam is controlled so that it releases yarn to the loom as it is needed. The *heedles* are wires or metal strips with an eye located in the center through which the warp ends are threaded. The *harness* is the frame that holds the heedles in position. Each loom has at least two harnesses; a majority of looms for regular fabrics have four to twelve harnesses, and some looms may have as many as thirty-two. Harnesses can be raised or lowered to produce the *shed* through which the filling yarn is passed and,

21.2 Diagram showing a simple loom.

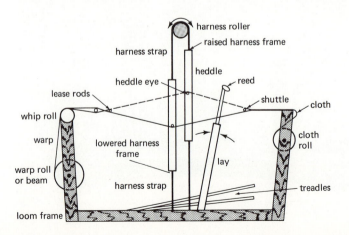

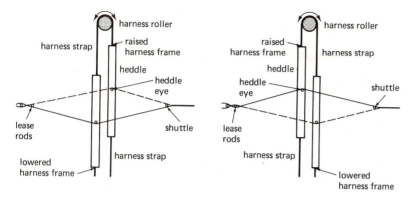

21.3 Movement of harnesses and warp yarns to form a shed.

thus, control the pattern of the weave (Fig. 21.3). The *shuttle* moves back and forth in the sheds created, passing the filling yarns between the warp yarns. The *reed* is a comblike device that helps to pack the filling yarns into position in the woven fabric. The openings in the reed through which the warp yarns are threaded are called *dents;* they maintain the warp yarns in a systematic relation and prevent yarns from tangling during the weaving process. The *cloth beam* is located at the front of the loom and holds the completed fabric. Regardless of the complexity of a loom, the method of weaving depends on these loom parts and on the following four basic weaving steps.

1. *Shedding* is the raising and lowering of the warp ends, by means of the heedles and harnesses, to form the shed of the loom so that the filling yarns can be passed from one side of the loom to the other. Filling yarns can be carried by a shuttle, a jet of water, a jet of air, a metal arm called a rapier, or a metal projectile or gripper.
2. *Picking* is the actual process of placing the filling yarn into the shed. The shuttle or other device moves the yarn across the shed, placing the pick or filling yarn as it goes.
3. *Battening,* sometimes called beating, beating in, or beating up, consists of evenly packing the filling yarns into position in the fabric.
4. *Taking up and letting off* involves taking up the newly manufactured fabric onto the cloth beam and letting off or releasing yarn from the warp beam. The operation maintains uniform distance and tension from warp beam to harness to completed cloth.

   Many fabrics are woven on looms with two to four harnesses; however, fabrics with woven-in designs require special looms or methods for controlling individual warp yarns. These complex looms differ only in the way in which sheds are formed and not in the general principles involved in weaving.

Looms: The State of the Art of Weaving

Shuttle Looms

For many centuries the basic loom used a shuttle as the means of placing or laying the filling yarn into position in the shed. Shuttle looms have reached a high level of efficiency and make fabric rapidly with a minimum number of flaws. The number of harnesses on shuttle looms can vary from two to thirty-two. Depending on the number of harnesses and the method

21.4 Example of loom with a shuttle. Note arm at right that hits shuttle across the shed. (Picanol)

for controlling the warp yarns, fabrics of nearly every type of weave can be made: plain, twill, satin, dobby, Jacquard, and others.

The shuttle (Fig. 21.4) moves across the shed and places a filling yarn in position. The shuttle stops at the opposite side, the shed is changed, and the shuttle returns to the previous location; the process is repeated until the fabric is completed. Shuttle looms are extremely noisy, as the hammer or bar that knocks the shuttle across the shed makes considerable noise each time it hits the shuttle. The width of fabric woven on shuttle looms is usually between 36 and 54 inches, partly because of the distance the shuttle can be moved by the shuttle hammer.

Although shuttle looms are still widely used, newer methods of weaving fabric are becoming increasingly important, and as weaving mills modernize and replace old, worn-out equipment, most mills are replacing shuttle looms with various types of shuttleless looms.

Shuttleless Looms

Shuttleless looms use some type of device, other than a shuttle, to place the filling yarn into position in the shed. These shuttleless looms are very fast, operate with less noise, and can weave fabrics as wide as 200 inches. The typical width for many shuttleless looms is between 72 and 110 inches.

Projectile looms   The projectile loom uses a small metal gripper that takes yarn from the supply package or source and carries it across the shed. Only sufficient yarn for the width of the fabric is carried across. There are two major types of projectile looms: One uses a single projectile that carries the yarn across, waits for the beating in of the filling yarn, and then picks up yarn from a supply source on that side of the loom and returns with that yarn to lay a second pick and start the operation over again. The most common projectile loom, however, uses multiple projectiles. Each one carries yarn for one pick and then falls into a conveyor system to be carried back to the side where the filling yarn supply is located. Figure 21.5 shows a projectile loom.

21.5 Projectible shuttleless weaving machine. (Springs Industries)

Rapier looms In the rapier system a metal arm carries yarn to the center of the weaving area, where the yarn is transferred to a second metal arm to be pulled across the remainder of the fabric width. Rapiers may be rigid or flexible. Some new rapier looms are designed to weave two distinct fabrics with the same rapier system. The rapier picks up yarn from the center between the two fabrics and carries it across one weaving area; as it finishes laying that pick, the opposite end of the rapier picks up another yarn from the center and moves back across the surface to lay a pick on the other half of the machine (Fig. 21.6).

Rapier machines are faster than shuttle looms but not as fast as projectile looms. However, they permit great flexibility in weaving designs, particularly in color. They are very effective in weaving fabrics 110 inches or more in width.

Jet weaving Jet looms lay the pick yarns by either a jet of air under pressure or a jet of water under pressure. The most popular are air jet looms. The air or water under pressure pulls sufficient yarn from the supply pack-

21.6 Two-phase rapier weaving machine. (Saurer Textile Machinery)

21.7 above. Air jet weaving machine. (Saurer Textile Machinery)
21.8 below. Modern weaving room with air jet weaving machine. Note protective coverings over filling yarn supply, used to reduce lint in the air. (Springs Industries)

age and then carries it across the shed. Supplemental air or water jets are placed along the shed area of the loom and serve to maintain the speed of placing the yarns in position. These jet looms are the fastest types available; they are less noisy than other types of looms; and there is little damage to filling yarns because there is no abrasion of the yarns during placement (Fig. 21.7).

Modern weaving rooms are well lighted. Lint is removed by various types of vacuum systems to maintain a relatively healthy environment, and the use of shuttleless looms has reduced the noise pollution to a great degree (Fig. 21.8). However, note that weaving fabrics does involve a noise level above that considered desirable for most working conditions.

Shuttleless looms result in fabrics without the selvage system that is found in fabrics woven with shuttle looms. These selvages can be made to look very similar to the consumer through the use of systems that tuck in the yarns at the edges of the fabric; or the yarn ends can be left so that the fabric has a ravel edge (Fig. 21.9).

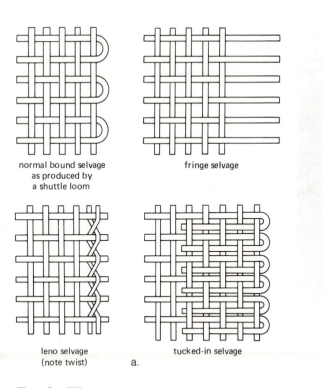

normal bound selvage
as produced by
a shuttle loom

fringe selvage

leno selvage
(note twist)   a.

tucked-in selvage

b.

21.9 a. Traditional selvage edges and selvage from some shuttleless looms. b. Fabric with fringe selvage.

Basic Weaves

Plain Weaves

Plain-weave fabrics can be produced from looms with two harnesses only or from looms with any even number of harnesses so they can be arranged to duplicate a two-harness loom in operation. The plain weave is the simplest form of weaving. It consists of the alternate interlacing of warp and filling yarns, one warp up, the other down, the entire width of the fabric (Figs. 21.10 and 21.11). This process is referred to as a 1/1 weave. In Figure 21.10 the black squares indicate that the warp yarn is on the surface (top side, or the face) of the fabric. The squares paralleling the verti-

21.10 left. Point diagram of a plain weave.
21.11 right. A plain-weave fabric.

cal direction of the diagram can be visualized as the warp yarns, whereas the horizontal rows represent the filling yarns.

The plain-weave interlacing is probably the major method used in weaving fabrics. The fabric as constructed is reversible, but the addition of special finishes, prints, or other surface designs gives a face, or right side, to some fabrics in terms of use. Considerable plain-weave fabric is reversible.

Yarns can be packed loosely or compactly in plain weaves. The warp yarns may equal the filling yarn in number per inch of fabric; this is considered a balanced plain-weave fabric. The number of yarns in one direction of the plain-weave fabric may be considerably greater than the number in the other direction; this is called an unbalanced fabric. The warp yarns may exceed the filling yarns in number per inch, or the filling may exceed the warp yarns in number.

Plain-weave fabrics are considered relatively inexpensive, yet they often are the most durable. Because of the uniformity possible in making plain-weave construction, this weave is the most common for making fabrics that are to be given print designs or special finishes.

Woven fabrics vary, depending on the number of yarns per inch in both the warp and filling directions. This property is known as the yarn or thread count and it is important in describing fabrics. It helps determine desirable end uses for the fabric, and it gives some information concerning how close the yarns are in each direction. This, in turn, provides information on the appearance, flexibility, compactness, density, and performance of woven fabrics.

Examples of plain-weave fabrics include muslin, percale, print cloth, cheesecloth, chambray, gingham, batiste, lawn, organdy, linen toweling, chiffon, challis, china silk, and some wool tweeds (Fig. 21.12).

Rib variation of the plain weave   An interesting modification of the plain weave is the rib weave, in which yarns in one direction give the appearance of being heavier, bulkier, or thicker than the yarns in the other direction. A diagram of the rib variation is identical to that of the regular plain weave. The rib appearance is produced by using such methods as inserting heavier yarns in the filling direction than those used in the warp; inserting groups of yarns in either the warp or filling so that the group of yarns produces a raised or rib appearance; and having more warp yarns per inch than filling yarns and having these packed tightly together so they create a raised effect in the fabric, giving the appearance of a rib.

Many rib-weave fabrics are made by inserting heavy filling yarns. Examples of this rib construction include fabrics identified as poplin, faille, bengaline, and ottoman. Dimity (Fig. 21.13) is constructed by alternating fine and heavy yarns at planned intervals in either the warp, the filling, or both directions. When such alternation is used in both warp and filling, the fabric is identified as a cross-bar dimity. The rib in dimity may also be created by placing several yarns together as though they were laying a single filling yarn.

Some tissue ginghams are made with this rib variation. Broadcloth, commonly found in men's shirts and women's blouses, is formed by a highly unbalanced yarn count in which there are many more warp yarns per inch than filling yarns.

The size of the rib is frequently used as one means of identifying the particular type of fabric. Rib-weave fabrics listed in order from a very fine rib to a relatively heavy rib include broadcloth, poplin, faille, grosgrain, bengaline, and ottoman.

21.12 above.   Example of plain-weave fabrics.

21.13 below.   Dimity, a rib variation of the plain weave.

  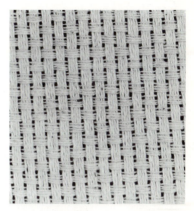

21.14 above left. Point diagram of a 2×2 basket weave.
21.15 above center. A basket-weave fabric.
21.16 above right. A 4×4 monk's cloth, a basket-weave fabric.

Basket variation of the plain weave   The basket weave is defined as having two or more warp yarns interlaced as a unit with one or more filling yarns. This construction is not as firm as either the regular plain weave or the rib modification; basket-weave fabrics, therefore, frequently have lower strength than other plain-weave fabrics. However, basket weaves are attractive and have interesting surface effects. A basket variation in which two warps pass over and under one filling, the simplest type of basket weave, is identified as a 2x1 basket weave. Other examples of basket-weave fabrics include interlacings of 2x2, 2x4, and 3x2 (Figs. 21.14 and 21.15).

Oxford cloth, frequently found in shirting fabrics, is an example of a 2x1 basket weave. In oxford cloth, the two warp yarns are equal in size to the one filling yarn. Some authorities have classified oxford cloth as a separate modification of the plain-weave construction, but technically it is a basket-weave modification because the two warp yarns are handled as one and lay flat in the construction.

Monk's cloth is one of the best known examples of the basket-weave modification (Fig. 21.16). It is available in such even arrangements as 2x2, 3x3, 4x4, and 8x8; in uneven arrangements it can be found in such groupings as 4x3 and 2x3. Coarse yarns are usually used in making monk's cloth, and frequently it is left a "natural" color, which is usually a light tan or cream.

A problem that consumers may encounter in basket-weave fabrics is a tendency toward yarn slippage. Because of the relatively loose weave, yarns may slip and tend to pack together where they should not. End uses where basket-weave fabrics may be encountered include coat and suit fabrics, particularly of wool; hopsacking, used in home furnishings; monk's cloth, used in home furnishings such as draperies and bedspreads; and duck, used in sportswear and for canvas.

Other plain-weave modifications   Variations can be produced in plain-weave fabrics without using any of the modifications just described. These design effects can be achieved by using complex yarns in the interlacing, at either regular or irregular intervals; using yarns of different fiber content; using yarns with different amounts of twist; using different colored yarns; and using yarns of different sizes. High-twist yarns can be used in the plain-weave structure to produce crepe fabrics; low-twist yarns may be used for making fabrics that are to be napped during finishing operations. Additional modifications can be made by varying the space between the yarns.

Consumers should be aware that plain-weave fabrics are usually maintained according to the fiber content of the fabric. However, other factors that influence care procedures include the amount of space between yarns—large spaces result in yarn slippage and snagging; the type of yarn construction involved—simple or complex; and various coloring processes and finishes. Durability is related to the number of yarns per inch, the type and size of yarns used, the type of fiber or fibers used, and finishes and coloring methods.

Twill Weave

The second basic weave is the twill. This technique is characterized by a diagonal line on the face of the fabric, and frequently this diagonal is visible on the back of the fabric as well. The diagonal can vary from a low 14° angle, called a *reclining twill,* to a 75° angle, called a *steep twill*. The most common twill is at 45°, and this is identified as a *regular twill* or *medium twill*. The angle is determined either by the closeness of the warp ends or filling picks or by the number of yarns and the actual pattern of repeat.

Twill-weave fabrics have a distinctive and attractive appearance, although some fine twill weaves are very faint and difficult to identify as twill weaves. Twills differ from the plain-weave construction in the number of harnesses required for weaving, which in turn, affects the number of filling picks and warp ends required for the particular interlacing pattern. The simple plain weave requires two filling and two warp yarns to complete the repeat pattern; the simple twill weave requires three filling picks and three warp ends (Fig. 21.17).

A ⅔ twill (Fig. 21.18) is an example of a simple twill; it requires the warp yarn to pass or float over two filling yarns and then under one filling yarn to form the basic repeat. At least three filling picks will be inserted before the interlacing repeats, with a filling going over and under the same warp yarns. In a regular twill each succeeding float begins one pick higher or lower than the adjacent float. In more complicated twills the progression may vary, but the diagonal effect will remain visible. The number of pick yarns required to complete the twill pattern determines the number of harnesses required for the loom. There must be at least three, and some twill patterns may require as many as fifteen harnesses.

Twill-weave fabrics have either a right-hand or a left-hand diagonal (Figs. 21.19 and 21.20). If the diagonal moves from the upper right to the lower left of the fabric, when viewing it in a longitudinal direction, it is re-

21.17 above. Point diagram of a 2/1 right-hand twill.
21.18 below. A 2/1 twill-weave fabric.

21.19 left. A point diagram of a 2/2 right-hand twill.
21.20 right. A left-hand twill fabric.

ferred to as right-hand twill; if it moves from the upper left to the lower right, it is a left-hand twill. Twill weaves may be either even or uneven; in even twills the filling yarns pass over and under the same number of warp yarns, whereas in uneven twills the filling yarns pass over either more or fewer warp ends than they go under. Uneven twill fabrics do have a right and wrong side (a face and a back); therefore, they are not considered reversible (Fig. 21.21). Even twills, unless altered by finishing or coloring processes, can be reversible.

The twill weave permits packing yarns closer together because of the fewer interlacings per inch than found in plain-weave fabrics. This close packing can produce strong, durable fabrics; but if the yarns are packed too closely, the fabric will have reduced breaking and tearing strength, abrasion resistance, and wrinkle recovery.

Twill weaves provide consumers with attractive, durable fabrics, and maintenance is not difficult; further, twill-weave structures tend to show soil less quickly than plain-weave fabrics because soil will tend to lodge between the diagonal lines. Twill weaves are frequently more expensive than plain-weave fabrics, probably because of the increased costs of manufacture, increased amount of raw materials used, and the difference in fiber costs.

Examples of twill-weave fabrics include denim, drill, jean, covert, gabardine, foulard, serge, surah, wool broadcloth, wool sharkskin, some flannel, and some wool tweeds.

Herringbone variation　A common variation of the twill weave is the herringbone structure. This pattern is made by reversing the direction of the twill at frequent intervals to form a series of Vs (Figs. 21.22 and 21.23).

Satin Weave

Satin-weave fabrics are characterized by yarns that float (pass over) over several yarns laid in the opposite, or perpendicular, position. These yarns usually float over a minimum of four yarns, and frequently the number is seven or more. The floating yarns are arranged so that parallel yarns do not interlace in a position of contact. This reduces the possibility of a diagonal effect occurring on the face of the fabric. Although either warp or filling yarns may float over the perpendicular yarns, acceptable terminology identifies fabrics where warp yarns are the floaters as *satin* fabrics, whereas those in which the filling yarns do the floating are called *sateen* fabrics. Satin fabrics are chosen for their attractive appearance, particularly their sheen; filament fibers are used, primarily, in the yarns combined to make these fabrics, particularly satin fabrics. Sateen fabrics tend to be selected for special characteristics other than sheen; thus, yarns made from staple length fibers are more typical than filament fibers for such fabrics.

The long floats in the satin weave help to create a shiny surface, which tends to reflect light. This effect is accentuated if bright filament fibers are used in making the yarns; further, yarns with a low amount of twist, as few as one or two turns per inch, tend to be used for satins.

Floats in satin structures tend to snag easily, which may result in a rough fabric surface and in reduced strength and, thus, a reduction in durability. In general, satin-weave fabrics are not considered as durable as twill- or plain-weave fabrics, especially when the number of yarns per inch is the same.

Two factors govern the length of the floats in either satin or sateen fabrics. The major control is the number of harnesses available for use, which determines the number of filling yarns over which the warp yarns

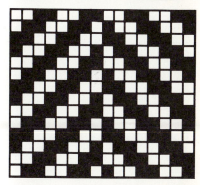

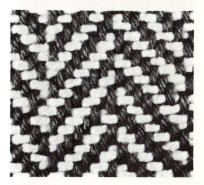

21.21 top.　Face of an uneven twill fabric.

21.22 center.　Point diagram of a herringbone twill, a variation of the twill weave.

21.23 bottom.　A herringbone twill-weave fabric.

21.24 left. Point diagram of a five-shaft satin weave.
21.25 right. A five-shaft satin-weave fabric.

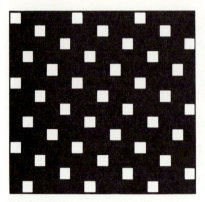

float. Other factors include the number of filling yarns and the number of warp yarns per inch and the size of the yarns used. A fabric with a high yarn count per inch will typically have shorter floats than one with a low yarn count.

The simplest satin- or sateen-weave fabrics require a minimum of five harnesses on the loom. This number produces what is called a ¼ weave or a ⁴⁄₁ weave; more complex satins and sateens may have ⁷⁄₁ or ¹⁄₇ weaves. The ¼ or ⁴⁄₁ satin weaves are called *five-shaft* satins or sateens, whereas the ¹⁄₇ or ⁷⁄₁ are eight-shaft satins or sateens. Figure 21.24 is a diagram of a ⁴⁄₁ satin in which the warp end floats over four filling yarns and under one. Figure 21.25 is an example of a five-shaft satin fabric. Because of the small number of yarns involved in this type of satin construction, there is often the appearance of a twill effect on the fabric surface. However, if the fabric is studied carefully, it can be seen that adjacent warp yarns do not go under adjacent filling yarns even in the diagonal direction. Satins made with eight or more yarns in the repeat pattern have sufficient distance between a repeating interlacing so that the twill effect is minimized.

Satin-weave fabrics are lustrous and attractive. People select them for their appearance and smoothness. Because of the smooth surface, satin fabrics are frequently used for lining coats and suits because they make it easy to slip the garment on or off over other materials. Satin and sateen fabrics have a definite face and back. Examples of satin-weave fabrics include antique satin, slipper satin, faille satin, bridal satin, moleskin, and Venetian satin. The typical fabric made with the sateen weave is called, simply, a sateen, or it may be used in making heavily napped fabrics.

Satins may be made in a wide variety of weights and can be used in apparel and a variety of home-furnishing fabrics. Heavy satins are frequently used for furniture upholstery. During 1985 and 1986 a fashion trend utilized highly lustrous satin fabrics for a wide variety of apparel items from bathing suits to evening gowns.

Crepe-backed satins   Fabrics identified either as a crepe-back satin or a satin-back crepe combine the satin weave with highly twisted yarns in such a manner that one side of the fabric has the characteristics of a satin structure and the other side has the appearance of a crepe fabric. These are usually made with highly twisted yarns in the filling direction. Either side of the fabric can be used as the face, or right side.

Decorative or Figure Weaves

Decorative or figure weaves may also be called fancy weaves or complex weaves. The major purpose of the name is to identify fabrics that have some type of design built into them as a part of the weaving operation. These weaves are formed by introducing changes in the interlacing patterns at various locations within the fabric construction. These weaves require some type of special control of the warp yarns to provide sheds that are not repetitious such as found in plain-, twill-, or satin-weave processes. These special controls may involve control of harnesses, such as used for dobby weaves; control of individual warp yarns, such as used for Jacquard weaves; or other types of controls that make it possible to weave in a variety of designs.

Dobby Weaves

Dobby fabrics have small figures, such as dots, geometric designs, and small floral patterns, woven into the fabric (Fig. 21.26). These decorative weaves are made with small patterns that repeat frequently. Looms for making dobby weaves require special attachments that permit individual control of each harness; the number of harnesses required will vary depending on the complexity of the dobby design, from as few as eight to as many as thirty-two. The control on the loom may be a dobby pattern chain, special pattern rolls that resemble the music for a player piano, or computer controls that direct the operation of the harnesses. Figure 21.27 is an example of a loom with a dobby attachment that is made of a pattern

21.26 Dobby-weave fabrics.

21.27 A loom with a dobby attachment. (Springs Industries)

sheet much like the roll for a player piano. Each horizontal line in the pattern sheet identifies which harnesses are to be raised or lowered at the same time to make a shed for the placement of a filling pick. Pattern rolls such as this may be made of plastic, metal, or heavy-duty paper. Originally the pattern roll was often made of wood strips fastened together by a chain so they could move around the control board. Many dobby looms today depend on computer controls, which send directions directly to the harnesses and which do not require the older type of mechanical controls.

Developments during the 1970s and early 1980s included not only the use of computer controls to operate the dobby loom but also the use of special cylinders, called double cylinders, which increased the number of potential sheds and thus increased the potential designs that could be made. The dobby weave may also be used in making decorative stripes in fabrics that are used for borders or for other spaced patterns.

Examples of fabrics made using the dobby attachment include Bedford cord, pique, waffle cloth, shirting madras, huck toweling, and a wide variety of decorative fabrics for apparel and home furnishings. The Bedford cord and many pique fabrics often use heavy *stuffer* yarns that help to give dimension to the design.

Jacquard Fabrics

Jacquard fabrics, frequently called Jacquard weaves, are large-figured designs that depend on considerable flexibility in the control of the warp yarns to form sheds for placing filling yarns in the fabric. These fabrics are made with the Jacquard attachment on the loom, which provides for individual control of each warp yarn. The Jacquard attachment was developed by Joseph-Marie Jacquard and was first exhibited at an industrial exposition in France in 1801. The major characteristic of this device is that each individual warp yarn can be controlled individually instead of in groups, as occurs with harnesses. This individual yarn control provides great freedom for the fabric designer, and large, intricate motifs or designs can be transferred to the fabric. Extremely elaborate patterns, including paintings, narrative scenes, and photographs, have been reproduced with the Jacquard attachment. The term *Jacquard loom* applies to those looms to which the Jacquard mechanisms have been securely attached (Fig. 21.28).

21.28 Jacquard loom using pattern cards to determine design. (Springs Industries)

The pattern used on a Jacquard loom is transferred to a series of perforated cards by punching the cards so that they resemble either a computer card or the roll on a player piano. There is one card for each filling pick that is to be inserted in any single pattern repeat. The punched cards are strung together so that they feed continuously to the area where the warp yarns are controlled. As each card passes over the control box, knives or controls push up against the card; where there are holes, the control passes through the card; where there is no hole, the control remains down. Those controls that pass through the cards raise warp yarns; the others remain down, creating a shed for placement of the filling yarn. After the pick is placed, the cards move forward; then the next card comes into position, and the next pick is placed. The process continues until each card is used, which means that the repeat for the pattern design is complete. The process then continues until the required yardage has been woven.

Many Jacquard designs are now made by using computer controls. These operate similarly to the use of cards; the difference is that computer tapes control the warp yarns that form the individual sheds. These computer controls for such looms are reducing maintenance problems, but individual threading of warp yarns for individual control is still required (Figs. 21.29 and 21.30).

The Jacquard loom is tall and requires a room with a very high ceiling, with catwalks near the top of the machine, or space where the loom can extend into a second floor or level. In the latter instance, there will be areas around the top of the loom where the Jacquard control can be reached for any adjustment that might be needed. Jacquard attachments are complicated to operate, expensive to build, and require considerable supervision to ensure that fabric is being formed without flaws. These factors combine to make Jacquard-weave fabrics expensive.

Jacquard fabrics are used in a variety of home furnishings, domestics, and apparel. They all have elaborate designs. Examples of fabrics typically woven with the Jacquard attachment include tapestry, brocade,

21.29 left. The Jacquard attachment on a rapier loom; a computer program control, which is lcoated in the box at the top, determines the formation of the design. (Sericulture Experiment Station, Japan)

21.30 right. Close-up of area where individual threads attach to individual warp yarns to control the formation of the design. (Springs Industries)

21.31 above. Damask, a fabric made with the Jacquard attachment.
21.32 below. A brocade, a Jacquard weave.

brocatelle, matelasse, and damask. Devices similar to Jacquard controls for looms have been developed for use on knitting frames (see Chapter 22).

Probably the most commonly encountered Jacquard fabrics include damask, brocade, and tapestry. Damask is used frequently for table coverings and for apparel. It may be made of different fibers, including cotton, silk, man-made fibers, and linen (flax). Damask tends to be a flat fabric and lays flat on a surface, which makes it practical for table coverings. In general warp floats form the design areas. These are usually perpendicular to filling floats, forming the base or background of the fabric, although a plain weave may be used for the background area of the fabric (Fig. 21.31).

Brocades are typically made by using satin floats on a plain or ribbed background fabric; but the design tends to stand away, very slightly, from the base, giving a slight dimension or depth to the design (Fig. 21.32). Brocatelles are heavier than brocades and are used almost entirely for home-furnishing fabrics.

Tapestry designs are fairly complex and involve a variety of colors. The yarns may be coarser than those used in other Jacquard fabrics, and designs may be very large. Tapestry fabrics are used for home furnishings, especially upholstery and heavy draperies; some tapestry fabrics are used for accessories, and some may find their way into fashion fabrics for special apparel items. Tapestry may be heavy, in which case apparel would be somewhat uncomfortable; it may be made of silk and used to make elaborate pictures (Fig. 21.33).

Leno Weaves

The leno weave may be called the *doup* weave or the *gauze* weave. The term *doup* is usually applied to the attachment on the loom that permits the construction of this fabric, whereas the tern *leno* is reserved for the fabric. The leno weave is made by means of an attachment on the loom that moves both horizontally and vertically and permits the warp yarns to be interlaced and crossed between the picks (Fig. 21.34). When a distinction is made between leno and gauze structures, the term *gauze* is applied to an open-mesh type of fabric, whereas the term *leno* is applied to

21.33 Two silk tapestries, Jacquard weave. a. Face. b. Back. c. Face.

a.

b.

c.

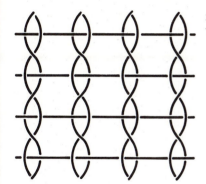

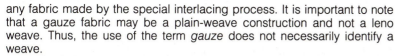

21.34 A diagram of the basic leno weave.

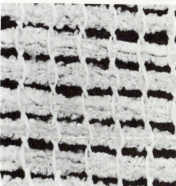

21.35 Leno-weave fabrics.

any fabric made by the special interlacing process. It is important to note that a gauze fabric may be a plain-weave construction and not a leno weave. Thus, the use of the term *gauze* does not necessarily identify a weave.

The leno weave is used to produce open-textured fabrics that may be sheer or heavy but that will have durability in specialized uses. The unusual warp interlacing and twisting prevents yarn slippage in the filling. This characteristic increases durability, stability, and strength of the sheer fabrics. The leno weave may be used with other weaves to produce some extremely complicated and decorative fabrics, particularly for draperies that will retain their shape after hanging for long periods of time.

Leno fabrics are used for a variety of purposes, probably the most common being for curtain and drapery fabrics, where it provides outstanding stability (Fig. 21.35). Other examples of end uses for leno construction include mosquito nets, laundry bags, food bags, shopping bags, and interlock needlepoint canvas.

Surface Figure Weaves

Many decorative and patterned fabrics can be made by inserting extra warp and/or filling yarns during the fabric-construction process. When extra warp yarns are used, they are wound onto an additional warp beam and threaded into separate heddles so that they can be controlled—depending on the complexity of the pattern—either by the dobby or the Jacquard attachment. Extra filling yarns are inserted by special shuttles or projectiles. Any type of loom may be used for these fabrics, but they must have numerous harnesses, or individual yarn control, in order to have sufficient warp control for the design to be formed. Controls for feeding the correct yarn color in the filling direction are usually a part of these construction processes. Controls for such fabrics permit great design flexibility; the use of several colors in the filling direction as well as the warp—which may be strung with several different colors of yarn—and the use of various types of yarns all provide methods for producing figure weaves in selected or spot areas of a fabric. The main types of fabrics made through the use of additional yarns are lappet, swivel, and spot or dot.

Lappet weave　Lappet is a form of weaving in which extra warp yarns are introduced to create a design over predetermined portions of the base fabric. Patterns are woven by means of an attachment to the loom, and the resulting designs resemble hand embroidery. If long floats are left on the back of the fabric during the actual construction, they are cut away before the fabric is placed on the consumer market. Short floats may be left in place; however, this can be a disadvantage because it is possible to snag such floats and damage the fabric. Within each design portion there is no break in the yarn used to produce the design.

The lappet weave is considered strong and durable, but because of high manufacturing costs, it is expensive to produce. There are no lappet fabrics being made in the United States; however, they may be found occasionally in fabrics imported from Europe, especially Switzerland, where some lappet weaving is still being done.

Swivel weave   The swivel weave is made with extra filling yarns. These yarns are wound onto special quills or shuttles and placed strategically on the loom to form the design at the points designated. The loom controls cause a shed to be formed; the special shuttles carry the yarn through this shed the distance of the specific pattern. Regular filling yarns are inserted to form the base fabric, and these run the entire width of the fabric; the design yarns are limited to the specific design area. The yarn is wrapped around warp yarns without a break until the pattern area is complete. The yarn will be floated to the next design area; after the weaving is finished the floating yarns may be cut away or they may be left on the fabric.

The swivel process permits the weaving of different colors in the same row because each vertical row of figures has its own shuttle or shuttles, depending on the number of colors involved in the specific pattern. In swivel weave, as in lappet, the yarns forming the pattern are securely fastened into the fabric. As with the lappet weave, there is almost no fabric made by the swivel process available on the consumer market, although some Swiss manufacturers are producing small amounts of swivel-weave fabric. It can be recognized by the fact that the design yarn wraps around a group of warp yarns to form the design.

Spot weave   Spot or dot designs can be fabricated with either extra warp or extra filling yarns. The yarns are inserted the entire length or width of the fabric in predetermined areas. If small, widely spaced dots or spots are made, the long floats on the reverse side between patterns are cut away, leaving dots that can be pulled out with a little effort. Design yarns usually differ in color from the base fabric; they may differ also in diameter, twist, and yarn type. Designs in which the floats on the back side between

21.36 below left. Face and back of fabric with clipped spot design.
21.37 below right. Face and back of a dotted swiss fabric.

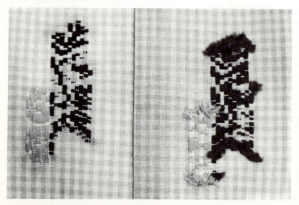

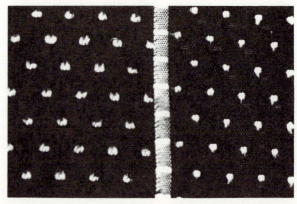

a.

b.

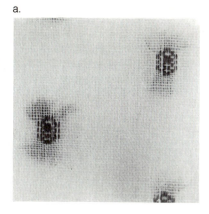
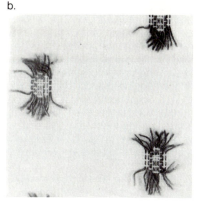

21.38 Fabric that may be called "eyelash." a. Face. b. Back. Either side may be used as the "right" side.

designs have been clipped away are called *clipped spot patterns* (Fig. 21.36).

The durability of a spot design depends on the compactness of the background yarns that hold the design yarns in place. Spots in compact weave structures are quite stable, whereas in loose weave structures they may be pulled out rather easily. Dotted swiss (Fig. 21.37) is made with extra yarns in a clipped spot weave. However, it should be pointed out that many so-called dotted swiss fabrics available on the market at the present time are really made by finishing techniques in which the dots are flocked onto and not woven into the fabric. Designs, called "eyelash" designs, are clipped spot structures in which there are considerable yarn ends left on the back side of the fabric when the floats are cut away. These ends are brushed up to form a fringe effect, and this becomes the face of the fabric (Fig. 21.38).

Spot designs in which floating yarns have not been cut are referred to as *uncut spot patterns* (Fig. 21.39). These are frequently border designs, and the repeat patterns are close together. In some instances these fabrics are reversible, with one side forming a mirror image of the other. Uncut spot designs can be made with either a dobby or a Jacquard attachment on the loom to control the yarn shed for the design area. In both cut and uncut spot fabrics, the yarns forming the design area can be removed without disintegration of the base fabric. However, the base fabric will no longer be as compact in those areas as it was prior to removal of the design yarns.

Most surface figure weaves are relatively durable fabrics. They are found in a variety of apparel and home-furnishing items. Unless given extremely hard wear or mishandling in use and care, these fabrics give satisfactory service and are attractive.

Pile Weaving

Woven pile fabrics have an extra set of warp or filling yarns interlaced with the ground warp and filling in such a manner that loops or cut ends are produced on the surface of the fabric. The base or ground fabric may be either a plain- or a twill-weave construction

Filling Pile Weaves

Filling pile fabrics have two sets of filling yarns and one set of warp yarns. Although the ground may be either twill or plain weave, the twill weave is

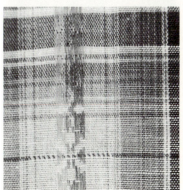

21.39 Both sides of an uncut spot pattern.

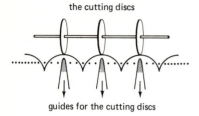

the cutting discs

guides for the cutting discs

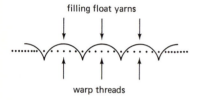

filling float yarns

warp threads

pile raised after floats are cut
these become corduroy ribs

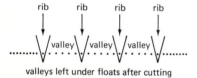

valleys left under floats after cutting
these become lines between ribs

21.40 Diagram illustrating the cutting of yarns to form the pile on corduroy fabrics.

21.41 Soft tailored jacket of corduroy.

preferred for durability. The extra set of filling yarns floats over a planned number of warp yarns, usually three or more. After weaving is completed the floats are cut and brushed to form the pile. Velveteen and corduroy fabrics are manufactured by this method. Corduroy differs from velveteen in that the floats are interlaced in such a manner that rows are formed, and when the pile is cut, it produces a ribbed effect (Figs. 21.40 and 21.41). Some fabrics on the market recently that have been advertised as corduroy have an even surface much like velveteen. These fabrics are made in such a way that the pile, when cut, forms a smooth fabric surface instead of the rib surface and resembles velveteen. The probable technique used is to have extremely fine ribs; after cutting each rib, the pile is brushed so that it gives the appearance of an overall uniform pile.

Velveteen floats are interlaced to produce an all-over effect that makes a smooth, uniform, and even pile surface. The depth of the pile is controlled by the length of the floats; the longer the float, the deeper the pile. Pile length must be kept short enough, however, so that the surface of the fabric is well covered with pile following the cutting operation.

Yarns forming the pile for either corduroy or velveteen may be interlaced into the base fabric with either a V- or a W-interlacing (Fig. 21.42). The W-interlacing is considered the more durable of the two as the pile is held down by two ground yarns instead of just one.

Corduroys and velveteens are prepared for cutting in the same manner. The floats are treated to give them cutting surface, and the fabric is stiffened so that it will remain smooth and firm. The fabric, held under tension, moves under sharp knife blades that carefully cut the floats without damage to the base fabric. For corduroy, circular knives revolve and cut the rows of floats. There may be a knife for each rib row, or more often, the fabric is fed through the cutter twice. The second time through the cutting unit, the knives are reset to cut those rows not cut during the first pass. Tandem cutters may also be used.

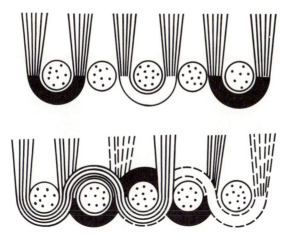

21.42 V- and W-interlacings for pile fabrics, after cutting.

Novel effects can be achieved by cutting the floats in some pre-planned pattern so that the resulting fabric may include some uncut as well as cut pile. This is more frequently done with special velveteens rather than any corduroy fabrics. Another modification is to cut the pile different lengths at different points to provide a surface with special patterns. Both corduroy and velveteen are usually made of spun yarns (Fig. 21.43).

Warp Pile Fabrics

In warp pile fabrics the pile is formed by extra warp yarns. Velvet, velour, rug velvet, and Wilton rugs are examples of warp pile fabrics. There are three general methods for making warp pile fabrics—double cloth, wire-cut pile, and looped pile.

The double-cloth technique is one of the most common procedures used to manufacture cut warp pile fabrics. In this construction five sets of yarns are necessary: two sets of warp; two sets of filling, which form the ground or base fabrics; and a third set of warp yarns that tie the fabrics together during manufacture and, after cutting apart, form the pile for each layer.

The pile yarns are interlaced with one set of ground ends and picks and then passed to the other ground set, where they interlace with those yarns. When the weaving is completed, the two layers of fabric are sev-

21.43 Examples of corduroy and velveteen fabrics.

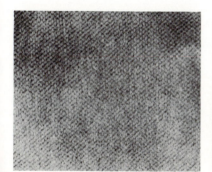

21.44 Diagram of warp pile weaving and cutting to form velvet fabrics.

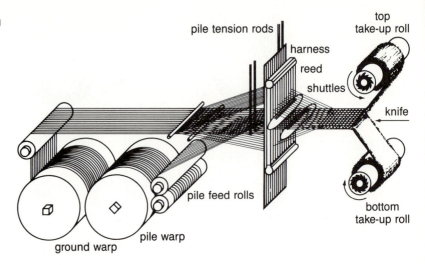

ered through the area between the two layers, and two distinct and separate fabrics are formed (Fig. 21.44). The pile can be further sheared or trimmed to form additional designs or to even the surface.

For many years one of the major methods for making carpeting was the process called the Wilton method, which formed what is known as Wilton rugs; some are still made by this process. Wilton rugs are made by a wire-cutting method. The loops are formed over wires; following the formation of the loops, the wire is removed, cutting the loops as it is pulled out. The manufacture of Wilton rugs involves the use of the Jacquard attachment as well as the formation of loops.

Terry pile constructions Terry pile fabrics are the best known type of warp pile fabrics. Terry cloth, used for toweling, robes, and many other end uses, is constructed with uncut loops of yarn on both sides of the fabric. These loops are formed by holding the ground warp yarns under tight tension and leaving the warp yarns that form the pile in a slack state. The shed is made and picks are inserted; this process is repeated for a specified number of picks, usually three, without any beating in. After the picks have been placed, they are battened into position, which causes the slack warp yarns to be pushed into loops between the picks. Although the typical terry cloth has loops on both sides, it is possible to make fabrics by this method with loops on only one side. Figure 21.45 illustrates the forma-

21.45 Formation of loops in a terry cloth pile construction. (Springs Industries)

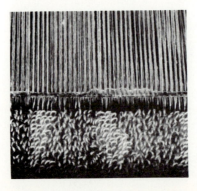

tion of loops as the pile yarns are being beaten into position. Figure 21.46 shows a typical loom used for making terry cloth in which considerable pattern is involved and therefore the Jacquard attachment is used.

Ply yarns are recommended for the ground warp yarns because they are strong. The warp pile yarns should be fluffy, soft, and absorbent. Low-twist yarns may be used, and often two yarns are placed together in each shed to have a pile that is soft and absorbent. Some terry cloth may have the pile cut, particularly on one side, to provide greater flexibility in design than would otherwise be possible. Some toweling, particularly, has loops cut on one side to provide a velour-type fabric. Typical uses for terry cloth include robes, toweling, upholstery fabrics, and carpeting.

Double Weaves

Double weaves are those in which at least two sets of filling yarns and two sets of warp yarns are interlaced so that the interlacing moves between the sets at various points. Some double weaves use a fifth set of yarns to tie two layers of fabric together at selected points during the weaving process. Double weaving used to make pile fabrics does not result in a double-weave fabric in terms of consumer use because the fabrics are severed following weaving, leaving two distinct layers of fabric. True double-weave fabrics are made up of two layers of fabric connected in some way through the interlacing process. Separating fabric layers in a double weave would tend to destroy the fabric unless it has been constructed specifically for that process, such as velvets. These fabrics are characterized by strength, extra weight, warmth, and a wide variety of design potential.

Some authorities discuss double weaves as a part of multicomponent fabrics. However, I wish to separate the two techniques because a true double weave is formed by the interlacing of warp and filling and is difficult, if not impossible, to separate without damage to the fabric. Multicomponent fabrics combine two or more layers of fabric that could stand alone before forming into the multicomponent fabric (see p. 241).

Double-cloth or double-weave fabric may be designed so that each side of the fabric is different but with coordinated appearances. It may have two distinct patterns, or each side may be so alike that the fabric is reversible (Fig. 21.47).

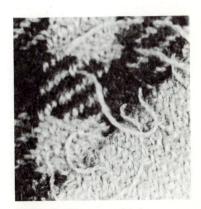

21.47 Double-weave fabric.

21.48 Matelassé type of double-weave fabric. a. Face. b. Back.

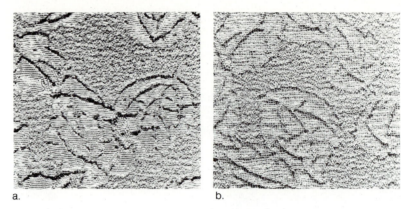

a.   b.

A fabric called *backed fabric* is sometimes misnamed a double cloth. This fabric is constructed by using either two sets of filling and one set of warp yarns or two sets of warp and one set of filling yarns. It is not true double-weave fabric, as there is no possibiity of separating the two layers at any point in the construction.

Double-weave fabric or cloth can be designed and constructed with dobby or Jacquard attachments on the looms to create complicated designs; various types of yarns—simple or complex—various fiber content, and different amounts of twist may be used to provide additional design possibilities. Double-weave fabrics are used where the following characteristics are desired: strength, design, weight, and warmth. Common uses for double-weave fabrics include coatings, blankets, matelassé, double brocade, and brocatelle. Backed fabric is often used for blankets and for heavy winter robes. Matelassé may be heavy or relatively light in weight; it is used primarily for the design potential (Fig. 21.48). Backed fabric is frequently used for blankets and for heavy winter robes.

Triaxial Fabrics

Woven fabrics discussed to this point are biaxial or orthogonal structures. That is, they are made from yarns laid at right angles to each other and forming a flat structure. Triaxial fabrics are comprised of three sets of yarns interlacing with angles of less than 90°. As seen in Figure 21.49, the

21.49 Diagram of triaxial weave structures. Numbers indicate the sets of yarns used in construction.

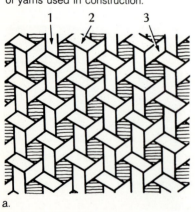

a.

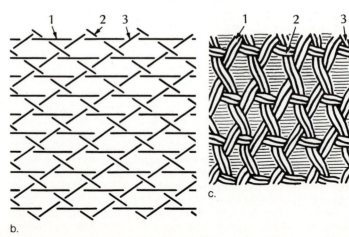

b.

c.

various sets of yarns interlace on a diagonal rather than at right angles. One set may be perpendicular to the edge of the fabric, but this is not necessary.

The preferred method for constructing these fabrics is to use two warp systems and one filling yarn system.* The interlacing is controlled by special cams, which provide for the diagonal direction of the warp yarns as they interlace with the filling yarns. The resulting fabric has a hexagonal mesh system. As yet these fabrics are used, primarily, for industrial purposes. They are characterized by excellent dimensional stability in both length and width and, in addition, are stable in the bias direction. They are being used for selected applications in aerospace vehicles.

As equipment for making this type of fabric becomes readily available at a reasonable cost, triaxial fabrics should become more common than they are. They do have remarkable stability and should prove to be valuable for a wide variety of end uses.

Care and Use of Woven Fabrics

Woven Fabric Care

The care of woven fabrics depends on the type of weave, the fiber content, and methods of coloring and finishing. Yarn structure may also influence care methods. In general, plain and twill weaves can be laundered if the fiber content permits. Satin weaves may require some special care because of the possibilities of snagging the floating yarns. This snagging could cause a loss of appearance and reduced durability and performance. Decorative weaves may require special handling because of floating yarns, irregular surfaces that result from the different weaves, and the tendency for decorative weaves to use yarns made from fibers that may require special handling or care.

Consumers should be cautious when selecting fabrics and make certain that care labels provide directions for laundering or dry cleaning.

Woven Fabrics in Use

Woven fabrics can be used for a wide variety of end uses. They tend to give good wear and durability. They provide a product that tends to hold its shape well and is relatively stable and firm. Woven fabrics are more stable than knitted fabrics. Fabrics for apparel, home furnishings, and business and industry may be of woven structures; they will tend to give good service in most types of textile products.

Study Questions

1. Prepare diagrams showing the basic weaves.
2. List the modifications of the plain, twill, and satin weaves, and describe how they differ from the basic structure.
3. Prepare samples of weaving from knitting or crochet yarns.
4. List and discuss ways woven fabrics can be modified other than by the actual interlacing of yarns.
5. List the six major techniques used in weaving decorative or novelty fabrics.

*Wayne C. Trost, "A Triaxial Weaving Machine Update," Barber-Coleman Co.

6. Describe each of the methods and the possible variations for weaving fabrics to be used in home furnishings and interior design.
7. Discuss the characteristics of fabric in use and care that are the result of weaving as opposed to other methods of fabric construction. (This will be answered more effectively following the study of Chapters 22, 23, and 24.)
8. Make a list of at least twenty-five different fabrics that are made by weaving, identify a potential end use for each, and state why it is appropriate for that use. Use the list of fabrics cited in various sections of this chapter and the Glossary at the end of this book as resources for this activity.
9. What are triaxial fabrics and how do you think they will be used in the future?
10. What is the difference between double-weave fabrics and multicomponent fabrics?

Knitted Fabrics

22

Knitted fabrics have enjoyed considerable success and been a popular type of fabric construction for many years. Known data support the fact that knitted structures date back to at least A.D. 256. There is inconclusive evidence that knitting actually was known in early civilizations. The use of machines to create knit structures dates from 1589, when William Lee developed the first mechanical knitting frame. The principles of knitting, like the principles of weaving, remain basically the same; only the sophistication of the equipment and modifications of techniques have changed over the years.

Knitting is the creation of fabrics by forming loops in the yarns and interlooping these to build fabrics. In machine knitting loops of yarn are formed with the aid of thin pointed needles, or shafts. As new loops are formed, they are drawn through those previously shaped. This interlooping and the continued formation of new loops produce knit fabric.

Production and consumption of knitted fabrics increased greatly during the mid-twentieth century. Technology of production has also increased because of the use of computer controls in the operation of the machines, which has created a wide design potential. Although knits have decreased slightly in use since the mid-1970s, they still account for a large proportion of all fabrics used, particularly for selected items of apparel and for some home-furnishing items.

There are several reasons for the popularity of knitted fabrics during the past thirty to thirty-five years. Knits can be made rapidly so that yarn-to-fabric expenses are lower than for woven fabrics. A quality fabric can be produced at comparatively low cost, and there is potential for a wide variety of fabric designs. The increase in travel, especially by air, resulted in the need for lightweight, comfortable apparel that requires little care and packs easily with retention of appearance; knitted fabrics fit these needs. The ability of knits to resist wrinkling and retain a desirable appearance has been an important factor in their use. Further, knit fabrics are recognized for the comfort they provide in apparel fabrics.

There are two general methods used in creating knit fabrics: *filling knitting* and *warp knitting*. Filling knitting may be called *weft knitting*. As these methods differ considerably they will be discussed under the two major headings. In the construction of knit fabrics there are two terms that are used for knits in general. *Wale* refers to a column of loops that are parallel to the loop axis and to the longer dimension of the fabric as it is formed. A *course* is a series of successive loops laying crosswise of the knit fabric, that is, at right angles to a line passing from the open throat to the closed end of the loops. Figure 22.1 diagrams a wale and a course; Figure 22.2 shows a knit fabric in which the wales and courses can be

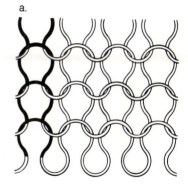

a.

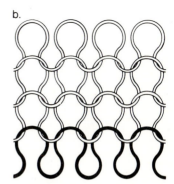

b.

22.1 Diagram of wales and courses. a. The darkened row indicates a wale. b. The darkened row indicates a course.

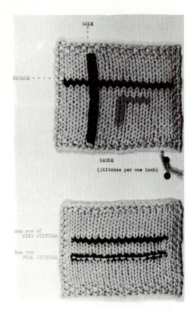

22.2 left.   Fabric showing vertical rows, wales, and horizontal rows, courses.

22.3 right.   A circular knitting machine. (Mayer and Cie)

clearly observed. Another important term is *gage. Gage,* or *gauge,* refers to the fineness of a knit fabric and is determined by the number of needles per unit of width, per inch or per 1½ inches.

Filling or Weft Knitting

Weft or filling knitting is a continuous process in which the fabric is formed by a yarn making loops across the width of the fabric or around a circle. Each yarn is fed at more or less a right angle to the direction in which the fabric is built. The term *weft* is taken from weaving terminology, in which weft refers to the crosswise yarns. Weft- or filling-knit fabrics can be made by machines or by hand processes. Most knit fabrics available on the market, either in end-use products or by the yard, are made by machines. A majority of weft-knit fabrics are made on circular knitting machines (Fig. 22.3), in which a series of needles is arranged around the circumference of a circle. Fabric is formed in the shape of a tube; when flat fabric is desired the tube is cut open. Many fabrics are made with a specific location for slitting the fabric open; this spot can be identified by the absence of complete wales and courses.

Weft knitting on circular machines uses a series of yarns rather than a single yarn; thus, the final fabric is built in a somewhat spiral manner. The slightly spiral character of circular knitted fabrics is seldom noticed by the consumer except when a design emphasizes this spiral characteristic, and it becomes difficult, if not impossible, to make the design appear parallel with either the lengthwise or crosswise of the knit fabric. As the fabric is formed it is pulled down through the center of the machine and taken up on rolls ready for further processing or marketing.

Weft knits may be made on flat-bed machines (Fig. 22.4). In this process the yarn is moved across the bed of the machine, from one side to the other, and forms a series of loops that are pulled through the previously formed row of loops. Flat-bed machines may have one bank of

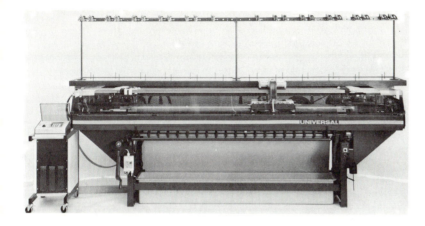

22.4 left. A flat-bed knitting machine. (Universal Maschinenfabrik)
22.5 right. Close-up of a section of needles on a flat-bed knitting machine. (Dubied Machinery Company)

needles (Fig. 22.5), or there may be two sets arranged to form a V-shape, with the open end of the V parallel to the base of the machine (Fig. 22.6).

Knitting requires four basic components: a yarn source; knitting elements or needles, which form the loops and build the fabric; fabric takedown, a device to pull the formed fabric toward the base of the machine; and fabric collection, a roll of some kind on which the completed fabric is collected. The yarn supply for weft knitting may be located above the knitting area or on large creels at the side. If at the side, the yarns are carried to the top of the knitting machine and then fed down to the knitting area. The knitting process requires the needles to pull the yarn to form loops, to hold the loops until new loops are formed, and then to "knock off" the loops to build the knit structure. The actual knitting elements include the

22.6 A V-bed arrangement of needles on a flat knitting machine. (Dubied Machinery Company)

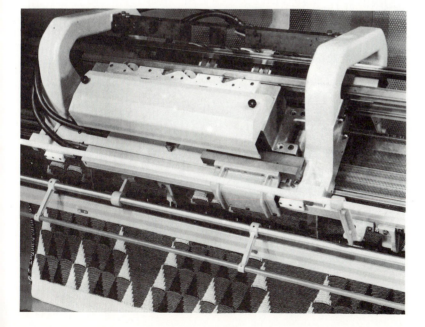

needles; the sinkers; the needle bed, or frame, which holds the needles; and the yarn carriers, which lay the yarn in knitting position. There are two basic types of needles, latch and beard. Although either may be used for weft knitting, the latch needle is more common. The action of the needles is controlled by cams of various types, which determine the appearance or pattern of the final fabric. Both circular and flat-bed machines can produce highly patterned as well as plain fabrics. Designs are created by special controls, often operated by computers. Final designs are often referred to as Jacquard knits because they involve elaborate patterns much like the elaborate weaves created using the Jacquard attachment on weaving looms.

There are two major types of weft knitting machines—single-knit frames and double-knit frames. Either circular or flat-bed machines can be designed as single- or double-knit frames; however, double-knit fabrics are made, primarily, on circular double-knit machines.

Four types of loops, or stitches, are used in making knit fabrics: the *knit,* or *plain, loop;* the *tuck loop;* the *purl,* or *reverse, loop;* and the *miss stitch,* or *float loop* (Fig. 22.7).

22.7 Knit loops and stitches. a. Regular plain stitch. b. Purl stitch. c. Tuck loop. d. Miss loop.

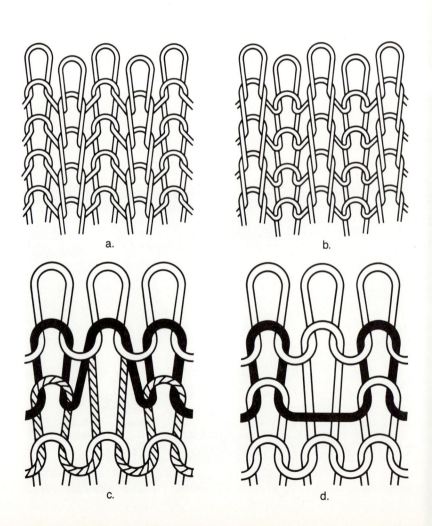

a.

b.

c.

d.

a.

b.

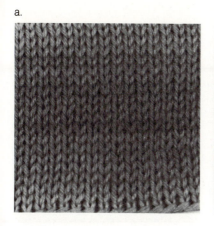

22.8 Plain jersey stitch. a. Face. b. Back.

The knit stitch shows the neck of the loop on the face of the fabric and the head of the loop on the back. These stitches produce a fine fabric with a smooth surface; there is a definite face and back, or reverse side (Fig. 22.8).

The purl, or reverse, stitch forms a fabric that resembles the reverse side of the knit, or plain, stitch on both front and back. The purl stitch produces a fabric that is fuller and puffier than that made by the plain stitch. The fabric is reversible as it does appear the same on face and reverse side (Fig. 22.9). The purl stitch is frequently used in the manufacture of bulky knits such as sweaters and a variety of other apparel fabrics. Recently this stitch has been popular in many fashion articles. Because the purl stitch produces fabric with the same appearance on both sides, there is no problem in cutting and preparing it for construction into end-use products.

The miss stitch or loop is characterized by yarns floating unlooped on the reverse side of the fabric. The needle in a miss loop does not move into position to accept new yarn and no actual stitch is formed.

The tuck stitch or loop is formed when the needle is raised only partially and retains the previous stitch as well as picking up yarn to form a second stitch in the same needle. Tuck stitches may hold more than two stitches for some designs. The tuck stitch tends to create open spaces and is used to form lace effects, mesh designs, open-work patterns, blister effects, and bumpy textures in knit fabrics.

Plain knit fabrics have distinct but flat vertical lines on the face and dominant horizontal lines on the reverse side (see Fig. 22.7). Hand knitters recognize this as the *stockinette* stitch. Flat or plain knits can be varied to produce run-resist and fancy patterned knit fabrics. Jersey or flat knits are used in making hosiery, lingerie, sweaters, sportswear, and a variety of fabrics, primarily for apparel.

A major disadvantage of regular plain knits is the ease with which they drop stitches when a yarn is broken and form "runs" or "ladders." These flaws destroy the appearance of the fabric; thus some plain knits have a modified pattern to reduce the danger of runs and help retain the appearance of the knit fabric (Fig. 22.10).

Other important stitches used in constructing knit fabrics include the rib-knit stitch and the interlock knit. The rib knit (Figs. 22.11 and 22.12) is usually made on a V flat-bed machine. The stitches intermesh in opposite directions on a walewise basis, and the frequency of intermeshing determines the type of rib. If intermeshing occurs at every other wale, it is a 1x1

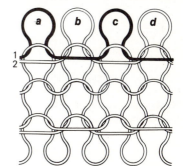

22.9 above. Purl-stitch knit fabric. Face and back of these fabrics are identical.

22.10 below. Diagram of a run-resist filling-knit stitch. Numbers indicate horizontal rows, or courses; letters indicate vertical rows, or wales.

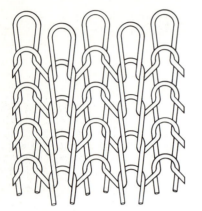

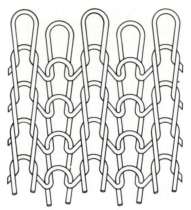

22.11 left. Diagram of rib knits.
a. 1×1 rib face. b. 1×1 rib back.
22.12 right. A rib-stitch fabric.

rib; if it occurs every two wales, a 2x2 rib is made. Uneven ribs can be produced by interlooping in one direction for a certain number of wales and a different number in the other direction. Rib fabrics can be knit on circular machines with two sets of needles—both dial and cylinder needles.

The rib pattern is used whenever stretch is desired, and rib knits do have excellent elasticity and elongation. Rib knits also tend to be warmer than flat knits. The primary disadvantage of rib knits is high cost because of the increase in fabric weight and the need for more yarns per area than used in regular flat knit fabrics. Rib-knit fabrics are found in such locations as necklines, wrists, and waistlines of sweaters and wherever considerable stretch is desired.

Interlock knits (Figs. 22.13 and 22.14) are a variation of the rib knit. In construction they resemble two separate 1x1 rib fabrics that are interknitted. Interlock fabrics are thicker and heavier than regular rib fabrics of the same gage.

Interlock-knit fabrics are constructed so that they appear identical on both face and back. This characteristic can be modified through surface design or the use of different colored yarns in selected locations. Interlock knits have a soft hand, good moisture absorbency, and high dimensional stability. They can be cut easily for construction, do not curl at the edges, and sew easily. The majority of interlock knits are constructed on circular double-knit machines.

22.13 left. Diagram of interlock stitch.
22.14 right. A double-knit interlock-stitch fabric.

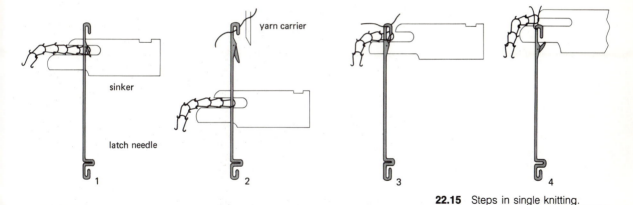

22.15 Steps in single knitting.

Single Knits

Single-knit fabrics may be plain, ribbed, highly patterned, or a combination of these. The knitting elements are latch needle, holding sinkers, and yarn carrier. The basic steps in stitch formation (Fig. 22.15) are as follows:

1. The needle is in the running or rest position. The last formed loop is on the latch of the needle, and the sinker is ahead holding the fabric in position.
2. The needle is pushed up by the cam to the uppermost or clearing position. The previous loop has slipped off the latch and lies on the stem of the needle. The sinker is still forward, holding down the formed loops. The yarn carrier feeds the yarn to the hook.
3. After the yarn is in the hook, the needle begins to lower. The holding sinker retracts to permit the needle to drop low enough so that the yarn in the hook is pulled through the previously formed loop. The old loop closes the latch, and thus the yarn is held securely in place, ready for a new loop.
4. The needle drops to its lowest position, forming the new loop. The sinker begins to move forward to push the old loop ahead and hold the fabric. The process is then repeated until the fabric is ready to be removed from the machine (Fig. 22.16).

a.

b.

22.16 Single-knit fabric with Jacquard pattern. a. Face. b. Back.

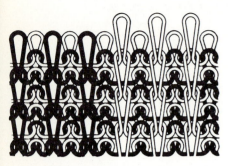

22.17 Diagram of a patterned double-knit fabric.

Double Knits

Double knits are produced by using the interlock stitch and by variations of that operation. Both surfaces of the fabric appear somewhat riblike. Decorative effects can be achieved with special Jacquard attachments for individual control of needles and yarns. Most of these attachments in use today are computer controlled. The flexibility provided by the individual control of the needles makes it possible to produce a wide variety of fabric designs.

The double knits can be made also by knitting two distinct filling or weft-knit fabrics that are periodically bound together by an additional set of yarns. Figure 22.17 shows a double knit in which two differently colored yarns have been used in developing a pattern that has been constructed by a computer program.

The manufacture of double-knit fabrics requires special circular machines with two sets of needles (Fig. 22.18). Dial needles lay parallel to the floor around the circumference of the central knitting area; the cylinder needles are perpendicular to the floor and to the dial needles. Cylinder needles lay against the cylinder on which the dial needles are placed. Steps in forming the stitches for double knits are as follows (Fig. 22.19):

1. The needles are in the nonknit or running position, with the previously formed loops in the hooks of both dial and cylinder needles.
2. The dial needles start their forward motion, and the cylinder needles start their upward motion. As the dial needles move, the cylinder needles hold the previously formed loop in place.

22.18 Diagram of a circular knitting machine. Yarns feed from creels to top controls, then down to center where knitting elements are located.

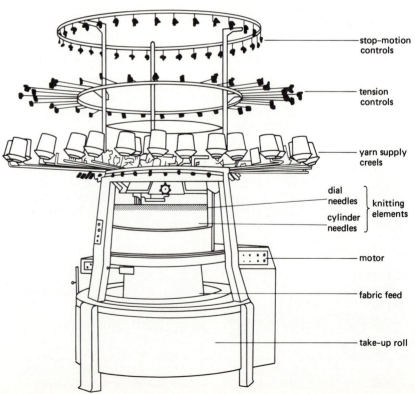

stop-motion controls

tension controls

yarn supply creels

dial needles ⎫ knitting
cylinder needles ⎬ elements

motor

fabric feed

take-up roll

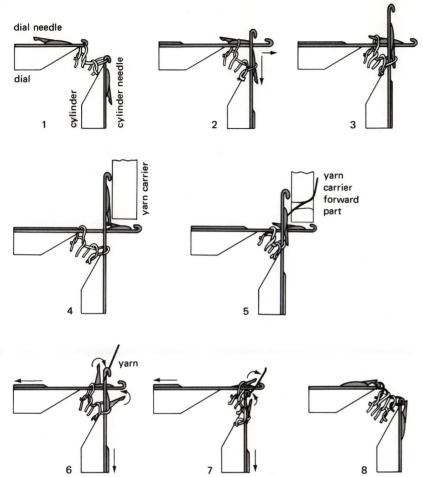

22.19 Diagram showing stitch formation in double knits.

3. The needles continue their motion; while the cylinder needles hold the stitch on the dial needles, the dial needles simultaneously hold the loops on the cylinder needles.
4. The two needles reach their forward and upward motion, and the yarn carrier moves into position to make certain the latches on the needles stay open. Note that the previously formed loops are on the needle stems behind the latches.
5. The yarn carrier continues its movement and lays new yarn in the hooks. The needles are moving back and down, and the old loops are beginning to lift the latches.
6. The needles continue their reverse motion; the old loops are moving up and partially closing the latches.
7. The yarn is in the dial hook and the cylinder hook. The latches are almost closed, and the old loops are almost ready to slide over the ends of the needles.
8. The needles are in the back or down position. The latches are closed, and the new loops have been pulled through the old loops. The last step is frequently called knocking off or knocking down the stitches.

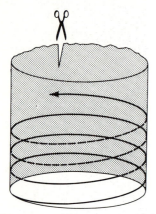

22.20 left. Diagram of a circular knit showing spiral yarn path that results from feeding many yarns nearly simultaneously.

22.21 right. Face, a., and back, b., of a Jacquard knit.

a.

b.

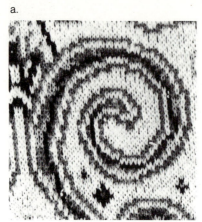
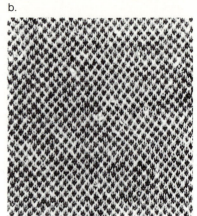

This action occurs simultaneously for each end of yarn being fed. For most double knits, about forty-eight ends of yarn feed to the knitting area, and there are about 1,800 needles in the cylinder and 1,800 in the dial. The fabric builds up in a spiral form rather than at a true 90° angle (Fig. 22.20). Single knits made on circular machines are also constructed so they form a spiral configuration.

Double knits are usually constructed on circular knitting frames; the interlock stitch is the basic stitch for double-knit constructions. All double knits require two sets of needles, whereas single knits need only one set. During the past two decades the production of patterned or Jacquard double knits has become highly sophisticated, and the types of designs may be extremely elaborate (Figs. 22.21 and 22.22).

Double knits have better stability than most single knits and resist the formation of runs. Double knits are easier to sew than single knits and do not tend to curl at the edges as many single knits do. Double-knit fabrics are firmer, heavier, less stretchable, and more resilient than single-knit fabrics. Single knits can be made considerably finer and sheerer than double knits.

Knitted Pile Fabrics

Knitted pile fabrics are usually made by the weft- or filling-knit process. Operations closely resemble double knitting. To produce the pile, an extra set of yarns is drawn out in long loops and then cut or left uncut depending on the desired effect. The base fabric is generally a plain stockinette stitch. Many pile fabrics made to resemble fur are actually made by using a knit pile construction (Fig. 22.23). Many pile fabrics now are constructed by using a soft yarn sliver for the pile rather than regular yarns. The sliver is fluffy and soft and creates a rich, luxurious fabric.

Yarn Insertion

Yarn insertion, or *laying-in* techniques, involves the addition of extra yarns as the fabric is being knitted. The process permits the use of a variety of novelty yarns that might not have the strength to be processed by the regular knitting operations. Further, yarns with considerable surface interest can be used for laying in, even though these yarns might not be acceptable to the action of feeding through the needles. Such fabrics tend to have a high surface interest. Laying in is also used as one method of in-

22.22 Patterned double knit—duplication of painting.

serting heavy duty yarns that will be held to the back of the fabric to provide additional strength, stability, and warmth without altering the appearance. Yarn insertion can be done on either single or double knits; furthermore, it can be used on both weft- or filling-knit fabrics and on warp-knit fabrics (discussed in the next section). A typical diagram of insertion is shown in Figure 22.24.

Warp Knitting

The term *warp knitting* is also adopted from weaving terminology. Warp knitting differs from weft or filling knitting in that the loops are formed in a vertical or warpwise direction and yarns laying side by side are interlooped. Machines used for warp knitting tend to look much like weaving machines. All the yarns are placed on beams that are then located behind and/or above the actual knitting area. All yarns feed into the knitting area at the same time. Each yarn is manipulated by its own specific needle as each interlooping action occurs. Guide bars control the placement of the

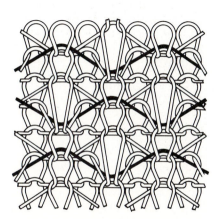

22.24 Diagram of weft yarn insertion.

22.25 Diagram of tricot (warp) knitting machine.

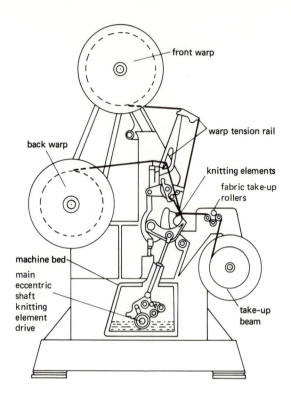

front warp

warp tension rail

back warp

knitting elements

fabric take-up rollers

machine bed

main eccentric shaft knitting element drive

take-up beam

yarn and identify the particular needle that will form a loop; these vary from one interlooping action to the next. Jacquard attachments or special computer controls can be used with warp knitting machines to construct warp knits with complex patterns and designs. Because of the appearance, the size, and the location of the yarn supply, the machines used in warp knitting are sometimes called *knitting looms* (Fig. 22.25).

Warp knitting is a system for producing fabric that is flat, has straight side edges, and is manufactured rapidly and in large quantities. Warp knits are classified according to the type of equipment or machinery used and special characteristics of the fabric. The types are tricot, raschel, milanese, and simplex. The most common types are tricot and raschel.

Warp-knit fabrics have some elongation, or stretchability, although it may be less than for filling knits. The amount of extension is influenced by the type of construction, the tightness of the knit, finishing techniques, gage, and type of yarns used. The strength of warp knits can be increased by using strong fibers, yarns of balanced construction, high gage, and yarns of ply construction.

The loop formed in warp knitting differs from that formed in weft knitting (Fig. 22.26). Note that in the warp loop the yarn comes into the loop from above and exits in a downward direction; the yarn enters the weft loop from one side and leaves on the other side, basically a horizontal movement.

Tricot Knits

Tricot knits originated in England during the latter part of the eighteenth century. Plain or decorative tricot fabrics can be made on the same ma-

weft   warp

22.26 Diagram of weft-knit loop and warp-knit loop.

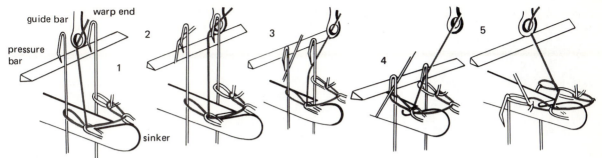

22.27 Diagram of five steps in formation of a warp-knit tricot fabric.

chine; the difference is determined by the patterns used in the interlooping operation and the number of guide bars involved. The interlooping of adjacent yarns can be controlled so that yarns laying next to each other are interlooped or yarns laying a few yarns away from each other can be interlooped. This flexibility helps to provide the different types of tricot knits and the variety in appearance and character.

Tricot fabrics can be made with either latch or beard needles; however, beard needles are most common and are used in the figure showing the steps in tricot knitting (Fig. 22.27).

1. Step 1 shows the various parts that make tricot knitting possible. Note the warp end, which would be coming from the beam of yarn on the knitting machine; the guide bar, which controls the placement of each yarn; the presser bar, which helps control the closing of the needle; the sinker, which helps control the movement of formed loops; and the fabric. The beard needles have a spring type of hook without any latch. In step 1 the needles are in their highest position, the previous loops are on the stems of the needles, and the sinker is holding down the formed fabric.
2. The guide bar carrying the yarn that formed the last loop on the left needle moves to the right to place the yarn in the needle to the right. A yarn from the far left is being placed in the left needle.
3. The yarn is against the needle stem, and the needles are starting their descent. As the needles move down, the yarn is trapped in the hooks. The presser bar moves toward the needles, and the sinker moves away.
4. The yarn is in the hook. The presser bar moves in and forces the tips of the needles against the stems to hold the yarn in place and to permit the needles to pull the yarn through the previously formed loops.
5. The needles have moved to their lowest position. The new loops are formed, and the old loops are knocked off. The sinker moves back in to hold the fabric. The needles will return to the upper position, and the steps will be repeated. The guide bar carries the yarn to either the right or left to form the vertical interlooping of stitches.

Tricot knits are identified as single guide bar, two guide bar, or more, depending on the number of yarns and guide bars used for each needle in making the interlooping pattern. The simplest is the single bar with movement between adjacent needles only (Fig. 22.28). A single-bar tricot in which the guide bar moves over two needles is shown in Figure 22.29. In making this fabric each guide bar carries the yarn over one needle and lays the yarn into the second needle from the one in which the previous loop was formed.

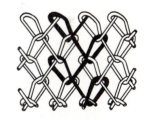

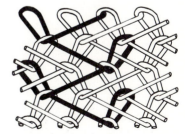

22.28 above. Diagram of the simplest single-guide-bar warp-knit fabric.

22.29 below. Single-bar tricot with two-wale underlap.

22.30 Diagram of two-guide-bar tricot fabric. Note: Two yarns and two guide bars work together to form the fabric.

A two-guide-bar tricot in which two different colors of yarn have been used is shown in Figure 22.30. With two or more guide bars, a variety of designs can be made by using different types and colors of yarns in each different guide bar. Most modern tricot machines use between two and four guide bars.

The characteristics of tricot knits include good air and water permeability, softness, crease resistance, good drapability, nonraveling properties, run resistance, and elasticity. Tricot fabrics can be given special finishes that control dimensional stability. Strength of fabric is influenced by the fiber used, the yarn type, and the closeness of yarns in the final fabric. Thickness of tricot fabric is influenced by the size of the yarns used, the tightness or compactness of the knit stitches, the length of the guide bar movement, and the finishing processes.

Prices for tricot knit fabrics are generally higher than for filling knits; however, they are usually less costly than woven fabrics. Price is influenced by the cost of the machinery and labor, the cost of preparing beams of yarn, and the cost of the fibers and yarns.

Tricot knit fabrics are used for a variety of end products. Typical applications include lingerie fabrics, nightwear, blouses, dresses, and other items of apparel (Figs. 22.31 and 22.32). Tricot may be used for some home furnishings, but because of the elongation or elasticity of such fabrics, this use is not common. Tricot is frequently used as a backing fabric in multicomponent structures, where it may serve as a built-in lining. Because tricot knits can be lightweight and less expensive than woven fabrics, they have been used as a lining for some quilted bedspreads.

Raschel Knits

Raschel knitting is a warp-knitting technique that offers the manufacturer tremendous flexibility in fabric design. It is one of the most versatile methods for producing fabrics and is particularly important in making highly patterned knit fabrics and crochet knits.

The machinery used is similar to that used for tricot knitting in that

22.31 left. Tricot-knit fabric used for lingerie. (Allied's Captiva nylon fibers)

22.32 right. Tricot-knit dress-weight fabric.

22.33 A raschel knitting frame. (Cidega Manufacturing, Inc.)

all the yarns required are placed on a beam located at the back or above the raschel unit (Fig. 22.33). The machines usually use beard needles, and there are several guide bars for each warp yarn; in addition there may be special guide bars to control the insertion of yarns that can be laid in during the knitting operation. Many raschel frames use computer units to control the movement of the guide bars, which determine the pattern that is to be knitted. Figure 22.34 shows a simple raschel-knit pattern.

Raschel machines may have as many as sixty-five guide bars, which provide for the tremendous choice of fabric designs. As raschel knits are formed, the fabric is pulled down from the knitting area at an angle of about 150° and then wound onto cloth beams.

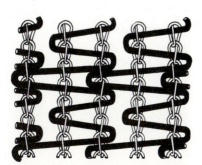

22.34 Diagram of a simple raschel crochet knit. (National Knitwear and Sportswear Association)

22.35 above left. Diagram of one type of knitted net.

22.36 above right. Raschel-knit fabric.

22.37 below left. Diagram of warp-knit insertion.

22.38 below right. Fabric, warp knit, with inserted yarns for design.

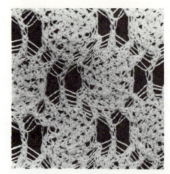

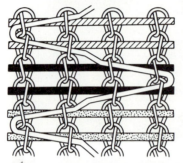

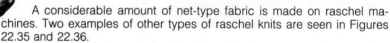

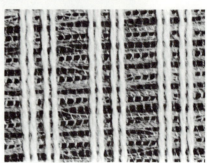

A considerable amount of net-type fabric is made on raschel machines. Two examples of other types of raschel knits are seen in Figures 22.35 and 22.36.

Yarn insertion is also popular with raschel knits. The extra yarns are laid in by means of special guide bars (Fig. 22.37). A typical raschel fabric with laid-in yarns is shown in Figure 22.38.

Milanese Knits

Milanese is a method of warp knitting similar to tricot. The resulting fabric is similar, but the machinery is quite different. Milanese equipment is not capable of producing a wide variety of patterns. Despite the fact that milanese knits are smoother, more regular in structure and elasticity, and higher in tear strength than tricot, they are disappearing from the market because the production rate is low and the pattern possibilities are limited. However, for special uses, where firmness is desired along with some flexibility, milanese knits meet an important need.

Simplex Knits

Simplex knits were popular in the early years of the twentieth century. They then disappeared almost completely; however, they are reappearing on the market for use in apparel, upholstery, accessories such as gloves, and moldable items in which the knit provides the fabric base.

Properties of simplex knits include the following: There is no running, splitting, or raveling; they have substantial bulk and compactness; they exhibit excellent snag and abrasion resistance; they possess good elastic recovery; they have a smooth, firm surface; they do not tend to curl at the edges; and they tailor well. It will be interesting to see what happens to these knits during the next few years.

22.39 Dress and coat of jersey knit fabric.

Use and Care

Knit Fabric Care

The care of knit fabrics depends on several factors. The fiber content should indicate whether the fiber should be laundered or dry cleaned. Also, the type of knit construction needs to be considered: Is it loosely or tightly knit? What type of yarns have been used? Will they snag during care? What finishes are present? Of most importance are the care labels attached to the product. These should be followed carefully. Knits tend to react well to automatic laundering and drying because the tumble action helps the fabric return to its original shape. Hanging is almost always a poor technique; the weight of moisture in the fabric and the natural tendency for the fabric to elongate combine to pull the fabric out of shape.

Knits may snag easily because of the fabric loop construction. Thus, care techniques should avoid the use of rough objects and abrasion action. Most knit fabrics do not require any ironing as the natural characteristic of the knit structure helps the product to return to its normal appearance.

Knits in Use

A wide selection of knitted fabrics is available to the consumer. They offer the user several important and desirable properties. The most important, probably, are excellent elongation or stretch combined with good elastic recovery or return to shape. They have an outstanding resistance to wrinkling and crushing. These properties make knit fabrics a good choice for travel because they pack well, hang out quickly, require small amounts of space, and are comfortable to wear.

Knit fabrics have many outstanding characteristics and are good choices for apparel (Fig. 22.39). However, consumers should make certain they select the best item for a particular use. It is important to note label information and to try to determine if the product will stretch or shrink during use and care. For home furnishings knits are being used for upholstery and for some domestic fabrics. Any knit upholstery must be firm enough to resist wear so that it will not stretch out of shape; however, this ability to stretch and conform to shape makes a knit fabric a good choice for furniture throws that need to be shaped around pieces of furniture.

Knitted structures are porous, permit good air circulation, are comfortable, and allow freedom of movement. Thus, they meet an important need for both apparel and home furnishings.

Study Questions

1. Describe the differences between filling (weft) and warp knitting.
2. What is the difference between a single knit and a double knit?
3. How do the differences between single and double knits influence use and care?
4. What are the major processes used in constructing warp-knit fabrics? Describe each.
5. What are the advantages and disadvantages of knitted fabrics?
6. What guidelines can you list to help consumers make intelligent choices for knit fabrics in relation to selection, use, and care?
7. What are the differences between woven and knit fabrics? How do these differences affect use and care?

8. What are the four basic types of stitches or loops used in knitting? Describe each.
9. What knit construction tends to develop runs very easily? What is a typical product in which such knits might be found?
10. Locate a variety of knit fabrics available on the market, indicate whether they are filling or warp knits, and note what care procedures might be recommended.

Felts and Other Nonwoven Fabrics

23

Felts

The construction of fabrics directly from fibers is the oldest as well as one of the newest processes for producing textile fabrics. The ingenuity of human beings in forming flexible covering materials first expressed itself in felt structures. These early textile fabrics were made from wool, hair, or fur fibers and depended on the special characteristics that made it possible to mat them together into a durable layer. The primary fiber for early felt was wool; although wool is still an important fiber in felt manufacture, much felt made today involves blends of wool and other fibers such as rayon. Fibers from several different types of animals may be used, also, in producing felt fabrics.

ASTM defines felt as

> . . . a textile (fabric) characterized by the densely matted condition of most or all of the fibers of which it is composed. There are two broad classes of felt: (1) fabrics relying for their construction upon the ability of the constituent fibers to mat together to form a composite body with neither warp nor filling; and (2) materials having a woven fabric structure.*

ASTM further describes felt as

> A textile composed wholly of any one or combination of new, reprocessed, or reused wool fibers physically interlocked by the inherent felting properties of wool and produced by a suitable combination of mechanical work, chemical action, moisture, and heat, but without weaving, knitting, stitching, thermal bonding, or adhesive.†

Fabrics that have a woven fabric structure are not usually considered to be felts; rather they may be felted to produce a dense fabric, but they would still carry the identification of a woven fabric. Thus, felt will be identified as a fabric made from the interlocking or intermatting of textile fibers without the use of yarns.

The ability of wool fiber (and many other hair fibers) to coil upon itself, interlock, and shrink when subjected to heat, moisture, and pressure (including friction and agitation) is responsible for the felting action. In ancient times, long before recorded history, it was discovered that when heat and water were applied to wool fibers and the resultant mass was pounded with rocks, a cloth was created that would hold together and conform to the general outlines of the body or add warmth to the near environment, such as the floors in caves or other habitats.

Today the manufacture of felt is highly mechanized and controlled. Wool fibers, alone or blended with other fibers, are cleaned, blended, and

*ASTM, *Annual Book of ASTM Standards,* Vol. 07.01, 1985, p. 32.
†Ibid.

carded. After carding, two or more layers of fibers are arranged at right angles to one another. The number of layers depends on the planned ultimate thickness of the felt, but every layer alternates in direction of fiber length in relation to the layer below or above. The final thickness can vary from $\frac{1}{32}$ inch to 3 inches or more. Apparel felts are usually between $\frac{1}{16}$ and $\frac{1}{18}$ inch in thickness; wools for home furnishings and accessories are usually between $\frac{1}{16}$ inch and $\frac{1}{2}$ inch (typical of a wool mat for use under carpeting). Most felt available today is composed of a blend of wool with some other fiber or fibers, frequently a cellulosic fiber of some type.

The layers of carded fibers are passed through machines where they are trimmed and rolled. Moisture and heat are applied, and the layers, or batts as they are called, are placed between heavy plates. The top plate vibrates, producing friction, agitation, and pressure, which cause the fibers to entangle and pack tightly together. The machinery is controlled so that it will stop when the desired thickness and stiffness or firmness is attained.

Next the layer is fulled; that is, the felt mat is shrunk into a compact mass by the application of a detergent and sulfuric acid and then is pounded with wooden hammers. Finally, the felt mat is neutralized, scoured, rinsed, dried, and stretched to the desired width. The amount of stretch is limited; however, the mat can be pulled somewhat to recommended dimensions. Following the final stabilization the felt will no longer stretch in use and care.

Wool from the sheep is the most frequently used fiber because it has the best felting properties. Wool may be used alone for some felt fabrics, but it tends to be relatively expensive; thus, most felt made at the present time does include other fibers. Rayon fibers are the most commonly used with wool, although short cotton fibers and other man-made fibers are sometimes combined with the wool fiber. The amount of wool required to make a felt fabric is not specified. Felts with as little as 25 percent wool appear to have desirable felt properties and characteristics.

Felts have many properties that make them desirable for a variety of industrial and domestic applications: They show good to excellent resilience; are good shock absorbers; are easy to shape; will not ravel, so edges need no finish; are sound absorbent; have good insulating properties with resultant warmth; will not tear, though fibers may pull apart; and can be finished to be mothproof, water repellent, fire resistant, and fungi resistant.

The breaking load of felt fabrics is low when compared with woven or knitted fabrics of the same general thickness and weight. However, with intelligent selection of type and thickness, the consumer can obtain a felt that will be satisfactory for a wide variety of end uses. The shopper seeking felts for apparel must remember that because of low breaking elongation, felt garments should be loose to be durable. Other properties that may cause dissatisfaction include the fact that holes cannot be mended very satisfactorily and there is little or no elastic recovery nor elongation in felt fabrics. If felt is deformed through forces that "stretch" the fabric, it does not return to the original shape.

Felt fabrics are used for wearing apparel, accessories, home-furnishing items, various types of crafts, decorative accents, and industrial purposes. The method of construction permits considerable variation in the thickness of the final fabric and, therefore, enables manufacturers to produce both very flexible felt fabrics as well as comparatively stiff materials. Thin felts that have considerable flexibility are found in such apparel items as skirts, jackets, and vests and in home furnishings such as table coverings, pillow covers, and various types of decorative accents (Fig. 23.1). Heavy thick felts are used for insulating materials, pads such as

23.1 Felt fabric used for decorative accent.

those placed under typewriters and other office equipment, and padding laid under carpeting or area rugs. Heavy felts are widely used in industry.

Proper care procedures for felts are similar to those required for any wool fabric. Because of the absence of yarn formation, the softer, thinner felts have comparatively little strength; therefore, they should be handled carefully and not subjected to pulling or twisting. Dry cleaning is frequently recommended for most felt products. When laundering is acceptable, it is best to wash carefully, either by hand or with a gentle wash cycle, and to dry in the air and not in automatic dryers. If dryers are used, temperatures should be kept low and tumbling action to a minimum; the combination of heat and tumbling on wet felt would increase the felting and result in a stiffer fabric than the original. The presence of some types of man-made fibers and of special finishing processes on felt may produce a product that can be safely and easily laundered; however, the consumer should make certain that label information supports laundering as an approved care procedure.

Needle-Punched Felts

Needle-punched felts resemble felt in appearance; they differ, however, in the fact that they are composed wholly of fibers other than wool or hair. These fabrics are characterized by an intimate, three-dimensional fiber entanglement produced by the mechanical action of barbed needles rather than by the application of heat, moisture, pressure, and agitation.

The fibers are blended by the same carding techniques used in other manufacturing processes. The blended fibers are then arranged into a web or batt by mechanical or air-lay systems. This arrangement may be completely random; that is, fibers lay in no established pattern, giving the fabric equal strength in all directions; or the fibers may be arranged so they are parallel to each other in each separate layer used to form the fabric, but each layer of fibers is perpendicular to the layer above and/or below. In addition, it is possible to make a needle-punched felt in which the fibers are all parallel to each other regardless of the number of layers of fiber needed to make the final fabric. Fabrics with layers that are placed at right angles to layers above and below provide good strength in both directions when the fibers are interlocked; fabrics with fibers all placed in the same direction provide good strength in that direction, but it may be somewhat weak in the direction perpendicular to the long dimension of the fibers.

Some needle-punched felts are made with a layer of *scrim* between the layers of fibers. This scrim is a very loosely woven fabric usually of filament fibers, or filaments are laid between the webs so that some of the filaments are parallel to the longer dimension of the fabric and others parallel to the shorter dimension of the fabric. Scrim increases the strength of the fabric.

To produce needle-punched felts the batt or mat of fibers, with or without scrim, is fed into the needle-punching equipment where barbed needles push through the layer of fibers and then pull out. The process tangles the fibers so they form a secure mat. For some fabrics the mat is put through a preliminary unit that "tacks" the fibers to prevent slippage during the actual needle-punching process. A tacking unit makes between thirty and sixty punches per square inch; this preliminary procedure tends to increase the uniformity of the final fabric.

There are several types of needle-punching machines, but the operation of all is very similar. The needles, which have barbs protruding from the shaft, move through the layer of fibers; as they move they push the fibers into distorted and tangled arrangements. The web moves slowly

23.2 Needle plate used in punching fiber mats to form needle felts. (Monsanto Fibers)

through the machine, and the needles punch as many times as desired for particular end-use fabrics (Fig. 23.2). The number of punches per square inch varies from as few as 800 to more than 2,500. The higher figure is typical of fabric to be used for blankets, whereas the lower number is typical of fabric to be used for carpet padding.

The characteristics of needle-punched felt fabrics depend on

1. The length and characteristics of the fibers used
2. The thickness, evenness, and weight of the fiber web
3. The arrangement of fibers in the web (whether parallel to one edge, crisscross, or random)
4. The density and pattern arrangement of needles in the needle board
5. The number of punches per second and the number of punches per square inch
6. The speed of movement of the web
7. The size of the needles and the number and arrangement of the barbs

Needle-punched felts, like other nonwoven structures, tend to be somewhat stiff and resistant to draping. They are relatively warm because they tend to reduce air circulation owing to thickness and fiber arrangement. This construction technique is particularly satisfactory for such end uses as blankets, industrial fabrics, indoor/outdoor carpeting, padding materials used in home insulation, padding for carpeting or rugs, selected home-furnishing items, and padding for selected upholstered furniture (Fig. 23.3). Needle-punched blankets, frequently called "fiber woven,"

23.3 Indoor-outdoor carpeting made by needle punching; used around a wave pool. (Courtesy Phillips Fibers Corporation)

have become widely used. They are relatively easy to care for and can be made for less cost than woven blankets. Manufacturers have successfully duplicated the appearance of such fabric constructions as velveteen, velour, and other pile structures with the needle-punching process. Consumers should be aware, however, that needle-punched fabrics do not have the stretchability that woven or knitted fabrics have.

Bonded Fiber Fabrics

Bonded fiber fabrics are made directly from fibers without the intermediate step of yarn construction. The term *nonwoven fabric* is generally considered synonymous with *bonded fiber fabric*. However, these terms should be distinguished from the term *bonded fabric* as that refers to a different procedure (discussed in Chapter 24).

Nonwoven or bonded fiber fabric is a textile material produced by the interlocking of fibers through a technique other than felting or needle punching. The general methods include the mechanical, chemical, thermal, or solvent bonding of fibers or the combination of two or more of these techniques.

Natural or man-made fibers can be used for these fabrics; fiber length can vary widely from as short as ½ inch to 2 inches. Filament fibers may also be used in some methods. A variety of different types of fibers can be blended and used in making bonded fiber fabrics; the choice depends on the planned use for the fabric. Cost of fibers may be important, particularly for fabrics that are to have limited use and durability.

The basic steps in manufacturing bonded fiber fabrics are (1) preparing the fibers by cleaning and carding; (2) forming the fibers into a mat or batt to form the web; (3) bonding the web; and (4) drying, curing, and finishing the fabric.

Fiber Preparation

Fibers are prepared much as they would be for yarn manufacture. They are cleaned, blended, and carded (see Chapter 17). Instead of pulling them from the carding frame into a sliver, the fibers are removed from the carding frame in a flat mat or batt. If filament fibers are used, the process differs in that the filaments are extruded onto a moving belt and formed directly into a mat that can be processed into the ultimate fabric.

Web Formation

The web is built of several layers of fibers, particularly if staple fibers are used. These fiber mats may be formed by mechanical means in which layers of fibers are placed on top of each other until the desired thickness is obtained. These layers may be placed so that the longer dimension of all the fibers is parallel to the longer dimension of the final fabric, or the layers may alternate so that fibers in each layer are perpendicular to the fibers above or below.

Fibers may be arranged by using an air-lay process, in which the fibers are suspended in an airstream and then blown onto a moving belt where they lay in a random manner. A wet process may be used in which the fibers are suspended in water and then deposited onto a special support, where the water is removed and the web is formed.

Binding

After the web is formed, the fibers are bonded to retain their position and to make the final product. Adhesives of various types or special fibers that are heat sensitive or solvent sensitive may be used. Adhesives are applied to the web, the web is dried, and finally the mat of fibers is cured. The adhesive chosen must not adversely affect the flexibility, resiliency, strength, and care performance required in the final fabric. The same considerations must be given when selecting binders. If fabrics are to be durable, the choice of a binding agent must be such that the product can be cared for without loss of the bonding material.

The two major methods used for bonding fiber mats are as follows:

1. An adhesive or bonding agent, either a dry powder or a liquid, is applied directly to the web. The powder is usually a thermoplastic substance that is fused into the web by the application of dry heat. If a wet solution is used, it is spread uniformly over the web and then set by chemical action or by heat.
2. Thermoplastic fibers are uniformly blended in the fiber mix and are evenly distributed within the web. Heat is applied, and the thermoplastic fibers soften and fuse over and around the other fibers. As the web cools, the fibers are held together with good durability. This method results in fabrics with good uniformity, good strength, and reasonable cost.

Drying and Curing

After the fiber mat has been bonded it is then dried and cured to ensure durability of the product, at least for the time needed for potential end uses. Some nonwoven or bonded fiber fabrics are designed for limited durability; for these, care is probably not important as the life of the product may be a one-time use only. However, if products are to be used for varying periods of time, they must be made to withstand the use and care to which they will be subjected.

Most nonwoven fabrics are designed for special types of end uses, and finishing procedures may be limited. Color may or may not be important. If dyeing and finishing are needed they would follow the drying and curing operation (Fig. 23.4).

Special Process for Producing Nonwoven Fabrics

Spunbonded Process

Spunbonding is a process by which fabrics are produced directly from the fiber solutions. One or several polymers, such as polyester, nylon, polypropylene, or polyethylene, are fed into fiber forming equipment and through a spinnerette. As they leave the spinnerette they are laid on a moving conveyor belt to form a continuous web. As the web cools the fibers seal together. This process is limited to fibers that can be formed by the melt spinning method.

Pattern in the final fabric can be determined by several factors. The spinnerette can be rotated so that it delivers filaments in different patterns and arrangements; a jet of air can be introduced to tangle the filaments, and the conveyor can be moved at different speeds to collect different amounts of filaments at different locations. The fabric is bonded through

23.4 Bonded fiber fabrics.

23.5 left. Spunbonded fabric.
23.6 right. Spunlaced fabric.
(Nexus from Burlington Formed Fabrics, a division of Burlington Industries)

the particular heat-sensitive properties of the fibers or through special chemical treatment, which alters the fiber slightly so that it will seal with other fibers. Fabrics made by this process have a wide variety of end uses. They are found in industrial fabrics, geotechnical applications, home furnishings, and apparel (Fig. 23.5).

Spunlaced Process

In the spunlaced process a fibrous web is subjected to a high-velocity water jet that entangles the fibers and forms a fabric by mechanical means. The process results in fabrics that are lightweight, soft, and drapable. The products that best identify this group are the Nexus fabrics made by Burlington. These fabrics are made from a variety of different types of fibers and, depending on the fibers used, may be washed, dry cleaned, or both. Fabrics range in weight from very light to medium and from very thin to medium thick.

Typical end uses for these fabrics include quilt backing, mattress pad covers, bases for coated fabrics, interlinings, curtains, table coverings, and a limited selection of apparel items (Fig. 23.6).

Melt-Blown Process

In this process the melted polymer is forced through spinnerettes, and as it emerges, a high velocity airstream hits the filaments as they form. This action breaks the filaments into short lengths, which are collected in a web form on a moving belt. The force of the airstream entangles the fibers, and thermal bonding is used to secure the web. These fabrics are comparatively new. It is expected that their use will be similar to spunbonded and spunlaced constructions.

Artificial Leathers

A product resembling suede was introduced to the market in the late 1960s; it has met with phenomenal success and is widely used in high-cost apparel, home furnishings, and accessories. This product was called Ultrasuede. Since its introduction, several other artificial suedes and leathers have appeared on the market. However, Ultrasuede represents the most successful product.

Ultrasuede is easily washed and dried in automatic laundry equipment and retains its appearance for long periods. It is strong and durable,

23.7 Suits of Ultrasuede fabric. (Springs Industries)

has the comfort of woven textiles, and has the appearance and feel of a top-quality suede leather. It is available in a variety of colors and in two weights. One weight carries the trade name of Facile and is lighter than the standard Ultrasuede fabric; thus it can be used in many products in which a high degree of flexibility and softness is desired. Ultrasuede and Facile are both expensive fabrics and are found, primarily, in high-cost items (Fig. 23.7).

Fabrics designed to be similar to Ultrasuede may be made by the typical bonded fiber processes, with the use of a finishing process to raise a surface similar to suede. They may also be made by using a woven or knitted fabric base, which is given special finishing processes. For the most part, these other artificial suede and leather fabrics require careful handling to prevent them from becoming stiff during care.

Films

Films are not true textiles in that they are not composed of fibers. However, they are made from the same type of polymers used in making fibers and may be used in the same type of products as textile fabrics from fibers. Thus, they are included in this discussion of nonwoven fabrics.

Films may be clear and transparent, colored and transparent, translucent, or opaque. Frequent applications for these fabrics include protective apparel such as rainwear and accessories and home furnishings such as shower curtains, upholstery, and wall coverings (Fig. 23.8).

Films are made by extruding the polymer solution in a sheet form rather than through spinnerettes to form fibers. This difference can be visualized if one compares Saran-Wrap, a film, with the saran fiber used in standard yarn- and fabric-making processes.

The films vary in thickness from very thin to relatively heavy. Thin films are frequently used for protective apparel, medium-weight films might be used for shower curtains, and heavy-weight films are more often used for furniture upholstery.

Many films are supported or laminated to another fabric, either a knitted or woven structure; the product then becomes a multicomponent fabric, which is discussed in Chapter 24.

Nonsupported films may not have a long life; however, some film fabrics that are not supported give outstanding service—particularly in such uses as place mats, shower curtains, or wall coverings.

Films are generally cleaned by wiping with a damp cloth or sponge. Some may be laundered in standard laundry equipment, but careful handling is required to prevent cracking and damage from the agitation. Automatic dryers are not recommended as the heat combined with the agitation can cause unwanted creases, folds, and cracks.

Tapa Cloth

Tapa is another early fabric. It was, and still is, created from the bark of the paper mulberry tree. Original tapa was made by natives in the South Sea Islands, particularly in the South Pacific. It is still made today in the same general areas.

The mulberry bark is cut into thin layers; soaked for a period of time; and then pounded into a thin, filmy layer. The layers are combined to produce the desired weight of the final fabric. Tapa cloth is generally printed by hand with native designs in tan and brown colors with touches of black (Fig. 23.9). The natural color of the tapa is a very light tan. The islanders make tapa into clothing, indoor matting, wall coverings, and other acces-

23.8 Clear vinyl printed with opaque enamel for drapery, wall covering, or shower curtains.

sories of various types. Tapa is a favorite purchase of tourists in Polynesia. Tapa, frequently, is used in business and commercial establishments selling Polynesian food and clothing. It is sometimes selected for recreation areas.

True tapa cloth cannot be laundered by usual methods. The fabric tends to break apart and separate if left in water for a short time. Thus, the recommended method for cleaning tapa is to wipe the surface with a sponge, using a mild detergent and rinsing with warm, not hot, water. The fabric should not be submerged in water, it should not be agitated, and it should not be wrung or handled excessively during care operations.

Fabrics of cotton or cotton blends have been printed to resemble tapa cloth and are available in end-use products and by the yard, especially in areas where tapa is popular.

23.9 Tapa fabric from Polynesia.

Use and Care

Care of Nonwoven Fabrics

Care of nonwoven fabrics depends on several factors: the fiber or fibers used; the method of forming the web, the thickness of the web, and the direction of the fibers in the web; the adhesives or bonding agents used to secure the fibers in position in the fabric; and the presence of finishes and coloring agents. Many nonwoven fabrics are made for one-time use only, so care of these fabrics is not an issue. Nonwoven fabrics designed for reuse can usually be laundered if directions are followed. Dry cleaning may be used, but it is frequently not suggested because of possible interactions between the adhesive or bonding agent and the dry cleaning solvents.

It is usually important to keep handling to a minimum when laundering such fabrics; thus, agitation in washers should be kept to the gentle cycle, or hand washing should be used. Wringing, creasing, or pulling, particularly when the fabric is wet, should be kept to an absolute minimum as it is possible to separate fibers and cause breaks in the fabrics.

Use of Nonwoven Fabrics

Nonwoven fabrics appear in a wide variety of products for apparel, home furnishings, business, industry, and specialized applications such as aerospace. The list of products made from nonwoven fabrics is long and growing each year. Some typical end-use items include diapers, handkerchiefs, skirts, dresses, apparel interfacings, bandages, curtains, decontamination clothing, garment bags, industrial apparel, lampshades, map backing, napkins, place mats, ribbon, upholstery backing, window shades, hospital gowns, hospital sheets, and many more. Figure 23.10 shows some of the medical uses of nonwoven fabrics.

When selecting nonwoven fabrics for use as apparel interfacings or underlinings or for home furnishings, it is important to determine whether the nonwoven fabric will be compatible with the main fabric. That is, the consumer should make certain that temperatures, detergents, and handling methods recommended for the outer or main fabric will not damage the nonwoven fabric used with it.

Consumers should consider characteristics required in the end-use product. What levels of softness or stiffness are desired? What about draping qualities? What strength is necessary? All these questions need consideration.

23.10 Nonwoven fabrics used for medical applications. (INDA, Association of the Nonwoven Fabrics Industry)

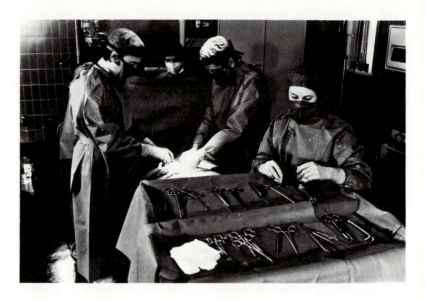

Study Questions

1. What is felt?
2. Describe how felt is made; identify its properties and characteristics that influence use and care.
3. How do felt and needle-punched felt constructions differ?
4. What are typical end uses for felt and for needle-punched felt?
5. Name the different types of nonwoven fabrics available.
6. Describe the major techniques used in making bonded fiber or nonwoven fabrics.
7. What factors might influence care of nonwoven fabrics?
8. Why are films discussed as a part of nonwoven fabrics?
9. How is tapa made? Why is it a part of nonwoven fabrics?
10. How would you care for products made of tapa?

Other Fabric-Construction Processes

24

Construction processes included in this chapter are those that do not fit easily into previous discussions. Included in this group are those composed of two or more previously constructed fabrics, those that involve stitch bonding, and those that are made by special equipment in limited amounts. Both very old and very new techniques find their niche in this location. Fabrics described here are manufactured in limited amounts and/or for highly specialized purposes.

Stitch-Bonded Structures

Stitch-bonded fabrics may be described as fabrics in which fibers, yarns, fibers and yarns, or fibers and a base (substrate fabric) are held together by stitching with additional yarn or thread. These fabrics are available in three basic types: (1) comparatively flat fabrics composed of yarns that are stitched together to form the fabric; (2) fabrics in which fibers are stitched together without the use of yarn or thread; and (3) fabrics made from a preconstructed fabric base into which other yarns, threads, or slivers are stitched, usually forming loops on one or both sides of the fabric.

Fabrics Made with Yarns and Threads

There are four types of fabric in this group. They are typically identified by such names as Malimo, Schusspol, Maliwatt, and Malifol. Each is described briefly.

Malimo   The Malimo process uses two layers of yarn, each at right angles to the other—or as close to right angles as possible; these layers of yarns are then securely joined together with lines of stitching. The stitching process resembles a chain stitch and looks very similar to a column of stitches in a tricot knit fabric. A modification of this process uses only weft yarns; the stitching lines form the warp direction. Various machines make it possible to interloop the columns of stitching to produce surface patterns. Figure 24.1 shows the basic structure used in this type of stitch-bonded fabric. Figure 24.2 is a typical fabric made by this technique.

    Characteristics of this type of fabric depend on several factors: the weight and diameter of the yarns used in the base layers and for the stitching operation; the closeness of the yarn arrangements and of the stitching lines; the type of yarns—simple or complex, single or ply or cord; the type of fiber or fibers; the elasticity or elongation of the fibers and yarns; and the strength of the fibers and yarns.

    When the stitching threads are fine and the base yarns are thick, the fabric resembles a woven structure because the stitching threads tend to

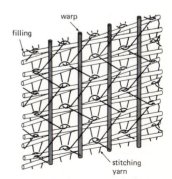

24.1   Diagram of the Malimo stitch-bond technique.

24.2 Stitch-bonded fabric, Malimo type.

disappear into the surface; when the stitching thread is dominant, the fabric surface tends to resemble a knit fabric.

Malimo fabrics are used for decorative textiles such as upholstery, wall coverings, pillow covers, draperies, and sheer window curtains; for apparel such as suitings and sportswear; and for technical fabrics such as conveyor belts, packing materials, and base fabrics for lamination.

Schusspol Schusspol fabrics require a sheet of weft yarns, yarns or thread for stitching, and a set of yarns that forms a pile surface. The stitching threads hold the base layer securely in place as well as the pile yarns, which form a raised surface on one side of the fabric only. The pile on these fabrics tends to be somewhat flat. The fabrics are used for home furnishings, particularly special floor coverings, upholstery, and wall coverings.

Maliwatt Maliwatt fabrics are made by stitching a layer or web of fibers with yarns or threads. A cross-laid or random fiber web forms the base and is held together by rows of stitching (see Figure 24.3).

24.3 Diagram of the Maliwatt web stitch-bond process. (Textimo)

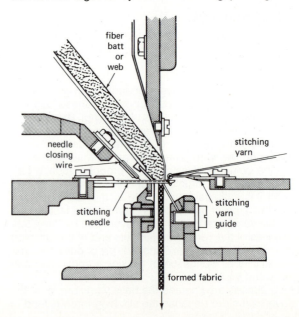

Maliwatt fabrics can range from very sheer and fine to relatively heavy products; however, the majority are in the medium-weight group. They are used for interlinings for apparel and for home-furnishing fabrics such as backing, wall coverings, insulation and temperature control fabrics, and padding for carpeting. These fabrics may resemble needle-punched felt fabrics (Fig. 24.4).

Malifol This construction is new, and little has been published about these products. It is believed that the base is made from tape yarns of polyester, which are stitched together to form the fabric.

Fabrics Made with Fiber Mats

The fabric type in this group is Malivlies. This fabric is made from a mat of fibers that is stitched without thread in the needles. Obviously it becomes very much like a needle-punched fabric. The difference lies in the fact that the method used for needle punching is such that the finished fabric has the look of actual threads stitched into the mat. Fabrics made with fiber mats are used, primarily, for packing and insulation.

Fabrics Made with a Preconstructed Base

The two major types of fabrics in this category are Malipol and Voltex.

Malipol The Malipol construction uses a prefabricated fabric as the base; to this base, yarns are stitched in to form a pile surface. Figure 24.5 shows the operation, and Figure 24.6 provides examples of these fabrics.

The pile stitches can be short or long, made with fine to heavy yarn, and left uncut or cut and sheared. Fabrics can be made to resemble terry cloth, velveteen, and other pile structures. The process can be used to produce fabrics that resemble woven or fiber-woven blankets.

These fabrics are less expensive to make than their woven counter-

24.4 Maliwatt-type stitch-bonded fabrics.

24.5 Diagram of the Malipol pile stitch-bond process. (Textimo)

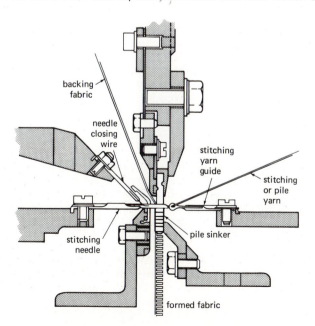

24.6 Face of two Malipol-type stitch-bonded fabrics.

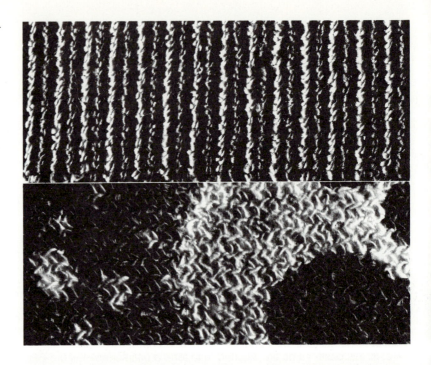

parts, which may help their eventual acceptance by consumers. They are used for the same type of end-use item as other pile fabrics, such as upholstery, imitation furs, floor coverings, and towels. Some of this type of construction has been used for women's coats and suits. The fabrics are durable.

Voltex This type of fabric is made with a preconstructed fabric base. Into the base a web of fibers is stitched, so the ultimate fabric is composed of a fabric base, a layer of fibers, and stitches that hold the two together. The method is designed to produce a fabric that appears similar to pile fabrics on one side; on the reverse the stitches can be clearly seen. The major use for this construction is for imitation furs, overcoating, upholstery, and plush fabrics for toys.

Use and Care

Care of these fabrics depends on several factors: the type of fiber or fibers in the yarns and threads, the closeness of the stitches, the type of construction, and the looseness or compactness of the structure. If a care label is included with the product, directions should be followed. In general, care for such structures is similar to that given to woven, knitted, or nonwoven structures, which the stitch-bonded product resembles and which are made of the same type of fibers.

Stitch-bonded fabrics are relatively new, and to date, the major consumer goods in which such fabrics are found are home furnishings: draperies, curtains, and upholstery. It is believed that these fabrics will increase in popularity for both apparel and home furnishings because of the variety of appearances that can be produced at a relatively low cost.

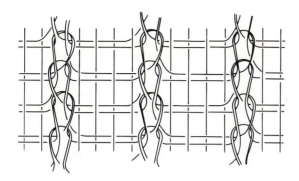

24.7 Diagram of the METAP fabric-construction process.

The Metap System

A type of fabric construction was introduced in the late 1970s that tends to combine knitting and weaving into one construction operation: the METAP system.

The machine uses a warp yarn arrangement much like any loom, with a shedding operation similar to standard looms. However, a number of weft or filling yarns are joined to the warp yarns by an operation similar to knitting (Fig. 24.7). Fabrics made by this system are recommended for apparel and home furnishings. The process offers several advantages, including design flexibility; added stretch in the filling direction; good drapability; firm edges, eliminating the need for special selvages; and rapid production, which saves money in manufacture.

Braided Fabrics

Braided fabrics are made by plaiting, or braiding, three or more yarns or strands of fabric that originate from a single location and that are parallel to each other before the interlacing occurs. The resulting fabric has a diagonal surface effect because the yarns intercross from one side to the other in a diagonal manner. A column of horizontal Vs is formed. Narrow braids can be joined together to form wide fabrics or large end-use items such as carpets. Braided fabrics can be produced that are either flat in form or circular.

Circular braids appear in such items as shoelaces, ropes, and insulation for wires. Flat braids serve for a variety of end uses, but one of the most common is that of trimming (Fig. 24.8). All braided fabrics have considerable stretch in the lengthwise direction and some in the width. This property may create problems in the application of braided trim because it is difficult to keep even. However, the stretchability enables a skilled operator to apply braid so that it lies smooth at corners and curved areas as well as along straight edges.

Fabrics made by the braiding process are not limited to the use of yarn forms. Braids may incorporate cut strips of already constructed fabric, leaves, leather strips, straw, or any other flexible product that can be braided and shaped to create attractive, distinctive, and unusual fabrics.

Braided fabrics should be given the care appropriate to both the fiber involved and the construction. If the braid is loose and extremely stretchy, it is wise to handle it carefully and to block it into the desired form before drying. Compact braids can be cleaned or laundered, using normal care procedures required by the fiber or fibers involved. If there is

24.8 Braided fabric for trimming.

24.9 Net fabric.

inadequate labeling for care, the consumer should select the method appropriate to woven or knitted fabrics of similar density or thickness and compactness, surface texture, and fiber content.

Nettings

Nets are open-mesh fabrics with large geometric interstices between the yarns (Fig. 24.9). Nets were originally made by knotting the yarns at each point of intersection, and this may still be done for limited production. These knotted nets may have a comparatively large mesh structure or a small opening; but because of the actual knotting at each intersecting point, there is minimal slippage or distortion during use and care. All net fabrics made before the 1800s were knotted by hand. In 1809 a machine was developed that duplicated the net construction so accurately that only an expert could distinguish the hand-tied from the machine-made product.

In recent years further changes have occurred. Today, a large proportion of the nets available on the market are made by knitting machines, either tricot or raschel units. They have the same open-mesh effect, but as there are no knots at intersecting points, only loops, these knitted nets are not as durable as those formed by the old knotting technique because of the possibility of yarn slippage at the point of interlooping; this slippage occurs most easily when yarns are very smooth and made of filament fibers. Heat setting these fabrics when they are composed of thermoplastic or heat-sensitive fibers increases the durability.

True nets are still made for a limited group of end uses. They are typical for fishing nets, sports equipment, hammocks, some curtain fabrics, and some veiling fabric.

The care of nets depends on the type of fiber used, the yarn structure, the size of the opening, and the size of the yarn. In general, it is best to use care procedures reserved for delicate fabrics to avoid snagging and abrasion damage. Nylon nets are relatively easy to care for; however, the openness of any net requires caution to prevent damage.

Laces

Lace has been defined in many ways, and authorities differ about what really constitutes true lace. However, most people agree that lace is an open-work fabric consisting of a network of yarns (or threads) that produce intricate designs (Fig. 24.10). There is no recorded evidence to indicate when lace was first made, but specimens in museums have been dated as early as 2500 B.C. Regardless of its origin, it is generally accepted that lace was developed for beauty and adornment for both apparel and home furnishings.

Lace is truly the aristocrat of textile fabrics. No other cloth is so difficult to make yet so delicate, requires so much skill in manufacturing, or demands so much creative ability in designing. Everything about lace indicates special characteristics. It is a product of a combination of construction procedures. Special yarns are made that have high strength but that are very fine; these are constructed into fabrics by a method that combines interlooping and knotting. In addition, surface embroidery may be added as a part of the actual construction procedure. The machinery used to make lace was designed by John Leavers and his brother in 1837 and is the most complicated textile machinery in use today.

Yarns used in making lace are stronger and more tightly twisted than those used for most other types of fabrics, particularly for fabrics of the same density. The use of nylon, with its inherent strength, has added

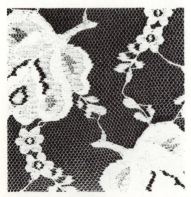

24.10 Lace fabric.

to the durability of lace. Lace can be made in very narrow widths or as wide as 72 or more inches.

Much lace available on the market today has been made with raschel knitting frames; these differ from real lace in that yarns are only interlooped, not knotted. Knitted lace is less expensive than true lace, and it can be produced much faster. For these reasons, there is little true lace on the market today. A majority of the lace available for consumers is made on knitting machines and not on lace-making equipment.

Lace fabrics tend to be fragile, at least in appearance, and require careful handling during use and care. Some laces are extremely delicate and do demand extreme caution in care; others are surprisingly strong and durable and can be laundered in automatic equipment with no problem. However, it is well to remember that delicate laces, or any lace in which there are open spaces that can be damaged by snagging or abrasion, should be handled carefully. The choice of detergent depends on the fiber content as does the use of other laundry additives such as bleaches and fabric softeners. Temperatures used depend on the fiber content and the finishing processes.

Lace is treasured for its decorative appearance, and its major function is to adorn. It is not a utility fabric. It is used for trimming on various types of apparel; for evening wear; for home furnishings such as curtains, table coverings, place mats, and bedspreads; and for other uses where a delicate and decorative fabric is desired. Any lace item should be given careful handling.

Multicomponent Fabrics

Multicomponent fabrics include *bonded fabrics, laminated fabrics, foam-backed fabrics,* and *quilted fabrics.* A multicomponent fabric is one in which at least two layers of material or fabric have been sealed together in some way. Adhesive may be used to seal the layers, or thread may be used to stitch them together.

It must be noted that some authorities classify double weave fabrics as a type of multicomponent. They are not included here; rather they are included with woven fabrics. Double-weave fabrics are made by a weaving process and may or may not be separated following construction. They do not involve either of the two techniques used in making multicomponent fabrics.

Definitions of a multicomponent fabric differ among authorities. It is generally considered a fabric in which at least two layers of previously constructed fabric are joined together by some means, such as an adhesive of some type, thermoplastic fibers, or stitching.

Multicomponents Using Adhesives

Fabrics joined by some type of adhesive are frequently identified as bonded fabric or laminated fabric. ASTM does indicate a difference between these two.

A bonded fabric is a layered fabric structure wherein a face or shell fabric is joined to a backing fabric, such as tricot, with an adhesive that does not significantly add to the thickness of the combined fabrics. A thin layer of foam is considered an adhesive when the cell structure is completely collapsed by a flame.

A laminated fabric is a layered fabric structure wherein a face or outer fabric is joined to a continuous sheet material, such as poly-

24.11 Tricot-backed bonded fabric.

urethane foam, in such a way that the identity of the continuous sheet material is retained, either by the flame method or by an adhesive, and this in turn normally, but not always, is joined on the back with a backing fabric such as tricot.*

Bonded fabrics frequently have a tricot knit as the backing, as indicated by the preceding definition. This provides a smooth inner surface and becomes a "self-lining" (Fig. 24.11). It is less costly than two separate fabrics when making into end-use products because only one operation is required in making "lined" products. Bonded fabrics have good stability, resistance to stretch or deformation, and a low incidence of raveling. However, the quality of the bond varies considerably, which may cause consumers serious problems in the use and care of these products. Fabric separation may occur during wear and/or care; uneven shrinkage of the two fabrics may occur because of differences in fabric structure and fiber content; and bubbles may appear where the bonding breaks away. Bonded fabrics have been improved over the past two decades, but there are still some difficulties in use and care that demand consumer caution in the purchase and handling of these fabrics.

For laminated fabrics the layer of foam adds both warmth and stability. These fabrics may be called foam-backed fabrics when there is only one layer of fabric attached to a layer of foam. When two layers of fabric are used with a layer of foam between, the fabrics are frequently called a sandwich construction. For either type of laminate, the layer of foam can vary in thickness from very thin, almost invisible, to as thick as 1/16 inch. When two layers of fabric are used with foam between, this construction gives a fabric a finished appearance on both sides (Fig. 24.12).

Laminated fabrics may also be made of a layer of film sealed to a woven or knitted fabric. Foam may or may not be used between them. Technically, if no foam is used the term *bonded fabric* is appropriate. Fabrics made with a layer of a film and a layer of fabric are called *supported films*. The woven or knitted fabric gives support and stability to the film. For many of these fabrics the film layer is the face, or right side. When films are used for upholstery and other home-furnishing fabrics, the supported film (bonded fabric film) is preferred because the support fabric contributes to the durability. Some fabrics, particularly for home furnishings, are made by sealing a layer of foam to a film such as vinyl.

*ASTM, *Annual Book of Standards,* Vol. 07.01, 1986, p. 31.

24.12 Fabric to foam to fabric laminate. a. Face. b. Back and foam.

a.

b.

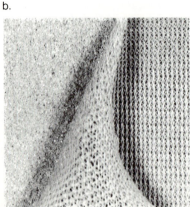

An additional type of bonded fabric uses a center sheet of fibers (a fiber web) instead of foam. The fabric formed provides lightweight structures that possess high levels of insulation. A majority of such fabrics are sealed by stitching and, thus, belong in the quilting group discussed later. However, in some of these fabrics the seal has been made by using adhesives. These are not recommended; the layer of fibers tends to weaken an adhesive seal because of the lack of contact between the main layers of the fabric.

Multicomponents Using Stitching

Multicomponent fabrics that are joined by stitching of some type are called *quilted* fabrics. Quilted fabrics have been made for centuries. They include a surface fabric of some type; usually a middle layer, which may be made of fibers in a mat form, foam, or a combination of the two; and a backing layer of fabric. The surface fabric may have considerable design, which has been imparted through various techniques; the backing fabric may be patterned or plain (Fig. 24.13). The middle layer may be very thin or somewhat thick, depending on the planned end use of the product.

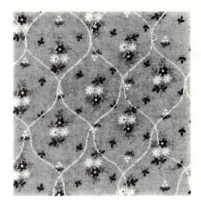

24.13 Quilted fabric.

Several factors need consideration in selecting quilted fabrics: The fabrics must be compatible in terms of care; they should have similar dimensional stability so they retain their size and shape; the stitching should be close enough to prevent slippage and movement of the inner layer, which could lead to unattractive products; the size of the stitch used for quilting should be relatively short to prevent breakage during use and care; fabrics of the same general weight, yarn count, and fiber content should be used.

Care of quilted fabrics depends on these factors plus the size of the end-use item. Some quilted products can easily be laundered and dried in standard automatic equipment; some require laundering or cleaning by professionals because of the size of the product or the type of fiber and fabrics used. If care labels have been attached, the directions should be followed carefully.

Multicomponents Using Ultrasonic Energy

Multicomponent fabrics may be made by using ultrasonic energy to seal the layers together. In this process either the fabric layers or the fiber mat used for the center must include heat-sensitive (thermoplastic) fibers that can be melted sufficiently to seal the fabrics and fiber mat together. In general, both the fabrics and the fiber mat include thermoplastic fibers such as polyester or nylon.

The final product appears similar to a quilted fabric except that the "stitches" are somewhat longer and wider than regular thread stitching. This process is called the "pinsonic" method. The structure includes a surface fabric, a fiber mat, and a backing fabric. The layers are fed into a machine with a patterned roll, which has a design formed by metal pins. Sonic (sound) vibration causes the pins to transmit enough heat at the point of contact with the layers so that the heat-sensitive fibers melt sufficiently at those points, sealing the sandwich of fiber and fabrics securely together (Fig. 24.14). The pins create the appearance of machine stitching except for the characteristics previously noted. These fabrics give adequate durability providing they are not subjected to pulling. When pulled they tend to separate at the bonding points and gradually will separate completely. They are used for products in which low cost and insulation or padding are desired. Typical uses are for mattress pads and table pads.

24.14 Pinsonic "quilted" fabric.

Use and Care

The care of multicomponent fabrics depends on a variety of factors. Consideration must be given to the fibers in the fabrics; the adhesives used, if any; and the types of fabric constructions. Another important aspect is the actual size of the end-use product.

Multicomponents are used for a wide variety of products, including home furnishings and apparel. They provide good insulation and attractive appearance. It is suggested that the consumer consider the following when purchasing multicomponent fabrics:

1. The layers should have been sealed together securely and firmly, so that it requires considerable pull to separate them.
2. When both fabrics are woven, the grain lines in each should be parallel to those of the other, and filling yarns in one fabric should be perpendicular to the warp yarns in the same fabric as well as to those in the second fabric.
3. Adequate care labels should be securely attached. It is hard to prescribe generalized care for multicomponent fabrics, as many different combinations are used; thus, care labels are essential.
4. There should be no odor, and the fabrics should not be stiff or brittle.
5. An adhesive, if used, should not be visible.
6. If foam is used, it should retain its light color unless it was dyed to blend better with the surface fabrics and their color.
7. For quilted fabrics, the stitching should be small, even in size, and have no breaks in the threads.

Tufted Fabrics

Tufted fabrics are examples of a very old type of construction coupled with modern procedures. Handmade tufted fabrics originated in the American Colonial period and included the early version of candlewick bedspreads and chenille-type coverlets and robes. Hand tufting, practiced as an art, was limited to making fabrics for special end uses. About 1900 the craft was revised when machines were developed to produce a tufted fabric at rapid speeds with a minimum of hand labor.

Tufting is a process of manufacturing a pile fabric by inserting loops into an already constructed base, or ground, fabric. This base may be of any type and made of any fiber, but most tufted materials use a base of cotton, linen, jute, or olefin fibers. If the fabric is woven, it has a close weave with a high yarn count; however, many tufted fabrics made today use a nonwoven fabric as the base. When nonwoven fabrics are used for the base, they must be firm and dense enough to hold the tufted yarns securely in place. Yarns that form the tuft, the pile effect, may be of any fiber, but a majority of tufting yarns today are composed of polyester, nylon, cotton, or acrylic fibers.

Yarns that form the loops are inserted into the ground fabric with needles, and the loops are held in place either by a special coating applied to the back or by untwisting the tufted yarn and shrinking the base fabric (Fig. 24.15). The loops may be inserted so that they vary in length and produce surface texture and designs (Fig. 24.16). This effect is achieved by controlling the amount of yarn fed to each needle and the distance the needle penetrates through the base fabric. A variety of controls can create interesting and unusual designs; these are frequently controlled by computers in modern tufting plants. The back of the fabric shows the yarns carried along the underside that form the loops during

24.15 above. Close-up of the tufting process. Yarns are punched through a base cloth to form loops on the face of the fabric. (Springs Industries)
24.16 below. Tufted area rug, Trevira polyester pile. (Hoechst Fibers)

the construction operation (Fig. 24.17). The tufts can be cut or left uncut to produce additional designs.

Tufted fabrics are less expensive than woven or knitted pile fabrics, which they resemble; they can be made more rapidly and with great design variety. Tufted carpets and rugs became popular in the 1950s, and their success has been phenomenal. Approximately 90 percent of all carpeting and rugs produced in the United States are made by the tufting process. It should be noted that the remaining 10 percent are divided about equally between needle-punching methods and weaving. Tufted fabrics are used in floor coverings because they are considerably less expensive than woven fabric; they may be made in a wide variety of textures and designs—far greater than available on needle-punching machines; they permit a wide choice of colors and yarn types.

Tufted fabric care depends on several factors: the type of fiber; the type of yarn structures; the length of the tuft, or "pile"; the base, or ground, fabric construction and fiber types; the compactness of the tufting; or closeness of tufts; and the size of the product. Tufted fabrics used in apparel and small home-furnishing items may be laundered in automatic equipment if the fibers permit. In fact, this method is recommended as it helps to fluff up the tufts and makes the clean fabric look like new. Large items such as carpeting and rugs require carpet-cleaning procedures and respond well to care typical for the fibers involved. It is essential that carpets and rugs be cleaned according to any care directions provided with the item; if no directions are available, care should depend primarily on the type of fibers used to make the product.

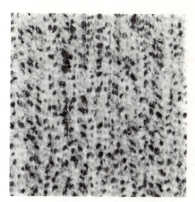

24.17 Back of tufted carpeting before backing fabric is sealed to it.

Study Questions

1. Describe the various methods of making stitch-bonded fabrics. How do these differ from nonwoven fabrics? How are they similar?
2. What type of end-use products may be made from stitch-bonded fabrics?
3. What are reasons for the use of stitch-bonded fabrics?
4. Describe each of the following fabric constructions:
   a. Braiding
   b. Netting
   c. Lace making
5. What are typical end uses for each of the fabric constructions cited in question 4?
6. What are care problems that might be encountered with nettings and laces?
7. What are multicomponent fabrics?
8. What are the differences between a multicomponent produced with adhesive and one produced with stitching?
9. What factors should consumers consider when selecting fabrics that are multicomponent?
10. How are tufted fabrics made? What proportion of floor coverings are made by this technique? What other end-use products may be made by tufting?
11. What type of end-use products might be made from quilted fabrics? What points need consideration in the care of these items?
12. What type of end-use products might be made from bonded or laminated fabrics? What points need consideration in the care of these fabrics?

Finish and Color Application

Fabric, as the average consumer knows it, does not exist until it has been subjected to various finishing processes. Most fabrics on the market for either apparel or home furnishings have undergone several finishing operations to produce a fabric that is pleasant to consumers and meets their various needs. In addition, a large proportion of fabric has been given color in some manner. The textile industry considers the application of dyes and finishes as wet processing. For convenience in understanding finishing and coloration, these techniques have been divided into several chapters.

The history of finishes and finishing processes is sketchy. Smoothing of fabrics on flat surfaces, such as stone slates, was the forerunner of calendering or ironing; application of white clay to make fabrics firm or stiff was an early sizing technique. The first recorded information concerning finishes dates from as recently as the mid-nineteenth century. It is to be assumed that before that time routine finishes were anything but routine. Mercerization is one of the oldest finishes in terms of written information. John Mercer discovered the effect of caustic soda on cotton in 1853. However, the process was not perfected to any degree until 1889, when H. A. Lowe found ways to control the caustic and handle the fabric during the mercerizing operation. Shrinkage control by processes such as sanforization was not developed until the early part of the twentieth century; and the development of durable-press finishes did not occur until the mid-twentieth century.

This text has divided the discussion of finishes into two major groups: Chapter 25 describes those finishes that are usually considered to be routine or general and a part of the normal preparation of fabric for sale. Chapter 26 describes those finishes that alter appearance and hand or that change the performance of the fabric in some way. These finishes are added to fabric to give it properties that consumers desire; they are not a part of the normal processing of every fabric.

Color application, unlike finishing, is a very old process. Color in some form was applied to the earliest examples of textiles. Fragments of fabrics found in archeological digs provide evidence of early coloration techniques. Modern dyestuffs, however, are only a little over 100 years old. The first synthetic dye was not developed until 1856, and most dyes used today are products of the years since 1920. Color can be added to textiles in many ways; this text has divided the application of color into two chapters. Chapter 27 describes methods used to dye fabrics or to apply color on an overall basis to fibers, yarns, or fabrics. Chapter 28 describes methods used to create pattern on the surface of fabrics.

Routine or General Finishes

25

The application of finishes is the province of the converting industry. Converters devote their research, development, and manufacturing facilities to the improvement and modification of fabrics through finishes. Their goal is to provide consumers with a product that will meet the particular needs to which the fabric will be applied. For the consumer this part of the textile industry may well be the most important. It is the finish that frequently determines the level of satisfaction or dissatisfaction that consumers feel in the selection, use, and care of textile products.

Fabrics before finishing are said to be in the *greige,* or *gray,* state. This term does not refer to the color of the fabric; rather it identifies fabrics that have not had any finishes applied.

Finishes can be classified in various ways. They can be identified as mechanical or chemical, permanent or nonpermanent (frequently identified as durable or renewable), and general or functional. Chapters 25 and 26 use the last division as the basis for classifying finishes by their common use—they are applied for routine or general purposes, or they are applied to serve some function or alter appearance. In addition, the discussion of finishes will identify those that are relatively durable and those that are renewable or nondurable.

In this chapter routine or general finishes are described, with some emphasis on care procedures required for retention of finish. The durability of the various finishes will be noted, and any effect they might have on hand and appearance of the final textile is included. The importance of selected finishes both in creating a desirable product and in pleasing consumers is noted.

Finishes are said to be durable if they can withstand a "normal" amount of wear. *Normal* is, obviously, a relative term, and one person's interpretation may be very different from another's. The industry measures the durability or permanence of a finish by its ability to withstand tests designed to simulate average use and care. Renewable finishes are those that rub off or are removed easily by washing or dry cleaning.

The following discussion starts with a brief look at the way routine finishing is achieved in modern converting plants. Then those finishes typically used on a majority of fabrics are discussed in the usual order in which they are applied. Next we will look at a few finishes that are somewhat specific to finishing wool or wool-blend fabrics, and finally, at a few that are used for some, but not all, fabrics to produce their typical appearance and develop their expected durability.

The inherent properties of staple length fibers, those short fibers as opposed to filament length fibers, require a variety of special finishing operations. The following discussion tries to identify such finishes wherever possible. The discussion follows the typical sequence of finishing for such fabrics as cotton; cotton and polyester blends; and other blends, including cellulosic fibers.

Finishing Processes

Finishes may be applied to textile fabrics by several different procedures. Any one or combinations of several may be used. These techniques are described briefly.

Water-Bath Finishing

Most finishes, until recently, were applied to fabrics from a water bath. The chemicals were dissolved in the water, the fabric was immersed in the solution, the finish was padded into the fabric, excess finish and liquid were removed, and the fabric was dried. This process is still widely used today; however, there have been changes in finishing because of the need to conserve water, avoid environmental pollution whenever possible, and conserve energy. As these requirements increased in importance, converters researched other ways to apply finishes; these new methods include solvent finishing and foam finishing. However, there are still a lot of finishes applied from a water bath, and this situation will probably continue for some time.

Solvent Finishing

Solvent finishes utilize a solvent into which finishing materials are dispersed; this solvent may be similar to those used for dry cleaning. This process reduces water pollution and energy consumption, although the same type of equipment as used in water-bath finishing may be used. Solvents are reclaimed when possible to reduce finishing costs. This process is frequently used on wool fabrics.

Foam Finishing

Foam finishing depends on the formation of foams, much like soap bubbles. These foams are applied to the fabric, and as the bubbles break, the finishing compounds are pressed into the fabric. This process reduces the amount of liquid required for applying the finish, reduces the energy requirement because of the lowered amount of liquid, and is very effective. Not only is the amount of required water reduced, but so is the amount of energy, and water pollution is also less.

Although water-bath finishing is still the most frequently used technique, it is probable that foam finishing and solvent finishing will increase rapidly in the future. Some finishes, however, are very difficult to apply without adequate water supplies; but it is likely that these will continue to be applied with water baths as long as there is sufficient water available for such procedures.

Basic Routine Finishes

Singeing and Desizing

Singeing and desizing are frequently combined operations. Singeing removes protruding fiber ends to produce a clear, smooth, uniform fabric surface. Desizing removes chemicals that were applied before fabric construction, particularly weaving, to reduce damage to yarns during the fabric construction process.

Singeing consists of burning off the fuzz or fiber ends on the surface of fabrics to obtain a smooth and flat fabric face (it may be applied to both sides so both face and back are smooth). Fabrics that are to have napped surfaces or raised surfaces of some type (discussed in Chapter 26) would not be singed. However, they would be desized.

A typical singeing and desizing operation includes the following steps:

1. Fabric is opened to full width and fed onto storage scrays (large tray-like holders) to allow ample fabric for feeding to the singers at the speed necessary to prevent fabric damage.
2. Fabric surfaces may be brushed lightly to raise unwanted fiber ends before singeing so that fabrics will be singed quickly and uniformly.
3. Fabric enters the singeing area, where it is held at full width and under tension to keep it flat and to minimize the formation of creases or wrinkles and to prevent curling at the outer edges. Singeing may be done with heated plates or open flames (Fig. 25.1).
4. Fabric leaves the singeing area and immediately enters the desizing bath. The desizing bath stops any singeing afterglow that might damage the cloth. The desize enzymes saturate the fabric, which moves into additional baths containing more enzymes and detergents that loosen the sizing present and prepare the fabric for the next step. Fabrics move through the singeing and desizing bath between 230 and 270 yards (210 to 247 meters) per minute.

The brushing that precedes singeing is a mechanical action, whereas the singeing is an oxidation process that literally burns away fiber ends. Desizing involves some chemical action as the desizing agents digest the sizing that was applied prior to fabric construction.

As the fabric leaves the desizing bath, it is either rolled onto large beams in full width or it is pulled into a rope form. Either method permits storage of the fabric prior to the next step; it puts the fabric into a form suitable for processing on the type of equipment that will be used for bleaching and scouring.

25.1 Open-flame singeing. (Springs Industries)

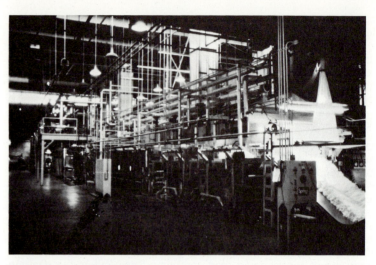

25.2 Overall view of an open-width finishing range for scouring and bleaching fabrics. (Springs Industries)

Bleaching and Scouring

Fabrics may be scoured and bleached in either rope or open-width form; the technique used depends on the fabric and the type of fibers in it. Any fabric that may be given creases or wrinkles that might be difficult, if not impossible, to remove during the finishing operation will be bleached and scoured in open-width or flat form; fabrics in which creases and wrinkles can be easily removed during later processing are usually bleached and scoured in rope form. The actual steps are the same for either; the difference lies in the equipment used and the handling of the fabric. Further, the speed of movement of fabric through the bleaching and scouring machines will differ: In rope processing, fabric moves between 100 and 200 yards per minute depending on fabric weight; in open-width processing, the speed is 80 to 120 yards per minute, also depending on fabric weight (Fig. 25.2).

Scouring procedures and the type of chemicals used for bleaching will depend on the type of fibers involved. Some fabrics will have considerable foreign matter such as natural waxes, dirt, processing oils, and sizing compounds that were not completely removed during the previous operation. For some fabrics fugitive colors (those that are used for marking) may have to be removed during this step.

Soaps or synthetic detergents with alkaline builders and with wetting agents are the most common scouring agents. If fibers are damaged by alkaline substances, alkaline builders are omitted and mild soaps or detergents are used. The bleaching substances depend on the fiber types. For many fabrics, chlorine compounds may be used along with caustic soda and hydrogen peroxide; for some fabrics, only hydrogen peroxide or perborate bleaching substances would be used. Refer to fiber chapters to determine which fibers could not use chlorine compounds. Other additives that might be a part of the bleaching and scouring process include optical brighteners and water softeners.

The general steps for bleaching and scouring include the following:

1. A prewash to remove any desizing chemicals that are still present in the fabric
2. Saturation with a caustic, wetting agents, and emulsifiers to remove waxes, foreign matter, and any discoloring materials present
3. Time for these agents to react—which varies depending on the fibers

present in the fabric, the weight of the fabric, and the compactness or looseness of the fabric structure
4. Washing to remove the various agents used and to cool the fabric prior to the next operation
5. Saturation with hydrogen peroxide, more caustic materials, and silicates; the temperature is raised to that appropriate to the fibers present
6. Another period of time to permit the chemicals to react
7. A final washing to remove all the chemicals and to give the fabric a final rinse so that it is completely free of any added chemicals used in the bleaching and scouring operations

Whiteness retention of textile products is important to consumers, and white fabrics may require frequent bleaching during their lifetime. This is much easier if the fabric was properly bleached during the finishing processes. Colored products should retain the color they had when purchased. This, too, is easier if the proper bleaching processes were used. Occasionally, incorrect bleaching may cause a fabric to regress to its natural color, which could alter the color applied and result in consumer dissatisfaction.

Bleaching of wool is a case in point. When bleached properly the wool will tend to retain a white or slightly off-white color; if the bleaching process included techniques that do not ensure a lasting white color, the product can return to its cream or yellow color and have, therefore, an undesirable appearance. Unfortunately, consumers seldom can determine such incorrect procedures when purchasing fabrics. Goods that have been given care specified on labels but that did not perform satisfactorily should be returned so that manufacturers are aware of the improper processing.

Tentering

Tentering is the mechanical straightening and drying of fabrics. For woven fabrics the tenter establishes the relationship between warp and filling yarns. Properly tentered fabrics will be straight, or "on-grain," which means that warp yarns and filling yarns are at a true 90° (right) angle. A tenter frame holds the fabric between two parallel chains with either clips or special pins. The chains spread apart to the desired fabric width, move with the fabric through finishing or drying units, and release the fabric to be rolled or folded onto cylinders (Fig. 25.3). The fabric is held horizontally

25.3 Tenter chains on tentering frame, used to maintain fabric dimensions and grain relation (keeping warp and filling at a true right angle to each other). (WestPoint Pepperell)

25.4 Fabrics printed off-grain.

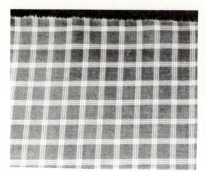 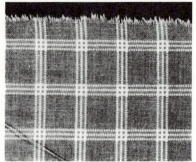

between the two chains. If the cloth is fed to the chains so that the filling yarns are not perpendicular to the warp yarns, an off-grain situation develops. This poses many problems to the consumer, for off-grain fabrics will not hang properly and may change shape after use and care. Tentering is applied to fabrics at several different times during the overall finishing operation. Any time that tentering results in off-grain fabrics the consumer will probably be dissatisfied with the product. When tentering follows the application of finishing compounds that are designed to help produce easy care fabrics, it is even more important to make certain that the fabric grain was true; these fabrics cannot be straightened after finishing and such fabrics will be unattractive during their use. Off-grain tentering during the application of prints or colors will also produce products that are going to be problems to consumers. Figure 25.4 is an example of fabrics that have been printed off-grain; when grain is straight, the design is not. Apparel fabrics or home-furnishing fabrics intended for items such as draperies or curtains with off-grain tentering will not be satisfactory.

To reduce the frequency of off-grain fabrics, several different types of machinery have been developed to be used with tentering equipment. These include sensors, much like electronic eyes, that stop the machine as soon as yarns are not in their proper relationships; some equipment identifies the off-grain situation, and stops or slows one chain until the grain is in its correct relationship, and then starts again with the fabric in proper position.

Fabrics are tentered following bleaching and scouring and many other finishing operations; thus this process is used frequently during the total converting procedure.

Mercerization

Mercerization is a process—applied primarily to cellulosic fibers, especially cotton, and to blends including cellulose fibers—that contributes luster to the fabric, enhances the ease with which cotton and other cellulosic fibers accept dyes, and increases the strength of the fiber, particularly of cotton. The steps include wetting the fabric thoroughly with water; saturating the fabric with a caustic solution, usually sodium hydroxide; leaving this solution on the fabric for a specified length of time; washing and neutralizing the fabric to eliminate action by the caustic; washing a second time to remove any materials left in the fabric; and drying on a tenter chain and feeding through a heat zone.

The wetted fabric is immersed in the solution of caustic (sodium hydroxide); the thoroughly saturated fabric is fed, under tension, around a

25.5 Mercerization frame—timing section. Fabric passes over timing cans, which control the length of time mercerizing solution is left on fabric. (Springs Industries)

series of metal rolls (called timing cans), where the solution swells the cellulosic fibers; after the necessary time on the timing cans, the fabric is fed onto a tenter chain and into the washing and neutralizing bath (Fig. 25.5). The fabric is thoroughly washed and rinsed and then fed into drying ovens or around large drying cans (heated metal rolls) that dry the fabric.

Mercerization swells cotton fibers, gives them a round cross section that reflects light better than the unmercerized fibers, creates a soft sheen or luster, and increases the strength of the fibers. In addition, mercerized fibers accept color more quickly and easily than nonmercerized fibers.

Calendering or Pressing

Calendering is applied to cotton, linen, silk, rayon, and other man-made fiber fabrics. *Pressing* is the term used for wool fabrics and those made from blends of wool and other fibers. This mechanical process flattens or smooths the surface of fabrics. If combined with certain performance or functional finishes, it may be relatively durable; however, the typical calendering or pressing finishing operation must be repeated following any application of moisture.

Calendering and pressing are much the same as ironing; the difference is in the equipment used. Calendering or pressing uses heavy equipment that can create much greater pressure on the fabrics than any iron. Calendering uses large metal rolls and a softer roll (Fig. 25.6). Some calendering uses only two rolls, one hard and one soft; others may use three (or more), with one roll soft and the others hard. The hard roll is heated, and as it rolls over the fabric, it flattens it much as the consumer

25.6 Calender machine, used to flatten and smooth (iron) surface of fabrics. (WestPoint Pepperell)

does when rolling an iron over the fabric surface. In pressing, moisture may be used to provide steam and reduce the possibility of damage to the fabric. Modifications to the calendering process allow a variety of appearance effects, which will be discussed in the next chapter.

Inspection

Fabric inspection involves three possible steps. Originally, only wool fabrics received complete inspection; today nearly every fabric is examined before it leaves the converting plant, and many fabrics are inspected several times. Inspection is becoming a highly sophisticated process with extremely sensitive equipment; however, considerable inspection is still done by the human eye. The most accurate inspection procedure in use today has laser beams that can spot flaws and damaged areas and mark them on a computer printout so that operators can locate them quickly and make repairs when possible. The typical steps in inspection include perching, burling, and mending.

Perching Perching is the visual inspection of fabric. The name derives from the frame, called a *perch,* of frosted glass with lights behind and above it. The fabric passes over the perch and is inspected visually. Flaws, stains or spots, yarn knots, and other imperfections are marked (Figs. 25.7 and 25.8). Depending on the flaw the marking may be on the fabric itself or in the selvage edge. Normally, if the flaw is easily repaired it is marked in the fabric with some marking material that is easily removed.

Burling Burling is generally limited to wool, wool blends, and fabrics made to resemble wool. Burling is the removal of yarn knots and other imperfections, occurring usually in the yarns and not in the fabric construction, and the replacement with flaw-free yarns so that the final fabric retains its first-quality status.

25.7 above. Perch used for inspection of fabric. (Springs Industries)

25.8 above left. Optical scanner used in inspecting yarns for defects as they are wound onto a warp beam. (Springs Industries)

Mending   Mending is the actual repair of imperfections and the removal of major flaws caused by fabric construction processes. The problem may leave marks that require a classification of "second quality" for some fabrics. The decision to mend depends on such factors as the seriousness of the flaw, the typical cost of the fabric, and the intended use.

Special Finishes for Wool Fabrics

Wool and wool-blend fabrics are subjected to a series of routine finishes that are specific to that fiber. These include carbonizing, crabbing, decating, and fulling.

Carbonizing

Carbonizing is the process by which vegetable matter found in wool fiber is removed. It is difficult, if not impossible, to remove all foreign matter found with wool fiber during the carding process when making wool or wool-blend yarns. Thus, remaining foreign matter is removed by carbonizing.

This finishing process involves the immersion of the wool fabric in a solution of sulfuric acid; it is then subjected to high temperatures for a brief period of time. The acid and heat react to convert the vegetable matter to carbon, which is easily removed by a final scouring and, if necessary, brushing. The process must be carefully controlled to prevent fiber damage, and it cannot be used on blends if other fibers in the blend are damaged by the acid solution.

Carbonizing is an important step in the manufacture of worsted fabrics. It may or may not be used on woolens, depending on the type of fabric. For example, some rough tweeds are not carbonized because the character of the fabric includes the presence of bits of vegetable matter in the wool yarns.

Crabbing

Crabbing is a finishing process designed to set the weave in the fabric permanently. The fabric is immersed in hot water and then into cold water; next, it is passed between rollers, where the water is removed and the warp and filling yarns are set at a true 90° angle to each other. Crabbing may reduce the amount of shrinkage in wool fabrics; it prevents uneven shrinkage in most fabrics.

Decating

Decating is a process used on wool to set the luster and to develop a permanent sheen. It may be used on other fibers, particularly on blends involving wool. Decating is, to some degree, a pressing process for wool and wool-blend fabrics.

The decating process involves pressure and moisture. In dry decating, steam and then cold air are forced through the fabric; in wet decating, hot and then cold water are forced through. For both types the final step is pressing. Decating is used to help set the grain in wool and wool-blend fabrics.

Fulling

Fulling is a finish applied to wool and wool-blend fabrics to make them more compact and to pull the yarns closer together. When wool fabric is removed from the loom, it often bears little resemblance to the fabric that the consumer finds on the market. The weave is usually loose, and the fabric feels hard and stiff. To make the fabric more compact and to soften it, it is fulled by applying moisture, heat, and friction in controlled situations. Fulling is somewhat similar to the process used to make felt; however, it is carefully controlled to prevent the yarns from packing so tightly together that a type of felt is made. Wool fabrics that have not been properly fulled will tend to shrink very badly during use and care.

Selected Other Finishes

The finishes discussed in this section are important in the preparation of many fabrics; they frequently are responsible for producing specific characteristics considered basic to selected types of fabric. A few are relatively new and are designed to replace older routine finishes.

Heat Setting

Heat-sensitive, or thermoplastic, fibers are frequently given a heat-setting finish to ensure a stable fabric or to create special shapes and designs in fabrics. Heat is used to build specific characteristics into these fibers so they become permanent features. Any fabric of either heat-sensitive fibers or blends in which heat-sensitive fibers are a part can be heat set.

One of the most important reasons for heat setting fabrics is to reduce or eliminate stretch or shrinkage in the fabric. The heat-setting operation produces a fabric that will not change size during normal use and care. Another important characteristic is to build in resiliency so that the fabric returns to shape and tends to be an easy care item. Heat setting can be used to build in planned creases, pleats, and surface designs such as embossing. It can be used to create special product shapes such as certain types of nylon hose.

Heat setting is durable providing the consumer does not exceed the heat-setting temperature during use and care procedures. It is most important to prevent the product from reaching the temperature used for heat setting; if such should happen the product would assume whatever shape it was at that time. Care during laundering and drying are important, as wrinkles can be formed in end-use items if the washing and drying temperatures are higher than the temperatures used for heat setting and the time of exposure to the high temperatures was longer than the time required for the original heat-setting operation. But without heat setting the thermoplastic (heat-sensitive) fibers would not be as attractive and would tend to shrink badly when exposed to normal care processes.

Brushing

Brushing involves the removal of short, loose fiber ends from the surface of the fabric. These loose fiber ends are brushed up to free them from the yarns and then brushed away from the surface. Cylinders covered with fine bristles rotate over the fabric; pick up the loose fibers; and pull them away, either by gravity or a vacuum. This operation is usually applied to fabrics of staple fibers to give them a smooth and uniform appearance. Brushing may precede the basic finishing operations of singeing, scouring, and bleaching; it may be used to help raise pile as a preliminary step to shearing; and it may be used to roughen the surface of the fabric.

Shearing

Shearing involves the cutting off of undesirable surface fibers or yarns that extend beyond the length desired. After singeing and subsequent processing, fiber ends or loose fibers may protrude from the fabric surface. Shearing cuts off these ends and permits a clear view of the fabric structure. For pile or napped fabrics, shearing evens the surface to give a uniform appearance. By manipulating the shearing machine, it is possible to cut designs into the fabric so that some areas are higher than others.

The shearing machine has a wide spiral cylinder to which cutting blades are attached, resembling a lawn mower in action (Fig. 25.9). The fabric passes over brushes that raise the fiber ends or the fabric nap or pile; then it moves over the cutting blades, where the shearing occurs.

Sizing and Slashing

Sizing is the application of materials to a fabric to produce stiffness or firmness. Slashing is a synonym in that it too involves the application of materials to produce stiffness and firmness; the difference, however, lies in the fact that *sizing* usually refers to fabrics that require stiffening, whereas *slashing* identifies the coating given warp yarns before weaving to make them resist the weaving action (Figs. 25.10 and 25.11).

Different types of materials are used for different types of fibers in fabrics. Cellulosic fiber fabrics may be starched or sized with resins, starch compounds, and dextrins. Sizing gives body and stiffness to fabrics and tends to add luster; it frequently reduces the speed with which the fabric shows soil.

Consumers should be aware that sizing compounds may be temporary or durable. If resins have been used, the stiff or firm finish is somewhat durable; if starches and dextrins have been used, the finish is probably removed during use and care. Labels concerning recommended care procedures should help consumers maintain desired stiffness due to sizing finishes.

25.9 Shearing blades used to smooth fabric surfaces or to even nap or pile. (Springs Industries)

25.10 above. Applying sizing (slashing) to warp yarns. (Springs Industries)

25.11 below. Winding slashed yarns onto the warp beam. (Springs Industries)

Weighting

Silk fabrics may be given a finish called weighting. After complete degumming of silk filaments the fibers are very soft. To make heavy or stiff silk fabrics, manufacturers resort to adding substances, usually metallic salts. It is the natural absorbency characteristic of silk fiber that makes this finishing process feasible. If weighting is overdone, silk fabrics tend to crack and split during use and care. Although weighted silk has body and density, the fabrics are not as durable for they are sensitive to damage by sunlight, perspiration, and deodorants.

Finishing Knitted Fabrics

The finishing processes described herein are applicable to woven fabrics and to some knitted fabrics. However, knit fabrics may not require all the finishes discussed to this point. The major difference between finishing knitted fabrics and woven fabrics is in the type of equipment used and the steps in the finishing procedures. Knit fabric must be carefully controlled during finishing to make certain that the fabric dimensions, both width and length, are maintained; further the density of knit fabric is determined to a great extent by finishing operations. Finishing of knit fabrics helps to determine the shape of the ultimate product, the density of the fabric, the thickness of the fabric, and easy care features.

Knit fabrics made of heat-sensitive fibers should definitely be given heat-set finishing. This process stabilizes the fabric and reduces shrinkage and loss of appearance during use and care.

Study Questions

1. List and describe the basic or routine steps in processing most woven fabrics. How would they differ for knitted fabrics?
2. What is the difference between rope and open-width finishing?
3. What points should consumers consider concerning care of fabrics that require bleaching at home?
4. What finishes are specific to wool and wool-blend fabrics?
5. What new developments in inspection have occurred recently?
6. Why would silk fabrics be weighted?
7. Why are fabrics sized?
8. What are the major ways in which finishes are applied to fabrics?
9. What is shearing and when is it done to fabrics?
10. For what types of fabrics is heat setting important and why?

26

Finishes for Appearance, Hand, and Performance

Finishes may be added to alter the appearance, the hand, or the performance of fabric. The discussion in this chapter is divided into two major sections: The first describes various finishes used to modify the appearance or the hand of fabrics to create either specific fabrics or those with special aesthetic interest; the second section describes those finishes added to modify the performance or function of fabrics. Those in the latter group are frequently called functional finishes. Most fabrics available to consumers have been given some type of special finish, and many consumers would not be interested in fabrics without these finishes.

There has been no attempt to identify the relative importance of the finishes discussed; rather, they are described in somewhat arbitrary order. Finishes that alter appearance or hand have been arranged by similarity of process. Functional finishes have been placed in modified alphabetical order, with related processes cited under a heading commonly recognized by consumers.

Many of the special finishes are used only on woven fabrics. The finishing of knit fabrics frequently requires special handling because of the nature of the knit construction and the tendency for it to stretch under tension. Some finishes that consumers want on woven fabrics may not be needed on knit fabrics because the knit construction may provide the property without added processing. When considered important, the use of a finish on various types of fabric construction is noted. Many functional finishes can be applied to any type of fabric construction, and if this is the case, no special mention will be made regarding fabric construction.

FINISHES THAT ALTER APPEARANCE AND/OR HAND

Special Calendering

Basic calendering, previously discussed (page 255), is a necessity for many fabrics to prepare them for consumer use. Special types of calendering are used to contribute special appearance or design characteristics. The permanence or durability of these special calendering processes is determined by several factors. When thermoplastic fibers are used in making the fabrics, calendering can actually soften them slightly and impart a permanent design effect. This effect remains durable unless higher temperatures than those used in calendering are applied. Resin materials can be added that, along with the calendering, produce appearance fin-

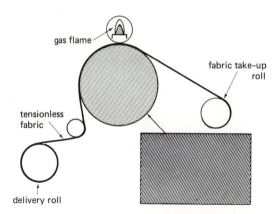

gas flame

fabric take-up roll

tensionless fabric

delivery roll

ishes; the resin makes it possible to build the design into the fabric so that it will be relatively durable. When the pressure of the calender rolls is the only process involved in applying the finish, it is not very durable; it may frequently be removed the first time the product is cleaned, especially when nonthermoplastic fibers are used in making the fabric. Consumers should look for labels that give information concerning care and, if possible, seek information about how the finish was applied and whether or not it is considered durable.

Schreinering

Schreinering is produced by a special calender (Fig. 26.1). The metal roll has a series of fine lines—about 250 per inch—engraved so they form an angle roughly 20° to the construction of the fabric. The angle is usually such that the lines are parallel to the twist in the yarns. This finish produces a soft luster and is used frequently on cellulosic fibers such as cotton and linen. In addition, the rolls flatten the yarns and create a smooth and compact fabric. Recently this finish has been applied to tricot knit lingerie fabric of nylon or polyester fibers to produce an opaque fabric. If properly done, the process does not affect care procedures.

Moiré

In the days before man-made fibers moiré was known as watered silk, and the finish was applied only to silk fabrics. Today, moiré is used on several fibers and fabric constructions. A moiré finish is characterized by a soft luster and a design created by differences in light reflection off the yarns. Rib fabrics, such as failles, taffetas, and bengalines, work best in producing the moiré effect (Fig. 26.2). However, knit fabrics with a slight rib character, which can be obtained from the interlock stitch, have been found on the market with a moiré finish.

Two rolls are involved, a large one covered with cloth and a smaller, heated one that often includes an engraved design. The fabric is doubled and fed between the two rollers; these rollers exert pressure and add heat. The ribs in one thickness impress images on the other thickness by flattening the ribs. If there is an etched pattern on the heated metal roll, the design is transferred to the fabric. Without the etching a bar or irregular, broken effect is formed on the fabric. A moiré finish on thermoplastic fibers such as acetate, nylon, or polyester is durable; if applied to cellulosic fi-

26.2 Moiré fabric.

26.3 Diagram of embossing rolls.

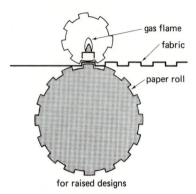

for raised designs

bers such as rayon or cotton, a moiré finish can be made relatively durable by using resins in the fabric, which tend to hold the appearance. A moiré finish on cotton or rayon applied without resin will disappear during the first care period.

Embossed Surfaces

Embossed fabrics have three-dimensional designs. Before the introduction of resin finishes, embossing lacked durability, but with resins it is possible to produce cotton and other cellulosic fabrics with durable embossing. Fabrics that can be heat set can also be given a durable embossed design. For best results the base fabric used for embossing should be a compact weave with a balanced structure.

The calenders used for embossing may have two or three rolls. One roll is of cotton or paper; a second roll is metal and holds the engraved design that is to be embossed into the fabric. If a third roll is used it is also of cotton or paper. The design is engraved onto the metal roll, the paper or cotton rolls are dampened, and the machine is run without fabric until the design has been impressed into the soft roll. The soft rolls are dried with the design securely set in place (Fig. 26.3). With the design securely established, fabric can be fed through the calender; the design is then impressed onto the fabric. Any type of design can be adapted to embossing (Fig. 26.4). Embossing that involves the use of resins or heat-

26.4 Embossed fabrics.

  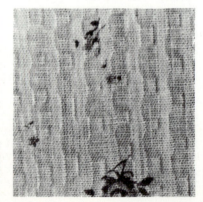

sensitive fibers will usually be easy care and durable. Such fabrics frequently require no ironing; in fact, for many embossed fabrics, ironing is discouraged because it can flatten the fabric and actually reduce the embossed character.

Polished Surfaces

Friction calenders along with special chemicals, such as resins, are used to produce fabrics with a high level of polish, gloss, or shine. The two most frequently encountered finishes in this group include glazed surfaces and ciré fabrics.

Glazed Surfaces

A friction calender and selected resins are used to produce a relatively durable polish or glaze on fabric surfaces. Without resins the finish is typically destroyed during the first care period. Fabrics that have a glaze or polish include glazed chintz and polished cottons. The process involves calenders with three rolls, the center one of cotton or paper, and the two outside rolls of metal. The fabric is fed around the center roll while the two outside rolls revolve on the fabric face. The outside rolls revolve at a very high speed and develop a polish on the fabric surface by friction. When resins are used, the glazed surface is relatively durable. Glazed surfaces are applied primarily to woven fabrics.

Ciré

Ciré is a high-polish finish often applied to silk or blends of silk and to thermoplastic fibers such as nylon, polyester, and acetate. The finish is formed by impregnating the fabric with wax or with a thermoplastic substance and passing it through a friction calender like that used for glazing. The finish is durable when applied to thermoplastic fibers because it can be heat set into the surface; it holds well on silk but can be removed during care procedures if not handled correctly. When applied to cotton or other cellulose fibers, the finish is not durable unless special substances have been used on the fabric to aid in producing lasting effects. This finish is sometimes called the "wet" look.

Some ciré finishes are applied with a vinyl-type substance instead of wax. This produces a high level of shine and is relatively durable.

Raised Surfaces

Gigging and napping are the two principal methods for raising fiber ends to the surface. Staple or short fibers in spun yarns are essential in fabrics that are to be napped. A nap finish hides the yarns and fabric construction and produces a soft, hairy appearance; the process can be used on either woven or knitted fabrics. A modification of the napping process is used to develop a suedelike effect on some fabrics.

Gigging

Gigging is a napping process used for wool, rayon, and other fibers when a short, lustrous nap is desired. Teasels, obtained from a special variety of thistle plant, are attached to a cylinder. The fabric is then fed into the machine, and the teasels gently tease or pull the fiber ends to the surface to produce the nap. The nap obtained by gigging is soft and short. The process is gentle and does little damage to the fabric. The nap is sometimes pressed flat, as for wool broadcloth, or it may be left full and fluffy, as in soft blankets. Gigging is seldom used at the present time because the teasels are difficult to obtain and the equipment is not as easy to operate as that operating with wires.

Napping

Napping is applied to fabrics made of almost any type of fiber; however, fabrics of cotton, cotton blends, rayon, and wool are those usually selected for napping. Staple length fibers are required to produce a good nap. The length of the nap is determined by the equipment controls and may vary from a short to a relatively long nap.

The process uses cylinders on which there are fine metal wires with small hooks (Fig. 26.5). These cylinders completely surround a large roll, and the length of the wires helps to determine the amount of nap that is formed. The hooks pull fiber ends to the surface of the fabric and create the nap. Napping can be done on one or both sides of the fabric.

Fabric used for napping should contain soft yarns of staple fibers with low twist. Plain-weave fabrics, soft-filled sheeting fabrics, soft twill-weave and satin-weave fabrics, and knit fabrics with soft, fluffy yarns are often used for napping. In woven fabrics it is the filling yarn that is designed for napping; warp yarns are kept strong to provide durability to the fabric. In knitted fabrics the soft yarns for napping are alternated with strong yarns for fabric durability. Soft yarns are easily roughened so that the fiber ends are pulled to the surface to form the nap.

When the raised fiber ends are to be even, the fabric may be sheared; the fiber ends are brushed into a standing position, and the fabric is fed through a shearing unit. Following the shearing the nap may be left standing or it can be brushed against the fabric surface to lay flat. By modifying the methods used in flattening or shearing the nap or both, interesting designs can be created.

Fabrics with napped surfaces include flannels, flannelettes, blankets, and some coating and suiting fabrics. Consumers should recognize the difference between napped fabrics and pile surfaces that have been created by weaving or knitting. Napping does not have pile yarns that may be removed; rather the yarns have a very rough surface. Napping obscures the fabric construction from the face of the fabric; it may obscure both sides if the napping has been done to both the right and wrong sides of the fabric (Fig. 26.6).

In addition to creating interesting and attractive appearances, the raising of fiber ends may modify performance characteristics. Fabrics with a napped surface are generally warmer than the same weight fabric without napping. The nap provides air pockets that increase the insulating properties of the fabric.

Fabrics with napped surfaces pose difficulties in construction into end-use products. The nap causes light reflection to vary, depending on the direction from which it is viewed; this, in turn, alters the appearance of the fabric as the direction changes. Consequently, cutting the fabric into garment pieces or into pieces for such items as upholstery requires that all parts be cut with the fabric facing the same direction so that the nap is going the same way in all parts of the item.

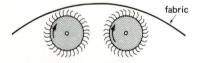

fabric

26.5 above. Diagram of napping rolls. The bent wires nap the surface of the fabric.

26.6 below. A napped fabric. Note that the weave is obscured by the surface finish. The nap has been pressed into a pattern.

Sueding

Sueding involves rubbing the fabric surface with a revolving roll that has been covered with a substance similar to sandpaper. The sandpaper cuts the fibers on the face of the fabric and produces a fuzzy surface. The amount of sueding depends on the tension of the cloth and the amount of contact between the fabric and the sueding rolls. Some "suede" cloth and fabrics such as duvetyn are made on a sueding machine rather than by napping.

Flocking

Flocking is sometimes considered a printing method, but because of its similarity to raised surface finishes, it is included with these finishes in this text.

Flocking is a process whereby short lengths of fibers are attached to the surface of a constructed fabric by means of an adhesive. The short fibers are identified as "flock" and may be attached in a design of some type or on an overall basis. The result is a textured appearance that resembles a pile or a napped surface, depending on the length of the fibers used for the flock and the way the flock is handled after it has been attached. For a surface that is to resemble a pile, the flock is left erect on the fabric face; for a fabric that is more like a napped surface, the flock is pressed somewhat so that it tends to lay flat. In designs some areas of the fabric are flocked and others are not; this creates interesting patterns (Fig. 26.7). The fibers used for the flock are generally of either rayon or nylon; these fibers are cut so that the ends are square and even. The length may vary, but the average is about ⅛ inch.

The adhesive is printed on the fabric surface in the desired pattern or on an overall basis, after which the flock is applied by one of two methods. The vibration, or mechanical, method can apply flock to one or both sides of the fabric (Fig. 26.8). The flock is circulated in a container through which the fabric passes. As the fabric moves, it vibrates and builds up static that attracts the flock. The flock adheres to the areas where the adhesive has been applied. The fabric then moves into a drying chamber, where the adhesive dries with the flock firmly embedded. Finally, the fabric is brushed to remove flock from areas where there is no adhesive and any flock that has not been securely attached to the fabric.

The second method uses electrostatic or electrocoating techniques. This process depends on the electric charge of the fibers and the presence of electrical fields above and below the fabric (Fig. 26.9). The fabric is printed with the adhesive, as for the mechanical method; it is then passed over an electrical field, which establishes an atmosphere that forces the loose fibers in the area away from one of the electrical fields and toward the second. With the fabric moving, the loose fibers strike the

26.7 below left. Fabric with flocked design.

26.8 below center. Diagram of mechanical flocking.

26.9 below right. Diagram of electrostatic flocking.

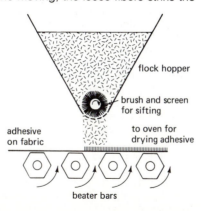

flock hopper

brush and screen for sifting

adhesive on fabric

to oven for drying adhesive

beater bars

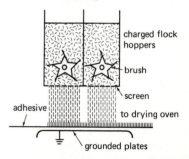

charged flock hoppers

brush

screen

adhesive

to drying oven

grounded plates

26.10 above.   Organdy with opaque design where finish was not applied.

26.11 below.   Fabric pattern created by burn-out process. Fabric is made of polyester and cotton.

adhesive, and the electrical field orients the fibers and pulls them into the adhesive. The fabric then moves into a drying area, where the adhesive is dried to hold the flock fibers in place.

Flocking is comparatively permanent in laundering as long as high temperatures and heavy rubbing or abrasion are avoided. Dry cleaning, however, may cause damage by softening or dissolving the adhesive. The consumer should check for loose fibers by rubbing a flocked fabric; if fibers easily rub loose, the fabric should not be purchased because it will not give good service.

Chemical Finishes

Acids

Transparent or parchmentlike fabrics of cellulose are produced by treatment with sulfuric acid. The cotton fabric is immersed in the acid base under controlled conditions for a brief time and then quickly neutralized. This type of finish can be applied to the entire fabric to produce a clear organdy. By printing an acid-resistant substance on the fabric before treatment, designs can be developed with both opaque and transparent areas (Fig. 26.10). The finish is most effective on mercerized cotton, but it can be used on any natural cellulosic fibers. The durability of organdy depends on the quality of the finish. A well-applied and controlled finish will be lasting and will not weaken the cloth. Organdy fabrics wrinkle during maintenance and require considerable ironing.

A second acid finish produces *burned-out designs* (Fig. 26.11). It uses a fabric composed of two different types of fibers—one that is easily destroyed by acid, such as rayon, acetate, or cotton, and another that is acid resistant, such as polyester or acrylic fibers. The fabric is exposed to an acid, usually sulfuric, which burns away the sensitive fiber to leave sheer areas in the fabric. The nonaffected fiber remains to provide integrity to the fabric. The acid can be printed onto the fabric in various designs so that the fiber affected by the acid is removed from selected areas only Careful planning and arrangement of the fibers in such fabrics are essential for satisfactory results.

Bases and Ketones

The application of chemical bases or alkalies—frequently called caustics—produces interesting fabrics. *Plissé* crepe, a crinkled or crepelike cotton fabric, results from the action of sodium hydroxide on cotton fabric in selected areas. Caustic soda in a paste form is printed onto the fabric in predetermined areas. This causes the coated areas to shrink and the untreated areas to pucker because of fiber shrinkage around the puckered areas (Fig. 26.12). After the caustic is removed, the crinkled effect is comparatively durable. However, ironing should be avoided whenever possible because it can stretch the fabric and flatten out the crinkled areas; this causes changes in the fabric dimensions and in appearance.

Crinkled effects can be obtained on nylon fabrics by using phenol instead of the sodium hydroxide. This organic base works the same way on the nylon.

It is important for consumers to distinguish between fabrics such as plissé, crinkled nylon or polyester, and seersucker fabrics made by weaving techniques (Fig. 26.13). Seersucker will have very clear and sharp rows that are smooth and even and other rows that are crinkled or wrin-

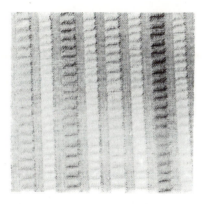

26.12 left. Plissé fabric. The design is created by finishing with a chemical base.

26.13 right. Seersucker fabric. The design is created by weaving and not by finishing.

kled. The effect in seersucker fabrics cannot be destroyed by ironing because it is part of the actual weave. Crinkled effects may be obtained in fabrics of nylon or polyester by using variants of the fibers in such a way that one variant shrinks during the final processing step and the other variant does not. The one that shrinks causes the part that does not to crinkle or wrinkle. Depending on the arrangement of the different fiber variants, the ultimate appearance of the fabric may be similar to a seersucker or plissé.

Stiffening Finishes

Sizings, discussed in Chapter 25, are one way to add stiffness to fabrics. Many of these sizings are not permanent or durable and are used for specific processing steps only. If nondurable products are used for fabric stiffness and then placed on the consumer market, consumers will probably be very unhappy when the stiffness is removed during the first use and care period. When fabric stiffness is desired as a part of the final fabric, it can be developed by thermosetting resins or other plastic materials. These may be applied with little or no damage to the fabric and they are durable. These resin finishes produce sheer fabrics with a crisp and attractive hand, help fabrics resist sagging and yarn slippage, keep fabrics from "wilting" during use and care, reduce the formation of lint, and help fabrics maintain a smooth surface that is resistant to snags and abrasions and, to some extent, to soiling. Resin finishes also contribute to dimensional stability of fabrics (see p. 281).

Softening Finishes

Softening finishes improve the hand and drape of the fabric. They may add some body; facilitate application of other finishes; subdue the coarseness imparted during some processing, especially durable press; and increase the life and usefulness of the fabric.

Softeners are common finishing materials and include a great variety of products. A wide selection is available to the consumer for home care. These products help to maintain fabric softness; restore softness lost during other finishing operations; and help reduce static electric charge, which may be unpleasant. The use of softeners on certain types of end-use products should be given consideration. Although such items as towels may need softening as a part of their care, it is important to note that softeners should not be used on towels every time they are cleaned. The softeners reduce absorbency and, thus, would reduce the effectiveness of the towels. However, to retain softness in these products, the use of softeners every third or fourth care period might help to maintain their original characteristics. It is also important to note that softeners inhibit the effect of flame-resistant finishes. If such finishes have been applied to fabrics, such as children's sleepwear, the use of softeners should be avoided.

A variety of fabrics routinely receive softening to produce the typical fabric characteristics. Batiste, for example, is always given a softening finish; other fabrics using softeners include those with durable-press properties.

Optical Finishes

Delusterants

Man-made fibers often have a high degree of luster, or shine, because they are relatively transparent and their cross-sectional shape helps reflect light. These fibers tend to reflect a few long light rays from their surface rather than many short rays characteristic of fibers with uneven cross sections and less transparency. Although luster can be diminished by intelligent selection of fibers and yarn-construction techniques, it is more often controlled in man-made fibers by pigments that alter the light-reflecting patterns. These pigments are incorporated into the fiber solution before extrusion through the spinnerette. The typical substance is a white pigment that reduces the luster by breaking up the reflected light rays; the resulting visual appearance of the fibers is opaque and somewhat dull. Such finishing materials are a part of the actual fiber manufacture.

Another method for delustering man-made fibers involves a special heat treatment that softens the yarn and fabric surface. This process modifies the fiber surface and reduces the light reflection characteristics.

External delusterants can be added to the surface of fibers, yarns, and/or fabrics to reduce luster. The solution is deposited on the fiber or yarn surface and forms a coating. These are easily removed by care procedures so they are not considered durable; thus, delusterants added prior to fiber formation are considered desirable for durability. Care of delustered fibers and fabrics should avoid high temperatures.

Optical Brighteners

Many fabrics lose their brightness, whiteness, and clearness during processing and maintenance. In an attempt to prevent this loss and to maintain white and bright fabrics, optical brighteners have been introduced. These are sometimes called *optical bleaches,* but the term in this case is inappropriate, for no bleaching action occurs. Optical brighteners are used by fabric converters during finishing processes, and they are added to many home-laundering agents. Thus, consumers can restore brightness each time a product is laundered. These substances attach themselves to the fabric and create an appearance of whiteness and/or brightness by the way in which they reflect light rays.

Beetling

Beetling is a mechanical finish applied to cotton and linen fabric and occasionally to rayon fabrics (Fig. 26.14). This finish increases the luster of fabrics by flattening the yarns to provide more area for light reflection. The

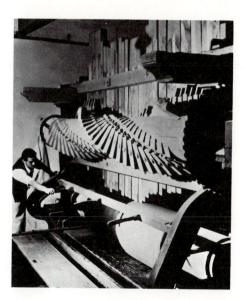

26.14 Beetling machine for flax fiber fabrics.

fabric is fed over rolls that rotate in a machine where large hammers rise and fall on the fabric surface. Continued pounding flattens the yarns and closes the weave. The beetled finish will withstand wear and maintenance if the fabric is laundered carefully and ironed with pressure to restore the flat appearance. Fabrics for table coverings are often beetled to add luster and to make them lay flat.

Other Finishes Affecting Appearance and Hand

Several finishes discussed in Chapter 25 also influence the appearance and hand of fabrics. Calendering, mercerizing, fulling, and singeing may change fabric appearance; sizing, fulling, and heat setting influence the hand of fabrics.

FINISHES THAT MODIFY OR CHANGE FUNCTION OR PERFORMANCE OF FABRICS

The finishing industry has developed a variety of special types of finishing processes to give consumers products that have the desired performance characteristics. These finishes are designed to produce the best combination of properties for selected end uses.

    Functional or performance finishes are of two basic types: external and internal. External finishes are those applied to the surface of fibers, and they do not penetrate into the fiber; internal finishes are those that do penetrate into the fiber and, in many cases, react chemically with the fiber molecules. Internal finishes are applied to fibers with porous surfaces. They include thermosetting resins, used for dimensional stability and durable press, as well as other modifying materials. External finishes may influence the appearance and hand of fabric; internal finishes influence the hand of fabric but seldom have any effect on the appearance except as the retention of appearance is a part of the performance of the finish. For example, durable-press finishes create fabrics that tend to be harsher than fabrics without the finish; however, the appearance is no different than the fabric without the finish. The finish helps to retain the original appearance through use and care.

Many functional finishes depended on urea formaldehyde as a part of their composition and/or application. This substance has been classified as a dangerous toxic material. Consequently, researchers are working hard to find other methods for imparting many of the finishes that previously required this toxic substance. The future of many functional or performance finishes, such as durable press, may depend on the success of researchers seeking alternate means to apply such properties to fabrics.

Abrasion-Resistant Finishes

Some manufactured fibers, particularly nylon, have excellent resistance to abrasion. However, natural fibers and some man-made fibers may be damaged by rubbing. To reduce this type of fabric damage, manufacturers may do one of two things: (1) blend fibers of high abrasion resistance with those of low resistance or (2) apply soft thermoplastic resins, which appear to increase the fabric's resistance to abrasion damage.

The problem of abrasion is complex. It is believed that a substantial part of the resistance produced by resins results from the fact that the resin binds the fibers more firmly into the yarns and thus increases the time and amount of abrasion required to roughen the surface by fiber breakage.

Recent information concerning these finishes indicates that abrasion-resistant finishes may increase the wet soiling of fabric. Thus, they should receive frequent care to reduce this type of damage.

Typical end uses for fabrics with abrasion-resistant finishes include trouser pockets, waistband linings, hat bands, and similar uses in which abrasion cannot be avoided. These finishes may be applied to fabrics for home furnishings, particularly for fabrics that will receive abrasion or rubbing during use and care, such as hems of draperies and upholstery fabrics.

Absorbent Finishes

Absorbent finishes increase the moisture-holding power of fabrics and accelerate the drying action of the product. Fabrics treated with these finishes can absorb more moisture than they normally would, but they will require longer to dry, either in the air or in dryers, because of the increased amount of moisture absorbed.

One type of absorbent finish causes the moisture to break up into small particles and evaporate readily into the surrounding air; a second type holds the moisture and disperses it into the yarns of the fabric. These finishes are used for such items as towels, underwear, and sports clothes.

Antipesticide Protective Finishes

Concern for people involved in the application of pesticides or who work in areas where there are large concentrations of pesticides has gained widespread attention. Antipesticide finishes are designed to prevent penetration of the pesticide through clothing and to permit easy removal of any pesticide on the surface of clothing by laundering. Special fabric constructions may also be used. Although little information is available concering these products, it is anticipated that they will become important materials for anyone involved in the application of pesticides and those who live in areas that require pesticide treatments.

Antislip Finishes

Antislip finishes are applied to fabrics as one method of reducing or eliminating yarn slippage; they may also be called slip-resistant or nonslip finishes. Antislip finishes help keep yarns in their proper position in the fabric, help maintain a 90° relationship between warp and filling yarns in woven fabrics, and reduce seam fraying or raveling. Many of these finishes have little durability.

Antistatic Finishes

Static buildup in fabrics has long been recognized as a problem both to the manufacturers and to consumers. Besides causing difficulties in the processing of fabrics, static buildup increases the ease and speed of soiling. Above all, however, static is annoying to consumers as well as a major problem in processing fabrics at all stages of manufacture.

Static is evident to consumers when garments cling to the body or to other fabrics, when sparks with sufficient force to be seen or felt jump from the wearer to metal after the person has walked across floor coverings or slid across upholstery, when crackling sounds are heard as a person walks or takes off a garment, or when a visible spark is produced by rubbing the fabric. It can develop in floor coverings, upholstery, and apparel. In areas where the static causes sparks that react with flammable vapors, major fires or explosions can result.

Antistatic finishes work by one or more of three basic methods. (1) The finish may improve the surface conductivity and thereby help the electrons to move either to the ground or to the atmosphere. (2) The finish may attract molecules of water to the surface, which in turn increases the conductance and carries away the static charge. (3) Chemical finishes may develop an electric charge opposite that of the fiber, which neutralizes the electrostatic charges. The most effective finishes work in all three ways. However, because fibers differ in the type of static charge they generate (some are positive, some negative), different finishing agents must be used for different types of fibers.

Many antistatic finishes are not durable because they are added to reduce static buildup during the various stages in textile manufacturing and finishing. Such finishes are either lost during care or during the final stages of fabric processing. Consumers can help control static buildup in fabrics that are washable. The addition of fabric softeners reduces the development of static. However, these are temporary, and manufacturers, as well as consumers, have indicated a need for antistatic finishes that will be durable.

One method has been to develop fibers with antistatic properties. Such fibers include Ultron nylon, Staticgard nylon, and variants of Antron nylon and Anso nylon. Fybrite is a type of antistatic polyester fiber. Research continues in antistatic textile products. Consumers have indicated a desire for products that retain antistatic properties regardless of the method of care given the item.

Bacteriostats

Bacteriostatic agents or antiseptic finishes also may be called antimicrobial or antibacterial agents. These materials are added to fabrics for three major reasons. They may be used to control the spread of disease and reduce the danger of infection following an injury; they may be included to help inhibit the development of unpleasant odors from perspiration and other soil on textile materials; or they may be added to reduce possible damage to fabrics that can occur from mildew-producing fungi and rot-producing bacteria.

Bacteriostats may be either durable or renewable. The renewable ones are external agents that produce a temporary climate unfavorable to the microorganisms. Durable finishes may be surface coatings applied to fabrics and made insoluble so they resist wear and care; or they may be substances that have been reacted with the fiber molecules to render them a part of the fiber, which makes them insoluble and resistant to wear and care.

Finishes to prevent the growth of microorganisms appear on fabrics for a wide variety of apparel, home-furnishing, commercial, and industrial products. Apparel items include socks, shoe linings, diapers, foundation garments, sportswear (particularly active sportswear), and baby clothes. In home furnishings the finishes may be found on fabrics for sheets, pillow cases, mattress padding and mattress coverings, carpet underpadding, carpeting, blankets, and towels. Fabrics for tents, tarpaulins, and auto fabrics will have a longer life when treated with some type of antimicrobial finish that reduces or prevents damage from rot and mildew.

A number of research projects have provided evidence of the value of bacteriostatic finishes. A lower incidence of reinfection from athlete's foot was noted when shoe linings were treated; a reduction in diaper rash was evident in a group of babies who were clothed in treated diapers. A group of homemakers noted the absence of musty odors that accompany mildew in hot, humid climates when floor coverings were protected with antibacteriostats.

Various trade names are in use for bacteriostatic finishes. For the most part, labels will indicate that the finish is antimicrobial, antibacterial, or bacteriostatic. Consumers may have such finishes added by many dry cleaners as a part of the dry cleaning process. Sanitone and Sanitized are two types of finishes available through dry cleaning. Carpet cleaners usually add bacteriostats to the cleaning solutions when cleaning carpets and rugs. Some detergents and other laundry aids may have bacteriostatic agents in their formulas. This is usually made clear to consumers by information given on labels.

Durable-Press Finishes

Durable press is the term used to refer to the ability of a fabric to retain its original surface appearance and/or shape following care, with little or no ironing required. *Wrinkle recovery* is a term used in technical literature to indicate the ability of a fabric to recover from folding deformation while it is dry. *Crush resistance* is used to describe the ability of a fabric to recover from crushing, especially pile fabrics. These characteristics can be imparted to fabrics by finishing processes or by the selection of fibers. This discussion is limited to the use of materials applied to fibers, yarns, or fabrics. It should be noted that the term *permanent press* is often used as a synonym for *durable press*.

A widely recognized defect of cellulosic fibers is their tendency to wrinkle badly during wear and maintenance. This results in unattractive products that require considerable ironing to restore to a neat appearance. Before the 1920s the only method known to minimize the wrinkling of cellulosic fiber fabrics was to apply starch, and this was only a temporary solution. Each time fabrics were laundered the starch had to be reapplied to the fabric and the item had to be ironed. In 1919 textile scientists developed techniques for measuring fabric creasing and recovery from creasing. During the decade of the 1920s, research was directed toward the development of processes that could reduce the creasing and wrinkling of cotton and linen; emphasis was placed on linen because it wrinkled so much more noticeably than cotton. Early finishes caused considerable loss of fiber strength, which resulted in reduced fabric strength, particularly in reduced resistance to tearing. Linen fabrics had some strength to spare, and thus the reduction in strength was not as noticeable to consumers as it might have been if cotton fabrics had been used. The finish made the fabrics look better, and consumers were so pleased with the appearance that they ignored the drop in durability. Cotton fabrics, however, had no extra strength, and fabrics treated with such finishes were unacceptable to consumers; as recently as the mid-1940s less than 1 percent of all cotton fabrics were treated with wrinkle-resistant finishes.

The researchers, however, were aware of how much consumers liked fabrics that required less effort to care for and retained a good appearance during wear. These researchers spent considerable time seeking processes that could be used to make fabrics, particularly cotton, wrinkle resistant. With new and better finishes their use increased, and by the mid-1950s a fair amount of cotton was given wrinkle-resistant finishes. It was not until the 1960s, however, that durable press was introduced to the market. The timing was due, in part, to the presence of man-made fibers that could be heat set to build in optimum shape and appearance and the fact that consumers now had alternatives from which to choose in order to have easy care and attractive fabrics.

Early examples of durable press were not an unqualified success. To obtain cotton fabrics that really had durable-press qualities, the amount of finishing chemicals used had to be high, and this reduced fabric strength, abrasion resistance, and tearing strength to a dangerous low. Some early fabrics tended to tear and develop abraded holes after only one wearing. In an effort to provide fabrics that did have sufficient strength to satisfy consumers, researchers decided to try fabrics in which man-made fibers that had some strength were blended with the natural fibers. Thus, the polyester and cotton blends became the popular combination of fibers for a wide variety of fabrics. These fabrics could be made and treated with finishes so that they did give outstanding behavior in use and care. Ironing almost became a thing of the past for some consumers. The polyester and cotton blend is still the most popular for durable-press fabrics. The polyester fibers contribute strength to the blend, and because they can be heat set, they also contribute to the easy care properties; cotton contributes comfort to the fabrics, and because durable-press finishes can be added to the fiber, it also contributes to the easy care qualities. Blends continue to be the most satisfactory process for creating durable-press fabrics; however, some fabrics of 100 percent cotton are now appearing on the market that do have durable-press properties, though usually at a lower level of performance than the blends.

Durable press requires the finish to be cured into the fibers. There are two basic techniques, precure and postcure—sometimes called deferred cure. For precured finishes a textile fabric is treated in a bath so the chemicals attach themselves to the fabric; the fabric is then dried and subjected to high temperatures to cure or seal the finish into the fibers. The fabric is washed to remove any excess chemicals and dried again. Textile products can then be made from this durable-press fabric.

For postcured fabrics the finish is applied in the same way as for the precured method: The fabric is dried, and the textile product is then made. After the product has been made it is subjected to curing temperatures to make certain the finish is sealed into the fibers. The product may be given a final wash to remove excess finishing chemicals, but this is not required. It should be noted that postcuring of finishes, following completion of the textile product, makes it nearly impossible to make alterations in the product because creases built in during finishing cannot be removed.

A serious problem in the application of durable-press finishes relates to the use of formaldehyde as a part of the process. This chemical has been identified as a possible carcinogen; thus, its use is under close observation and limited in terms of the amount of vapor that can be in the air. Research continues to find other materials that are successful and will not be an environmental pollutant. Some are currently in use, but to date, formaldehyde is still an important component in the application of durable-press finishes.

Despite the widespread acceptance of durable-press fabrics, these fabrics do pose some serious problems in use and care. It is impossible, or nearly so, to alter apparel items made by the postcure process. Seams and construction lines cannot be removed. For precured fabrics it is difficult to press in creases and lines because the fabric has already been given the final processing prior to use. For consumers who sew, the use of postcured fabrics presents a problem because the typical consumer has no way to perform the postcure operation after an apparel item has been constructed.

Nonetheless, consumers like the easy care characteristics of durable-press fabrics, and they are widely used for both apparel and for home furnishings, particularly domestics such as sheets and pillow cases. During the 1980s, a variety of fabrics have been designed, particularly for apparel, to have a wrinkled appearance. These fabrics may or may not have some durable-press properties, but care is easy because the fabric is supposed to appear wrinkled.

Fabrics and textile items made of fabrics with durable-press finishes can be laundered in washers and dryers; they require little or no ironing. A fabric softener in the laundering operation helps to maintain a smooth surface and reduce static cling in these fabrics. Consumers should read care labels carefully to determine if the finish has any special care requirements. One important item to watch for is information concerning bleaching. Some durable-press finishes are discolored by chlorine bleaches, and white fabrics become yellow when exposed to chlorine. Perborate bleaches can be used on most durable-press fabrics without any discoloration.

The majority of durable-press fabrics on the market are blends of polyester and cellulose—usually cotton. However, considerable 100 percent cotton fabric is available now that has been given durable-press finishes. For the most part these fabrics give adequate wear, partly because of improvements in the finishing process and the use of new chemicals that do not have the negative effect on cotton and other cellulose fibers that early durable-press finishes had.

Flame-Resistant Finishes

Finishes that reduce the flaming, charring, or afterglow of fibers and fabrics are important for safety. Most fabrics finished with flame retardants will still burn in the direct path of flame; however, they self-extinguish when the source of flame is removed. The important characteristic is that they do not propagate the flame. A truly fireproof fabric will not burn even in the path of direct flame, but actually only asbestos and glass fibers have this property. Finishes cannot provide completely safe products. They can, however, reduce the danger of complete destruction of the treated fabric, and they do provide a margin of safety that may prevent serious harm to individuals.

There have been several recorded incidents of serious damage and death as a result of flash burns from brushed cellulosic fiber fabrics, such as rayon negligees or sweaters, ignited by cigarette ashes. As a result of group disasters (i.e., the Coconut Grove nightclub fire in Boston and the circus tent fire in Hartford, Connecticut), Congress enacted legislation designed to control the sale of highly flammable wearing apparel. This legislation was passed in 1953, and several amendments to strengthen it in relation to specific types of products have been passed (see p. 41).

Definitions concerning flame resistance and flame-retardant chemicals have been clarified by the legislation and by groups interested in standards for textile items, such as the American Society for Testing and Materials (ASTM). The definition for *flame resistance* is that property of a material whereby flaming combustion is prevented, terminated, or inhibited following application of a flaming or nonflaming source of ignition, with or without subsequent removal of the ignition source. *Flame resistant* identifies the property of having flame resistance. *Flame retardants* refer to the substances used to impart flame resistance to a textile fabric (see p. 41).

Flame-resistant finishes are of two general types. The first is the most important and comprises those finishes considered to be durable. These can meet legislation requirements for children's sleepwear only if the product can withstand at least fifty launderings without loss of performance. However, consumers should be aware that the actual durability of these finishes is somewhat variable, and they should study any label information that details performance and care requirements. A second group of flame retardants is not durable. These finishes are removed by normal care procedures. Though they do not satisfy the legislation and, consequently, are not acceptable for fabrics that must meet the specified requirements, they can be used on fabrics for one-time use.

The durable flame-resistant finishes include insoluble salts applied by dissolving in a suitable solvent; oils, waxes, and resins that incorporate chlorinated or bromine substances; and substances that react with the fiber to produce molecular change that causes flame resistance. The manufacturer or converter must select the type of finish that is most suitable for the particular fiber or fibers involved in the product. The fiber type is critical in the selection of flame-retardant chemicals; fabric structure may influence the choice to some extent, and the intended end use determines what level of flame resistance a product must meet before it can be sold.

Consumers should be aware of the problems related to flame resistance. If fiber blends are involved, flame resistance may be extremely difficult to attain. For example, cotton can be made flame resistant fairly easily, and so can polyester; however, blends of these two fibers are very difficult to treat so that they meet flame-resistance standards for children's sleepwear. As yet, there is no really good method for making polyester and cotton blends sufficiently flame resistant to be used in children's sleepwear. They do, however, meet the basic flammable fabric legislation, as do all fabrics sold on the U.S. market.

Flame-resistant finishes may influence the hand of fabrics and result in fabric that is stiff and rough in texture. This can be a problem, particularly with fabrics for sleepwear. The dimensional stability of fabric may be improved by such finishes.

Flame-resistant finishes delay the speed of fire spread in fabrics and

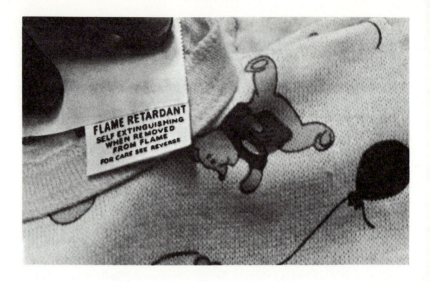

26.15 Typical label in flame-resistant sleepwear for infants. (U.S. Consumer Products Safety Commission)

can make it possible to extinguish the flame before major damage occurs. Nonetheless, such fabrics can give a false sense of security. These fabrics do burn, and they may give off toxic fumes that can be hazardous. Some finishes may increase the amount of smoke produced. Further, flame-resistant fabrics tend to cost more than similar fabrics without such finishes. However, it is important that they be available to consumers who want them, as they do provide a safety factor. Whether they should be mandated for all fabrics for selected end uses is a philosophical question that cannot be easily answered.

The care of flame-resistant fabrics requires attention. Soaps mask the effectiveness of the finish and render it inactive within three launderings. Bleaches destroy the finish, and fabric softeners destroy the effect and increase the ease of burning. Calcium in hard water reduces the effectiveness of flame resistants, and nonphosphate detergents may stop the flame-resistant action. It is important to remember that the property of a fiber in relation to its behavior in flame may be changed by the presence of normal processing substances such as dyestuffs. The presence of soil may increase flammability.

The most satisfactory method of care for flame-resistant fabrics is to launder with phosphate detergents and to avoid fabric softeners and chlorine bleaches. When bleaching is necessary, perborate bleaches may be used. If phosphate detergents cannot be used in the geographical area because of legislation that has banned that type of detergent, citrate detergents or nonionic commercial detergents should be tried.

Consumers may find informative labels attached to products that meet special flame-resistant standards. Figure 26.15 is an example of a product label for flame-resistant sleepwear for infants. Before laundering or providing care for any fabric, especially items that are flame resistant, it is essential that the consumer read any care labels. Some detergent packages also carry specific directions for use with flame-resistant textiles.

Fume Fading-Resistant Finishes

Certain dyestuffs on certain fibers are subject to color loss or change as a result of exposure to atmospheric fumes that include oxides of nitrogen and various sulfur compounds. Such fumes may be the result of improperly vented home heating units or stoves; they may occur outside as contaminants found in smog.

Dyes applied to acetate fibers are particularly susceptible to fume fading, and the same type of dyestuffs may cause problems when used on nylon or polyester fibers. A major step in efforts to reduce fume fading was taken when pigments were introduced into the fiber polymer solution before extrusion (see p. 291). However, not all fabrics subject to fume fading can be dyed economically by pigment coloration.

For fabrics that are colored after construction of either the yarns or the fabric, finishes can be added to reduce damage from fume fading. Label information may inform the consumer that the product has been treated to reduce or prevent fume fading, but this type of information is not common. Too often, the consumer discovers the potential for fume fading after the fact; in such a case it is recommended that consumers return the product to the store or send it to the manufacturer to indicate their dissatisfaction.

Metallic and Plastic Coatings

In an effort to produce fabrics that reflect heat, fabric converters developed finishes in which an aluminum coating is applied to the back of fabrics. This coating modifies the warmth or coolness of the fabric. Today, converters may use the aluminum coating or they may use a plastic coating. These are frequently applied to fabrics to be used for draperies, especially drapery linings. The fabric helps maintain constant room temperatures; the aluminum coating will reflect sunlight in summer and retain heat in winter, and the plastic coating closes the interstices of the fabric and delays the passage of heat through the fabric. Fabrics with an aluminum coating have been used as lining materials for coats. It is said that they help maintain comfort in cold weather with a relatively lightweight item. Evidence indicates that some of the insulative value is psychological rather that physical; however, these coatings do reflect some heat and may produce comfort otherwise not felt.

Aluminum finishes with adhesives that resist solvents will dry clean fairly well; some, however, are lost during dry cleaning. Fabrics with closely packed yarns and smooth surfaces serve as good substrates (base fabrics) for such finishes. Plastic coatings help reduce the amount of soil that will penetrate the fabric as well as the passage of air.

A different use of plastic coatings on fabrics is the creation of designs. Plastic coatings can be treated to resemble leather. Depending on the end use of the fabric, coatings can be applied either to the face or to the back of the fabric. For drapery linings and similar uses, the coating is attached to the back, or wrong side, of the cloth; when the coating is to provide appearance value, such as the leather effect, it will become the face of the cloth.

A problem with either metallic or plastic coatings is that they may crack and peel off the base fabric, especially plastic coatings that are cleaned incorrectly. As with all fabrics, it is important to read care labels and follow directions.

Mothproofing Finishes

Fibers containing protein, such as wool and silk, are especially susceptible to damage by moth and carpet beetles. The protein keratin in wool and other hair fibers is believed to be what the moths prefer; carpet beetles will eat either the keratin in wool or the protein fibroin in silk. Some other fibers may be damaged by moths and carpet beetles if they are caught within the folds of the fabric and try to reach desirable food. Wool is the most susceptible and most frequently damaged fiber. The U.S. Department of Agriculture reports indicate that damage to wool and other protein fibers by moths and carpet beetles results in an annual loss valued between $200 and $500 million.

Damage may be caused by any one of a group of moths that are known to damage protein fibers. The larva of the moth is the culprit. During the eating period the larvae increase their weight approximately 300 times. The moth itself does not damage the fiber; however, it will lay eggs on the fibers, which, as soon as they hatch, will start to eat the protein fibers.

Finishes to reduce or prevent damage by moths can be renewable or durable. The substances may be effective because (1) they give off an odor that repels the mature moth and prevents the deposit of eggs. Naphthalene crystals or moth balls are examples. They are comparatively unsuccessful in preventing damage as they do not last for any great length of time, nor do they destroy any eggs that might have been deposited before the crystals were used. (2) The agent gives off a gas, which may or may not be noticeable to humans, that is toxic to the mature moth and to the destructive larvae as well. It is this second type of product that is the most successful and should be used whenever there is a possibility of damage from moths or carpet beetles.

Many wool products are sold with moth-preventive finishes incorporated into the fabric, particularly wool carpeting and upholstery. Further, moth preventives can be added to wool fabrics as part of the dry cleaning operation. These may not be as durable as the type that is added during the processing or finishing of wool fabrics, however.

Good care practices are important in the care of wool, wool blends, or other hair fibers. Fabrics should be brushed frequently; soiled fabrics should always be cleaned before storage or hanging in a closet for any length of time. Spraying closets is an extra precaution. Carpets must be cleaned frequently to avoid damage from moths, especially when the carpeting is of wool or wool blends.

Soil-Release Finishes

With the proliferation of synthetic fiber fabrics and with durable-press finishes, the difficulty of removing soil has increased. In an effort to alleviate the problem, manufacturers have incorporated soil-release finishes with durable-press finishes or have supplied soil-release finishes alone. These finishes operate on one of two principles: They provide a hydrophilic surface that attracts the water and permits it to lift off soil, or they coat the fibers so that the soil does not penetrate.

Many soil-release finishes are nearly identical to soil- and stain-repellent finishes. They often provide several side benefits, such as preventing soil redeposition during care, introducing antistatic qualities, and improving the softness and hand of fabrics.

Research on soil-release finishes is continuing. The problem has not been solved to the satisfaction of textile experts or the consumer. A true soil-release finish should make it possible for the consumer to remove all types of soil by home laundering with common detergents, including the removal of both oil- and water-borne stains. Further, the finish should not affect dyes and result in color change during use and care.

Consumers should read labels carefully to determine if a soil-release finish might be present. Adhering to care directions that accompany such finishes should prevent dissatisfaction with the product.

Stabilization Finishes

One of the most frequently asked questions about a textile item is whether the fabric will shrink. This is true for apparel, home furnishings, and many other applications. The problem of fabric shrinkage is as old as fabrics. Some solutions to the problem were developed by consumers themselves; they simply washed the cloth before converting it into an end-use item. During the 1930s, fabric manufacturers became aware that stabilization of fabric was extremely important to consumers, apparel manufacturers, and makers of home furnishings. Stabilization finishes not only reduce the possibility of fabric shrinking in size; these finishes also reduce the danger of fabric stretching out of shape.

Fabric converters and processors recognize two distinct types of shrinkage: relaxation, or residual, shrinkage and felting shrinkage. *Residual* shrinkage, sometimes called *relaxation* shrinkage, is that shrinkage remaining in a fabric when it is purchased, that is, the actual shrinkage that can occur during use and care. *Felting* shrinkage is caused by certain fiber characteristics and may occur over a long period of time. *Shrinkage* indicates a change in dimensions of a fabric in either the length or the width measurement or both. The term *dimensional change* refers to either a loss or reduction in measurement or a growth or enlargement of measurement.

Relaxation shrinkage is rather complex. It is the most common type and occurs when some operation, such as laundering, releases the tensions imposed during fabric manufacture, so that the yarns return to their original length. This type of shrinkage is sometimes progressive in that all the potential shrinkage may not take place during the first laundering. The delay may be caused by the presence of various finishing agents, and as they are gradually removed, the additional relaxation shrinkage occurs. Dry cleaning can also cause relaxation shrinkage, especially if a wet cleaning process is used.

A second problem with relaxation shrinkage is that although shrinkage occurs during laundering, ironing will often restretch or strain the fabric. This may continue for the life of the garment, so that the size will vary with each care period.

Some fabrics shrink or stretch with changes in humidity. This is a fiber property, but it is reflected in the fabric. It occurs when a fiber is more easily stretched or elongated when humidity is high and the weight of the fabric causes the fibers and yarns to extend or stretch. As humidity decreases, the fiber returns to position. This type of shrinkage is visible in some drapery fabrics. Chain weighting in draperies increases the effect, which is sometimes called the "elevator effect." Rayon is particularly susceptible to this behavior.

If a fabric has been held under tension on the lengthwise yarns during drying, it may shrink in that direction upon release of stress and stretch in the perpendicular direction. Nearly all fabrics composed of natural fibers and many of man-made fibers exhibit relaxation shrinkage; the amount will vary, but if left uncontrolled it will result in an unsatisfactory product. Such shrinkage is seldom the result of fiber characteristics. Rather, the stress put on fibers when making yarns as well as the stress applied in making fabrics cause relaxation shrinkage when such stresses are released.

Felting shrinkage is primarily a characteristic of hair fibers. It occurs when fibers entangle as a result of heat, moisture, pressure, and/or agitation. Wool fabrics are particularly susceptible to felting shrinkage. Although this property is used to advantage in fulling wool fabrics, it is disappointing when it occurs during use and care of wool items.

26.16 Compressive shrinkage frame. (Springs Industries)

Shrinkage Control

Cellulosic fiber fabrics The primary method for eliminating shrinkage in cellulosic fiber fabrics is mechanical. A simple method, frequently employed by consumers, is to wet the fabric thoroughly, dry it in a tensionless state, then smooth it out by calendering or ironing. Another method involves feeding the cloth into the tenter frame in a slack condition and applying stretch to the filling. However, the method that is probably most commonly used and most successful is called *compressive shrinkage*. This method produces fabrics with no more than 2 percent shrinkage, and the typical shrinkage is less than 1 percent.

In compressive shrinkage the fabric is fed in open width to the shrinkage area (Fig. 26.16). Fabric, slightly damp, and a thick rubber blanket are fed over a roller and then against a heated cylinder. As the fabric and blanket pass over the roller, the outer surface of the blanket is extended and the fabric tightly adheres to the blanket surface. As the blanket and fabric leave the unit, the blanket retracts and the fabric is forced to comply. Thus, the fabric is compressed or physically shortened. Fabrics carrying the trade names of Sanforized and Rigmel are examples of compressive shrinkage. Other chemical treatments to control shrinkage in cellulosic fiber fabrics involve resin impregnation, which is often a part of durable-press finishing.

Nylon and polyester Man-made fibers, particularly nylon and polyester, can be controlled for shrinkage by heat setting. This process stabilizes the fabrics, and unless care procedures are such that the heat setting is altered, the fabrics tend to retain their shape.

Wool fabrics Wool has always posed many problems in relation to shrinkage. In addition to relaxation shrinkage, wool has a high degree of felting shrinkage. Sponging and steaming of wool fabric will eliminate much of the relaxation shrinkage, but treatment to prevent felting shrinkage demands more drastic treatment. One of the more common techniques is to coat the fibers with a polymer, somewhat like that used to make nylon. This coating reduces the chance of the wool fibers felting and, as a result, reduces the felting shrinkage. The use of a small proportion of nylon fiber blended with wool tends to reduce felting shrinkage; this is often combined with the polymer coating technique. Other processes for eliminating felting shrinkage in wool fabrics are under investigation.

Use and care of shrink-resistant fabrics The advantages of shrink-resistant finishes are obvious. A fabric that shrinks or stretches and changes size or dimensions results in a product that no longer meets the need for which it was purchased. There are cautions, however, that consumers should know. Fabrics that have been given shrink-resistant finishes may be difficult to work with in home sewing. Loose weaves or knits, which have potential for packing yarns closer together, may be easy to work with when constructing items at home; however, close weaves and compact knits may pose difficulties and need pattern alterations before sewing.

Despite the many advances in the finishing of fabrics, dimensional change is one of the most frequent causes of consumer dissatisfaction. Thus, consumers should be alert and request information concerning fabric performance during use and care, and it is equally essential that consumers follow all care directions provided on labels or those that have been learned through a study of textiles.

Stain- and Soil-Resistant Finishes

Removal of stains from fabrics has been, and is, a constant problem for consumers. Thus, finishes that reduce staining and soiling are always welcome. These finishes reduce the rate of soil deposition on fabrics and help prevent spot staining—a real aid to consumers. These finishes increase the surface tension so that liquid stains bead up and roll off or make it easy for the consumer to absorb the spot with tissue or a sponge (Fig. 26.17).

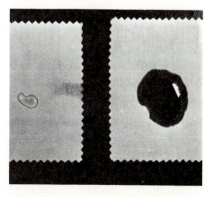

26.17 Fabric with stain-resistant finish (left) and same fabric without finish (right). Finish causes stain to "bead up" and roll off fabric.

Although these finishes delay the penetration of stains and soil into fabric, it is important to remove any stain as quickly as possible to prevent it from being set into the fabric. Once soil or stains have become embedded into the fabric they are nearly impossible to remove. Frequent cleaning will maintain these finishes.

Water-Repellent and Waterproof Finishes

Water-repellent finishes result in a fabric that resists wetting while retaining a porous characteristic that permits air circulation. The finish alters the surface tension properties of the fabric, which causes moisture to form into tiny balls or beads of water and roll off without passing through the fabric. Waterproof finishes are those that coat or seal a fabric so that water or moisture does not pass through it. Such fabrics are impermeable to air and thus, in general, are not comfortable in items of wearing apparel. They may serve an important function for specialized fabrics for the home or for industrial applications.

Early methods used to produce a waterproof fabric included a coating of rubber, oxidized oil, or varnish on the fabric surface. Though they prevented water from passing through, most were heavy and bulky. Oiled silks were light in weight, but they were not as durable as rubber- or varnish-coated fabrics. Today some fabrics are coated with plastic to produce a waterproof finish. They may be used for upholstery for homes or automobiles or for heavy raincoats.

Water-resistant or water-repellent finishes are popular in consumer goods because the fabrics are comfortable and the finish does not alter the original appearance of fabric and seldom alters the hand of the fabric. Both durable and nondurable or renewable water-repellent finishes are available on consumer goods. Durable water-repellent finishes will withstand considerable use and care. They will take laundering better than dry cleaning, but the latter process may be employed if the cleaner is informed that the fabric has such a finish. It is important to study labels concerning water-repellent finishes as the same trade name may be used for either durable, semidurable, or renewable finishes. For example, Cravanette is a trade name that is used for both durable and renewable finishes. Most water-repellent fabrics will have some type of tag or label that identifies the type of finish or the trade name for the finish and will provide care information.

Study Questions

1. List and describe the main types of finishes used to modify fabric appearance and hand.
2. List and describe the major functional or performance finishes used on fabrics.
3. Indicate which finishes would be desirable for a variety of end uses, such as for draperies, carpeting, furniture upholstery, coats and suits, dress fabrics, sweaters, and lingerie.
4. What are some of the characteristics that functional finishes impart to fabrics?

5. For each of the following list any special care requirements, indicate any special considerations concerning the use of the finish, and identify typical end uses for fabrics that have been given the finish.
   a. Bacteriostatic finishes
   b. Durable-press finishes
   c. Mothproofing finishes
   d. Stabilization finishes
   e. Soil-release finishes
   f. Stain-resistant finishes
   g. Water-repellent finishes.
6. Flame-retardant finishes are applied as a safety precaution. Identify typical end uses for products with these finishes.
7. Refer to the chapter on textile legislation (p. 37) and determine the special items covered by the Flammable Fabrics Act.

27

Dyestuffs and Their Application

The color of textile products, particularly apparel and home-furnishing textiles, is one of their most important properties. Consumers are more concerned, usually, with selecting the right color than they are with selecting a product that will give good durability and performance. Color is universal in its appeal; it serves as a common language across many barriers.

The textile industry is aware of the consumer's desire for appealing colors. Manufacturers and retailers know that the consumer who selected an item because of its color will be extremely annoyed if the color is not maintained for the anticipated life of the product. Consequently, research by dyestuff manufacturers has resulted in coloring agents that satisfy the aesthetic demands of consumers and provide lasting pleasure if the color is properly selected and applied and the fabric carefully maintained. This last point is critical. No matter how good the coloring agent is and no matter how well applied to the textile fabric, if improper care occurs, the color may fail. Further, certain dyes work on certain fibers and only certain fibers; thus it is essential that the dyer select the best dyestuff for the specific fiber or fibers used in any textile fabric. A further note is important: Dyes vary widely in cost, and manufacturers intent on marketing low-cost merchandise or merchandise that will bring a large profit may select dyes that are not the best for the particular textile. In such a situation the durability of the color may be severely limited.

Historical Review

Dyestuffs and dyeing are as old as textiles themselves and predate written history. Fabrics dated from 3500 B.C. have been found in Thebes, Egypt, that still possess the remains of blue indigo dye. Other fabrics, discovered in the ancient tombs of Egypt, were colored yellow with dye obtained from the safflower plant. Beautifully colored fabrics dating back several thousand years have been unearthed in China, eastern Mediterranean countries, and some areas of Europe.

Prior to 1856 all dyestuffs were made from natural materials, mainly animal and vegetable matter. A bright red was obtained from a tiny insect native to Mexico. This insect was used by the Aztecs to color their fabrics, and when the Spaniards invaded Mexico in 1518, they called the insect and the dyestuff *cochineal*. A tiny mollusk found on the Phoenician coast near the city of Tyre produced a beautiful purple color. By 1500 B.C. Tyre had become the center for the trading and manufacture of this purple dye. The dye was tremendously expensive to produce because approximately 12,000 of these tiny shellfish were needed to obtain a single gram of dye. Thus, the expression "royal purple" or "born to the purple" arose as an indication that only the wealthy could afford the dye. Other ancient dyes included madder, a red dye, from the roots of a plant; blue indigo from the leaves of a plant; yellow from a stigmata of a plant; and logwood from the pulp of a tree.

Early efforts at coloring fabrics were hampered by the fact that few of the natural dyes formed colorfast combinations with fibers. Eventually, scientists found that this defect could be partially overcome by the use of *mordants*—compounds that render the dye insoluble on the fiber. These mordants are primarily mineral matter.

During the Dark Ages there was little advancement in fabric coloring, and most dyeing was done in the home. The beginning of the Italian Renaissance saw the art of dyeing revived, and the first books on the subject were published during the fifteenth century A.D. Dyeing techniques were constantly being improved during the ensuing centuries, and written materials have provided valuable information to fiber scientists and technicians as well as to consumers.

As long as people were dependent on animal and vegetable matter for their dyestuffs and on minerals for the mordanting agents, progress was limited by the skill of the operator in mixing the natural dyes and in perfecting the techniques used to apply them. As with many of nature's products, the quality of materials varied considerably, and consequently, the results were somewhat unpredictable. It should be noted, however, that throughout these periods the only fibers to be colored were the natural ones. Thus, coloring was not as difficult as it became after the development of man-made fibers.

The year 1856 marked the turning point in the history of dyes. Sir William H. Perkin, while trying to make artificial quinine from coal tar, accidentally produced the first synthetic dyestuff—*mauve*. This discovery launched the modern dyestuff industry. Today, nearly all dyes are chemically compounded and, in most cases, are superior in every way to natural dyes.

The development of artificial dyes has been rapid, and the available dyes number in the thousands. However, research in the development of dyes continues. New fibers and fiber modifications frequently require a new type of dye; various finishes influence the dye used, and the desire for new and different colors makes it important to develop dyes that will produce these new colors in a durable form. During the past few years, several types of synthetic dyes have had to be discontinued because it was found that they either were or used chemicals believed to be carcinogenic. Thus, dye scientists have had to locate new products that would not be hazardous to health to replace the colors previously provided by these toxic chemicals.

Seeing Color

Color is a visual sensation. It results from the reflectance of certain visible light rays that strike the retina and stimulate cells in the nerves of the eye. The nerves send a message to the brain, which in turn produces the sensation of a specific hue. Thus, if the nerves and brain operate correctly, we see color. When all the visible light rays are reflected, an object appears to be white; if none of the rays are reflected, it appears to be black. When one or more rays are reflected, the viewer senses, or sees, the color produced by the specific reflected ray or combination of rays.

The purpose of a dye is to absorb light rays on a selective basis, causing the substrate or fabric to reflect those rays that are not absorbed; in other words, if all the rays except those producing blue are absorbed, the viewer sees blue. The ability of a compound to create a desired color derives from the presence of chemical groups called *chromophores*. Substances that include chromophores in various arrangements will produce the sensation of different color hues.

Though chromophores confer color on a substance, the intensity or brilliance of the color depends on the presence of one or more chemical groups called *auxochromes*. The auxochromes also can give water solubility to the dye and provide the chemical groups that form associative bonds with the fiber. Dyestuffs themselves, or combinations of dyes with other additives, contribute both chromophores and auxochromes to the dye operation.

The technical definition of a *dye* is a compound that can be fixed on a substance in a more or less permanent state and that evokes the visual sensation of a specific color.

Types of Dyestuffs

Dyes can be classified in a variety of ways. The system used here depends on the names commonly given to the different types of dyes. These names are based on both the method of application and the common group terms that have become accepted. Dyes are discussed in relation to the fibers to which they are normally applied and the relative colorfast properties.

Substantive or Direct Dyes

Substantive or direct dyes comprise the largest and most commercially significant group of dyestuffs. Direct dyes are water soluble, and they are applied primarily to cellulosic fibers. When the dye is dissolved in water, a salt is added to control the absorption of the dye by the fiber. The fiber, yarn, or fabric is immersed into a solution of the dye; this solution includes the dye, salts of some type, water, and other additives that may improve the absorption to some degree. The amount of dye absorbed depends on two factors—the size of the dye molecule and the size of the pore opening in the fiber. Direct dyes do not react chemically with the fiber.

To improve the colorfastness of direct dyes, finishing chemicals may be added. Some of these react chemically with the dye to create an insoluble compound that has good colorfastness. These are called *developed direct dyes*.

There is a large market for direct dyes because they are inexpensive, easy to apply, and available in a large range of colors. These dyes exhibit good colorfastness to sunlight, but unless they are developed, their colorfastness to laundering is poor. The application of durable-press finishes tends to increase the colorfastness of direct dyes, and they also help to lock or attach the dye onto the fiber surface.

Direct dyes are used, primarily, for low- to medium-priced cellulosic fiber fabrics. They are good choices for drapery and curtain fabrics because of their good lightfastness (colorfastness to daylight and artificial light).

Azoic or Naphthol Dyes

Azoic or naphthol dyes are used, also, for cellulosic fibers and to a limited extent for man-made fibers such as nylon, acrylic, polyester, and polypropylene. These dyes are sometimes called "ice" colors because they are applied from a low-temperature water bath.

Azoic dyestuffs produce brilliant and fast colors at relatively low cost. They exhibit good colorfastness to laundering, bleaching, and light, so they often serve to color fabrics used for towels, sheets, pillow cases, and other fabrics that require clear, bright colors or that may require bleaching.

Acid Dyes

Acid dyes can be used on protein, acrylic, nylon, and certain modified polyester fibers; some work satisfactorily on spandex and polypropylene fibers. The dye forms an association with the fiber that results in good colorfastness. These dyes are applied from an acid bath, rather than a water bath; therefore, their use is limited to fibers that are not damaged by the type of acid solutions required. The range of colors varies from bright to light and from pale to dark tints and shades.

Colorfastness of acid dyes varies widely. Some of these dyes fade quickly in light, as a result of laundering or dry cleaning or perspiration. Others exhibit excellent colorfastness. The best method for care of such products should be cited on care labels; directions should be followed.

Cationic or Basic Dyes

Cationic or basic dyes are among the oldest synthetic dyes. They are excellent for coloring acrylic fibers and are successful on modified nylon and polyester fibers. When properly selected for the right fibers, they produce brilliant colors with good colorfastness to most environmental and laundering conditions. These dyes are not colorfast on cellulosic or protein fibers; however, they are sometimes used as topping colors to increase the brightness of a textile. Such brightness on cellulosic or protein fibers is seldom durable and disappears during the first care period. However, these dyes do give outstanding colorfastness on acrylic, nylon, and polyester fibers.

Disperse Dyes

Disperse dyes, formerly called acetate dyes, were originally developed for acetate fibers. They are used for coloring acetate, polyester, acrylic, and nylon fibers. These dyes are dispersed into a solution and then into the fiber. When disperse dyes are applied to polyester fibers at temperatures below the boiling point, carriers are required to bring about penetration of the dye into the fiber. A combination of high temperature with pressure (Fig. 27.1) accomplishes successful application of disperse dyes as an alternative to the use of carriers. The thermosol process is also successful; in this technique the dye is applied to the fabric, which is then passed into a heated oven where high temperatures bake the color into the fibers. This procedure is often used in dyeing the polyester fibers in blends with cotton.

Colorfastness of disperse dyes to light, laundering, and dry cleaning is excellent. However, on acetate and some nylons, the dyes are subject to fume fading—a reaction to nitrogen oxide fumes found in the atmosphere, particularly where there is smog and where large quantities of gas are used for heat. Some fabrics are given fume fading finishes (see p. 278) to reduce this type of color loss.

Disperse dyes are frequently applied with vat dyes to color polyester and cellulosic fiber blends. Special techniques have been developed that make it possible to apply these different types of dyes in a continuous operation.

27.1 Pressure dye unit.

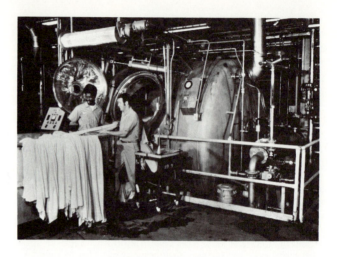

Vat Dyes

The type of dyes that have frequently been advertised as having the best colorfastness is the group identified as vat dyes. In general, these dyes do exhibit excellent colorfastness, particularly to laundering; however, their colorfastness to light may not be as good. Today there are many different types of dyes that have outstanding colorfastness, but vat dyes still remain a good choice for those types of fibers to which they can be applied.

Vat dyes were developed originally about 1910 and took their name from the large vats used for applying the dye to yarns or fabrics. Today vat dyes can be applied in either vats or in continuous feed methods (Fig. 27.2). Vat dyes are insoluble in water unless chemically modified, but they will dissolve in an alkaline solution. It is their insolubility in water that makes vat dyes colorfast to laundering.

Vat dyes are adaptable to all cellulosic fibers; they may be used under certain conditions on protein fibers and on some of the man-made fibers. They are available in a wide choice of colors.

27.2 Vat dyeing equipment.

Reactive Dyes

Reactive dyes were first introduced in 1956. These dyes actually react chemically with the fiber molecule, thus producing a high degree of color-fastness. Although they are used primarily on cotton, some types have been developed for rayon, nylon, acrylic, and protein fibers. Reactive dyes have also been developed, in a few colors, for some polyester fibers.

Bright colors with excellent resistance to laundering are available in reactive dyes; some have good colorfastness to light as well as laundering. One of the major problems with reactive dyes is that they are susceptible to damage from chlorine bleaches. Thus, consumers should avoid the use of chlorine bleach with fabrics colored with such dyestuffs. Labels indicating that perborate bleach should be used are usually attached to fabrics with these dyes. As with any textile item, consumers should seek care labels to determine the recommended methods of maintenance.

Pigment Colors

Pigment colors technically are not true dyestuffs. However, they are included here as they are used in coloring some textile fabrics and, thus, serve as coloring agents. Pigment colors have no affinity for fibers; they are attached to fibers or fabrics by means of some type of adhesive resin, or bonding agent. The resultant colors are relatively permanent, but their durability is directly related to the durability of the bonding agent. As the latter wears away so will the pigment. Pigments are frequently used in printing colored designs on fabrics.

Pigments may be mixed with the fiber solution; when this is done the fiber is colored as it is formed. These colors have outstanding colorfastness properties. Fibers colored by these substances may be identified as dope-dyed fibers, solution-dyed fibers, or mass-pigmented fibers.

Application of Color

Color, through the proper choice of dyes, can be applied to textile products at various stages of manufacture. Color can be added to the fiber solution before the formation of man-made fibers; it can be added to fibers prior to formation into yarns; it can be added to yarns prior to formation into fabric; it can be added to completed fabrics; and it can be applied to finished textile products. The major differences are in relation to the types of equipment used. Further, the proper dye must be selected for the particular fiber type involved. The following discussion highlights the stages at which color can be applied.

Solution or Dope Dyeing, Mass Pigmentation

In the manufacture of man-made fibers, color can be added to the solution before it is forced through the spinnerette. If the pigment or dye is well chosen, this method ensures even and colorfast dyes, as the color becomes an integral part of the fiber. Because it is a part of the fiber it is not easily affected by any outside environmental conditions. This method of coloration is somewhat expensive and results in fibers that cannot be changed in color if fashion decrees new colors. However, the colorfastness frequently is considered more important than being able to change colors quickly. Some man-made fibers are extremely difficult to dye; for those fibers this method of applying color is important. This is particularly important for olefin fibers because the best way to add color to these is by mass pigmentation.

27.3 Dye kier with fiber. (Morton Machine Works, Inc.)

Fiber Dye

Raw fiber stock may be dyed in large kiers, or vats. These vats can be operated either at atmospheric pressure or under increased pressure (Fig. 27.3). The use of pressure increases the depth of penetration of the dye into the fiber and increases the uniformity of coloration and, to some degree, the colorfastness. Consumers should recognize, however, that the ultimate colorfastness depends on having the right type of dyestuff for the fiber or fibers used, regardless of how or when the dye is applied.

Yarn Dye

One of the oldest systems of dyeing textiles is to color the yarns. Yarns can be dyed in skein form (Figs. 27.4 and 27.5), rolled on tubes (called

27.4 Package dyeing machine for dyeing yarn in cones. (Morton Machine Works, Inc.)

27.5 Yarn dyeing in skein form.

package dyeing), or rolled onto warp beams (called beam dyeing). In skein dyeing, the yarn is moved through the dye bath while at the same time the dye is forced through the arms holding the skeins. Package dyeing involves placing many packages or tubes of yarn into a large vessel, where the dye is forced through the yarn. Beam dyeing is similar to package dyeing except that large beams of yarn are placed in the dye vessel and the dye is forced through the yarns. The dyed beam can be moved directly to weaving looms or warp knitting frames for use in fabric construction.

Yarn dyeing provides good color absorption and adequate penetration for most textile items. It permits the use of various colored yarns in one fabric and gives the fabric designer wide latitude in designing plaids, checks, stripes, muted color arrangements, and iridescent effects. A variation of yarn dyeing, called *space dyeing,* applies color to selected areas of the yarn in the skeins. When made into fabric, interesting color arrangements can be created.

Piece Dye

A large proportion of solid color fabrics are dyed after the fabric has been constructed. This is the easiest and least expensive method for adding color to textile items. Fabrics can be dyed in a rope form or flat, depending on the type of fabric. Open-width dyeing is usually carried out on a continuous basis. These dye frames are large and include the dye application, a first rinse, a final rinse, and drying operations. These dye frames are large and require careful monitoring to make certain procedures are done accurately. Rope dyeing involves the same general procedures and the same level of control, but the space needs are somewhat less.

Piece dyeing permits manufacturers to dye fabric as they are ordered by product manufacturers; thus there is no need to carry large stocks of colored fabric that may or may not sell. Piece dye does not always produce as thorough a penetration of dye into fiber or yarn as previous methods of application, but for many uses the end product is satisfactory. New machines that use a vacuum to pull the dye solution through fabric have increased the level of dye penetration and, consequently, improved colorfastness to some degree.

Normally piece-dyed fabrics are a solid color. However, when fabrics contain more than one type of fiber, a pattern can be produced by using different types of dyes. Each fiber type will absorb the dye intended for that specific fiber, resulting in multicolored fabrics. The number of colors depends on the number of fiber types and fiber variants within a single fabric.

Two general techniques are used when dyeing fabrics of two or more fiber types. These are identified as *union dyeing* and *cross dyeing*.

Union dyeing   The term *union dye* indicates that a fabric containing two or more fiber types or fiber variants has been dyed a single uniform color. Various dyestuffs are applicable only on certain fiber types, as discussed previously. When a fabric that contains two or more types of fibers is to be colored a single solid color, it is necessary to select the dyes appropriate to each fiber type. These different dyes may be applied from a single dye bath, or they may be applied in stages. Simultaneous application of the dyes means that the dye bath is designed to accommodate both (or all) types of dyes that are required to color the fabric; each fiber will selectively absorb the dyestuff appropriate to that specific fiber. Sequence dyeing, or stage dyeing, means that each color is applied individually from its own dye solution. Care must be taken in union dyeing to make certain that none of the processes used will harm any of the fibers in the fabric.

Cross dyeing   Fabrics of two or more different fiber types or variants of a single fiber type may require different types of dyestuffs. In cross dyeing the fabric designer identifies a color for each fiber type or fiber variant. Dyes are chosen so they will color only one of the fiber types or fiber variants involved. When finished, each fiber type has received a particular color. One type of fiber may be left white in this type of processing.

The end product in cross dyeing is a fabric of two or more colors. These colors may be arranged in a variety of designs including plaids and stripes, or they may be blended in such a way that muted color effects are formed or even tweed effects. The final color design depends on the types of fibers involved, the types of dyestuffs selected, and the arrangement of the fibers in the yarns and fabrics.

Product Dyeing

It is possible to complete a textile product and then color it. For example, many items for the home are colored in this way. Carpeting is frequently colored after the carpet has been finished and is ready for use. Towels, sheets, pillow cases, and bedspreads are frequently dyed after the product is made. Some couture houses create their designs, make them up, and then add color. However, product dyeing is more frequently used for home furnishings than for apparel. Different fiber types makes it possible to use union or cross dyeing on final textile products and create fabrics with interesting color arrangements. Product dyeing is not as common as piece dyeing, but it does have its place. It is particularly helpful when manufacturers receive orders for a limited number of items in a variety of colors.

Other Methods of Color Application

There are several other methods of applying dyestuffs to products that do not seem to fit into the discussion here. They are not true applied design and they are not true dyeing operations. These techniques, which include batik, tie-n-dye, and various types of jet dyeing, are discussed with applied design because they are used to create interesting patterns on the surface of fabrics.

Study Questions

1. What types of dyestuffs were used up to the mid-nineteenth century?
2. What was the first synthetic dyestuff, who discovered it, and how was it discovered?
3. List the different types of dyestuffs discussed, describe each briefly, and indicate the fibers to which they are applied.
4. What are pigments and how are they applied?
5. Dyes can be applied at various stages in textile manufacture. Cite each stage and describe each briefly.
6. Which method of dye application would give the most colorfast product? Why?
7. Which method of dye application would probably be the most expensive? Why?
8. Which method of dye application is best adapted to fashion change? Why?

28   Applied Design

Applied design is defined as a pattern that has been added to the surface of fabrics. These may be printed by using various types of dyestuffs, colored yarns, or finishing processes. Finishes used for altering appearance were discussed in Chapter 26. In this chapter applied designs that involve dyestuffs and printing processes of various kinds will receive the major consideration; however, mention will be made of the application of designs with colored yarns.

The term *printing* is frequently used synonymously with applied design; this is not truly correct, although printing of patterns onto the fabric surface is the most important method for applying designs to fabrics.

PRINTING

The art of printing color onto fabrics originated thousands of years ago, immediately following the development of some type of fabric. Primitive peoples decorated garments and home furnishings with paints as they did their bodies. At that time colors were not securely attached to the fabric so they frequently were lost during use and care. Fortunately, however, some early printed textiles have survived. There are examples of early printed textiles in museums throughout the world; and there are examples of illustrations showing painted textiles on walls of excavated tombs, pottery, and other artifacts found in archeological digs. One of the oldest remnants of printed fabric was found near Thebes, Egypt, and has been dated about 1600 B.C.

The oldest printed textiles found in Europe were dated about A.D. 600, and old examples of printed fabrics were found in Peru that are believed to have been part of the Inca civilization; these have been dated between A.D. 300 and A.D. 500 (Fig. 28.1).

During the latter part of the fifteenth century textile printing attained general acceptance. Printing became a fine art in France during the eighteenth century when Christophe Phillipe Oberkampf opened his textile printing factory at Jouy and began production of the famous "Toile de Jouy," considered by many to be the finest patterned fabrics in the world (Fig. 28.2).

There are many different ways to print fabrics today. These have been grouped into four major and three less-important categories. The major categories include resist, discharge, direct, and transfer printing; the other three are photographic, jet, and bubble printing.

Resist Printing

Resist printing is considered one of the oldest methods for applying color to form surface designs on fabric. Early Javanese batiks, Japanese stencil prints, and Plangi tie-dye are examples of this technique. The basic principle of resist printing is the protection of certain areas of the fabric by some device to prevent color or dye penetration. Both early and modern methods of resist printing are described.

Tie-dye Processes

Plangi tie-dye Plangi resist methods were used by primitive peoples in the Far East. Early designs were extremely delicate, and many from Asian countries today are fine and delicate in nature. In this process, tiny puffs of fabric were pulled over a pointed object, tied tightly with waxed thread below the puff, and then dipped into color. The entire fabric may have been dipped for certain effects. Where the fabric was tied by the thread, it resisted the dye and remained the original color. If more than one color was applied, the fabric was retied before the second color was added. Each tying would be at different locations. Many colors could be used, but retying was needed prior to each application (Fig. 28.3).

Modern tie-dye Tie-dye designs can be made by folding the fabric so that certain areas are protected from the dye; by knotting or plaiting the fabric to prevent dye penetration in selected areas; by inserting lines of stitching, which are then pulled into a tight unit; or by using foreign materials to prevent dye from reaching the fabric. When fabric is folded for tie-dyeing, it is arranged in various types of folds or accordion pleats, and then certain areas are further tied off with cord or thread to prevent penetration of color into the fabric at those locations. Fabrics may be refolded and retied several additional times for each color that is to be applied.

28.1 above left. Painted linen textile fragment from Nazea, southern Peru, c. A.D. 300–500. (Staatliche Museum fur Volkerkunde, Munich)
28.2 above right. Typical pattern found on Toile de Jouy.

28.3 Plangi tie-dye.

28.4 Example of modern tie-dyed fabric.

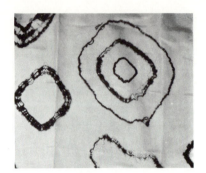
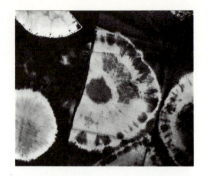

Fabrics may be plaited or tied into knots to prevent dye penetration. These designs tend to be large and bold, whereas the type obtained from the folded and tied areas are smaller (Fig. 28.4). The use of stitching is often called *tritik*. In this process a row of stitching outlines the design; then the thread is pulled tight, drawing the fabric together into bunches or puffs. The puffed areas will accept the color, whereas the stitched areas will resist it. Fabrics may be "tied off," using such devices as paper clips, pins, rubber bands, or other instruments available.

Commercial tie-dye prints are available that can be made by one of the true tie-dye processes or by imitation processes using one of the common printing methods, such as screen printing or roller printing. The design of such fabrics is difficult because dyes may diffuse differently. However, the characteristic of tie-dye patterns is relatively easy to identify. Tie-dyed fabrics from one of the true tie-dye methods are frequently expensive; they are often used for decorative accents in homes and offices or commercial buildings. Occasionally, they may be used for apparel fabrics for special items.

Batik

Batik is a resist dye method perfected by the Javanese. Today, batik is made in many countries, but the most typical and probably the best comes from Indonesia, Malaysia, and parts of Micronesia. This method of printing fabrics involves sealing sections of fabric with wax to prevent dye penetration; after color is added the wax is removed. This process is repeated for as many colors or dyes as needed to finish the pattern. Any smooth fabric can be printed with this method; however, it is not effective when applied to fabrics with a nap or a pile or made with rough-textured yarns.

The fabric is washed thoroughly to remove any dirt, wax, oil, or processing residues that might have been left in the fabric; then the cloth is stiffened with a special starch to produce a smooth, even surface.

1. Wax is melted in small containers; it is picked up either by small knives, blocks with wires protruding, or a tjanting and is applied to areas that are not to receive the color (Fig. 28.5).
2. The cloth is either dipped into a dye bath or dye is painted onto the fabric with a large brush or block. The portion that has not been covered with wax absorbs the dye; the portion covered with wax resists the dye.
3. The fabric is dried carefully and then immersed in boiling water to remove the wax. Some may be removed by cracking it off prior to the boiling water bath. As the water cools, the wax solidifies, floats to the

28.5 Tjanting being used to paint wax on fabric.

28.6 left. Painting dye onto fabric that has been waxed to resist at design areas.
28.7 right. Batik design from Malaysia.

surface of the water, and is recovered for reuse until the wax has picked up so much color that its application would actually put color onto the fabric.

4. The process is repeated for each color that is needed for the design. It can be repeated many times or only a few.

Prior to submersion in the dye bath, wax may be cracked to permit passage of dye through the fine lines, which gives a weblike set of lines. When designers want sharp and clear lines, they usually color the fabric on a flat surface with a large brush of some type to reduce the chance of cracking (Fig. 28.6). As noted, wax may be applied with a large block in which the design has been implanted by copper wires and metal bands (Fig. 28.7). The block is dipped in wax, the wax is transferred to the fabric, where it hardens; color is applied to the fabric; and it is absorbed by the areas where there is no wax. Each time a new color is to be added, the fabric is rewaxed. Combinations of blocks and the tjanting are sometimes used to create interesting designs. The tjanting is the typical method of applying wax when designs are to be hand drawn.

Ikat

Ikat, also called kasuri, is a resist method in which only the warp yarns are printed. The areas not to receive color are tied, and the yarns are dipped in dye; the tied areas remain white, and the untied areas pick up the color of the dye. If more than one color is to be used, several tyings will be necessary. After the yarns are colored they are placed on the warp beam and threaded into the loom. The fabric is then woven with solid-colored filling yarns. The resulting design is soft and somewhat hazy in character.

Stencil Printing

Stencil printing was first developed by the Japanese and was the precursor of modern screen printing. Today it is considered primarily a handcraft process. In stencil printing, design areas are cut from sheets of paper coated with oil, wax, or varnish, or they are cut from thin sheets of metal. A separate stencil is prepared for each color. The stencils are arranged or planned so that all stencils for a single design fit together, or register, so that the resulting pattern is a perfect copy of the original design. A difficulty with screen printing is that the design areas must be connected to prevent parts of the stencil from falling out. To offset this problem, Japanese stencil artists developed a method of tying the various sections of a

28.8 Stencils used in creating a stencil resist design.

design together with silk filament or human hair. Today, when stencils are used, the design is usually rather bold, and lines of the stencil base hold parts together (Fig. 28.8).

In producing stencil prints one can apply the color by hand brushing through the openings in the stencil or by spraying the color onto the fabric with an air brush or spray gun. Stencil printing is used for special designs where the yardage needed is limited or where designs are to be applied directly to textile products—either items of apparel or fabrics for interiors.

Screen Printing

Screen printing is considered by many to be the newest technique for decorating fabrics. Developed from stencil printing, it is essentially a stencil process that has been refined. The screen is made by covering a frame with a fine-mesh fabric of silk, metal, nylon, or polyester filament. The screen fabric is covered with a film; then the design areas are cut out of the film, leaving the fine-mesh fabric open for the dyestuff to pass through the print area. There is a screen for each color to be used. Equipment for screen printing utilizes either a flat-bed unit or a rotary unit. The older screen-printing process uses a flat bed. Fabric is securely attached to a table, a frame holding the screen for a specific color is laid on top of the fabric, and dye is forced through the screen with a squeegee. As soon as one color has been placed on the fabric another screen is placed on top of the location and the second color is forced onto the fabric. This process continues until all colors have been applied. Flat-bed printing is relatively time consuming, but it does permit the making of very large-scale patterns.

Most screen printing today uses rotary screens. The screen is placed on a cylinder, instead of being flat, and dye is fed through the openings from the center of the cylinder (Figs. 28.9 and 28.10). Rotary screens are placed on a printing frame, usually in an order from lightest color to darkest or from the color with the least amount of space to the color with the greatest amount of space. Rotary screen printing limits the size of the design repeat to the diameter of the rolls; however, these rolls are large, and the design often can be up to 24 to 30 inches in length. Flat-bed screen printing is limited in size only by the width of the fabric and the ability of operators to handle large screens.

Screen printing is preferred for the production of large patterns and for fabrics that require considerable dye, such as uncut pile. Screen printing is a versatile process; it is economical when limited yardage is to be produced.

Flat-bed screen printing is limited to the production of small amounts

28.9 Modern frame for rotary screen printing. (Springs Industries)

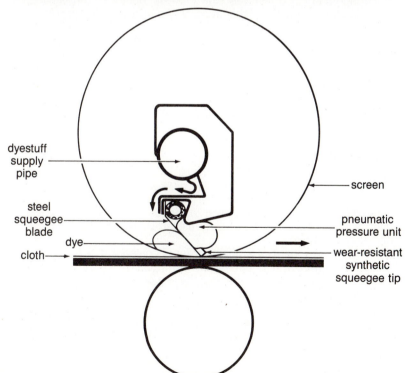

dyestuff supply pipe

steel squeegee blade

dye

cloth

screen

pneumatic pressure unit

wear-resistant synthetic squeegee tip

28.10 Inside schematic of print roll for rotary screen printing. (Stork Screens America, Inc.)

28.11 Screen-printed fabrics.

of yardage and it is a relatively slow process. Rotary screen printing can produce large amounts of fabric quickly and economically. In some companies, rotary screen printing is replacing direct printing, which was long considered the fastest and most economical method of printing fabric.

Screen printing offers many advantages: Designs can be large, small amounts of yardage can be produced economically, color changes are made easily, a variety of dyestuffs can be used successfully, wide fabrics are printed easily, fabric such as knits that might stretch during direct printing can be screen printed with no stretch or distortion, and a wide variety of patterns can be produced (Fig. 28.11).

Discharge Printing

Discharge printing involves the removal of dye from a fabric in such a manner that a pattern is formed. The area where the dye has been removed may be left white, or another color may be placed in the pattern area. Discharge printing is applied to fabrics that have been previously dyed a solid color; it is particularly useful when print fabrics with dark backgrounds are to be made.

To remove the dye, a design roller is coated with a bleach that removes the base dye and leaves the white pattern on a dark background (Fig. 28.12). If the designer wishes to have a color replace the white area, a second roll applies the color to the section that has been discharged or bleached.

Discharge printing may reduce fabric strength if the chemical used to remove the dye is not properly selected, promptly removed following the bleaching action, and thoroughly rinsed away. Sometimes a neutralizing chemical may be applied in the final rinse to prevent any latent effect of the discharge chemical.

28.12 Discharge-printed fabric. (Larsen Textiles/Jack Lenor Larsen incorporated)

28.13 A block used for block printing (left) and printed fabric (right).

Direct Printing

Direct printing has been the most common method of applying surface designs to fabric. Recently, however, the increase in the use of screen printing and the development of transfer printing have reduced the amount of direct roller printing. Nonetheless, direct printing is still one of the most important methods for applying color patterns or designs to fabric. There are two general methods used for direct printing: block and roller.

Block Printing

Actual samples of fabric stamped with blocks to produce block prints have been dated as far back as 1600 B.C. Wall paintings indicating the possible application of pattern by blocks appear to have been made as far back as 2100 B.C. Some of the early blocks were up to 18 inches square and more than 3 inches thick. Blocks used today may be of any manageable size.

In block printing a separate block is required for each color. On the block the design area is raised, whereas the background area, which is not to be printed, is carved away (Fig. 28.13). The procedure for printing is more or less standard. The fabric is laid flat on a smooth, padded surface and anchored securely. Next the dye is applied in a uniform layer to the raised portion of the block. Then the block is pressed onto the fabric so that the dye is transferred to the fabric. Extra pressure is exerted on the block to produce clear prints. Today, block printing is primarily a craft or art form.

Roller Printing

Direct roller printing had its origin in the use of flat plates or blocks on a flat printing press. This was a natural development from block printing. The flat-bed direct printing press was used by Oberkampf to produce his famous printed fabrics. Thomas Bell invented the roller print machine in 1783. His process combined metal engraving with color printing. The major difference between block and roller printing is that in blocks the design area is raised; in roller printing the design area is etched away so it is lower than the surface.

In roller printing the design size or repeat cannot exceed the circumference of the rolls used; and as these rolls are considerably smaller than

28.14 Etching a design into a copper roll for direct roller printing.

the rolls used in screen printing, designs for direct roller printing are generally smaller than those produced in screen printing. The process involves the following steps: After the design has been made and the colors to be used have been selected, the portion of the design for each specific color or dye is identified. The design for a specific color is transferred to a metal roll with an instrument called a pantograph (Fig. 28.14). The roll is coated with an etch-resistant paint; after the design is transferred to the roll the coating is removed from the design area; the roll is then dipped in acid, which etches or burns away the surface layer of the metal where there is no coating. After etching the resist coating is removed and the roll is polished. The engraved rollers, one for each color, are locked into place on the printing machine. Most direct print machines will carry up to sixteen different rolls. The roll rotates in a paste of the dye; a blade removes dye from the smooth surface of the roll, leaving color in the etched areas; the roll rotates on the surface of the fabric, depositing color from the design areas onto the cloth.

Roller printing is fast and economical; it can print large amounts of fabric rapidly and accurately, and designs are clear and well matched. Controls on modern roller printing machines reduce the chance of colors not matching or registering with other colors so the quality of the product is high. There is considerable variety in designs for roller printing machines; however, the size of the repeat is limited by the circumference of the rolls (Fig. 28.15).

Transfer Printing

Transfer printing is a new method of printing fabric; this technique was developed in the late 1960s and early 1970s. The process involves the transfer of color from one surface, usually paper, to a second surface, the textile fabric. There are three basic methods used for transfer printing: vapor phase transfer, wet transfer, and melt transfer. They all operate in somewhat the same manner. A design is printed onto paper or similar surface; it is then transferred to the fabric by one of the methods listed. The system depends on the fact that the dye has a greater attraction for the cloth than it does for the paper; thus it will move from one to the other.

Transfer printing has become an important process, particularly for knit fabrics, because it does not distort the fabric during the printing operation. Further, transfer printing can be used on fabrics of almost any width;

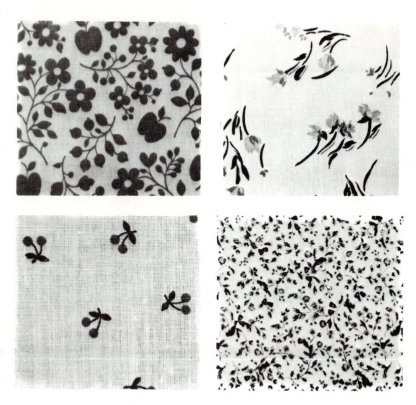

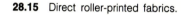

the only limits are the way the transfer paper has been prepared and the width of the transfer printing frame. Transfer printing can be used on small pieces of fabric, such as pillows and shirts, just as easily as it can on yardage.

The advantages of transfer printing include the following: The process is highly efficient and economical; the amount of second-quality goods is reduced or nearly eliminated; a wide variety of patterns can be prepared on the printing paper; unskilled labor can operate the transfer machines (but not regular printing frames); there is less pollution of water and considerable less water and energy required in the operation of the equipment; fabrics can be printed as needed so losses due to unsold yardage are reduced; and there is less space required for the operation, which reduces overhead costs as well as energy and labor costs.

Transfer printing can be used successfully on fabrics made of fibers that can be dyed with disperse dyes, with a new class of dyes that were developed specifically for transfer printing, and with selected reactive dyes. It is highly successful on knit fabrics.

A major advantage is that transfer printing provides for a wide variety of designs. It is possible to transfer large scenic photographs, pictorial prints such as found in tapestries, and other large designs to fabric with little difficulty (Fig. 28.16). One must not forget, however, that the paper for transfer printing must be printed and prepared, and this does require the use of equipment similar to rotary screen or roller printing machines. However, printing paper is less costly than printing fabric, and there are economies associated with the process.

28.16 Transfer-printed fabrics.

Jet Printing

Jet printing is achieved by controlling continuous dye streams. The dye streams are deflected by air or mechanical devices in such a way as to be directed onto or away from the fabric, depending on the pattern desired. Only three of these are discussed, briefly, in this text.

The TAK Method

The TAK method applies two or more colors in a random shower, and rotating wire chain bands break the dye streams into tiny droplets, which fall onto the fabric surface. Variations are further achieved by modifying the consistency of the dye solution. Sharp and distinct or large and diffused color spots can be obtained. The system frequently is used in printing carpeting.

The Polychromatic Process

The polychromatic process produces patterns that may be similar to screen printing designs; they may also resemble some tie-dye patterns. There are two basic techniques involved: the dye-weave method and the flow-form process. In the dye-weave method the dye is forced through jets onto a metal plate at a 45° angle to the fabric. The dye runs down the plate and onto the fabric. The design is influenced by the distance the dye must flow before it hits the fabric. A short distance gives sharp, clean patterns; longer distances produce more indistinct and blurred designs. In the flow-form process the dye is fed onto a roller, which in turn rolls the color onto the fabric. This method tends to give a marbled effect.

The polychromatic printing method is used for fabrics for apparel and home furnishings; however, it is used more often for carpeting and other home-furnishing fabrics than for apparel. The process is good for printing tufted carpeting because it penetrates the pile satisfactorily.

The Millitron Process

The Millitron process is similar to screen printing. The fabric is carried on an inclined plane under a series of jets, one for each color. There are ten jets per inch across the bar. The pattern is controlled by computer systems that generate electronic signals to jets of air blown at right angles to the dye jets. When dye from a jet is to hit the fabric, the air jet is off; when no printing is to occur the air deflects the dye into a trough, where it is carried back to the dye holder. Patterns can be changed rapidly by merely changing the airflow. This process, too, is frequently used for carpeting and other heavy fabrics.

Photographic Printing

Photographic prints are produced in a manner very similar to that used in making photographs. The fabric is treated with a light reactive dye. A negative is placed on the fabric, light is transmitted through it, and the design is developed—just as photographic prints are developed. The print is stabilized, and the fabric is thoroughly washed; this makes the print permanent. Either black and white or colored designs can be produced by this process (Fig. 28.17).

Bubble Printing

Bubble printing is a relatively new process. The dye is dispensed onto the fabric in the form of bubbles—like foam. The majority of designs using bubbles involve geometric shapes similar to hexagons or modified geometric figures. The dye is dispensed in the foam according to the planned pattern, the bubbles are pressed into the fabric, and the dye is set. One or several different colors may be used. As this is still a new process, there is little information available concerning the type of fabrics that will be printed in this manner.

28.17 Photographic print.

EMBROIDERY

The application of yarn, thread, or floss is a very old method of applying design to fabric (Fig. 28.18). Exquisite embroideries were made during the fourteenth, fifteenth, and sixteenth centuries; some of these are treasured

28.18 Fabric with embroidery.

28.19 Embroidery on canvas; fabric for interior accents.

museum pieces. Embroidery is still a popular method of applying design to fabric. It can be done either by machine or by hand; it can be done on very fine and sheer fabrics to heavy fabrics; and yarns used can vary from very fine to relatively heavy wool or man-made fiber yarns. Fabrics can be covered with embroidery so that they closely resemble prints from a distance (Fig. 28.19); or small areas can be embroidered to create isolated designs for apparel or home-furnishing items.

Study Questions

1. Evidence indicates that some type of design was painted onto fabric as early as _____ . What other dates help to identify various events of interest in relation to coloring fabric by applied design?
2. What is resist printing?
3. What methods or techniques are used in resist printing? Describe them.
4. How do stencil and screen printing differ? Which is the more common? Which provides the greatest flexibility of design?
5. Describe the differences between flat-bed and rotary screen printing. Which is the fastest?
6. What is discharge printing? What hazards might exist in this process and in the use and care of discharge printed fabrics?
7. What is direct printing? Describe the different types. How do they compare with each other and with resist methods?
8. Describe transfer printing and indicate the advantages of this method. What possible problems might occur with this method?
9. What is jet printing? Describe at least one of the types discussed.
10. What is bubble printing?
11. What is photographic printing?
12. Why is embroidery discussed in a chapter on applied design? What is involved in adding embroidery to fabrics?

PART VI

Fabric Selection, Use, Care, and Testing

Fibers, yarns, fabrics, finishes, dyes—all are directed toward one important goal: the development of a product that will meet the needs of the consumer for some specified end use. Most consumers select textile fabrics to meet some specified need such as apparel or home furnishings. Fabrics were developed to provide comfort and aesthetic properties; many consumers expect them to be durable and easy to maintain. Some fabrics provide protection from environmental conditions or special situations that might occur. The knowledge needed to determine how a product will perform and what consumers might do to achieve such knowledge are discussed in Chapter 29. Chapter 30 discusses the application of textiles and notes how consumers can evaluate products for possible end uses, citing points to consider in relation to selection, use, and care.

The major purpose of these two chapters is to help consumers use information gathered from observation and the study of textiles to make informed decisions concerning textile products.

Testing Fabric Performance

29

Textile fabrics may be subjected to a wide variety of tests prior to their sale to consumers. These tests provide information to manufacturers that is often used in meeting specifications that have been identified for various end uses; they may provide information for consumers that can be used in determining expected performance of the product in the intended use; they do provide information used by various product manufacturers in developing labels, such as care labels, that are attached to the product.

Many tests for fabric performance cannot be made by consumers; they require testing instruments available only in well-equipped laboratories. There are some things, however, consumers can do in their homes to obtain information concerning use and care of textile products; suggestions for these home tests are included in this text, and standard laboratory tests are discussed. The discussion of fabric performance and testing has been divided into three sections: tests used to determine fiber, yarn, and fabric characteristics; tests used to determine performance of fabric finishes; and tests used to determine colorfastness of dyes. In some instances tests used for finish or color characteristics may provide additional information concerning fiber, yarn, and fabric characteristics.

Standard test methods described have been taken from test manuals published by the American Association of Textile Chemists and Colorists (AATCC) and the American Society for Testing and Materials (ASTM). These organizations publish standard testing procedures on a yearly basis. AATCC calls its publication simply *Technical Manual;* ASTM calls its publication the *Annual Book of ASTM Standards.* Full reference information is cited in the Bibliography, page 352. Many different organizations may test fabrics. The company who markets the products may have testing laboratories (Fig. 29.1), private testing companies may perform various tests, and textile manufacturers themselves frequently have large testing laboratories for quality control.

In addition to testing procedures to determine the level of various characteristics and properties of textile fibers, yarns, and fabrics, ASTM publishes a set of *Performance Standards.* These standards recommend requirements for various textile fabrics in selected end uses.

Tests for Fabric Characteristics

When purchasing fabrics, buyers of large quantities frequently cite a list of specifications to which fabrics must conform. These specifications are determined by various types of testing procedures. Although the consumer would not be able to perform most of these tests, any consumer might be interested in the information obtained from them. This information

311

29.1 above left. Merchandise testing center, a product-evaluation laboratory. (J. C. Penney)
29.2 above right. Testing for abrasion and pilling. (J. C. Penney)

may be provided on tags or labels that accompany the item at the point of sale.

A woven textile fabric is described by the following information: The average width of the fabric is the average distance between selvage edges, the distance across the fabric; the number of yarns per inch, or yarn count, indicates how many yarns have been placed per inch in both the warp and the filling direction; yarn size or yarn number gives the size of the yarns used in making the fabric; the weight of the fabric indicates how much the fabric weighs in ounces per square or linear yard; fiber identification provides the information necessary for labeling the fabric. These data are important to product manufacturers, who are billed for the fabric, because they provide a basis for price comparison and for identification of potential end uses. For example, average fabric width helps determine how patterns for end-use products can be cut efficiently.

The number of yarns per inch and yarn size give some idea of the compactness and density of the fabric. Balanced thread or yarn counts tend to give more uniform wear than unbalanced counts; however, this is influenced by yarn size and type.

Knitted fabrics are tested for fiber content, weight, width, number of wales and courses per inch (instead of yarns per inch), and yarn size. Test procedures differ from those used for woven fabrics, but the information is used in the same general way.

Other fabric constructions may be tested by tests specifically designed for those constructions. In addition, several tests apply to fabric of any structure.

Fabrics are tested for thickness, which provides some help in determining warmth and flexibility of the textile. Air permeability determines the ease or difficulty of air movement through the fabric, which helps determine comfort properties. Thermal transmission tests also provide information on comfort, particularly for fabrics used for insulation and protection.

Abrasion resistance of fabrics indicates how well fabrics resist damage from rubbing. Testing for pilling and snagging determine how well fabrics withstand damage from objects that can catch yarns on the fabric surface or wear fibers and yarns that make up the product (Fig. 29.2).

Fabrics are tested to determine the amount of pull required to break the fabric (Fig. 29.3). Woven fabrics are measured in terms of force required to break a 1-inch-wide strip of fabric; knit fabrics are measured in terms of force required to rupture them. Other constructions may be evaluated by one of these testing methods. Breaking strength provides manufacturers and consumers with information that helps in selection, use, and care by indicating what type of treatment the fabric can withstand. As a part of strength, fabrics may be tested to determine tearing resistance. This test is extremely important for fabrics with durable-press finishes because these finishes tend to reduce tearing strength considerably and to some extent reduce breaking strength.

Evaluation of Properties Enhanced by Finishing

Finishes can modify and alter fabric properties to provide consumers with characteristics and performance they believe to be desirable. Tests to determine the performance, durability, and maintenance of fabrics in relation to the presence, or absence, of finishes have been developed by the organizations mentioned, AATCC and ASTM. However, consumers have the option of performing some simple testing procedures in the home that help identify fabric properties that may be influenced by finishes. It should be noted that the tests described here are not limited to special finishes; they can be used on any fabric to determine how it performs in the property being tested. The following discussion describes a selected group of tests that consumers can perform in their home or laboratory without standard testing equipment. It is important to emphasize that any test that does not use standard testing equipment cannot be used in making comparisons with other fabrics on the market; they can, however, be used to compare fabric samples tested in the same way and at the same time.

These simple "home" tests give limited information about fabric and finish behavior. They may help consumers make decisions concerning care; and if fabric can be tested prior to purchase, they aid in the decision-making process at that point.

Dimensional Stability

To laundering   The possibility of shrinkage or stretch in a fabric is very important to consumers. Even if a maximum percent is stated on the label, consumers may wish to verify this figure. The following two tests may be used to determine how much fabrics will shrink or stretch.

Test 1   This test depends on the availability of a piece of fabric that is at least 12 inches square. For woven fabrics the warp must be clearly identified.

1. Mark a 10-inch square within the sample and clearly indicate warp direction on woven fabrics (Fig. 29.4).
2. Launder the sample with a regular load of laundry, using the procedure typical for the test fabric.
3. Dry and press if necessary. Consumers may wish to launder two samples, one to be air dried and the other to be dried in an automatic dryer. Frequently automatic drying causes considerably more shrinkage than air drying.
4. Measure the marked square to obtain the amount of change. To obtain an average of any change, measure the square at three points in each direction; then obtain an average of the three for each direction.
5. Calculate the percentage of shrinkage or stretch with the following formula:

% stretch or shrinkage = (original measurement − final measurement)/ original measurement) × 100

29.3 above. Testing for strength and elongation of fabrics. (J. C. Penney)
29.4 below. Fabric sample marked for determination of dimensional change, shrinkage, or stretch.

29.5 Small sample to test for shrinkage by comparison with marked outline of original before laundering.

The original measurement should be 10 if the square was accurately marked.

A shrinkage of more than 3 percent is said to cause a full size change in wearing apparel; in home furnishings such as draperies and curtains the product might no longer fit the windows; if it were slipcover fabric it probably would no longer fit the furniture for which it was intended.

Many consumers would not have adequate fabric for such a test. In that case an alternate procedure is given.

Test 2 This test requires a small sample of the fabric; it should be at least 4 to 5 inches, as nearly square as possible.

1. Trim the sample so the cut edges are parallel to the lengthwise and crosswise structural lines of the fabric. Clearly identify the lengthwise dimension, if possible. If the fabric tends to ravel badly, a stitching line can be placed around the edge; however this does tend to alter the results somewhat; however, raveling will alter results even more drastically than the line of stitching.
2. Place the sample on a piece of paper and draw around it so there is a clear record of the original sample (Fig. 29.5).
3. Wash the sample by hand or in a washing machine if confined in a small laundry bag, using recommended detergents and washing temperatures.
4. Make certain the sample is thoroughly rinsed, dry (usually in air), and press if needed.
5. Compare with the original size by placing the sample on top of the drawing. Calculate the amount of change that has occurred.

To dry cleaning Shrinkage in dry cleaning is usually caused by water used to remove water-borne soil and stains prior to the use of cleaning solvent, by agitation in the presence of such water, or by steam pressing. The consumer can obtain some idea of the potential shrinkage of a fabric in cleaning by following these steps:

1. Mark a sample, using directions given in either of the tests for laundering.

2. Wet the sample in water and remove excess moisture.
3. Place the sample in cleaning solvent and agitate frequently by stirring or shaking or rubbing. Continue this action for eight to ten minutes.
4. Remove from the solvent, squeeze out excess fluid, and dry.
5. Measure the cleaned sample, compare with the original, and determine how much shrinkage or stretch has occurred.

When using dry cleaning solvent, it is essential that the consumer note any precautions associated with use of the substance.

In addition to determining the possible stretch or shrinkage that laundering or dry cleaning might cause, these tests can help consumers observe the effect of care on any appearance finishes that have been applied to the fabric. The effect of the care procedures on such finishes as glazing, embossing, moiré, and other appearance finishes can be observed to some degree through these tests.

Durable Press

Samples similar in size to those used for shrinkage can be used to obtain some evidence of the durability of durable-press finishes. The standard test procedures use plastic replicas of different degrees of wrinkling as a basis for determining the durable-press properties (Fig. 29.6). The consumer can obtain some idea of the quality of durable press by comparing samples to other fabrics.

1. Select a sample of the fabric and launder it according to the recommended care procedures.
2. Dry carefully either in air or in an automatic dryer. If the sample is large enough, it should probably be dried in the dryer at durable-press settings. If the dryer does not have such settings, it is better to air dry. However, durable press performs better when tumble dried because the tumbling action tends to remove wrinkles formed during the laundering.
3. Evaluate by visual inspection. If pressing appears to be needed, the quality of durable press may be poor.

Even the standard test for evaluation of durable press is subjective because it involves visual comparisons among fabrics.

29.6 Testing for performance of durable-press finishes. Standards are in lower row; fabric for test are in upper row. (Springs Industries)

29.7 Forty-five degree angle testing for flame resistance; standard test for all fabrics. (Springs Industries)

Water Repellency

With a clothes sprinkler or eyedropper, drop or shake water onto fabric that has been placed on a smooth surface or in an embroidery hoop and held at a 45° angle. If the water forms tiny beads and rolls off the fabric surface without penetrating, the fabric is considered to have some water repellency.

Oil Repellency

Place a drop of salad oil on a scrap of fabric. If the drop of oil forms a bead and can be removed easily with a blotter or a tissue, and if the drop leaves no evidence of staining, the fabric has some resistance to oily stains.

Flame Resistance

There are several different standard tests for flame resistance; the one selected depends on the proposed use of the product. For example, standard testing uses the angle test (Fig. 29.7), whereas children's sleepwear is tested by vertical tests. Both the size of the samples tested, the angle of the specimen, and the length of time for application of the flame differ among the different tests. It is not possible to duplicate standard test procedures for flame resistance; however, consumers can gain some idea of the flammability of fabrics by following these steps:

1. Obtain a small sliver of fabric; this may be from a seam in apparel, draperies, or similar products.
2. Hold the sliver of fabric in tongs, make sure the substance is at a safe distance from your fingers and that the test is carried out in a area free from fire danger. A good spot to do such testing is in a sink, where water is easily obtained.
3. Place a lighted match or candle or some other source of flame at the lower edge of the fabric until it starts to burn. Time this step. If the fabric does not burst into flame within a reasonable length of time, four to five seconds, it can be considered flame resistant; however, if it does flame up, it is important to determine how long that took.
4. When the sliver of fabric starts to burn, remove the source of flame immediately and observe what happens to the fabric sample. If the entire sliver of fabric burns, determine the time it took to move from the point of ignition to the end of the sliver. If the flame extinguishes itself, determine the amount of time needed from ignition to extinction.

When the flame extinguishes itself, the fabric is considered flame resistant. Of equal importance, however, is the time involved. Flame-resistant fabrics are difficult to ignite and tend to self-extinguish. This test cannot be considered a replacement for standard methods, and results cannot be used to make comparisons with published test results. This test does provide some information about fabrics that could reduce danger when they are used where fire poses a possible threat.

It is important to follow extreme caution in conducting a flame test to prevent any possible damage to person or property.

Resistance to Other Environmental Conditions

Many other characteristics of fabrics are altered by finishes. For these there are various standard testing procedures. There are, however, few

29.8 Color difference meter. (Hunter Laboratories)

methods for testing such substances in the home. When laboratories are available, there are tests to determine the resistance of textiles to insect damage such as moths, carpet beetles, and silverfish; to determine resistance to mildew and rot-producing bacteria; and to determine the durability of many finishing substances considered important by consumers.

Evaluation of Colorfastness

The durability of color on fabrics has long been an important factor for consumers. Many consumers believe that color is the most important factor when purchasing textile products. The durability of that color is responsible for much of the satisfaction or dissatisfaction consumers have with textiles. Again there is a wide choice of standard tests for colorfastness. These include tests to determine colorfastness to laundering, bleaching, crocking or rubbing, light, weather, perspiration, salt water, dry cleaning, and pressing. Several different pieces of equipment can be used in testing for colorfastness. One type of machine is designed to measure the actual color change and can be applied to the results of any test (Fig. 29.8). Consumers do have an opportunity to determine a little about colorfastness if they wish to try any of the following tests designed to be performed in the home or in a simple laboratory.

To Laundering

Standard testing for colorfastness to laundering requires special test equipment. The Launder-Ometer is one such instrument (Fig. 29.9). These tests use small samples, about 2 by 4 inches, and well-defined procedures.

Any consumer can test for colorfastness to laundering with a small sample of fabric. If yardage is available the sample should be about 2 by 2 inches; if only tiny scraps can be obtained, a small sliver might be cut from a seam, hem, or other hidden location.

1. Use a pint jar and water at the temperature suggested for the particular fiber content.
2. Put one cup of water and one teaspoon of soap or detergent in the jar.
3. Add the sample
4. Shake the jar frequently to simulate washing action, and allow the fabric to remain in the solution for eight to ten minutes.
5. Observe the color of the washing solution.

29.9 Launder-Ometer. (Atlas Electric Devices Company)

6. Remove the sample and rinse in water at least twice. Use the jar for this rinsing, and determine if any color is lost into the solution during this step.

7. Dry the sample and compare it with the original fabric if possible. If no original fabric is available, determine the general acceptability of the sample. If the sample is large enough and facilities are available, it might be possible to measure the fabric sample with a color difference meter of some type.

To Laundering with Other Fabrics

Some fabrics may lose color and discolor other fabrics with which they are washed. To determine if such behavior would occur, it is necessary to wash a sample of the fabric along with samples of fabrics made of other fibers. Follow the steps outlined for the preceding test, but this time include small samples of white fabrics of other fiber content in the glass jar. These might include samples of cotton, nylon, polyester, and other fabric typical of that which might be laundered with the sample. Observe the white samples after the laundering to see if they have picked up any color. If so, the fabric being tested should not be washed with other fabrics because it could stain them.

To Dry Cleaning

To determine how a fabric will react to dry cleaning solvent, the following procedure should be tried. Cut a small sample of fabric to be tested; if possible obtain a sample about 2 by 4 inches; if this is not possible, use a sliver of fabric.

If a sample of about 2 by 4 inches is available, immerse it in dry cleaning solution in a small jar. Shake frequently. Let it remain in the solution for about ten minutes. Observe the color of the solution, remove the sample, and blot out excess solvent. Compare the color of the sample with the original to determine any color change.

If only a small sliver of fabric is available, sponge the fabric with a cloth moistened with the dry cleaning solvent. See if color bleeds onto the cloth and if the sample appears to change color from the solvent.

Dry cleaning solvents should be used in well-ventilated areas and away from any open flame; vapors should not be inhaled as they may be somewhat toxic.

To Light

Textile products that are exposed to considerable sunlight for many hours each day should have colorfastness to light. This is especially true for home furnishings that will be in the light for long periods of time, such as draperies and curtains. Carpeting may also be exposed to light. Apparel worn in the sunlight, such as sports clothes and items like swimwear, should have superior colorfastness to light. Standard testing for colorfastness to light is done in special instruments called Fade-Ometers or Weather-Ometers (Fig. 29.10). Although testing equipment is not available to most consumers, it is possible to gain some idea of the colorfastness of a textile to light. However, such testing does require considerable time and therefore may well be of little or no value.

1. Obtain a small sample of fabric. Maintain a sample of the original for comparison purposes; the original sample should be stored away from light.

29.10 Fade-Ometer. (Atlas Electric Devices Company)

2. Expose the test sample to light, either outside or through window glass, between 10:00 A.M. and 4:00 P.M., standard time, from May to September.
3. Keep a record of the number of hours of exposure.
4. Compare the sample with the original at frequent intervals.

Fabrics to be used for draperies or curtains should not fade within a minimum period of 120 hours. For other fabrics to be used in the light, the same time period provides a sound basis; however, apparel may be satisfactory if it lasts 80 hours before color change. Fabrics that change color within 20 to 40 hours should not be used where they will be exposed to sunlight; at least consumers should not expect that they will retain their color in such a situation.

29.11 Perspiration tester.

To Perspiration

Fabrics for apparel should be colorfast to perspiration, especially if they are to be worn at times when the body may excrete considerable perspiration. Units to test for this property are relatively simple (Fig. 29.11). When these testers are used, they require the preparation of a chemical solution developed to duplicate, as closely as possible, body perspiration.

When such testing equipment is not available, consumers may get some idea of the colorfastness of a fabric to perspiration from the following procedure. Obtain a small sample of fabric; roll it into a tiny roll; place it in a location on the body where it will be exposed to perspiration, such as under the arms; and leave it until it has become moistened from the perspiration. Let it stand for a few hours, at least until dry, and then compare it to an original piece of the fabric to see if color change has occurred. As perspiration frequently causes color to bleed onto other fabrics, such as white lingerie, the test specimen can be rolled in a white fabric. If color appears on the white fabric, the consumer has some idea of what might happen when the fabric is worn.

To Ironing or Pressing

Although ironing or pressing may produce noticeable color change, the fabric will usually return to its normal color after cooling. However, occasionally, fabrics do change color from heat, either wet or dry. As this change can occur when the consumer is caring for the textile item, it is possible to check for this property. The following procedure will test for either wet or dry heat or both.

1. Select a sample of fabric, perhaps a seam area that will not be visible after testing.
2. Press the area with an iron set at the recommended temperature, with no steam. This step provides information concerning dry heat.
3. Observe any color change.
4. If color does change, let the fabric cool and see if it returns to its original color. Frequently, fabrics that change color when warm will return to their original color as they reach room temperature.
5. To determine if wet heat affects the color, apply a wet press cloth and/or a heavy amount of steam to the fabric. Make the same comparisons as with dry heat.

If the color change is permanent, consumers should contact the store from which the product was purchased or the manufacturer.

29.12 Crockmeter.

To Rubbing or Crocking

Color may be lost by rubbing or abrasion. This type of loss may be called "frosting," as the rubbed edges become lighter. It may occur on durable-press fabrics as a result of action among dyestuffs, finishing agents, environmental factors, and care procedures. Color loss from rubbing or friction may occur when other fabrics do the rubbing. For example, upholstery fabrics could stain apparel fabrics; outerwear apparel fabrics could stain underwear items; cloth belts of contrasting color could stain garments. Standard tests for color loss because of rubbing utilize a crockmeter or similar instrument (Fig. 29.12). For a home test to determine potential color loss from rubbing there is a simple test:

1. Place a small square of white cotton fabric over the forefinger.
2. With even pressure rub the white fabric at least ten times over the colored item.
3. See if the color rubs off onto the white fabric and if there is a color loss in the fabric being tested.
4. Repeat the process with a white piece of fabric that has been moistened thoroughly.

Performance Standards

A group of established standards or specifications for various textile items may be used as voluntary guidelines or standards for fabrics. These specifications define performance levels of textile products in specific types of end-use products. Although these standards are not required by any legislation, many retailers and purchasing agencies follow them when ordering merchandise in large quantities. These performance standards concern such characteristics as fabric strength; dimensional stability; tearing strength; colorfastness to laundering and dry cleaning, crocking, perspiration, and light; flammability; and durable-press performance where applicable.

The performance standards may be used as part of a sales contract, in advertising, and in the development of labels—including care labels—for the product. A few of the items for which specifications have been developed include men's and boys' woven dress shirt fabrics, bedspread fabrics, career apparel fabrics, coat fabrics, drapery and curtain fabrics, swimwear fabrics, and upholstery fabrics.

Regardless of the information provided at the point of sale of any textile product, consumers should have a body of knowledge that they may use in making decisions concerning the selection, use, and care of these products. A basic knowledge of fibers, yarns, fabrics, finishes, and coloring agents can be of value when selecting textile products. Information concerning performance, which can be gained from labels or simple tests, can increase the possibility of long-term satisfaction with the textile product. Consumers must remember that the only label information that must accompany a textile product includes its fiber content and care requirements. This information may be adequate for some products but quite inadequate for others. Being able to supplement required label information with knowledge about textiles will help consumers select products that will give expected durability and performance.

1. Cite several reasons that standard test procedures cannot be carried out by consumers in their own homes.
2. Describe simple home tests for identifying possible fabric shrinkage or stretch during laundering or dry cleaning.
3. What properties can consumers test at home sufficiently to have a general idea about performance during use and care?
4. What is a major caution concerning home tests?
5. Describe testing procedures consumers might use to test for colorfastness to
   a. Laundering
   b. Dry cleaning
   c. Sunlight
   d. Dry heat
   e. Wet heat
   f. Rubbing or abrasion
6. What should a consumer do if a product fails to perform satisfactorily during use and care?
7. What are performance standards? Who uses them?
8. What type of label information is required on textile items? What type of information would you like to have included on labels?

30

Fabric Performance: Selection, Use, and Care

Fibers, yarns, fabrics, finishes, and dyes all contribute to the final textile product. Each has a part in determining what the product will look like, how it will perform, how it will be maintained, and how durable it will be. Textile products are designed for a wide variety of end uses. They are selected by consideration of many factors, including appearance of the product, how it will be maintained or cared for, what its expected and needed useful life will be, and what level of durability is needed or desired. Furthermore, each of these factors has different priorities depending on what the textile product is to do; and each of these factors is interrelated, which adds complications to the decision-making process.

This chapter will establish some guidelines concerning the application of textiles and how textile information may be used in choosing textile products for a group of selected end-use applications; also it will provide some specific details concerning care or maintenance of textile products. This chapter, therefore, is divided into two major sections: One is directed toward fabric performance and selection of textiles for different end uses; the other will discuss various products used in care and some specifics concerning care procedures.

FABRIC APPLICATION

Fiber content, fiber arrangement and/or yarn structure, fabric structure, finishes, and color comprise the basic component parts of a textile; these all need consideration in determining which fabric or fabrics to purchase for a specific end use. Emphasis is placed, here, on information related to decision making at the consumer level.

The consumer must identify the priorities and objectives in the selection of a textile product for a proposed end use. Some decisions might have relatively clear-cut objectives; for example, when selecting drapery fabrics the major concerns might be appearance, resistance to damage from light, flame resistance, insulative properties, and potential durability; an evening gown will probably be selected because of appearance, with little or no concern for durability or care; children's play clothes might well be selected for strength and durability, and then appearance and comfort. In other words choices are based on how the consumer sees the order of the various factors involved in making the decision. Furthermore, any decision concerning textile products is laden with individual judgments. Each individual consumer will have a different set of priorities for different textile products. Nonetheless, it is hoped that the following discussion will help establish some guidelines related to the application and selection of textile products. This first part of the discussion will summarize factors that relate to appearance, durability, and comfort of textile items, followed by a set of examples of decision making for a group of end uses. The second part of this chapter will discuss care or maintenance of textiles.

Fabric Appearance

The appearance of a fabric refers to both the visual effect it has on the consumer and to the effect of touch. The latter enhances comprehension of what is seen. All end-use components have some influence on the appearance of fabrics. The luster of the fiber is responsible for the amount of sheen, gloss, or dullness that comes from the fiber itself; fiber length and cross-sectional shape influence appearance, particularly in relation to light reflection and soiling. The method used in making yarns is extremely important in appearance as simple yarns contribute to smooth, flat fabrics; complex yarns add texture and surface interest. Fabric structure is extremely important to appearance; knitted fabrics have a different appearance than woven fabrics, braids are different from knitted or woven, and nonwoven fabrics are nothing like fabrics made from yarns. Finishes may influence appearance directly by altering the fabric surface, or they may influence the retention of appearance by altering behavior in use and care. Color is an obvious factor in appearance; it provides the variability in design that determines how a product will look in various situations. All these factors are interrelated, and the final appearance of a textile depends on each component part and how those parts are combined.

Fabrics may be rough or smooth, light or dark, delicate or coarse, lustrous or dull, bulky or sheer, soft or stiff—or any point in between. The importance of appearance and of any of the various factors that influence appearance is based on the individual judgment of the consumer.

Fabric Durability

Durability is defined as the ability to last or endure. Consumers, in general, do not wish to have fabrics last a lifetime. Thus, for purposes of this discussion, fabric durability is considered to be the ability of a fabric or textile product to retain properties and characteristics for a reasonable period of time or for the time desired by the consumer.

Properties of fibers, yarns, and fabrics that influence durability include fiber strength; yarn strength; fabric strength; resistance to abrasion by fiber, yarns, and fabric; resistance to pilling of fibers, yarns, and fabrics; resistance to snagging of yarns and fabrics; and resistance to care products and procedures. Each of these is discussed in the following paragraphs—except for care, which is discussed in the special section on maintenance.

Fiber Content

Fiber content influences durability. The strength of fibers, as well as their other properties, will determine how long fibers will resist use and care; strong fibers tend to provide longer life for a product than the weaker fibers; the chemical behavior of fibers will influence the use of various cleaning agents and will affect the choice of finishing and coloring materials.

Some fibers, such as acetate, are valued for their beauty of hand and drape and not for their strength; nylon is often selected for strength and abrasion resistance; polyester is frequently chosen for its easy care;

cotton is prized for its comfort. All these factors contribute to the consumer's interest in durability because products must provide their special characteristics for the life of the product if they are to be considered durable.

Strong fibers influence durability and appearance in an obvious way. Fibers tend to form pills on the surface of a fabric as a result of rubbing or abrasion; strong fibers retain these pills on the surface, creating an unattractive product that may no longer be considered durable; weaker fibers will break off as pills are formed, retaining the fabric appearance and giving the consumer the idea that the product is wearing well and is durable. It must be said, however, that such durability may be false as the fabric may indeed give less life in its planned use if pills fall off than if pills are retained; however, the consumer tends to discard the product because of the pills, an interaction of appearance and durability factors.

Yarn Structure

Yarn structure determines durability to a noticeable degree. For example, complex yarns with loops and similar surfaces are easily snagged, producing damage, altering appearance, and reducing fabric usefulness. Simple ply yarns with medium twist will give good durability. Single yarns with medium or high twist are less likely to show wear than those with slubs or irregular areas of very low twist. The latter may pull apart easily, resulting in fabric breakdown.

Both yarns and fabric structure are important considerations in abrasion damage; yarns may show wear and break because of rubbing. This can occur at folded areas, called edge abrasion; on the fabric surface, called face abrasion; or as a result of continued bending or flexing, called flex abrasion. The interaction between factors affecting durability and those affecting appearance is important because a product that no longer provides the desired appearance will seldom be considered to have continued durability.

Fabric Structure

Fabric structure is an important factor in durability. Plain and twill weave fabrics are usually more durable than satin weaves; the floating yarns in satins are subject to damage from snagging, breaking, and abrasion. Decorative weaves that include long floats are easily damaged by rough or sharp objects, which may snag and break the floating yarns. Decorative weaves with short floats, high thread or yarn counts, and strong yarns and fibers may be more durable than loose plain weave fabrics. Compact weaves using smooth simple yarns are, typically, more durable than any fabric of complex yarns and loose construction.

Filling- or weft-knit fabrics of plain design are subject to the formation of runs when the yarns are broken. The runs spread rapidly when the fibers are of a filament type and smooth. Nylon yarns in women's hosiery are an example of smooth yarns that run quickly when broken, particularly when the fabric is a plain weft knit. Complex knit structures resist runs; knits made from yarns that are rough, such as wool or textured man-made fibers, tend to adhere to each other, and the formation of runs is reduced. Mesh constructions are not as subject to the development of runs; however, if a yarn is broken, the fabric tends to spread at that point and form unattractive holes. Warp-knit fabrics and double-knit fabrics are comparatively run resistant. Most knit fabrics have sufficient fabric give or stretch to resist damage from continued bending, stretching or elongation, or crushing.

Felt fabrics usually have good durability unless they are subjected to considerable pulling force or abrasion. Heavier felts give longer service than lightweight felts. Felts tend to have great strength in the direction the fibers lay but less strength in the direction perpendicular to the length of the fibers. Nonwoven fabrics may be made for one-time or limited use, where durability is of no concern; they may be constructed to be durable in selected end uses. Nonwoven interfacings should be able to withstand various methods of maintenance in order to last as long as the outer fabrics.

Decorative fabrics such as lace are not usually purchased with durability in mind. Although laces tend to be fragile, they may last for many years if made of strong fibers. Nylon lace, for example, is usually relatively durable.

The durability of fabrics such as brocades and other Jacquard-weave constructions will depend on several factors: the type of fibers, the type of yarn construction (simple or complex), and the closeness of the weave. Many Jacquard-weave fabrics will provide outstanding durability; however, consumers should consider the proposed end use, the strength of the fibers involved, the amount of yarn surface that can be snagged or pilled, and the possibilities of abrasion damage to the fabric surface or folds in the product.

In general, basic weave constructions and plain knits are considered more durable than complicated fabric constructions. The latter may show signs of wear as a result of surface distortion, abrasion, or other types of damage. Fabrics with medium to high yarn count are usually more durable than fabrics with a low yarn count; however, this factor is influenced by the type of yarn structure and the type of fiber involved.

It should be evident that the properties of a fabric are determined by complicated interrelationships; therefore, it is not easy for consumers to predict ultimate durability. However, an understanding of the various interrelationships may help consumers understand performance and resulting durability or lack thereof.

Finishes

Finishes, whether applied for appearance or to alter performance properties, often affect fabric durability. Surface finishes such as glazing can be removed by improper care; performance finishes are gradually removed over time as a result of both wear and care. Finishes may reduce durability while they provide the consumer with a desired characteristic.

Durable-press and other minimum-care finishes reduce fabric tear strength and abrasion resistance—both important factors in fabric performance and durability. An abrasion damage, called *frosting,* is evident at edges of textile items where color tends to abrade away or to change in hue. This type of abrasion is more prevalent in durable-press finished fabrics than in other types. Many consumers, however, are willing to accept reduced durability in exchange for easy care properties.

Color

The selection of and application of dyestuffs influence durability of color. Choosing the proper dye for each fiber type is essential if the fabric color is to give good service in use and care. The consumer should be aware of scientific, economic, and fashion effects on color and design. It is impossible to find all colors in all types of dyes, and this may mean selection of an inferior dye to obtain a current fashion color. Moreover, not all dyes within any one type are equally colorfast; it is difficult to find dyes in all colors that prove resistant to all degrading environmental conditions.

Dyestuffs differ in cost and in the expense involved in application; thus, it is necessary to select the dye that will be on a level with a reasonable competitive price. Dye selection should be based on the planned end uses of the fabric, which may necessitate a compromise. Fabrics intended for apparel may not be sunfast, but fabrics intended for draperies should be sun- or lightfast.

Color loss during maintenance of any textile item results in consumer dissatisfaction and premature discarding of the product. Thus, the durability of color is of considerable importance to the selection and use of textile fabrics. The level of importance is best judged by the individual consumer in relation to the proposed end use for the textile.

Fabric Comfort

The importance of fabric comfort will vary according to the predetermined end use of the textile product and the personal preference of the consumer. Factors that influence comfort include texture and tactile characteristics, heat retention, moisture absorbency, fabric weight, wicking properties of fibers and fabric structures, air permeability of the fabric, and the degree of softness or stiffness. Although these characteristics can be measured accurately by standard test procedures, the actual relationship between the properties and human comfort has not been clearly established. Recently, considerable research has been designed and undertaken concerning fabric comfort, but ultimately, comfort remains a very personal factor.

Comfort is both a physical and a psychological characteristic. For example, color loss would hardly influence physical comfort, but it might create a psychological atmosphere leading to an illusion of physical discomfort. The end result can be very real and should not be dismissed as irrelevant. Both sensual and mental comfort should be assessed in considering textile products for various end uses; and it must be recognized that this is a matter of individual preferences and individual differences.

Specific characteristics that play an important role in fabric comfort for apparel and to some degree for interior fabrics include air permeability and moisture absorbency. Fabrics that carry air through the fabric will be more comfortable for apparel in warm weather than in cold weather; fabrics that carry moisture away from the body, either by wicking or absorbency, will tend to be more comfortable in warm weather than in cold. Fabrics with good air permeability will be good for curtains at windows where air is to circulate in or out; fabrics with poor air permeability will tend to retain air in a room or prevent air from moving into the room, and thus can either help heat or cool the area. Fabrics with rough surfaces may be undesirable for upholstery because of the possible irritation that can occur, which would reduce comfort considerably. Carpeting with short uncut pile that is packed tightly together might give good service, but if children are to play on the floor, it might prove to be uncomfortable. Here is where individual differences and preferences become important in establishing priorities for particular end uses.

Textile Selection for Various Applications

It is impossible in a book this size to describe all possible end uses for textile fabrics and to identify factors that might be used in the selection of a textile product. The following discussion considers a small group of possible applications for textile products and notes factors that play an important role in the decision-making process.

Apparel

As there are many different items of apparel for men, women, and children, and as it would be impossible to discuss every possible item, what follows is necessarily limited. The factors discussed, however, can be applied when considering textile products for any item of apparel; the importance of each factor rests on the individual's preferences and needs.

Men's woven fabric shirts Several types of fabrics are available for men's shirts, for example, all-cotton broadcloth or oxford cloth with a durable-press finish, blends of cotton and polyester with a durable-press finish in which the proportion of polyester varies from 20 to 80 percent, and fabrics with color or patterns or those that are white. If comfort is the most important property, the consumer would probably select the all-cotton fabric with a durable-press finish; if easy care is the most important, the consumer would probably select a fabric with at least 65 percent polyester; if a balance between comfort and easy care is important, a blend of 50 percent polyester and 50 percent cotton would probably be acceptable. Care label tags should indicate recommended care procedures, and for colored shirts, information on colorfastness would be desirable.

Men's dress suiting fabrics A wide choice of fabric is available for men's dress suits. However, points to consider include comfort, appearance during wear, required care, and durability. A fabric of worsted wool would retain appearance, would dry clean well, would be warm, and would have good durability. A fabric of worsted and polyester blend would retain appearance, would be somewhat easier to clean and maintain than all wool, would be cooler and more adaptable to a variety of climates, and would provide good durability. Fabrics of woolen yarns instead of worsted would have a casual appearance rather than a dress appearance and might have somewhat wider use, but these fabrics do not hold a press as well as worsted. Fabrics of wool with a small amount of nylon would perform quite well, hold their appearance well, and be easy to clean; however, they would be considerably warmer than the wool and polyester blend.

Women's dress fabrics So many different fabrics are available for women's dresses that it is impossible to name just a few. They could be considered, however, on the basis of some of these points: Blends of polyester and cotton would tend to be comfortable and would retain a good appearance; fabrics of 100 percent polyester would retain an excellent appearance but might not be as comfortable as the blend. Cotton fabrics could be attractive and comfortable but more difficult to maintain. Rayon and/or acetate fabrics can be used to provide a variety of appealing appearances and will drape well; care is more difficult. Wool fabrics would provide warmth and good appearance but require careful maintenance. Silk is attractive and relatively comfortable, but it demands care in maintenance and can be expensive.

Swimwear Swimwear should be selected according to some of the following factors. If spandex is present, it will tend to hold its shape, but it may fade in chlorine water in swimming pools. If textured yarns are used to provide the holding power, the fabric can eventually stretch out of shape. If the suit is made of nylon or polyester, with a small percentage of spandex, it will be easy to clean and it will dry quickly—either after cleaning or after exposure to swimming—and it will hold its shape well during wear.

Children's sleepwear   Children's sleepwear must meet special federal regulations concerning the flammability of the fabrics used; thus, determining the presence of such finishes and/or fabric behavior is important. Then consideration for the type of care that must be given the item is important, particularly if the consumer lives in an area where phosphate detergents cannot be purchased and the recommended care states that only such detergents should be used. Comfort of the fabric is important and feeling to determine if the item is harsh and rough should be routine.

General apparel concerns   The factors that should be considered in the purchase of apparel items or fabrics for apparel are many and varied. Few consumers will have the same priorities for the same type of item, although they will consider many of the same factors. Factors, therefore, that are usually involved in the purchase of apparel textiles include the following, which have been listed with no concern for which is most and which is least important:

Consider the importance of appearance, particularly color and design, and the expected durability of that appearance.

Consider the importance of comfort and the type of environmental conditions in which the item will be worn; this will involve determining such information as the need for warmth or coolness, light weight versus heavy weight, moisture repellency or absorbency, flexibility versus stiffness.

Consider the situation for which it will be worn and arrive at some order of importance for comfort, appearance, maintenance, and durability.

Many other factors are involved when selecting textiles for apparel items, and each consumer should develop his or her own list of factors and criteria.

Home-Furnishing Fabrics

As with apparel there are many different uses for fabrics in interiors and home furnishings. These include fabrics for window coverings, bedding, towels, upholstery, carpets, wall coverings and wall upholstery, and decorative accents. Factors that could be used in selecting a few of these items are discussed.

Carpeting   When selecting carpeting, the consumer should consider the type of wear it will receive, the appearance, the desired durability, and the maintenance involved. For example, wool fiber would tend to give a look of luxury and elegance, warmth, and good durability, but care might be complex because the fiber is difficult to spot clean. Nylon wears well, can be made into a wide variety of designs and styles, and provides relatively easy care; but the surface may have a sheen that is unattractive to some consumers and in some types of decoration. Polyester gives good wear, can be made into a variety of designs and styles, is an easy care floor covering, and does not have the same type of sheen that nylon tends to have. Olefin provides good wear, is easy to clean, is available in a variety of designs and styles, but frequently does not have as wide a style range as either nylon or polyester.

The type of yarns used in carpeting affects use and care. Yarns for the pile of carpeting should be fairly soft but highly resilient so they will recover quickly from crushing; yarns for backing should be strong and firm. A nonwoven base may be used successfully for tufted carpeting rather than a woven base. The fabric added to the carpet to form the backing should be made with yarns that tend to prevent slipping and reduce stretching of the carpeting so that it will hold both its shape and its place. Fibers that work well for carpet pile include wool, nylon, polyester, and olefin. Fibers that work well for carpet base include olefin, nylon, and polyester. Fibers for backing fabrics that provide good service include jute and olefin.

Fabric structures for carpeting include pile weaving, tufting, and needle punching. Woven carpeting is limited in use because of cost; when available, woven carpets are long wearing and have considerable design flexibility. Tufted carpets are the most common, and these may be made with cut pile, uncut pile, or combinations of the two. Uncut pile may hold soil in the loops and be more difficult to clean; however, for low-pile carpeting it will usually give superior wear; cut pile may wear more rapidly than uncut pile because the fiber ends can be abraded and worn by walking as well as by furniture placement. Pile-tufted carpeting can be obtained in a wide variety of designs and color combinations as well as in a wide variety of pile heights and densities. Needle-punched carpeting is usually less decorative, but it will give good wear in many situations. It is not typically used for interiors except in kitchens, garages, and other utility locations.

Finishes on carpeting involve flame-resistant materials, moth proofing for wool carpeting, antistatic materials, and spot- and stain-resistant materials. Carpeting must meet specified flame resistance, which can be achieved either by selection of flame-resistant fibers or by the addition of finishes. Wool carpeting is typically finished with a substance to prevent moth and insect damage. Most carpeting in use today has been given some type of finish to reduce staining and to make it easy to remove soil and stains. Another finish that may be applied to carpeting is bacteriostatic substances; these are used to reduce the spread of infection, reduce damage from mildew and rot-producing bacteria, and eliminate odors that might develop from microorganisms.

Color and applied design on carpeting are available in a wide range. Information on colorfastness of carpeting may be difficult to obtain, and even more difficult to ascertain from looking at the product. However, when possible, carpeting should be colorfast to light, to abrasion, and to care procedures.

To date, there is little carpeting on the market that utilizes blends of different types of fibers for the pile. Most carpeting is limited to one fiber in the pile; however, carpeting as a unit often involves several different types of fibers: one or more for the base, one for the pile, and one or more for the backing.

Upholstery Upholstery fabrics are available in a wide variety of fiber types and in various blends of fibers. Some of the fibers and fiber combinations used for upholstery are wool; nylon; cotton; acrylic; linen; olefin; and blends of rayon and cotton, polyester and cotton, nylon and wool, and linen and polyester or rayon. Some upholstery fabric actually contains three or more fibers.

Factors to consider for upholstery include which fiber or blend of fibers, yarn structures, and fabric structures will give the appearance needed for the particular interior design plan; which product will give the type of wear desired; and which product will be the best in terms of planned maintenance procedures. If long-term wear is important, upholstery of nylon, olefin, or polyester should probably be selected; if a luxurious appearance is most important, upholstery of wool, acrylic, polyester, silk, linen, or blends including these fibers could be a satisfactory choice.

In relation to yarn structure, complex or fancy yarns tend to show signs of wear from abrasion damage, whereas simple yarns resist this type of damage. Fabric structures that involve complex weaves such as highly patterned Jacquards and satins with long yarn floats will show wear more quickly than plain or twill weave fabrics. Stain-resistant finishes will tend to prevent staining from liquid stains if removed quickly; but if dry soil gets rubbed into the surface of the fabric, it is more difficult to remove from stain-resistant fabrics than from the same fabric without such a finish. Upholstery fabric may have backing material added to give stability and reduce stretch when applied to the furniture. These backings may be laminated or bonded to the surface or face fabric; concern for the behavior of bonded fabrics is required when this occurs (see p. 244). Finishes on upholstery fabric include spot and stain resistance, moth and insect resistance, flame resistance, and antistatic properties.

Draperies and window coverings   Fabrics for draperies and window coverings are chosen to complete the interior design, to provide some privacy, and, in some cases, to provide some insulation. Many fibers are used in draperies and curtains; however, factors that need consideration here include the following: Fibers should be selected that have good resistance to light, have good flexibility, and are not affected by moisture. Nylon is not recommended for window coverings because of its low resistance to sunlight; polyester, cotton, linen, rayon, and acetate provide good durability for window coverings; polyester is particularly good for sheer curtains. Draperies may be coated or backed with plastic or metallic coatings to increase the insulative value and resistance to soil and sunlight. Coatings, however, may increase the difficulty involved in maintenance.

Drapery and curtain fabrics need to be flexible so they will hang and drape well at windows; thus fibers, yarns, and fabric structures must be selected that do not result in stiff products. Further, fabrics designed to resist abrasion are desirable to reduce damage when drapes are pulled across or rub against other surfaces. Rayon may present some problems in draperies or curtains because of its characteristic of stretching when humidity is high and shrinking when humidity is low; this factor is controlled to some degree when rayon is blended with other fibers.

Numerous blends of fibers are available for window coverings. These include rayon and acetate; cotton, rayon, and polyester; rayon, acetate, and linen; rayon, acetate, and saran; and many other combinations.

Bedding   Bedding includes a variety of end-use items: sheets, pillow cases, mattress pads, bedspreads, and blankets. Each of these has some specific properties that consumers might want. A few considerations include the following.

Sheets and pillow cases are selected for appearance, comfort, and easy care. The most common fabric is a balanced plain weave structure—either muslin or percale—with a smooth surface and made of a blend of polyester and cotton fibers. These tend to give good wear, require little or no ironing and launder easily, can be found in a wide variety of colors and designs, and feel comfortable. Silk sheets are available for luxury use; they have a smooth surface and consequently a smooth feel; they frequently require professional care; and they are generally expensive. Linen sheets are long wearing, attractive, and expensive; they may not be as comfortable as cotton or silk. Nylon sheets have a feel somewhat like silk but tend to be slippery; they wear well and are easy care items.

Bedspreads may be found in a wide variety of fabric structures, fiber contents, finishes, and colors. As they tend to be selected primarily for their decorative appearance, consumers often base their choice on appearance. Thought might be given, however, to the size of the bedspread that is needed and its weight, to possible methods of care (Can it be laundered in home equipment or must it be sent to professional cleaners because of its size or its fiber content or fabric structure?), and to its use (Is it strictly decorative or must it provide warmth as a part of the bed coverings?).

This is just a brief look at the application for fabrics in various end uses. Regardless of what the end use might be, consumers should give thought to their needs and the factors of importance relative to the particular product. They should think about comfort, durability, appearance, and care and then determine which fiber or fibers will be good for the specific product; which type of yarn structure will meet the criteria; which fabric structure will be best for the purpose; what finishes are needed; and what type of color and design is desirable and how colorfast, and to what, are the dyes.

FABRIC MAINTENANCE

The care or maintenance of any textile product depends on the fiber or fibers, yarn structures or fiber arrangements, fabric structures, finishes, and methods of imparting color and types of dyestuffs. Each fiber chapter has included a brief summary of the care recommended for the specific fibers; discussions of other components of the final textile have also included some comments on care. It is the purpose of this section to identify typical products and processes used in the care of textile products. The consumer and reader are reminded that federal legislation requires care labels to be securely attached to most apparel items; however, as yet, such labeling is not required on home-furnishing products, although some manufacturers do include care information as a help to the consumer. When care labels are available, they should be used as the guide to maintenance procedures for the labeled product.

Fabrics may be cleaned by laundering or dry cleaning. Both of these can be done in the home, although dry cleaning is best done by professionals. Soil found on textile products is made up of various materials. Some of the materials are soluble in water; some are not; some may be soluble in cleaning solvents. Typical products found in soil on fabrics include mineral matter; starches; dust; and accidental soil such as blood, food stains, and the like. Water and some type of detergent are successful in removing most of the soil from fabrics; some soil may require treatment with other materials, such as special stain removers. As laundering is the typical method for cleaning fabrics in the home, that process is discussed in some detail.

The Laundering Process

Laundering means wetting fabric in water with additives included, agitating the solution and fabric, and rinsing away the materials used. The trick in laundering is to use additives that help lift the soil off the fabric, retain that soil in the water solution until it can be rinsed away, and prevent any soil from redepositing on the fabric during the operation. Laundering uses a variety of products—soap or detergents, water softeners and conditioners, bleaches, fabric softeners, optical brighteners, wetting agents, and disinfectants.

Soaps and Synthetic Detergents

Soaps and detergents are the major products in laundering. These substances establish an environment that releases or dissolves the soil and pulls it into suspension in the wash water. Soaps are natural cleaning agents made from fatty acids and an alkali of some type; synthetic detergents are those made from petroleum and natural fats and oil; both soaps and synthetic detergents are correctly identified as detergents.

Soaps work well on many fabrics providing they are used in soft water. In hard water soaps form a curd with the mineral in the water, which becomes a deposit that may attach itself to the fabric and result in products that look gray and discolored. In soft water the curd is not formed, and soap can be a good cleaning agent. Synthetic detergents are made to work well in hard or soft water and do not form a curd. Many synthetic detergents are built, which means they have added materials to make them clean better on heavily soiled fabric.

Synthetic detergents are made by combining some or all of the following:

Surfactants are a part of all synthetic detergents; these are the substances that are responsible for removing the soil. The surfactant breaks up water droplets into small units, which penetrate into the fabric more easily; then the surfactant surrounds the soil and carries it away from the textile. This is a highly simplified description of the action of these materials.

Builders may be added to detergents to create a product with greater cleaning power. The amount of builder is directly related to the ability of the product to clean; the stronger the builder, the stronger the cleaning power. Builders include such products as phosphates, citrates, carbonates, sulfates, and silicates. The best builder is a phosphate; however, the use of phosphates is controlled in most states in the United States. Some areas have banned phosphates completely, so consumers in those areas must depend on other builders. Most areas that permit phosphates have reduced the amount allowed. This does pose problems in some care situations; however, the phosphate was found to cause water pollution, and limits on its use appear to be necessary.

Silicates may be added to the detergent as a protection against corrosion of the parts of the washer exposed to the water and detergents.

Antiredeposition agents, such as carboxymethyl cellulose (CMC), are added to detergents to help prevent soil from reattaching itself to fabric after it has been removed.

Fluorescent whiteners or optical brighteners are added to increase the ultraviolet light reflection and create an appearance that seems to be whiter and brighter than it would be without these additives.

Perfumes are added to give an appealing scent to the detergent and to leave the clean clothes with a pleasant odor.

Color may be added to help identify various products as being from specific manufacturers. In most cases this color is no problem; however, color may be a hazard when cleaning nylon because nylon is a scavenger and may pick up the color during the laundry operation.

Fabric softeners may be added to the detergent; it is more common, however, to use these additives separately.

Bleaches

Bleaches are of two major types, oxidizing and reduction. The most common types used in the home are of the oxidizing variety and include chlorine bleaches, perborate bleaches, and hydrogen peroxide. Chlorine and perborate comprise the vast majority of bleaching agents used by consumers. Chlorine bleaches are the strongest and must be used with caution. It is not an all-purpose bleach and cannot be used on every fiber type. A review of the different fibers will indicate which ones can be bleached with chlorine and which ones cannot. Chlorine bleach may react negatively with some finishing agents, which negates its use with such products; also, chlorine bleach may remove color. It is best to use chlorine only when there is considerable discoloration of the fabric and then only on fibers known to be unaffected by this type of bleach. Typical mistakes that consumers may make when using bleach and that may cause serious damage to fabrics include the following:

1. Pouring the bleach, undiluted, directly onto the fabrics to be bleached. Bleach should be diluted and added to the water in such a way that fabric does not come in contact with the concentrated liquid.
2. Using too much bleach for the amount of liquid in the washer. Care labels and information on bleach containers should be checked to make certain the amount added is appropriate for the size of the washer, the amount of fabric in the load, the type or types of fibers, the type of finishes, and the dyes.
3. Using too much bleach for the item. Consumers should make certain a product that needs heavy bleaching can withstand the bleach; application should be limited, even to heavily soiled textiles, to about ten minutes; heat should not be used when soaking textiles in bleach.
4. Using bleach on items that cannot be bleached safely. Labels should be read carefully on both the textile product and the bleach container.

Perborate bleaches can be applied to most products without damage. They are not as strong as chlorine bleaches but they do help maintain clean and bright products. If used on colored fabrics, it is important to dilute the bleach before it is added to the laundry bath.

Any bleach should be thoroughly rinsed away from the fabrics before they are dried. Any residue of bleach remaining in the fabric can cause deterioration and result in breaks in the fabric.

Disinfectants

Bleaches are a type of disinfectant and help to destroy bacteria on fabric as well as prevent its growth. Other disinfectants may be used in laundering when bleaches are not appropriate and when there is a need to make certain that products are free of bacteria and other microoogranisms. Other disinfectants sometimes used in fabric care include pine oils and phenolic compounds such as Lysol.

Fabric Softeners

Fabric softeners may be a part of the detergent; they may be added separately to the wash or to the rinse water; they may be added while the fabrics are being dried. The purpose of fabric softeners is to make fabrics feel softer; in addition they reduce the development of static electricity. These substances are important when laundering durable-press fabrics because they help to keep the fabric soft and pliable, keep it from wrinkling, and reduce the potential for static charges. They are helpful when laundering pile fabrics as they help fluff the pile and improve the appearance. Any fabric that may stiffen during laundering probably can profit from a fabric softener; however, there are a few situations in which they should not be used: They counteract the effect of flame retardants and increase the flammability of textiles that have been treated for flame resistance; they reduce absorbency of fabric, and thus when used on towels, reduce their effectiveness.

Laundering Guidelines

The laundering process involves washing, rinsing, and drying. It is extremely important that all textile products be thoroughly rinsed following the washing. Temperatures of washing and rinsing solutions should not exceed those recommended for the particular fibers involved. Drying involves removal of moisture from the fabric. Items can be air dried or dryer dried. Label information should be followed in relation to laundering procedures. Some fibers cannot be washed or dried at high temperatures; some require gentle handling; some must be laundered alone. The following guidelines should be helpful in ensuring that the laundry operation will be successful.

1. Sort fabrics before laundering and do like fabrics together; keep light colors together and dark colors together; keep fabrics that require special handling together; keep durable-press items together when possible; keep fabrics that might shed lint separate from other fabrics.
2. Pretreat any stained areas prior to laundering.
3. Check all items of clothing to make sure there are no tissues, coins, or other objects left in pockets. Tissues may be particularly bad as they can leave a vast amount of lint on the fabrics.
4. Use the proper amount of detergent, bleach, and any other laundry additive considered necessary for the particular load.
5. Make certain all items in a load can be bleached before using bleach, especially chlorine bleach.
6. Wash each load according to the best temperature settings and agitation levels for the particular type of product in that load.
7. Make certain the load is thoroughly rinsed.
8. Dry according to the recommended temperatures and special controls.
9. Make certain that the laundry tub and the dryer unit are free from rough surfaces. Any rough area in the washer or dryer can cause serious damage to fabric.

Dry Cleaning

Dry cleaning may be done professionally or consumers may use coin-operated cleaning units. Many products can be dry cleaned satisfactorily by consumers providing they follow directions very carefully. Professional cleaning is recommended whenever feasible. Dry cleaning uses a solvent as the liquid in which the fabric is placed and which will dissolve the soil and then carry it away. When only dry cleaning solvents are used, there is minimal damage to most fabrics, although some fibers and some finishes are adversely, in fact seriously, affected by dry cleaning solvents. Make certain the fiber can be dry cleaned before pursuing this method. When products are heavily soiled, dry cleaners may use a wet cleaning process to remove water soluble substances. This results in fabric change if water can damage it. Shrinkage may occur with wet cleaning but seldom with dry cleaning. All solvents should be thoroughly removed from fabric after cleaning and the product dried so that no residual cleaning liquid remains in the fabric. Caution must be exercised in dry cleaning to avoid inhaling cleaning agents that might be toxic to some individuals.

Pressing

When fabrics require ironing or pressing, it is important to verify the temperature appropriate to the fiber content. In addition, some finishes may require lower ironing temperatures than would be needed for the same fabric without such finishes. Check care labels in relation to ironing or pressing apparel; use a press cloth and steam when in doubt with a low temperature setting. Pressing or ironing may be required following either laundering or dry cleaning.

Tips Concerning Maintenance

The following suggestions are given to help readers avoid problems in care of fabrics:

Most woven fabrics constructed from the plain or twill weaves do not require special handling during care procedures. Yarns are tightly interlaced and are not subject to snagging or abrasive damage. Satin fabrics, however, with the floating yarns, may be damaged from rubbing and agitation; they should be handled carefully. Fancy or figure weaves may require special handling if they have long yarn floats, if there are irregular surfaces, or if the yarn count is low.

Knitted fabrics may need care in drying, particularly if the knit requires blocking; then dryers cannot be used. Some knits require the use of dryers for the fibers and yarns to return to their original size; then air drying is not acceptable. Fiber content is important in deciding care procedures for knit fabrics. Cotton knits may shrink when laundered; wool knits should probably be dry cleaned; polyester knits may shrink if not properly heat set but when processed properly they are easy to wash and dry in automatic equipment. Any knit should be handled carefully to prevent snagging of the loops of yarn in the fabric surface.

Sheer fabrics made by leno construction or by knotting should receive gentle handling. The spaces between yarns may cause snagging and abrasion damage. However, the interlocking of yarns in both the leno and knot constructions reduces the danger of yarn slippage and makes care somewhat easier than for an open-weave or knit construction.

Nonwovens may be easy to care for if they have been properly bonded. However, some adhesives used in nonwovens are damaged by dry cleaning solvents and some may be lost during laundering. When this occurs the nonwoven tends to disintegrate and the fibers separate. Care labels are important on nonwovens, and any care for the fabric when it is thin should be gentle. Heavy-duty nonwoven fabrics should require no special handling.

Pile fabrics, woven, knitted, or tufted, can be laundered if the fiber is launderable and if the adhesive on tufted constructions is not damaged by laundering. These fabrics look best when dried in a dryer because the tumble action fluffs up the pile to produce a fabric that looks much like it did when new.

Most floor coverings are not adaptable to washing and drying or even to coin-operated dry cleaning. They require special equipment. However, consumers who wish to rent the heavy-duty cleaning machines can clean carpets and rugs providing the fiber content is not damaged. Polyester, nylon, acrylic, and olefin rugs can be cleaned in the home with little or no problem.

Stain-removal chart

Stain	Bleachable Fabrics: White and colorfast cotton, linen, polyester, acrylic, triacetate, nylon, rayon, permanent press. Removal Procedure	Nonbleachable Fabrics: Wool, Silk, Spandex, non-colorfast items, some flame retardant finishes (check labels). Removal Procedure
Alcoholic Beverages	Sponge stain promptly with cold water or soak in cold water for 30 minutes or longer. Rub detergent into any remaining stain while still wet. Launder in hot water using chlorine bleach.	Sponge stain promptly with cold water or soak in cold water for 30 minutes or longer. Sponge with vinegar. Rinse. If stain remains, rub detergent into stain. Rinse. Launder.
Blood	Soak in cold water 30 minutes or longer. If stain persists, put a few drops of ammonia on the stain and repeat detergent treatment. Rinse. If stain still persists, launder in hot water using chlorine bleach.	Same method, but if colorfastness is questionable, use hydrogen peroxide** instead of ammonia. Launder in warm water. Omit chlorine bleach.
Candle Wax	Rub with ice cube and carefully scrape off excess wax with a dull knife. Place between several layers of facial tissue or paper towels and press with a warm iron. To remove remaining stain, sponge with safe cleaning fluid. If colored stain remains, launder in hot water using chlorine bleach. Launder again if necessary.	Same method. Launder in warm water. Omit chlorine bleach.
Carbon Paper	Rub detergent into dampened stain; rinse well. If stain is not removed, put a few drops of ammonia on the stain and repeat treatment with detergent; rinse well. Repeat if necessary.	Same method, but if colorfastness is questionable, use hydrogen peroxide** instead of ammonia.
Catsup	Scrape off excess with a dull knife. Soak in cold water 30 minutes. Rub detergent into stain while still wet and launder in hot water using chlorine bleach.	Same method. Launder in warm water. Omit chlorine bleach.
Chewing Gum, Adhesive Tape	Rub stained area with ice. Remove excess gummy matter carefully with a dull knife. Sponge with a safe cleaning fluid. Rinse and launder.	Same method.
Chocolate and Cocoa	Soak in cold water. Rub detergent into stain while still wet, then rinse thoroughly. Dry. If a greasy stain remains, sponge with a safe cleaning fluid. Rinse. Launder in hot water using chlorine bleach. If stain remains, repeat treatment with cleaning fluid.	Same method. Launder in warm water. Omit chlorine bleach.
Coffee, Tea	Soak in cold water. Rub detergent into stain while still wet. Rinse and dry. If grease stain remains from cream, sponge with safe cleaning fluid. Launder in hot water using chlorine bleach.	Same method. Launder in warm water. Omit chlorine bleach.
Cosmetics (Eye shadow, lipstick, mascara, liquid make-up, powder, rouge)	Rub detergent into dampened stain until outline of stain is gone, then rinse well. Launder in hot water using chlorine bleach.	Same method. Launder in warm water. Omit chlorine bleach.
Crayon	Rub soap (Instant Fels, Ivory Snow, Lux Flakes) into dampened stain, working until outline of stain is removed. Launder in hot water using chlorine bleach. Repeat process if necessary. For stains throughout load of clothes, wash items in hot water using laundry soap and 1 cup baking soda. If colored stain remains, launder with a detergent and chlorine bleach.	Same method. Launder in warm water using plenty of detergent. Omit chlorine bleach. If colored stain remains, soak in a presoak product or an oxygen bleach using hottest water safe for fabric; then launder.
Deodorants and Antiperspirants	Rub detergent into dampened stain. Launder in hot water using chlorine bleach. Antiperspirants that contain such substances as aluminum chloride are acidic and may change the color of some dyes. Color may or may not be restored by sponging with ammonia. Rinse thoroughly.	Rub detergent into dampened stain. Launder in warm water. Antiperspirants that contain such substances as aluminum chloride are acidic and may change the color of some dyes. Color may or may not be restored by sponging with ammonia. (If ammonia treatment is required, dilute with an equal amount of water for use on wool, mohair, or silk.) Rinse thoroughly.
Dye (Transferred from a non-colorfast article)	May be impossible to remove. Bleach immediately using chlorine bleach. Repeat as often as necessary. Or use a commercial color remover.	Use a commercial color remover.
Egg, Meat Juice, and Gravy	If dried, scrape off as much as possible with a dull knife. Rub detergent into stain while still wet. Launder in hot water using chlorine bleach.	Same method. Launder in warm water. Omit chlorine bleach.
Fabric Softener	Rub the dampened stain with bar soap (such as Ivory or Lux) and relaunder in the usual manner.	Same method.
Fingernail Polish	Sponge white cotton fabric with nail polish remover; other fabrics with amyl acetate** (banana oil). Launder. Repeat if necessary.	Same method.
Formula	Soak in cold water, then launder in hot water using chlorine bleach. If stain persists, soak in a presoak product.	Soak in warm water using a presoak product. Launder in warm water using plenty of detergent.
Fruit Juices	Soak in cold water. Launder in hot water using chlorine bleach.	Soak in cold water. If stain remains, rub detergent into stain while still wet. Launder in warm water.
Grass	Rub detergent into dampened stain. Launder in hot water using chlorine bleach. If stain remains, sponge with alcohol. Rinse thoroughly.	Same method. Launder in warm water. Omit chlorine bleach. If colorfastness is questionable or fabric is acetate, dilute alcohol with two parts water.
Grease and Oil (Car grease, butter, shortening, oily medicines such as oily vitamins)	Rub detergent into dampened stain. If stain persists, sponge thoroughly with safe cleaning fluid. Rinse.	Rub detergent into dampened stain. Launder in warm water using plenty of detergent. If stain persists, sponge thoroughly with safe cleaning fluid. Rinse.

30.1 Stain-removal chart. (Maytag Corp.)

Stain	Bleachable Fabrics: White and colorfast cotton, linen, polyester, acrylic, triacetate, nylon, rayon, permanent press. Removal Procedure	Nonbleachable Fabrics: Wool, Silk, Spandex, non-colorfast items, some flame retardent finishes (check labels). Removal Procedure
Ink (Ballpoint)	Sponge stain with rubbing alcohol, or spray with hair spray until wet looking. Rub detergent into stained area. Launder. Repeat if necessary.	Same method.
Ink, Drawing	May be impossible to remove. Rub cold water through stain until no more color is being removed. Rub detergent into stain, rinse. Repeat if necessary. Soak in warm sudsy water containing one to four tablespoons of ammonia to a quart of water. Rinse thoroughly. Launder in hot water using chlorine bleach.	Same method. Launder in warm water. Omit chlorine bleach.
Ink from Felt Tip Pen	Rub household cleaner such as 409 or Mr. Clean into stain. Rinse. Repeat as many times as necessary to remove stain. Launder. Some may be impossible to remove.	Same method.
Iodine	Make a solution of sodium thiosulfate crystals.** Use solution to sponge stain. Rinse and launder.	Same method.
Mayonnaise, Salad Dressing	Rub detergent into dampened stain. Rinse and let dry. If greasy stain remains, sponge with safe cleaning fluid. Rinse. Launder in hot water after drying.	Same method. Launder in warm water. Omit chlorine bleach.
Mildew	Rub detergent into dampened stain. Launder in hot water using chlorine bleach. If stain remains, sponge with hydrogen peroxide.** Rinse and launder.	Same method. Launder in warm water. Omit chlorine bleach.
Milk, Cream, Ice Cream	Soak in cold water. Launder in hot water using chlorine bleach. If grease stain remains, sponge with safe cleaning fluid. Rinse.	Soak in cold water. Rub detergent into stain. Launder. If grease stain remains, sponge with safe cleaning fluid. Rinse.
Mustard	Rub detergent into dampened stain. Rinse. Soak in hot detergent water for several hours. If stain remains, launder in hot water using chlorine bleach.	Same method. Launder in warm water. Omit chlorine bleach.
Paint and Varnish	Treat stains quickly before paint dries. If a solvent is recommended as a thinner, sponge it onto stain. Turpentine or trichloroethane can be used. While stain is still wet with solvent, work detergent into stain and soak in hot water. Then launder. Repeat procedure if stain remains after laundering. Stain may be impossible to remove.	Same method.
Perfume	Same as alcoholic beverages.	Same as alcoholic beverages.
Perspiration	Rub detergent into dampened stain. Launder in hot water using chlorine bleach. If fabric has discolored, try to restore it by treating fresh stains with ammonia or old stains with vinegar. Rinse.	Same method. Launder in warm water. Omit chlorine bleach.
Ring Around the Collar	Apply liquid laundry detergent or a paste of granular detergent and water on the stain. Let it set for 30 minutes. A prewash product especially designed for this purpose may be used. Follow manufacturer's directions. Launder.	Same method.
Rust	Launder in hot water with detergent and RoVer® Rust Remover. Follow manufacturer's instructions. RoVer is available from authorized Maytag dealers and parts distributors; specify Part No. 57961.	Same method. If colorfastness is questionable, test a concealed area first.
Scorch	Launder in hot water using chlorine bleach or RoVer Rust Remover. (See Rust). Severe scorching cannot be removed; fabric has been damaged.	Cover stains with cloth dampened with hydrogen peroxide.** Cover with a dry cloth and press with an iron as hot as is safe for fabric. Rinse thoroughly. Rub detergent into stained area while still wet. Launder. Repeat if necessary.
Shoe Polish (Wax)	Scrap off as much as possible with a dull knife. Rub detergent into dampened stain. Launder in hot water using chlorine bleach. If stain persists, sponge with rubbing alcohol. Rinse. Launder.	Scrape off as much as possible with a dull knife. Rub detergent into dampened stain. Launder in warm water. If stain persists, sponge with one part alcohol and two parts water. Rinse. Launder.
Soft Drinks	Sponge stain immediately with cold water. Launder in hot water with chlorine bleach. Some drink stains are invisible after they are dry, but turn yellow with aging or heating. This yellow stain may be impossible to remove.	Same method. Launder in warm water. Omit chlorine bleach.
Tar and Asphalt	Act quickly before stain is dry. Pour trichloroethane through cloth. Repeat. Stain may be impossible to remove. Rinse and launder.	Same method.
Urine	Soak in cold water. Rub detergent into stain. Launder in hot water using chlorine bleach. If the color of the fabric has been altered by stain, sponge with ammonia; rinse thoroughly. If stain persists, sponging with vinegar may help.	Same method. Launder in warm water. Omit chlorine bleach. If ammonia treatment is necessary, dilute ammonia with an equal part of water for use on wool, mohair, or silk.
Wine Yellowing Of White Cottons And Linens	Same treatment as for alcoholic beverages. Wait 15 minutes and rinse. Repeat if necessary. Fill washer with very hot water. Add at least twice as much detergent as normal. Place articles in washer and agitate for four minutes on regular cycle. Stop washer and add one cup of chlorine bleach to the bleach dispenser or dilute in one quart of water and pour around agitator. Restart washer at once. Agitate four minutes. Stop washer and allow articles to soak 15 minutes. Restart washer and set ten minute wash time; allow washer to complete normal cycle. Repeat entire procedure two or more consecutive times until whiteness is restored.	Same treatment as for alcoholic beverages.
Yellowing of White Nylon	Soak 15 to 30 minutes in solution of ⅛ cup of chlorine bleach and one teaspoon of vinegar thoroughly mixed with each gallon of warm water. Rinse. Repeat if necessary.	

Stain Removal

Stain removal is not nearly as difficult as it appears. A few important guidelines aid in successful stain removal.

1. Remove any stain as soon as possible. Promptness is one of, if not the, most important aspect of successful stain removal. The longer a stain is allowed to stand on a fabric, the more difficult removal becomes.
2. Take time to remove the stain. Follow procedures carefully and repeat, if necessary, when the first attempt is not successful.
3. Maintain a few key stain-removing agents in your laundry so that they can be found easily and quickly.
4. If the stain is one you have not removed before, determine the preferred method for removal and follow it carefully.

The steps in removing stains are these:

1. Soak the stain, if necessary, in cold water. A few stains require warm water, and reviewing procedures for particular stains may help in this respect. Also, make certain that the fabric color will not run in water and spoil the appearance. If this can happen, it is best to try cleaning solvents and not water.
2. Pretreating stains before washing in detergent may be helpful and, for some, is very important. These pretreatments loosen the stain and make it easy to remove during the laundry operation. Such treatments are extremely important for oily stains. A good pretreatment is a clear liquid detergent, shampoo, or special prewash product.
3. After soaking, wash the item in detergent. It may be helpful at this point to cover the stain with a prewash, even though one has been used in a pretreatment step, which will surround the stain particles and help the detergent solution lift them off during the washing operation.
4. If the fabric can be bleached safely, this is a common treatment for many stains. The bleach will remove the color of the stain and render it invisible.
5. Stains on fabrics that cannot be laundered can be treated with special spot removers made of cleaning solvent. These products are available as spot removers and work well if applied as soon as possible after the fabric is stained and if directions are followed.

When the identity of a stain is known, consumers should follow the specific directions for removing it. Directions are available from a variety of sources. Figure 30.1 is an abbreviated chart for stain removal. Many others may be obtained from manufacturers of laundry equipment and soaps and detergents. Extension services in many states have prepared booklets on stain removal that may be obtained through the county or the state extension office.

If a stain is not known, the following procedure might help:

1. Soak the stain in cold water. Work a liquid detergent into the stained area and allow to stand for thirty minutes; rinse carefully. Launder in an automatic washer, using the regular cycle, if the fabric is washable. Chlorine bleach may be used for white cotton, nylon, acrylic, polyester, or rayon. Use a perborate bleach for other fibers. Agitate briefly, rinse thoroughly, and air dry.
2. If step 1 was not successful try step 2. Soak the stained article overnight in an enzyme presoak. Launder with the regular washing cycle in hot water; air dry.
3. If a product cannot be laundered, sponge the stained area with a

cleaning solvent such as trichloroethane. Let the stained area stand for about twenty minutes. Rub the spot with a solution of laundry detergent, rinse thoroughly, and air dry. This step should be eliminated if the fabric can be seriously damaged by water.

4. Any fabric that can be bleached might be treated as follows: Mix a solution of equal parts of chlorine bleach and water, and apply with an eye dropper to the stained area. Launder immediately with a regular wash cycle and hot water; air dry.

The reader should note that these rules specifically state the item should be air dried. Dryers use sufficient heat in drying that any stain may be set so thoroughly that it can never be removed. Therefore, do not use dryers until a stain is removed.

The Care Label

One of the most important items provided consumers on apparel is the care label. This may be available on some home-furnishing fabrics; however, it is not required for most of these. Products that should have care labels and do not should be reported to the store; if consumers receive no satisfaction, they should notify the Federal Trade Commission. The number or name of the manufacturer of the product should be included in the report as well as the retail source.

Consumers should make certain care labels are included with the textile product. In turn, they should make certain that they adhere to the care directions. Much dissatisfaction with textile items is due to the fact that the consumer fails to follow care directions.

Study Questions

1. Discuss the factors that influence fabric appearance.
2. Discuss the factors that influence comfort of fabrics.
3. Discuss the factors that relate to the durability of textile products.
4. What is involved in the care of fabrics? Suggest a set of guidelines for consumers that would be important to follow in the maintenance of textile items.
5. What are government responsibilities in relation to providing consumers with information concerning textile products?
6. What information must be given to the consumer on labels attached to apparel items?
7. What type of information do you believe should be given consumers in relation to fabrics for use in interior design and home furnishings?
8. What can the consumer do to remove a stain that is unknown?
9. What is probably the most important thing to do when a textile is stained?
10. Suggest a set of guidelines for consumers for care procedures for items that can be washed.

Metric Conversion Table

When dealing with foreign suppliers or consulting references printed abroad, the textile manufacturer, scientist, or student should be able to convert readily from the American system of weights and measures to the metric system, employed by virtually every country outside the United States. The following tables provide multipliers for converting from metric to the U.S. system and the reverse; the multipliers have been rounded to the third decimal place and, thus, yield an approximate equivalent.

	metric to U.S.			U.S. to metric	
to convert from	to	multiply the metric unit by	to convert from	to	multiply the U.S. unit by
length					
meters	yards	1.093	yards	meters	.914
meters	feet	3.280	feet	meters	.305
meters	inches	39.370	inches	meters	.025
centimeters	inches	.394	inches	centimeters	2.540
millimeters	inches	.039	inches	millimeters	25.400
area and volume					
square meters	square yards	1.196	square yards	square meters	.836
square meters	square feet	10.764	square feet	square meters	.093
square centimeters	square inches	.155	square inches	square centimeters	6.451
cubic centimeters	cubic inches	.061	cubic inches	cubic centimeters	16.387
liquid measure					
liters	cubic inches	61.020	cubic inches	liters	.016
liters	cubic feet	.035	cubic feet	liters	28.339
liters	U.S. gallons*	.264	U.S. gallons*	liters	3.785
liters	U.S. quarts*	1.057	U.S. quarts*	liters	.946
weight and mass					
kilograms	pounds	2.205	pounds	kilograms	.453
grams	ounces	.035	ounces	grams	28.349
grams	grains	15.430	grains	grams	.065
grams per meter	ounces per yard	.032	ounces per yard	grams per meter	31.250
grams per square meter	ounces per square yard	.030	ounces per square yard	grams per square meter	33.333

*The British imperial gallon equals approximately 1.2 U.S. gallons, or 4.54 liters. Similarly, the British imperial quart equals 1.2 U.S. quarts, and so on.

Glossary of Textile Terms

absorption The attraction and retention of gases or liquids within the pores of a fiber; also, the retention of moisture between fibers within yarns and between fibers or yarns within fabrics.

adsorption The retention of gases, liquids, or solids on the surface areas of fibers, yarns, or fabrics.

antique satin A satin-weave fabric made to resemble silk satin of an earlier century. It is used for home-furnishing fabrics.

art linen A heavy plain-weave fabric used for tablecloths and as the basis for many types of embroidered household items.

balanced yarns Yarns in which the twist is such that the yarn will hang in a loop without kinking, doubling, or twisting upon itself.

barathea A closely woven dobby-weave fabric with a characteristic pebbly surface. It is generally made from silk or rayon, often combined with cotton or worsted. The fabric is used for dresses, neckties, and lightweight suits.

batiste A fabric named for Jean Baptiste, a French weaver. (1) In cotton, a sheer, fine *muslin,** woven of combed yarns and given a mercerized finish. It is used for blouses, summer shirts, dresses, lingerie, infants' dresses, bonnets, and handkerchiefs. (2) A rayon, polyester, or cotton-blend fabric with the same characteristics. (3) A smooth, fine wool fabric that is lighter than *challis;* very similar to fine nun's veiling. It is used for dresses and negligees. (4) A sheer silk fabric, either plain or figured, very similar to silk mull. It is often called *batiste de soie* and is made into summer dresses.

Bedford cord Lengthwise-ribbed durable cloth for outer garments or sports clothes. The corded effect is secured by having two successive *warp* threads woven in plain-weave order. Heavier cords are created with wadding—a heavy, bulky yarn with very little twist—covered by *filling* threads.

*Italics denote a cross-reference within the Glossary.

beetling A finish primarily applied to linen whereby the cloth is beaten with large wooden blocks to flatten the yarns.

bengaline A ribbed fabric similar to *faille,* but heavier, with a coarser rib in the *filling* direction. It may be silk, wool, acetate, or rayon *warp,* with wool or cotton *filling.* The fabric was first made in Bengal, India. It is used for dresses, coats, trimmings, and draperies.

bicomponent fibers Fibers in which two *filaments* of different composition have been extruded simultaneously.

bouclé A fabric woven with bouclé yarns, which have a looped appearance on the surface. In some bouclés, only one side of the fabric is nubby; in others, both are rough. Sometimes the bouclé yarn is used as a *warp* rather than a *filling.* Bouclé yarn is very popular in the knitting trade; there are many varieties and weights.

breaking load The minimum force required to rupture a fiber, expressed in grams or pounds.

brins The two adjacent silk *filaments* extruded by the silkworm.

broadcloth A term used to describe several dissimilar fabrics made with different fibers, weaves, and finishes. (1) Originally, a silk shirting fabric so named because it was woven in widths exceeding the usual 29 inches. (2) A tightly woven, high-count cotton cloth with a fine crosswise rib. Fine broadcloths are woven of *combed* yarns, usually with high thread counts, such as 136 x 60 or 144 x 76. They are usually mercerized, Sanforized, and given a soft, lustrous finish. (3) A closely woven wool cloth with a smooth nap, velvety feel, and lustrous appearance. Wool broadcloth can be made with a two-up-and-two-down twill weave or plain weave. In setting up a loom to make the fabric, the loom is threaded very wide to allow for great shrinkage during the fulling process. The fabric takes its name from this wide threading. High-quality wool broadcloth is fine enough for garments that are to be closely molded to the figure

341

or draped. Its high-luster finish makes it an elegant cloth. Wool broadcloth is 10 to 16 ounces per yard and is now being made in chiffon weights. (4) A fabric made from silk or man-made *filament fiber* yarns, woven in a plain weave with a fine crosswise rib obtained by using a heavier *filling* than *warp* yarn.

brocade   Rich Jacquard-woven fabric with an allover interwoven design of raised figures or flowers. The name is derived from the French word meaning "to ornament." The brocade pattern is emphasized with contrasting surfaces or colors and often has gold or silver threads running through it. The background may be either satin or twill weave. It is used for dresses, draperies, and upholstery.

brocatelle   Supposedly an imitation of Italian tooled leather, in which the background is pressed and the figures embossed. Both the background and the figures are tightly woven, generally with a *warp* effect in the figure and a *filling* effect in the background. Brocatelle is used mainly in upholstery and draperies.

cambric   A closely woven, white cotton fabric finished with a slight gloss on one side.

Canton flannel   A heavy, warm cotton material with a twilled surface and a long soft nap on the back, produced by napping the heavy soft-twist yarn. It is named for Canton, China, where it was first made. The fabric is strong and absorbent; it is used for interlinings and sleeping garments.

carding   A process by which natural fibers are sorted, separated, and partially aligned.

card sliver   A ropelike strand of fibers about ¾ inch to 1 inch in diameter; the form in which fibers emerge from the *carding* machine.

cavalry twill   A sturdy twill-weave fabric with a pronounced diagonal cord. It is used for sportswear, uniforms, and riding habits.

challis or challie   One of the softest fabrics made, named from the Anglo-Indian term *shalee,* meaning "soft." It is a fine, lightweight, plain-weave fabric, usually made of worsted yarns. Challis was formerly manufactured with a small flower design, but now it is made in darker tones of all-over prints and solid colors, in the finest quality fabrics.

chambray   (1) A plain-woven fabric with an almost square count (80 x 76), a colored *warp,* and a white *filling,* which gives a mottled, colored surface. It is used for shirts, children's clothing, and dresses. The fabric is named for Cambrai, France, where it was first made for sunbonnets. (2) A similar but heavier carded yarn fabric used for work clothes and children's play clothes.

cheesecloth   A very loosely woven, plain-weave

cotton fabric. The yard width is called tobacco cloth. It is used for curtains, costumes, and cleaning cloths.

chiffon   A term used to describe many light, gossamer, sheer, plain-weave fabrics. Chiffon can be made of silk, wool, or man-made fibers. It is an open weave with tightly twisted yarns.

china silk   A lightweight, soft, plain-weave silk fabric used for lingerie, dress linings, and soft suits.

chino   A type of army twill made of combed, two-ply, mercerized yarns in a vat-dyed khaki color. It is now available in a variety of colors.

chintz   A highly lustrous, plain-woven cotton with a bright, glazed surface, generally made by finishing a print cloth construction.

cohesiveness   The ability of fibers to adhere to one another in yarn-manufacturing processes.

combing   A process by which natural fibers are sorted and straightened; a more refined treatment than *carding.*

copolymer   A *polymer* composed of two or more different *monomers.*

corduroy   A ribbed, high-luster, cut-pile fabric with extra filling threads that form lengthwise ribs or *wales.* The thread count varies from 48 x 116 to 70 x 250.

core yarn   A yarn in which a base or foundation yarn is completely wrapped by a second yarn.

cotton linters   Cotton fibers that are too short for yarn or fabric manufacturing.

course   A series of successive loops lying crosswise in a knitted fabric.

covert   Generally called covert cloth; a closely woven *warp*-face twill. Its characteristically flecked appearance is produced by using a two-ply yarn so that one dark thread alternates with a light thread. Covert is generally made of wool or cotton, but man-made fibers and blends can also be used.

crepe   A lightweight fabric of silk, rayon, cotton, wool, man-made, or blended fibers, characterized by a crinkled surface that is produced by high-twist yarns, chemical treatment, weave, or embossing.

cretonne   A plain-weave fabric similar to unglazed *chintz,* usually printed with large designs.

crimp   The waviness of a fiber, usually visible only under magnification.

crystallinity   The degree to which fiber molecules are parallel to each other, though not necessarily to the longitudinal fiber axis.

damask   A firm-textured fabric with patterns, similar to *brocade* but lighter and reversible. Table damasks are Jacquard woven in lustrous designs.

denier A unit of yarn number equal to the weight in grams of 9,000 meters of the yarn.

denim A twilled fabric made of hard-twist yarns, with the *warp yarns* dyed blue and the *filling yarns* undyed. Sports denim is softer and lighter in weight. It is now available in many colors and in plaids and stripes.

dimensional stability The degree to which a fiber, yarn, or fabric retains its shape and size after having been subjected to wear and maintenance.

dimity Literally, double thread; a fine checked or corded cotton sheer made by bunching and weaving two or more threads together.

dotted swiss A sheer, crisp cotton fabric with either clipped spot or swivel dots.

doupion Silk yarns made from two cocoons that have been formed in an interlocked manner. The yarn is uneven, irregular, and larger than regular *filaments*. It is used in making *shantung* and doupioni.

drawing The process by which slivers of staple fibers are pulled out or extended after *carding* or *combing.*

drill A strong cotton material similar to *denim,* which has a diagonal 2 x 1 weave running up to the left *selvage.*

duck A durable plain-weave, closely woven cotton, generally made of *ply yarns* in a variety of weights and thread counts. Often called canvas, it is used for belting, awnings, tents, and sails.

duvetyn A very high-quality cloth that resembles a compact velvet. It has a velvety *hand* resulting from the short nap that covers its surface completely, concealing its twill weave. It is used for suits and coats.

elastic recovery The ability of a fiber, yarn, or fabric to return to its original length after the tension that produced elongation has been released.

elongation The amount of stretch or extension that a fiber, yarn, or fabric will accept.

faille A soft, slightly glossy silk, rayon, or cotton fabric in a rib weave, with a light, flat, crossgrain rib or cord made by using heavier yarns in the *filling* than in the *warp.*

felt A nonwoven fabric in which the fibers develop a tight bond and will not ravel. It is used for coats, hats, and many industrial purposes.

fiber morphology The form and structure of a fiber, including its biological structure, shape, cross section, and microscopic appearance.

fibrils Bundles of fiber cells.

filament fibers Long, continuous fibers that can be measured in meters or yards, or in the case of man-made fibers, in kilometers or miles.

filling yarns Yarns that run perpendicular to the longer dimension or *selvage* of a fabric.

flannel A catchall designation for a great many otherwise unnamed fabrics in the woolen industry. Flannel is woven in various weights of worsted, woolen, or a mixture of both. It can even be made of man-made fibers. The surface is slightly napped in finish. A wide range of weights is available: An 11-ounce flannel is made for suits, and there are tissue-weight flannels for dresses.

flannelette A soft, plain- or twill-weave cotton fabric lightly napped on one side. The fabric can be dyed solid colors or printed. It is popular for lounging and sleeping garments.

fleece Wool sheared from a living lamb.

flexibility The property of bending without breaking.

foulard A lightweight silk, rayon, cotton, or wool fabric characterized by its twill weave. Foulard has a high luster on the face and is dull on the reverse side. It is usually printed, the patterns ranging from simple polka dots to elaborate designs. It is also made in plain or solid colors. Foulard has a characteristic *hand* that can be described as light, firm, and supple.

frosting Frequently called "color abrasion," frosting is color change in localized areas because of differential wear resulting from unlike fibers or dye failure. Frosting is most often evident where durable-press finishes have been applied.

gabardine A hard-finished, clear-surfaced, twill-weave fabric made of either natural or synthetic fibers. The diagonal lines are fine, close, and steep and are more pronounced than in serge. The lines cannot be seen on the wrong side of the fabric.

gauze A plain-weave fabric with widely spaced yarns, used for such things as bandages. Some weights of gauze can be stiffened for curtains or other decorative or apparel purposes.

gingham A light- to medium-weight plain-weave cotton fabric. It is usually yarn dyed and woven to create stripes, checks, or plaids. The fabric is mercerized to produce a soft, lustrous appearance; it is sized and calendered to a firm and lustrous finish. Gingham is used for dresses, shirts, robes, curtains, draperies, and bedspreads. The thread count varies from about 48 x 44 to 106 x 94.

greige The state of a fabric before a finish has been applied.

grenadine A tightly twisted *ply yarn* composed of two or three *singles.*

grosgrain A closely woven, firm, corded fabric often made with a cotton filling. The cords are heavier than in *poplin,* rounder than in *faille.*

habutai   A soft, lightweight silk dress fabric originally woven in the gum on hand looms in Japan. It is sometimes confused with *china silk,* which is technically lighter in weight.

hackling   A *combing* process that separates short fibers from long fibers.

hand   The "feel" of a fabric; the qualities that can be ascertained by touching it.

herringbone   A fabric in which the pattern of weave resembles the skeletal structure of the herring. It is made with a broken twill weave that produces a balanced, zigzag effect and is used for sportswear, suits, and coats.

homespun   A coarse, plain-weave fabric, loosely woven with irregular, tightly twisted, and unevenly spun yarns. It has a hand-woven appearance and is used for coats, suits, sportswear, draperies, and slipcovers.

homopolymer   A *polymer* composed of one substance or one type of molecule.

honan   Originally a fabric of the best Chinese silk, sometimes woven with blue edges. It is now made to resemble a heavy *pongee,* with slub yarns in both *warp* and *filling.* Honan is manufactured from silk or from man-made fibers. It is used for women's dresses.

hopsacking   An open basket-weave *ply yarn* fabric of cotton, linen, or rayon. The weave is similar to the sacking used to gather hops; hence the name. It is used for dresses, jackets, skirts, and blouses.

huck or huckaback   A toweling fabric with a honeycombed surface made by using heavy filling yarns in a dobby weave. It has excellent absorbent qualities. Huck is made in linen, cotton, or a mixture of the two. In a mixture it is called a "union" fabric.

hydrophilic   Water loving; having a high degree of moisture absorption or attraction.

hydrophobic   Water repelling; having a low degree of moisture absorption or attraction.

jean   A sturdy cotton fabric, softer and finer than *drill,* made in solid colors or stripes. It is used for sport blouses, work shirts, women's slacks, children's play clothes, and men's pants.

jersey   Elastic knitted fabric in a stockinette stitch. It was first made on the Island of Jersey off the English coast and used for fishermen's clothing. Jersey can be made from wool, cotton, rayon, nylon, other man-made fibers, or a combination of any of these. The term is frequently applied to tricot-knitted fabrics used for dresses.

kersey   A thick, heavy, pure wool and cotton twill-weave similar to *melton.* It is well fulled, with a nap and a close-sheared surface. Kersey is used for uniforms and overcoats.

lace   An openwork cloth with a design formed by a network of threads made by hand or on special lace machinery, with bobbins, needles, or hooks.

lamb's wool   Wool clipped from sheep less than eight months old.

lawn   A lightweight, sheer, fine cotton or linen fabric, which can be given a soft or crisp finish. It is sized and calendered to produce a soft, lustrous appearance. Lawn is used for dresses, blouses, curtains, and lingerie, and as a base for embroidered items.

linear polymer   A *polymer* formed by end-to-end linking of molecular units. The resulting polymer is very long and narrow. It is typical of fibrous forms.

loft   The springiness or fluffiness of a fiber.

longcloth   A fine, soft cotton cloth woven of softly twisted yarns. It is similar to *nainsook* but slightly heavier, with a duller surface. Longcloth is so called because it was one of the first fabrics to be woven in long rolls. It is also a synonym for *muslin* sheeting of good quality. The fabric is used for underwear and linings.

luster   The gloss, sheen, or shine of a fiber, yarn, or fabric.

macromolecule   A large molecule formed by hooking together many small molecule units. The term can be used synonymously with polymolecule or *polymer.*

madras   (1) A finely woven, soft, plain- or Jacquard-weave fabric with a stripe in the lengthwise direction and Jacquard or dobby patterns woven in the background. Some madras is made with woven checks and cords. It can be used for blouses, dresses, and shirts. (2) A fabric handwoven in India from cotton yarns dyed with native vegetable colorings. The designs are usually rather large, bold plaids that soften in color as the dyes fade and bleed.

marquisette   A light, strong, sheer, open-textured curtain fabric, often with dots woven into the surface. The thread count varies from 48 x 22 to 60 x 40.

matelassé   A soft double or compound fabric with a quilted appearance. The heavier type is used in draperies and upholstery, whereas crepe matelassé is popular in dresses, semiformal and formal suits and wraps, and trimmings.

melton   A thick, heavily felted or fulled wool fabric in a twill or satin weave, with a smooth, lustrous, napped surface. In less expensive meltons the warp yarn may be cotton instead of wool.

micronaire fineness   The weight in micrograms of 1 inch of fiber.

moisture regain   The moisture in a material determined under prescribed conditions and expressed as a percentage of the weight of the moisture-free specimen.

molecular orientation The degree to which fiber molecules are parallel to each other and to the longitudinal axis of the fiber.

monk's cloth A heavy, loosely woven basket-weave fabric in solid colors or with stripes or plaids woven into the fabric. It is used chiefly for draperies and slipcovers.

monofilament yarn Yarn composed of only one fiber *filament*.

monomer A single unit or molecule from which *polymers* are formed.

mousseline de soie Literally, "muslin of silk"; silk organdy, a plain-weave silk, chiffon-weight fabric with a slight stiffness.

multicomponent fabric A fabric in which at least two layers of material are sealed together by adhesive or stitching.

multifilament yarn Yarn composed of several fiber *filaments*.

multilobal A fiber with a modified cross section exhibiting several lobes.

muslin A large group of plain-weave cotton fabrics ranging from light to heavy weight. The sizing may also be light or heavy. Muslin can be solid colored or printed. It is used for dresses, shirts, sheets, and other domestic items.

nainsook A fine, soft cotton fabric in a plain weave. Better grades have a polished finish on one side. When it is highly polished, nainsook may be sold as polished cotton. In low-priced white goods, cambric, longcloth, and nainsook are often identical before converting; the finishing process gives them their characteristic texture, but even so it is often difficult to distinguish one from the other. Nainsook is heavier and coarser than *lawn*. It is usually found in white, pastel colors, and prints and is used chiefly for infants' wear, lingerie, and blouses.

ninon A smooth, transparent, closely woven *voile*, with the *warp yarns* grouped in pairs. It is available in plain or novelty weaves. Man-made fibers are generally used for glass curtains and dress fabrics.

nonthermoplastic Not capable of being softened by heat.

oleophilic Tending to absorb and retain oily materials.

oleophobic Tending to repel oily materials.

organdy A thin, transparent, stiff, wiry cotton *muslin* used for dresses, neckwear, and trimmings. Organdy, when chemically treated, keeps its crispness through many launderings and does not re-

quire restarching. It crushes readily but is easily pressed. Shadow organdy has a faint printed design in self-color.

organzine A yarn of two or more plies with a medium twist.

orientation See *molecular orientation*.

Osnaburg Named for the town in Germany where it was first made, a coarse cotton or blended fiber fabric in a plain weave that resembles crash. It is finished for use in upholstery, slacks, and sportswear. It was originally used unbleached for grain and cement sacks.

ottoman A heavy corded silk or synthetic fabric with larger and rounder ribs than *faille;* used for coats, skirts, and trimmings. *Fillings* of the cloth are usually cotton or wool, and they should be completely covered by the silk or man-made fiber *warp*.

outing flannel A soft, lightweight, plain- or twill-weave fabric usually napped on both sides. Most outing flannels have colored yarn stripes. Outing flannel soils easily, and the nap washes and wears off. It is used chiefly for sleeping garments.

Oxford shirting A cotton or blended fabric in a basket weave first made in Oxford, England, and used for shirts, blouses, and sportswear.

percale A medium-weight, plain-woven printed cotton, such as 80 x 80; a staple of dress goods. Percale sheets are high quality, with a count of at least 180 threads per square inch. Most percales are made of combed yarns with a count of 84 x 96 or 180 threads per inch. Some fine percale sheets count 200 threads per inch or more, such as 96 x 104 or 96 x 108.

picks See *filling yarns*.

pilling The formation of tiny balls of fiber on the surface of a fabric.

piqué Strictly, a ribbed or corded cotton with wales running across the fabric, formed by *warp* ends. The term is often used in the trade to refer to Bedford cord or warp piqué, in which the cords run lengthwise.

plissé Usually a print cloth treated with chemicals that cause parts of the cloth to shrink, creating a permanently crinkled surface.

ply yarn A yarn in which two or more single strands are twisted together.

polymer A large molecule produced by linking together many monomers.

polymerization The conversion of *monomers* into large molecules or polymers.

pongee (1) A thin, natural tan-colored silk fabric originally made of wild Chinese silk with a knotty rough weave, named for the Chinese *Pun-ki,* meaning "woven at home on one's own loom." It is used primarily for summer suits and dresses, and both plain fabrics and prints are used for decorative purposes. (2) A staple fine-combed cotton fabric finished with a high luster and used for underclothing. (3) A man-made fiber fabric simulating pongee.

poplin   A tightly woven, high-count cotton with fine cross ribs formed by heavy *filling yarns* and fewer, finer *warp yarns*. Poplin has heavier ribs, heavier threads, and a slightly lower count than broadcloth, ranging from 80 x 40 to 116 x 56.

pulled wool   Wool pulled from the hide of a slaughtered animal.

raw silk   Silk that has not been degummed.

reeling   The process of winding silk filaments onto a wheel.

reprocessed wool   Wool fibers reclaimed from scraps of fabric that have never been used.

resiliency   The ability of a fabric to return to its original shape after compressing, bending, or other deformation.

retting   The removal, usually by soaking, of the outer woody portion of the flax plant to gain access to the fibers.

reused wool   Wool fibers reclaimed from fabrics that have been worn or used.

roving   The process by which a sliver of staple fibers is attenuated to between ¼ and ⅛ of its original size; also, the product of this operation.

sailcloth   A very heavy, strong, plain-weave fabric made of cotton, linen, or jute. There are many qualities and weights. Sailcloth can be used for sportswear, slipcovers, curtains, and other heavy-duty items.

sateen   A cotton or spun-yarn fabric characterized by floats running in the *filling* direction. It is usually mercerized and used for linings, draperies, and comforters.

saturation regain   The moisture in a material at 95 to 100 percent relative humidity.

scroop   A characteristic rustling or crunching sound acquired by silk that has been immersed in solutions of acetic or tartaric acid and dried without rinsing. It is probably caused by acid microcrystals in the fiber rubbing across each other.

scutching   The separation of the outer covering of the flax stalk from the usable fibers.

seersucker   A lightweight cotton or cotton blend with crinkled stripes woven in by setting some of the *warp yarns* tight and others slack.

selvage   The long, finished edges of a bolt of fabric.

sericulture   The raising of silkworms and production of silk.

shantung   Originally, a handloomed plain-weave fabric made in China. Made of *wild silk,* the fabric had an irregular surface. Today the term *shantung* is applied to a plain-weave fabric with heavier, rougher yarns running in the crosswise direction of the fabric. These are single complex yarns of the slub type. The fabric can be made of cotton, silk, or man-made fibers.

sharkskin   (1) A cotton, linen, silk, or man-made fiber fabric with a sleek, hard-finished, crisp, and pebbly surface and a chalky luster. *Filament yarns,* when used, are twisted and woven tightly in either a plain-weave or a basket-weave construction, depending on the effect desired. *Staple fiber yarns* are handled in the same manner, except for wool. (2) A wool fabric characterized by its twill weave. The yarns in both *warp* and *filling* alternate white with a color, such as black, brown, or blue. The diagonal lines of the twill weave run from left to right.

shed   The opening between *warp yarns* through which *filling yarns* are passed.

shoddy   See *reused wool.*

silk noil   Short ends of silk fibers used in making rough, textured, spun yarns or in blends with cotton or wool; sometimes called *waste silk.*

singles   A strand of several filaments held together by twist.

specific gravity   The density of a fiber relative to that of water at 4° C.

spinning quality   The ease with which fibers lend themselves to yarn-manufacturing processes; cohesiveness.

spun silk   Yarns made from short fibers of pierced cocoons or from short ends at the outside and inside edges of the cocoons.

spun yarns   Yarns composed of staple fibers.

staple fibers   Short fibers that are measured in inches or fractions of inches.

suede fabric   A woven or knitted fabric of cotton, man-made fibers, wool, or blends, finished to resemble suede leather. It is used in sport coats, gloves, linings, and cleaning cloths.

surah   A soft, usually twilled fabric often of silk or man-made fibers, woven in plaids, stripes, or prints. It is used for ties, mufflers, blouses, and dresses.

swiss   See *dotted swiss.*

synthetic fiber   A fiber made from chemicals that were never fibrous in form; more frequently referred to as "man-made synthesized fiber."

taffeta   A fine, plain-weave fabric, smooth on both sides, usually with a sheen on its surface. It is named for the Persian fabric "taftan." Taffeta may be a solid color or printed or woven so that the colors appear iridescent. It is often constructed with a fine rib; this fabric is correctly called *faille taffeta.*

tapestry A fabric in which the pattern is woven with colored *weft* threads. It is used extensively for wall hangings and table covers.

tenacity The tensile strength of a fiber, expressed as force per unit of linear density of an unstrained specimen. It is usually expressed in grams per *denier* or grams per *tex.*

tensile strength The maximum tensile stress required to rupture a fiber, expressed as pounds per square inch or grams per square centimeter.

terry cloth A heavy, absorbent cotton made with extra heavy *warp* threads woven into loops on one or both sides.

tex A system of yarn numbering that measures the weight in grams of 1 kilometer of yarn.

textile Any product made from fibers.

thermoplastic Tending to become soft and/or moldable upon application of heat.

thermosetting A procedure in which a substance is softened by heat, whereupon the substance undergoes chemical change, becomes firm, and assumes a completely different structure and different properties. The substance cannot be softened by reapplication of heat.

three-dimensional polymer A *polymer* formed when molecules unite in both length and width, producing a relatively rigid structure. This is typical of polymers used in finish processing.

ticking A heavy twill made with a colored yarn stripe in the *warp.* It is used for mattress covers, home furnishings, and sportswear.

trademark A word, letter, device, or symbol used in connection with merchandise and alluding distinctly to the origin or ownership of the product to which it is applied.

trade name A name given by manufacturers or merchants to a product to distinguish it as one produced or sold by them. It is called a trademark name and may be protected as a trademark.

tram silk A low-twist, ply silk yarn formed by combining two or three single strands.

trilobal A fiber with a modified cross section having three lobes.

tropical suiting A lightweight plain-weave suiting for men's and women's summer wear. It has various weaves and is made of a variety of fibers. If called *tropical worsted,* it must be an all-wool worsted fabric.

tweed A term derived from the river Tweed in Scotland, where the fabrics were first woven. It is now used to describe a wide range of light to heavy, rough-textured, sturdy fabrics characterized by their mixed color effect. Tweeds can be made of plain, twill, or herringbone weave, in almost any fiber or mixture of fibers.

Tussah silk See *wild silk.*

unbalanced yarns Yarns in which there is sufficient twist to set up a torque effect, so that the yarn will untwist and retwist in the opposite direction.

velour A soft, closely woven, smooth fabric with a short, thick pile. It is named for the French word for *velvet.* Velour is often made of cotton, wool, or mohair.

velvet A fabric with a short, soft, thick, warp-pile surface, usually made of silk or man-made pile fiber with a cotton back. It is sometimes made of all silk or all cotton. The fabric is often woven double, face to face, and then, while still on the loom, it is cut apart by a small shuttle knife. There are several varieties of velvet, which differ in weight, closeness of pile, and transparency.

virgin wool New wool that is made into yarns and fabrics for the first time.

voile A sheer, transparent, soft, lightweight plain-weave fabric made of highly twisted yarns. It can be composed of wool, cotton, silk, or a man-made fiber. Voile is used for blouses, dresses, curtains, and similar items.

waffle cloth A fabric with a characteristic honeycomb weave. When made in cotton, it is called *waffle pique.* It is used for coatings, draperies, dresses, and toweling.

wale A column of loops that is parallel to the loop axis and to the long measurement of a knit fabric.

warp yarns Yarns that run parallel to the *selvage,* or long dimension of a fabric.

waste silk See *silk noil.*

weft yarns See *filling yarns.*

whipcord A twill-weave fabric similar to *gabardine* but with a more pronounced diagonal rib on the right side. It is so named because it simulates the lash of a whip. Cotton whipcords are often four-harness, warp-twill weaves.

wickability The property of a fiber that allows moisture to move rapidly along the fiber surface and pass quickly through the fabric.

wild silk Silk produced by moths of species other than *Bombyx mori.* It is tan to brown in color and is coarser and more uneven than ordinary silk. It is usually called *Tussah silk.*

woof yarns See *filling yarns.*

Care Terms Used in Labeling

1. Washing, Machine Methods

a. *Machine wash*—a process by which soil may be removed from products or specimens through the use of water, detergent or soap, agitation, and a machine designed for this purpose. When no temperature is given, e.g., *warm* or *cold,* hot water up to 150° F (66° C) can be regularly used.

b. *Warm*—initial water temperature setting 90° F to 110° F (32° C to 43° C) (hand comfortable).

c. *Cold*—initial water temperature setting same as cold water tap up to 85° F (29° C).

d. *Do not have commercially laundered*—do not employ a laundry that uses special formulations, sour rinses, extremely large loads, or extremely high temperatures or which otherwise is employed for commercial, industrial, or institutional use. Employ laundering methods designed for residential use or use in a self-service establishment.

e. *Small load*—smaller than normal washing load.

f. *Delicate cycle* or *gentle cycle*—slow agitation and reduced time.

g. *Durable-press cycle* or *permanent-press cycle*—cool-down rinse or cold rinse before reduced spinning.

h. *Separately*—alone.

i. *With like colors*—with colors of similar hue and intensity.

j. *Wash inside out*—turn product inside out to protect face of fabric.

k. *Warm rinse*—initial water temperature setting 90° F to 110° F (32° C to 43° C).

l. *Cold rinse*—initial water temperature setting same as cold water tap up to 85° F (29° C).

m. *Rinse thoroughly*—rinse several times to remove detergent or soap and bleach.

n. *No spin* or *Do not spin*—remove material at the start of final spin cycle.

o. *No wring* or *Do not wring*—do not use roller wringer nor wring by hand.

2. Washing, Hand Methods

a. *Hand wash*—a process by which soil may be manually removed from products or specimens through the use of water, detergent or soap, and gentle squeezing action. When no temperature is given, e.g., *warm* or *cold,* hot water up to 150° F (66° C) can be regularly used.

b. *Warm*—initial water temperature 90° F to 110° F (32° C to 43° C) (hand comfortable).

c. *Cold*—initial water temperature same as cold water tap up to 85° F (29° C).

d. *Separately*—alone.

e. *With like colors*—with colors of similar hue and intensity.

f. *No wring or twist*—handle to avoid wrinkles and distortion.

g. *Rinse thoroughly*—rinse several times to remove detergent or soap and bleach.

h. *Damp wipe only*—surface clean with damp cloth or sponge.

3. Drying, All Methods

a. *Tumble dry*—use machine dryer. When no temperature setting is given, machine drying at a hot setting may be regularly used.

b. *Medium*—set dryer at medium heat.

c. *Low*—set dryer at low heat.

d. *Durable press* or *permanent press*—set dryer at permanent-press setting.

e. *No heat*—set dryer to operate without heat.

f. *Remove promptly*—when items are dry, remove immediately to prevent wrinkling.

g. *Drip dry*—hang dripping wet with or without hand shaping and smoothing.

h. *Line dry*—hang damp from line or bar in or out of doors.

i. *Line dry in shade*—dry away from sun.

j. *Line dry away from heat*—dry away from heat.

k. *Dry flat*—lay out horizontally for drying.

l. *Block to dry*—reshape to original dimensions while drying.

m. *Smooth by hand*—by hand, while wet, remove wrinkles and straighten seams and facings.

4. Ironing and Pressing

a. *Iron*—Ironing is needed. When no temperature is given iron at the highest temperature setting.

b. *Warm iron*—medium temperature setting.

c. *Cold iron*—lowest temperature setting.

d. *Do not iron*—item not to be smoothed or finished with an iron.

e. *Iron wrong side only*—article turned inside out for ironing or pressing.

f. *No steam* or *Do not steam*—steam in any form not to be used.

g. *Steam only*—steaming without contact pressure.

h. *Steam press* or *Steam iron*—use iron at steam setting.

i. *Iron damp*—articles to be ironed should feel moist.

j. *Use press cloth*—use a dry or a damp cloth between iron and fabric.

5. Bleaching

a. *Bleach when needed*—all bleaches may be used when necessary.

b. *No bleach* or *Do not bleach*—no bleaches may be used.

c. *Only nonchlorine bleach, when needed*—only the bleach specified may be used when necessary. Chlorine bleach may not be used.

6. Washing or Drycleaning

a. *Wash* or *dryclean, any normal method*—can be machine washed in hot water, can be machine dried at a high setting, can be ironed at a hot setting, can be bleached with all commercially available bleaches, and can be dry cleaned with all commercially available solvents.

7. Drycleaning, All Procedures

a. *Dryclean*—a process by which soil may be removed from products or specimens in a machine that uses any common organic solvent (e.g., petroleum, perchlorethylene, fluorocarbon) located in any commercial establishment. The process may include moisture addition to solvent up to 75 percent relative humidity, but tumble drying up to 160° F (71° C), and restoration by steam press or steam-air finishing.

b. *Professionally dryclean*—use the drycleaning process but modified to ensure optimum results either by a drycleaning attendant or through the use of a drycleaning machine that permits such modifications or both. Such modifications or special warnings must be included in the care instruction.

c. *Petroleum, Fluorocarbon,* or *Perchlorethylene*—employ solvent(s) specified to dryclean the item.

d. *Short cycle*—reduced or minimum cleaning time, depending on solvent used.

e. *Minimum extraction*—least possible extraction time.

f. *Reduced moisture* or *Low moisture*—decreased relative humidity.

g. *No tumble* or *Do not tumble*—do not tumble dry.

h. *Tumble warm*—tumble dry up to 120° F (49° C).

i. *Tumble cool*—tumble dry at room temperature.

j. *Cabinet dry warm*—cabinet dry up to 120° F (49° C).

k. *Cabinet dry cool*—cabinet dry at room temperature.

l. *Steam only*—employ no contact pressure when steaming.

m. *No steam* or *Do not steam*—do not use steam in pressing, finishing, steam cabinets, or wands.

8. Leather and Suede Cleaning

a. *Leather clean*—have cleaned only by a professional cleaner who uses special leather or suede care methods.

Bibliography

General Interest

Alexander, Patsy R. *Textile Product Selection, Use and Care.* Boston: Houghton Mifflin, 1977.

Bendure, Z., and G. Pfeiffer. *American Fabrics.* New York: Macmillan, 1947.

Collier, A. M. *A Handbook of Textiles,* 3d ed. New York: State Mutual Book and Periodical Service, 1982.

Corbman, Bernard P. *Textiles: Fiber to Fabrics,* 6th ed. New York: McGraw-Hill, 1983.

Creekmore, Anna M., and Ila M. Pokornowski. *Textile History.* Washington, D.C.: University Press of America, 1982.

Encyclopedia of Textiles, 3d ed. Englewood Cliffs, N.J.: Prentice-Hall, 1980.

Hall, A. J. *Standard Handbook of Textiles,* 8th ed. New York: Halstead Press, 1975.

Hollen, Norma, Jane Saddler, and Ann Langford. *Textiles,* 5th ed. New York: Macmillan; and London: Collier Macmillan, 1979.

Joseph, Marjory L. *Introductory Textile Science.* New York: Holt, Rinehart and Winston, 1986.

Joseph, Marjory L., and Audrey Gieseking-Williams. *Illustrated Guide to Textiles,* 4th ed. Canoga Park, Calif.: Plycon Press, 1985.

Linton, George E. *The Modern Textiles and Apparel Dictionary,* 4th ed. Plainfield, N.J.: Textile Book Service, 1973.

Lyle, Dorothy Siegart. *Modern Textiles,* 2d ed. New York: Wiley, 1982.

Man-made Fiber and Textile Dictionary. New York: Celanese Corp., 1974.

Pizzuto, J. J. *Fabric Science,* 4th ed., rev. Arthur Price and Allen C. Cohen. New York: Fairchild Publications, 1980.

Seagroatt, Margaret. *A Basic Textile Book.* New York: Van Nostrand Reinhold, 1975.

Smith, Betty F., and Ira Block. *Textiles in Perspective.* Englewood Cliffs, N.J.: Prentice-Hall, 1982.

Textile Handbook, 5th ed. Washington, D.C.: American Home Economics Association, 1975.

Tortora, Phyllis G. *Understanding Textiles,* 3d ed. New York: Macmillan, 1987.

Wingate, Isabel. *Dictionary of Textiles,* 6th ed. New York: Fairchild Publications, 1979.

Wingate, Isabel, and June Mohler. *Textile Fabrics and Their Selection,* 8th ed. Englewood Cliffs, N.J.: Prentice-Hall, 1984.

Textile Fibers

Chapman, C. B. *Fibers.* Plainfield, N.J.: Textile Book Service, 1974.

Cook, J. Gordon. *Handbook of Polyolefin Fibers.* London: Merrow Publishing Co., 1967.

Cook, J. Gordon. *Handbook of Textile Fibers,* 5th ed., 2 vols. London: Merrow Publishing Co., 1985.

Leggett, W. S. *Story of Linen.* New York: Chemical Publishing Co., 1945.

Leggett, W. S. *Story of Wool.* New York: Chemical Publishing Co., 1947.

Moncrieff, R. W. *Man-Made Fibers,* 7th ed. Woburn, Mass.: Butterworth, 1984.

Textile Yarns

Lord, P. R. *Spinning in the '70s.* Watford, Eng.: Merrow Publishing Co., 1971.
Studies in Modern Yarn Production. Manchester, Eng.: The Textile Institute, 1968.
The Yarn Revolution. Manchester, Eng.: The Textile Institute, 1976.

Fabric Construction

Buresh, Francis M. *Nonwoven Fabrics.* New York: Reinhold, 1962.
Emery, Irene. *The Primary Structures of Fabrics.* Washington, D.C.: The Textile Museum, 1966.
Gioello, Debbie Ann. *Profiling Fabrics.* New York: Fairchild Publications, 1981.
Gioello, Debbie Ann. *Understanding Fabrics.* New York: Fairchild Publications, 1982.
Lennox-Kerr, Peter, ed. *Needle Felted Fabrics.* Manchester, Eng.: Textile Trade Press, 1972.
Reichman, Charles, ed. *Knitting Dictionary.* New York: National Knitted Outerwear Association, 1967.
Reichman, Charles, J. B. Lancashire, and K. D. Darlington. *Knitted Fabric Primer.* New York: National Knitted Outerwear Association, 1967.

Finishing and Coloring

Clarke, W. *An Introduction to Textile Printing,* 4th ed. New York: Wiley, 1974.
Dempsey, E. P., and C. E. Vellins. *Heat Transfer Printing.* Sale, Cheshire, Eng.: Interprint, 1975.
Miles, L. W. C. *Textile Printing.* New York: State Mutual Book and Periodical Service, 1983.
Pettit, Florence. *America's Printed and Painted Fabrics.* New York: Hastings House, 1970.
Storey, Joyce. *Textile Printing.* New York: Van Nostrand Reinhold, 1974.

Performance and Testing

Annual Book of ASTM Standards (published annually), vols. 07.01 and 07.02. Philadelphia: American Society for Testing and Materials, 1985.
Lyle, Dorothy Siegart. *Performance of Textiles.* New York: Wiley, 1977.

Recommended Periodicals

American Dyestuff Reporter
American Fabrics and Fashions
America's Textile Reporter
Journal of the Society of Dyers and Colourists
Journal of the Textile Institute
Knitting Times
Modern Textile Business
Textile Chemists and Colorists
Textile Industries
Textile Organon
Textile Research Journal
Textile World
Textiles

Index